Tales from the

PLANET

ST. MARTIN'S PRESS

By Nicole Hollander

Introduction by Barbara Ehrenreich

SYLVIA

NEW YORK / EARTH

TALES FROM THE PLANET SYLVIA. Copyright © 1990 by Nicole Hollander. All rights reserved. Printed in the United States of America. No part of this book may be used or reproduced in any manner whatsoever without written permission except in the case of brief quotations embodied in critical articles or reviews. For information, address St. Martin's Press, 175 Fifth Avenue, New York, NY 10010.

Design by Tom Greensfelder

Library of Congress Cataloging-in-Publication Data

Hollander, Nicole.
    [Sylvia. Selections]
    Tales from the planet Sylvia / Nicole Hollander.
        p.   cm.
    ISBN 0-312-05166-2
    I. Title.
    PN6728.S97H659   1990
    741.5'973—dc20   90-8642
                                                               CIP

First Edition: October   1990

10 9 8 7 6 5 4 3 2 1

INTRODUCTION
by Barbara Ehrenreich

First of all, it is not true that I am jealous of Sylvia. There's room for all kinds in the social commentary business—my aunt in Iowa, for example, who covered the entire S&L crisis from a strategic position at her ironing board and still managed to get a high-fiber meal on the table every evening before "Jeopardy." I am sure Sylvia could cook if she *wanted* to, and I never once suggested that there was something untoward about her rapid rise to fame—her spot in forty-five newspapers (very few of which are mimeographed), her cult following of millions (many of whom are able to follow complex ideas even without visual aids). It certainly wasn't me who hinted darkly that no one could be so phenomenally successful if they didn't have friends in very, *very* high places.

No, it must have been George Will who said those things. And what working commentator can confront Sylvia's range of subject matter—from macro-economics to stretch marks, from foreign policy to kitty litter—without gnawing anxiously on his or her writing instrument—pencil or personal computer, as the case may be? We leave aside the startling range of *media*—taped phone messages, letters of advice, bathtub monologues, science fiction—that Sylvia deploys with such ease and versatility. I could write on my refrigerator too. I just don't *choose* to.

Nor does it bother me that America's top-flight intellectuals will one day hold entire conferences and seminars devoted to Sylviology. That they will deconstruct her frame by frame with straight edge and compass, attempting to identify each tiny object as an Artifact of Our Time and a clue to our condition. That they will bring in leading neurologists, phrenologists and psychoanalysts to study the blabbermouth pets, the thimble-sized martinis, the neurotic superheroes, to answer the inescapable question: *What kind of a mind...?*

But with that out of the way, let me make it clear that I have not gone to the other extreme and accepted Sylvia as my personal guru and mentor. Many, many women have. That's their choice. I'll admit, though, that, like Sylvia, I have a problem with food stains (which is why I never buy a shirt that isn't the color of marinara sauce). And, yes, I too am standing by encouragingly, waiting for some household pet, some goldfish, perhaps, or gerbil, to vacuum the floors. But these are superficial similarities, widespread among the population, and hardly the result of conscious imitation.

The fact is that I have criticisms. I maintain a boundary. I say, How is it possible to totally admire and worship someone who is afraid of food and a fool for cats? The reason cats are so smug is that they have a plan for world domination—a plan which, as the pages ahead suggest, may already be in effect.

Now, of course there are commentators—very famous and important ones whose names I could drop if I wanted to—who *are* jealous of Sylvia. I have witnessed the great weeping and grinding of teeth that occurs in the National Press Club and the Corridors of Power whenever a new "Sylvia" hits the news-stands. These famous and important commentators complain that she has sources that are inaccessible to the average working journalist. They point to her obvious familiarity with the heavenly hosts, the Evil One, with winged superheroes and extraplanetary deadbeats. They mention her supernatural insight into matters of public policy, her ability to see, as with x-ray vision, through the stupefying drone of media rhetoric.

For we all know—let us be honest—that there *is* a Planet Sylvia. We know that it is a place where cats write passable fiction, where ham has no cholesterol, where women are free to go out of doors without eyeliner and eat large portions of fries in public. We know that this distant world is the true source of Sylvia's insights, and that it is a place where one's wildest dreams— as for a tasty diet beverage or a race of humble, kindly public officials—are readily realized. We know that it is terribly far away, but not so far that every detail on earth cannot be seen from it, with stunning clarity and perspective. And we know that its atmosphere is not only breathable, but induces a delirious sense of lucidity, unknown on our own dank orb, except to the mystically enlightened and abusers of nitrous oxide.

So go there if you want. I don't care. Just one warning (and if Sylvia had the least sense of social responsibility she would have told you this herself): Once you've been there, it's not that easy to get back to this wretched place, or to ever fit in again with the yuppies, the health snobs, the couch potatoes, the two-faced insurance executives and purveyors of military hardware. Unless you take the cats' advice, as they prepare to send the little lost girl back to the world of humans, and—pointing to a UFO in the sky—tell her, *"Pretend you didn't see it."*

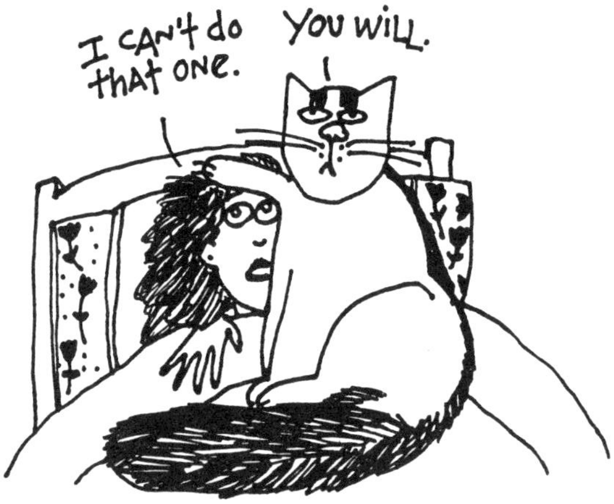
I can't do that one.
You will.

IDEAS THAT COME FROM ANIMALS ARE OFTEN BIZARRE AND MUST BE RESISTED.

WHERE I GET MY IDEAS

I'm often asked where I get my ideas. I am torn between saying I find many of them stuffed in meat loaf (a path closed to vegetarian cartoonists) or the truth, that I just write and write until something good shows up.

Most of my ideas are the result of hard work (eavesdropping at restaurants, reading tabloids), but I like the easy way as much as the next guy. My favorite ideas are those that arrive, fully formed out of nowhere, usually when I'm sure I'll never have another good one again.

Here's one of those cartoons that came as a gift from the universe.

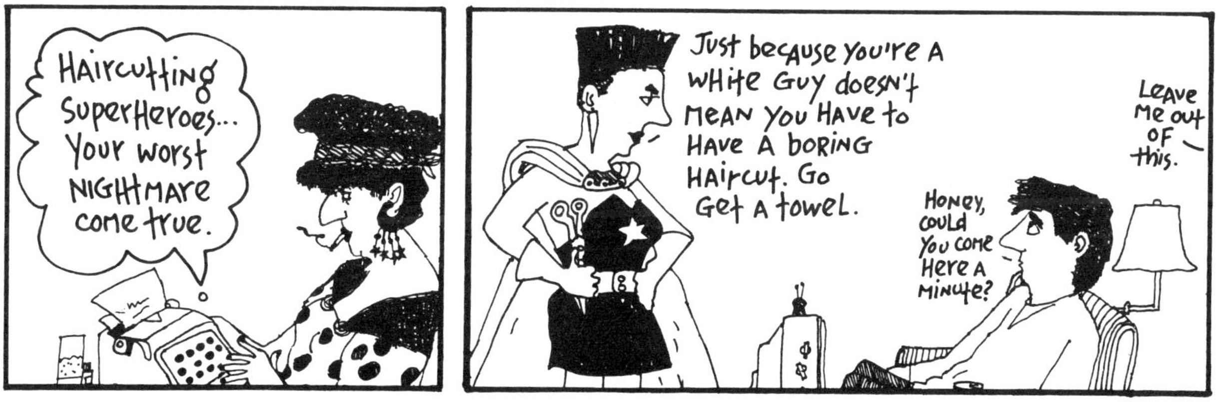

Haircutting SuperHeroes... Your worst NIGHTMARE come true.
Just because you're A WHITE GUY doesn't MEAN YOU HAVE to HAVE A BORING HAIRCUT. Go Get A towel.
HONEY, COULD YOU COME HERE A MINUTE?
LEAVE ME OUT OF this.

I'd like to take this opportunity to thank the three graphic designers I share office space with, who often moan and shriek out loud at the outrageous fate that forces them to work for a living, for providing me with a congenial atmosphere in which to write cartoons.

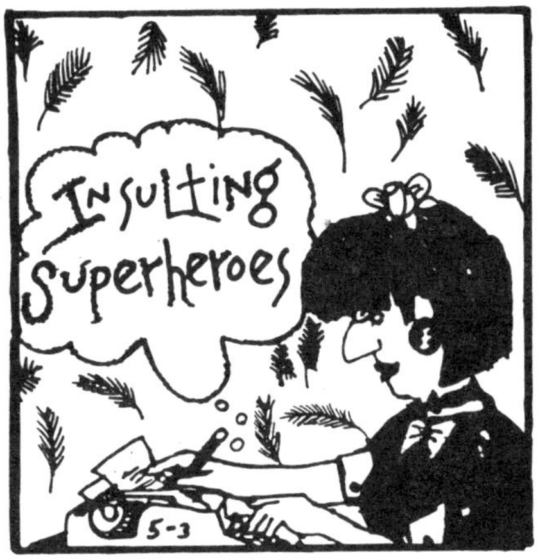
Insulting Superheroes
5-3

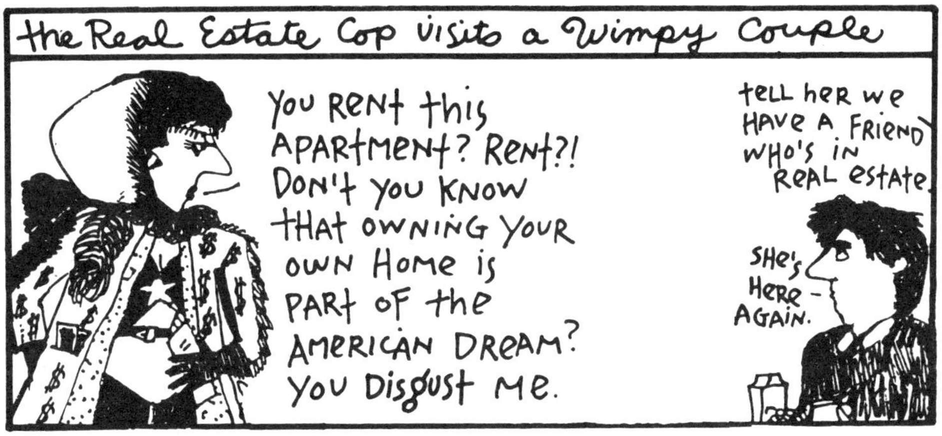
the Real Estate Cop visits a Wimpy Couple
You Rent this Apartment? Rent?! Don't you know that owning your own Home is part of the American Dream? You Disgust me.
tell her we have a friend who's in real estate.
She's Here Again.

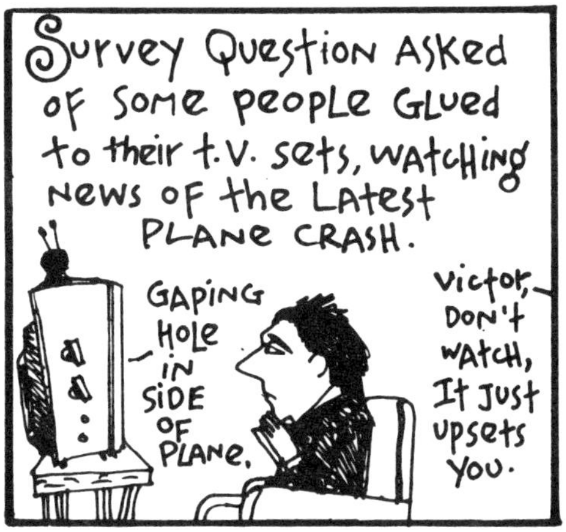
Survey Question asked of some people glued to their t.v. sets, watching news of the latest plane crash.
Gaping hole in side of plane.
Victor, don't watch, it just upsets you.

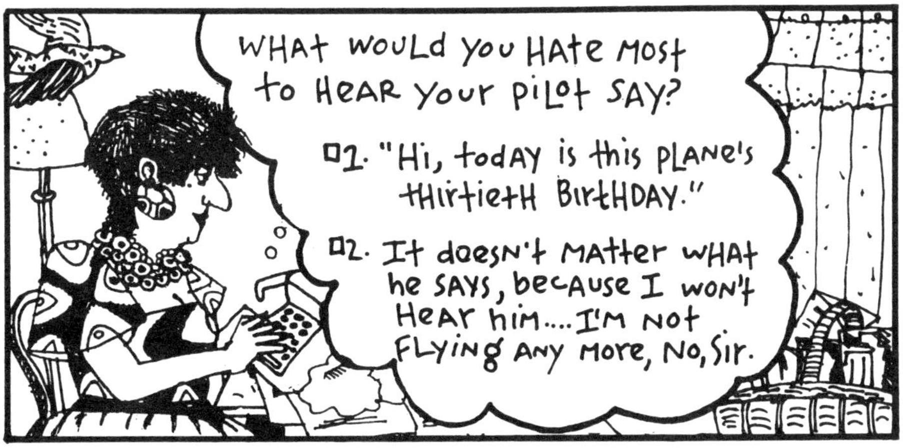
What would you hate most to hear your pilot say?
☐1. "Hi, today is this plane's thirtieth Birthday."
☐2. It doesn't matter what he says, because I won't hear him.... I'm not flying any more, No, Sir.

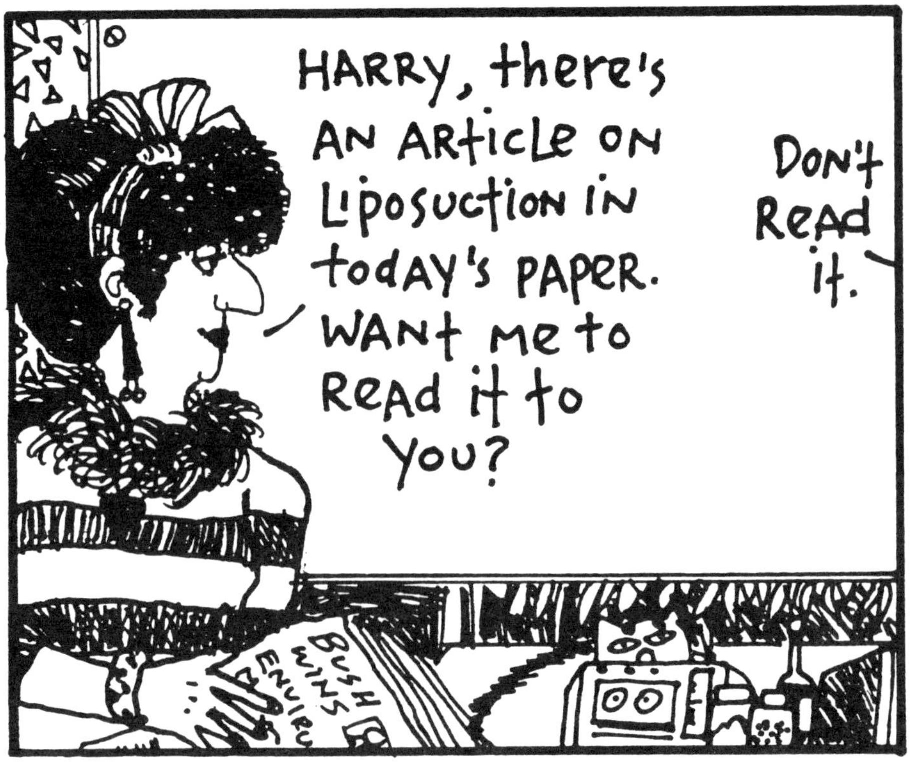
Harry, there's an article on Liposuction in today's paper. Want me to read it to you?
Don't read it.
BUSH
WINS

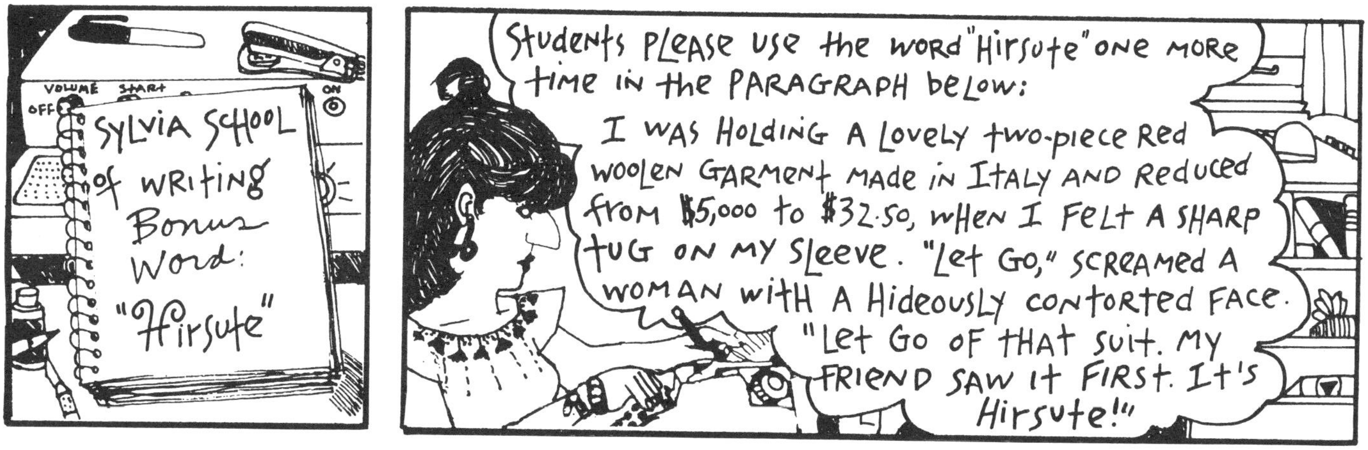
VOLUME START ON OFF
SYLVIA SCHOOL of WRITING Bonus Word: "Hirsute"
Students PLease use the word "Hirsute" one more time in the PARAGRAPH below:
I was Holding A Lovely two-piece Red woolen Garment made in Italy and Reduced from $5,000 to $32.50, when I Felt A Sharp tug on my Sleeve. "Let Go," screamed A woman with A Hideously contorted Face. "Let Go of that suit. My Friend saw it First. It's Hirsute!"

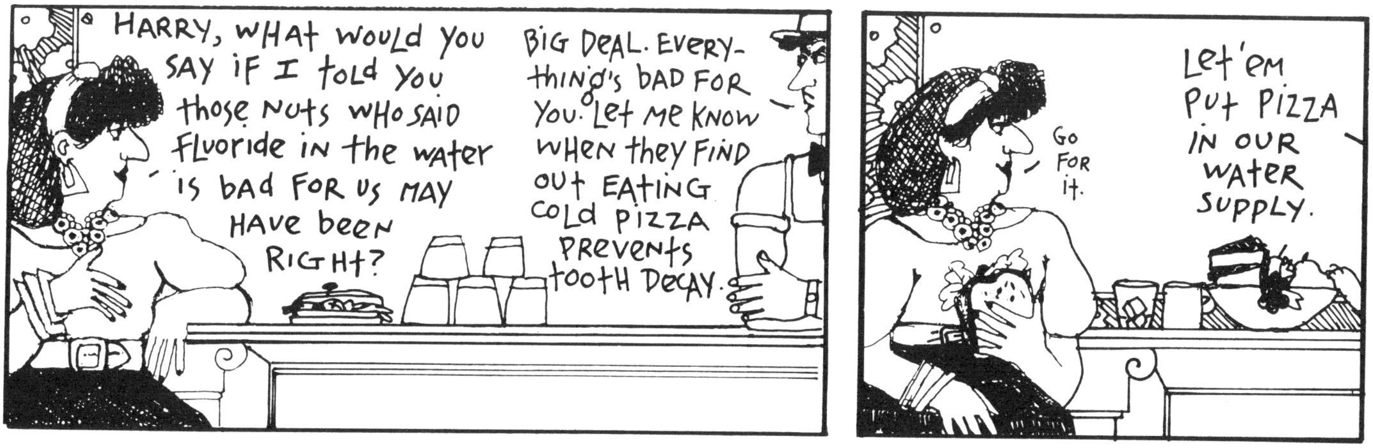
HARRY, WHAT would you say if I told you those nuts who said Fluoride in the water is bad for us may have been Right?
Big Deal. Everything's bad for you. Let me know when they find out eating cold pizza prevents tooth decay.
Go for it.
Let 'em put pizza in our water supply.

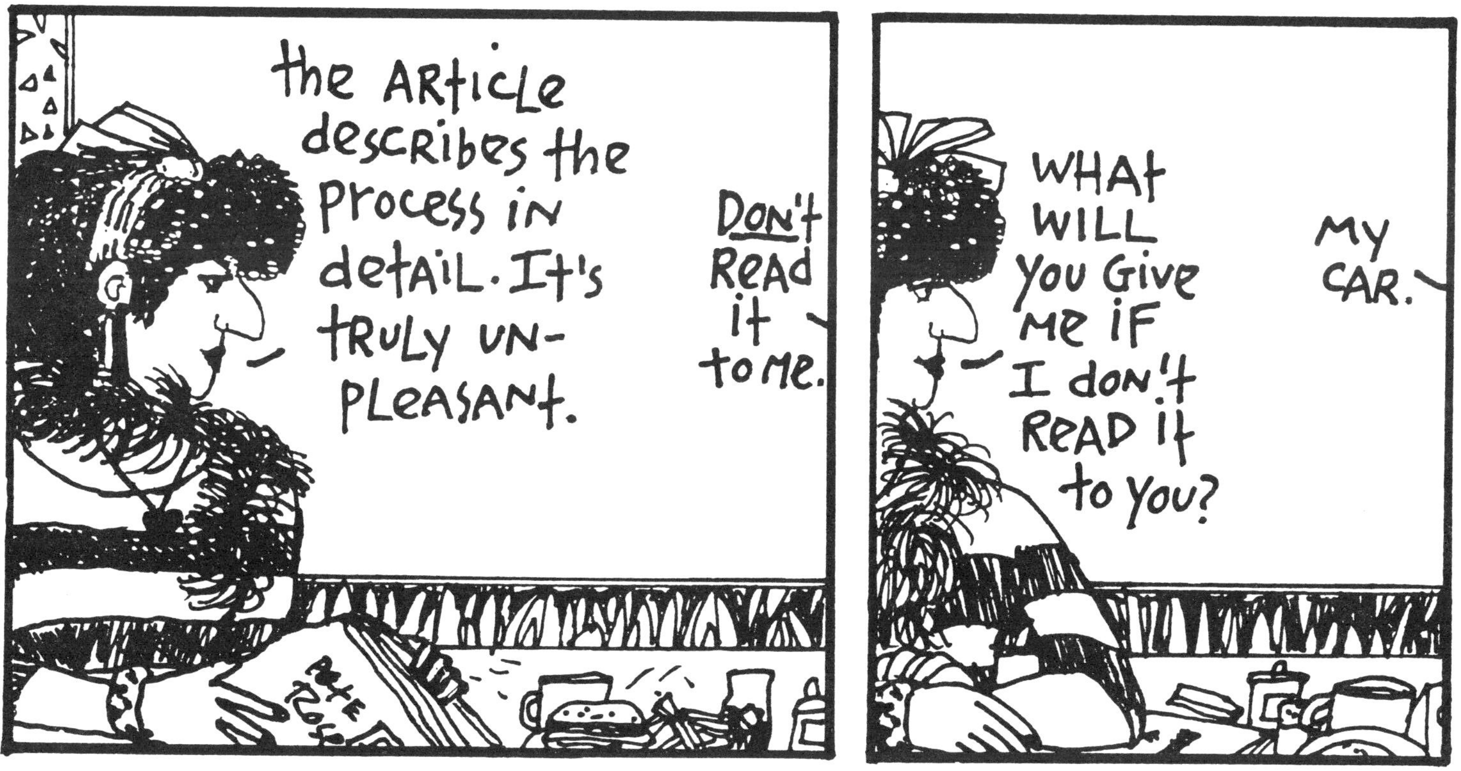
the Article describes the process in detail. It's truly un-pleasant.
DON't Read it to me.
WHAT WILL you Give me if I don't Read it to you?
My CAR.

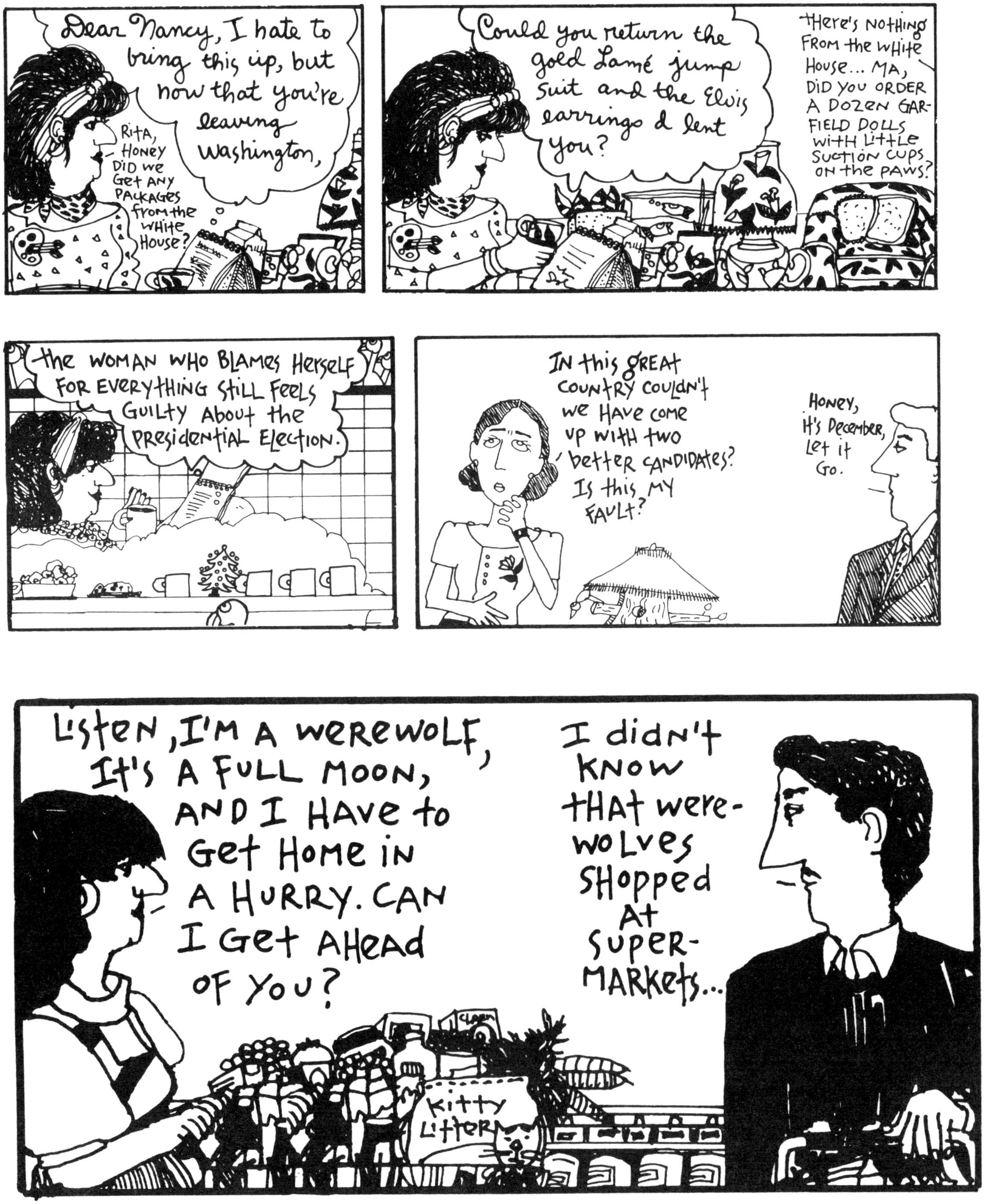
Dear Nancy, I hate to bring this up, but now that you're leaving Washington,
Rita, Honey did we get any packages from the White House?
Could you return the gold Lamé jump suit and the Elvis earrings I lent you?
There's nothing from the White House... Ma, did you order a dozen Garfield dolls with little suction cups on the paws?
The woman who blames herself for everything still feels guilty about the presidential election.
In this great country couldn't we have come up with two better candidates? Is this my fault?
Honey, it's December, let it go.
Listen, I'm a werewolf, it's a full moon, and I have to get home in a hurry. Can I get ahead of you?
I didn't know that were-wolves shopped at super-markets...
Kitty Litter

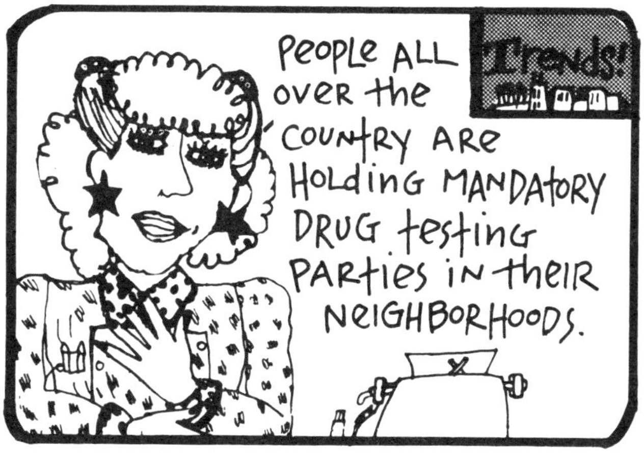
Trends!
People all over the country are holding mandatory drug testing parties in their neighborhoods.

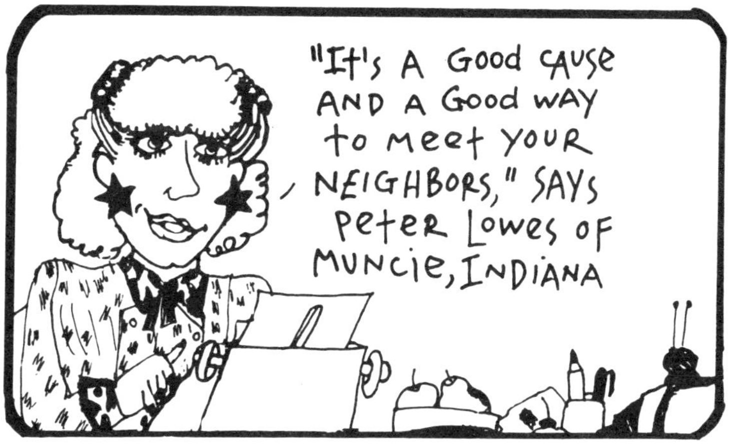
"It's a good cause and a good way to meet your neighbors," says Peter Lowes of Muncie, Indiana

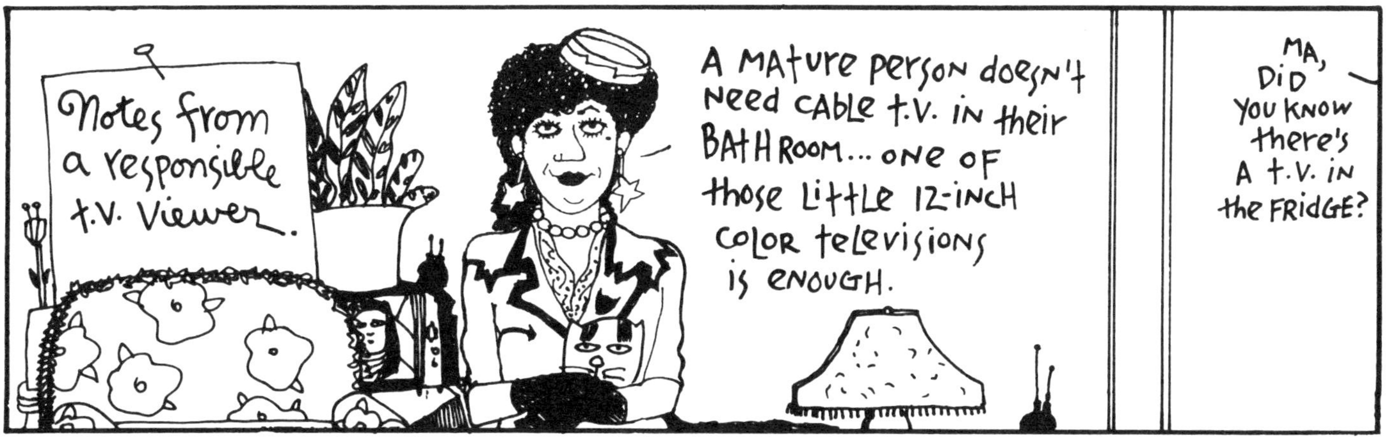
Notes from a responsible t.v. viewer.
A mature person doesn't need cable t.v. in their bathroom... one of those little 12-inch color televisions is enough.
Ma, did you know there's a t.v. in the fridge?

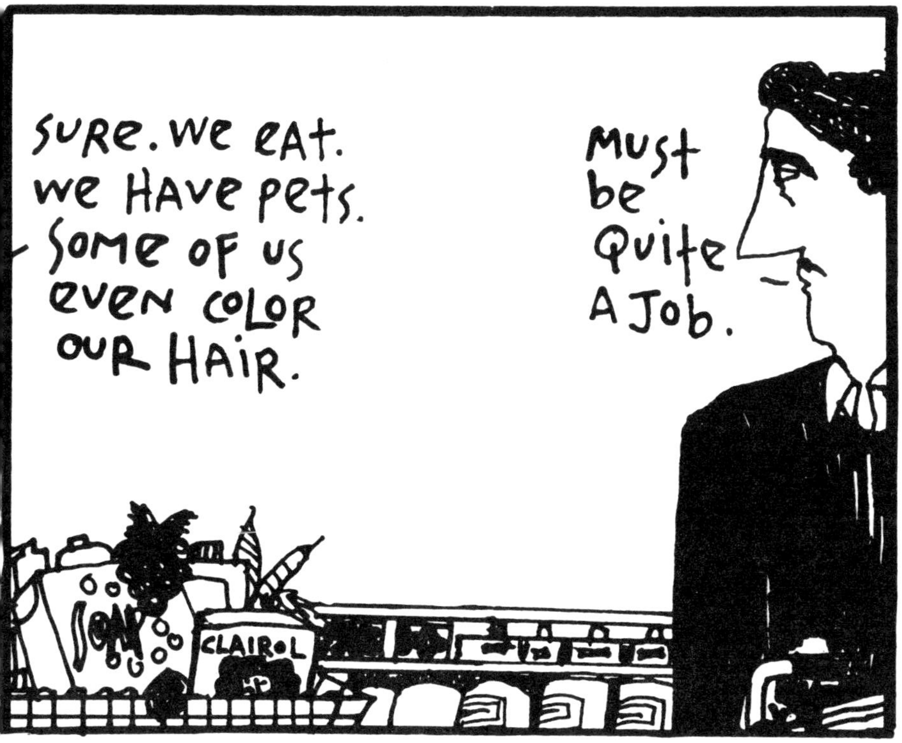
Sure. We eat. We have pets. Some of us even color our hair.
Must be quite a job.
SOAP
CLAIROL

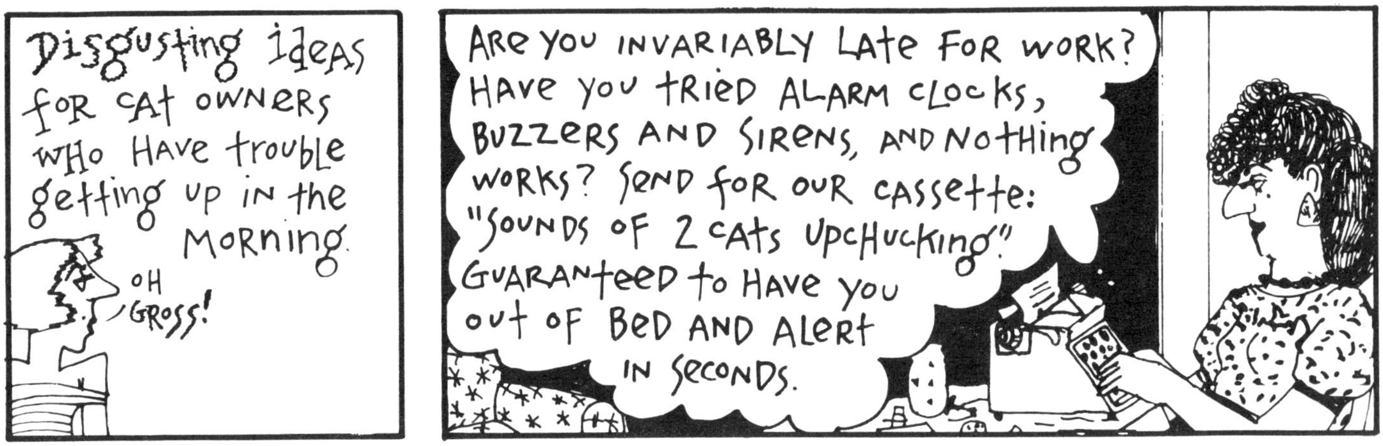
Disgusting ideas for cat owners who have trouble getting up in the Morning.
OH GROSS!
Are you invariably late for work? Have you tried alarm clocks, buzzers and sirens, and nothing works? Send for our cassette: "Sounds of 2 cats upchucking." Guaranteed to have you out of bed and alert in seconds.

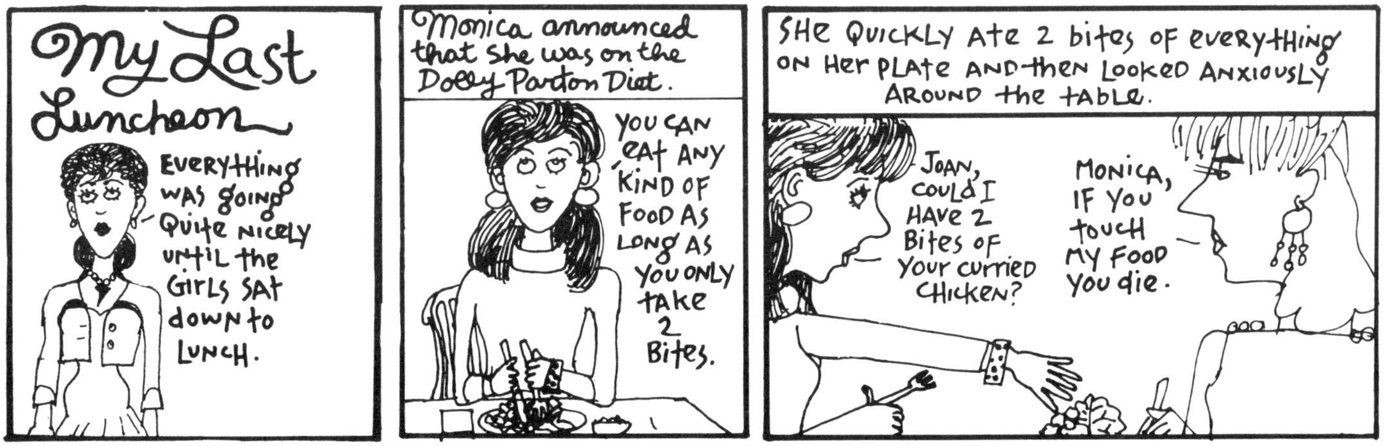
My Last Luncheon
Everything was going quite nicely until the girls sat down to lunch.
Monica announced that she was on the Dolly Parton Diet.
You can eat any kind of food as long as you only take 2 bites.
She quickly ate 2 bites of everything on her plate and then looked anxiously around the table.
Joan, could I have 2 bites of your curried chicken?
Monica, if you touch my food you die.

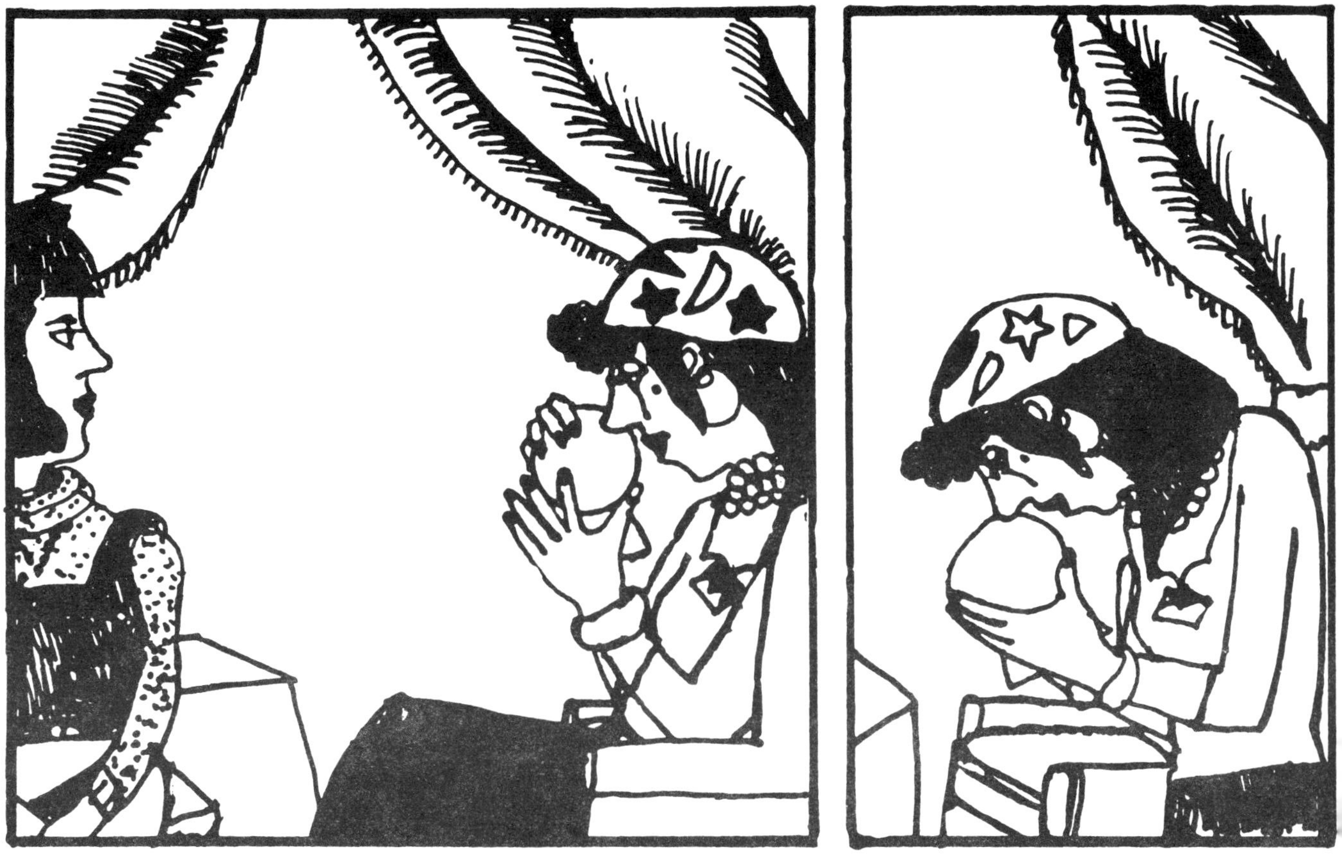

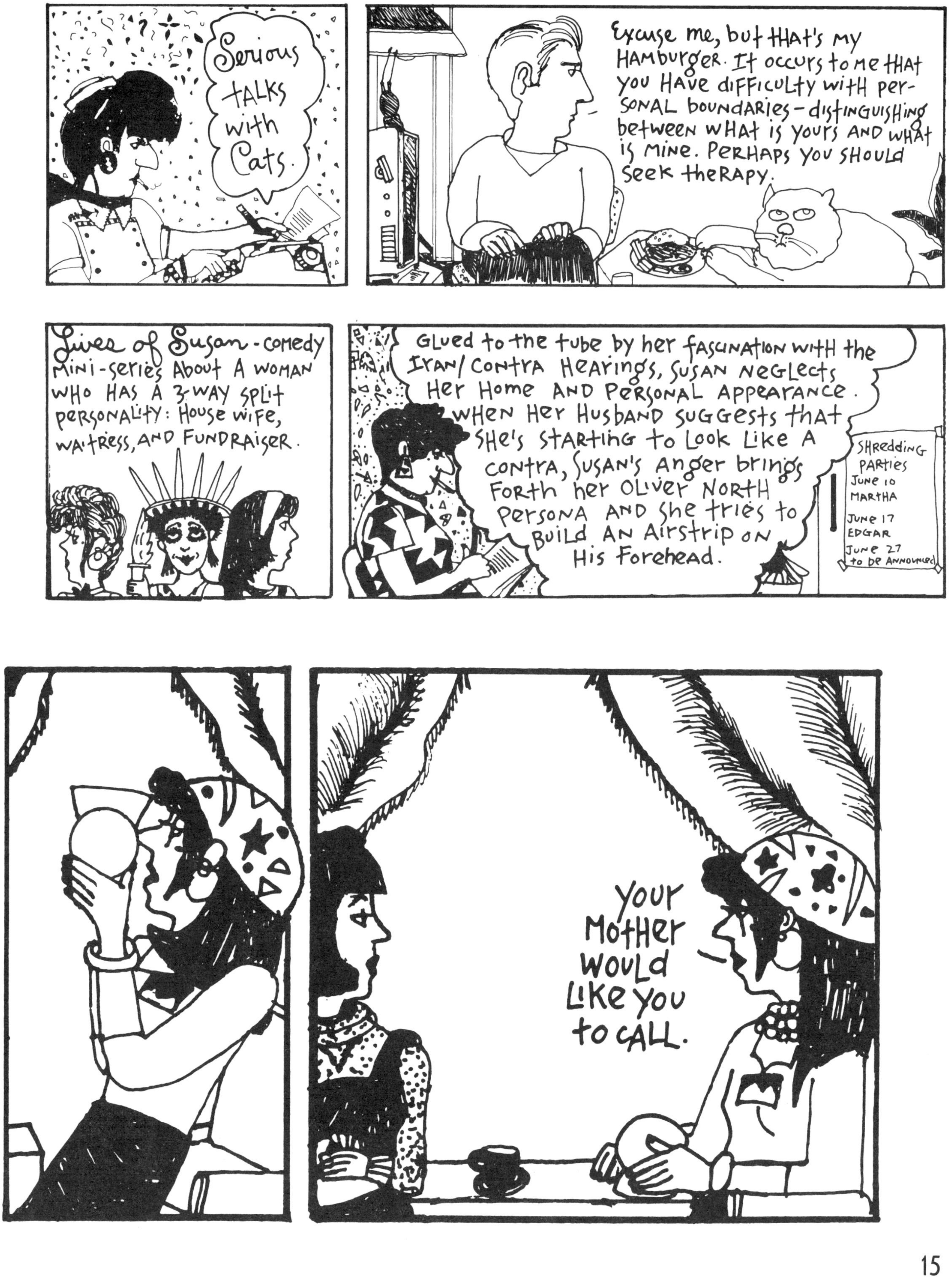
Serious talks with Cats.
Excuse me, but that's my hamburger. It occurs to me that you have difficulty with personal boundaries—distinguishing between what is yours and what is mine. Perhaps you should seek therapy.
Lives of Susan - comedy mini-series about a woman who has a 3-way split personality: housewife, waitress, and fundraiser.
Glued to the tube by her fascination with the Iran/Contra Hearings, Susan neglects her home and personal appearance. When her husband suggests that she's starting to look like a contra, Susan's anger brings forth her Oliver North persona and she tries to build an airstrip on his forehead.
Shredding Parties
June 10 Martha
June 17 Edgar
June 27 to be Announced
Your Mother would like you to call.

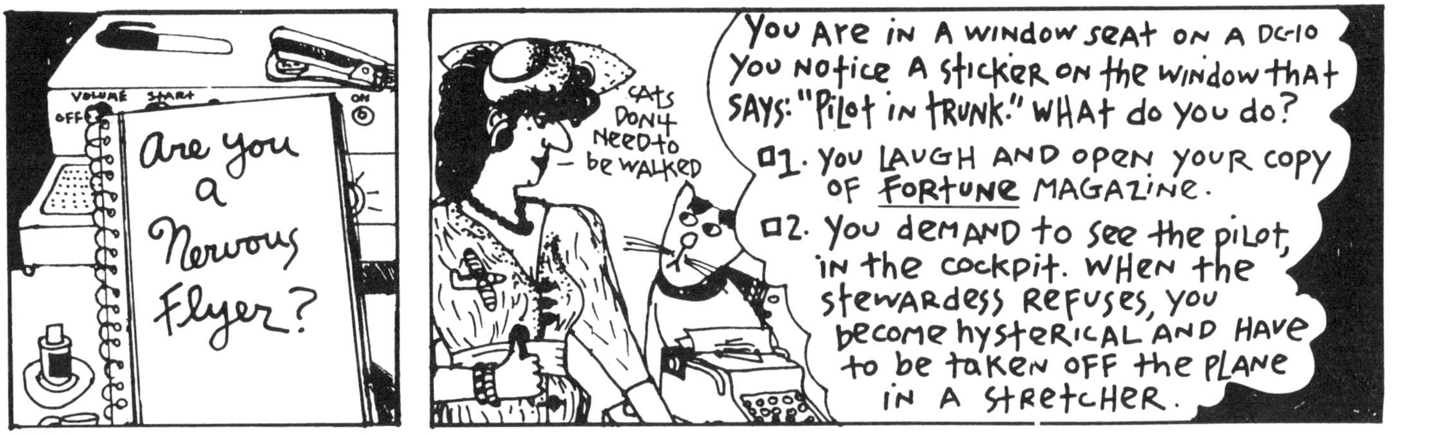
VOLUME
START
OFF
ON
Are you a Nervous Flyer?
CATS DON'T NEED to be WALKED
You Are in A window seat on A DC-10 You Notice A sticker on the window that says: "Pilot in trunk." WHAT do you do?
1. You LAUGH AND open your copy of FORTUNE MAGAZINE.
2. You demand to see the pilot, in the cockpit. When the stewardess refuses, you become hysterical and have to be taken off the plane in a stretcher.

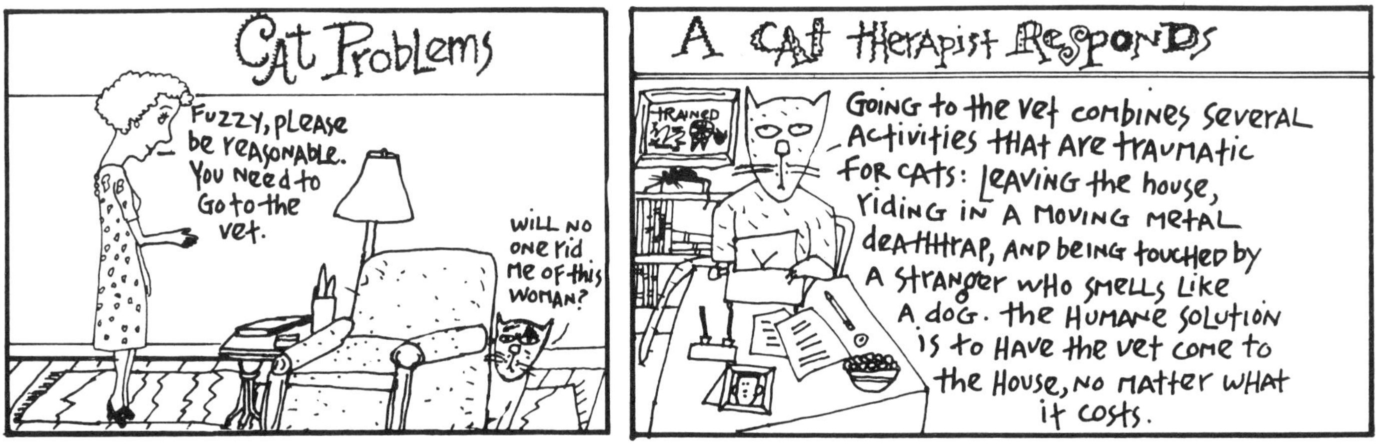
CAT Problems
Fuzzy, please be reasonable. You need to Go to the vet.
WILL NO ONE rid Me of this WOMAN?
A CAT therapist Responds
TRAINED
Going to the vet combines several Activities that are traumatic for cats: leaving the house, riding in A moving metal deathtrap, and being touched by A stranger who smells like A dog. the Humane solution is to have the vet come to the House, no matter what it costs.

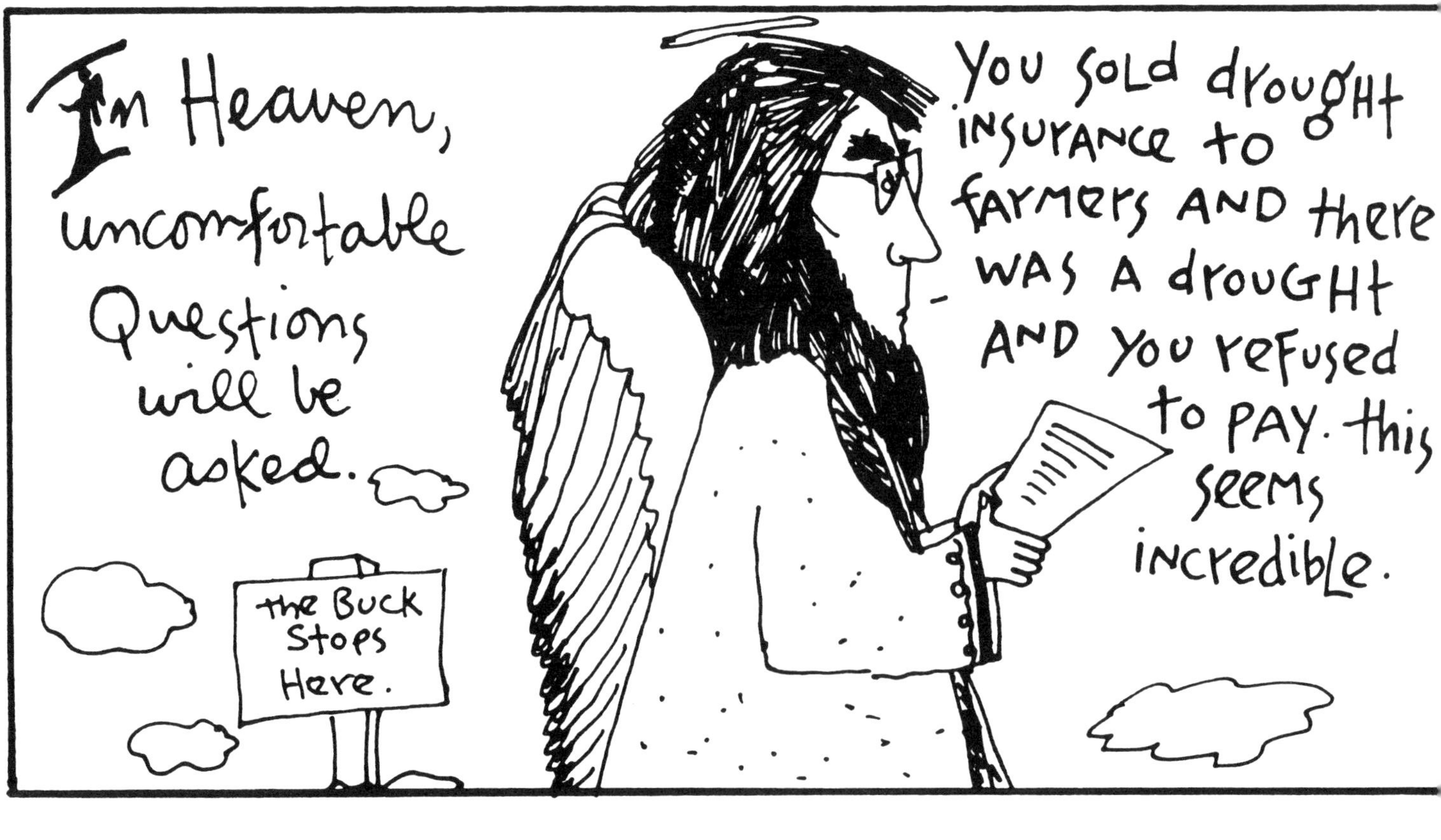
In Heaven, uncomfortable Questions will be asked.
You sold drought insurance to farmers and there was a drought and you refused to pay. this seems incredible.
the Buck Stops Here.

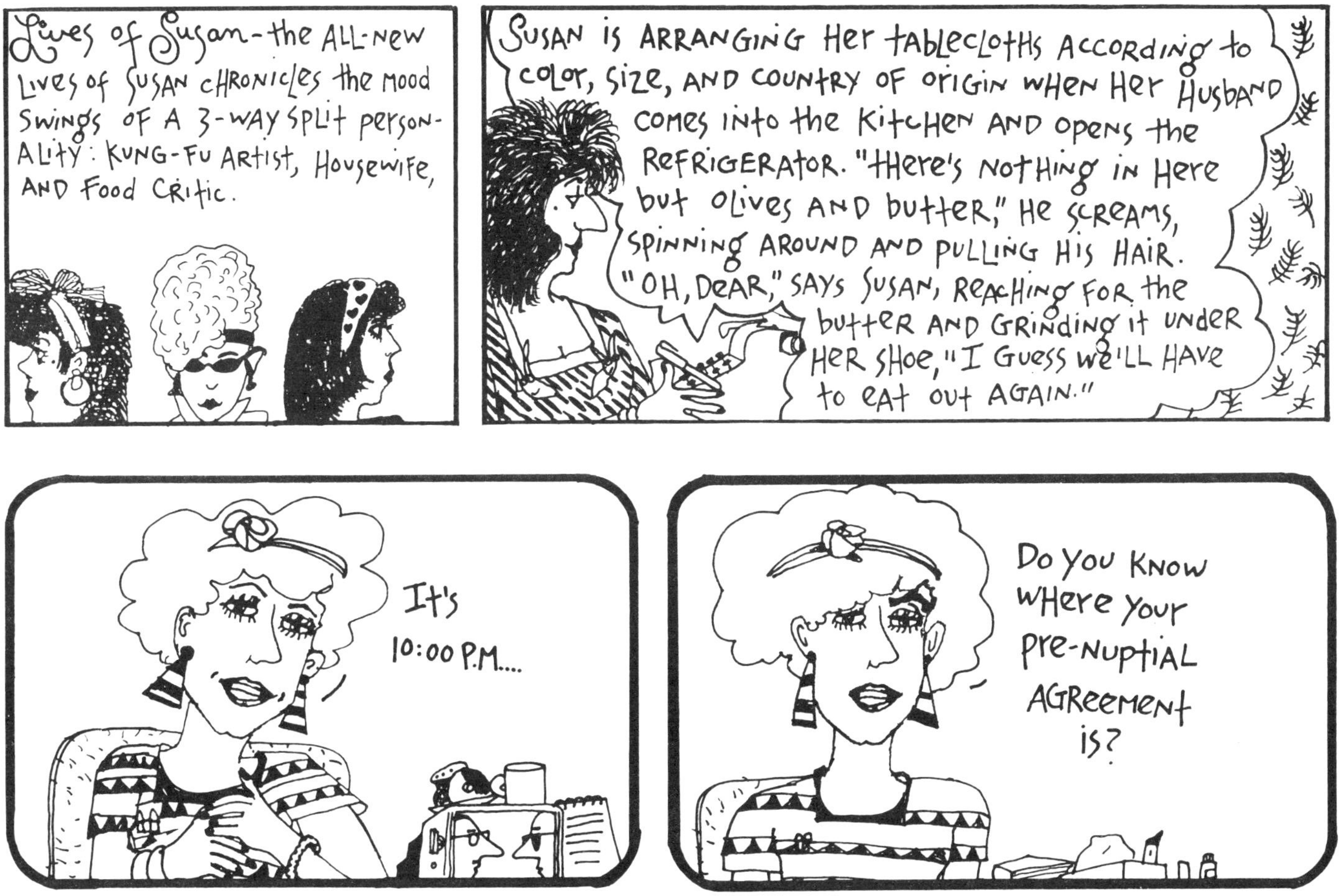
Lives of Susan - the ALL-NEW Lives of Susan chronicles the mood swings of a 3-way split personality: Kung-Fu Artist, Housewife, and Food Critic.
Susan is arranging her tablecloths according to color, size, and country of origin when her husband comes into the kitchen and opens the refrigerator. "There's nothing in here but olives and butter," he screams, spinning around and pulling his hair. "Oh, dear," says Susan, reaching for the butter and grinding it under her shoe, "I guess we'll have to eat out again."
It's 10:00 P.M....
Do you know where your pre-nuptial agreement is?

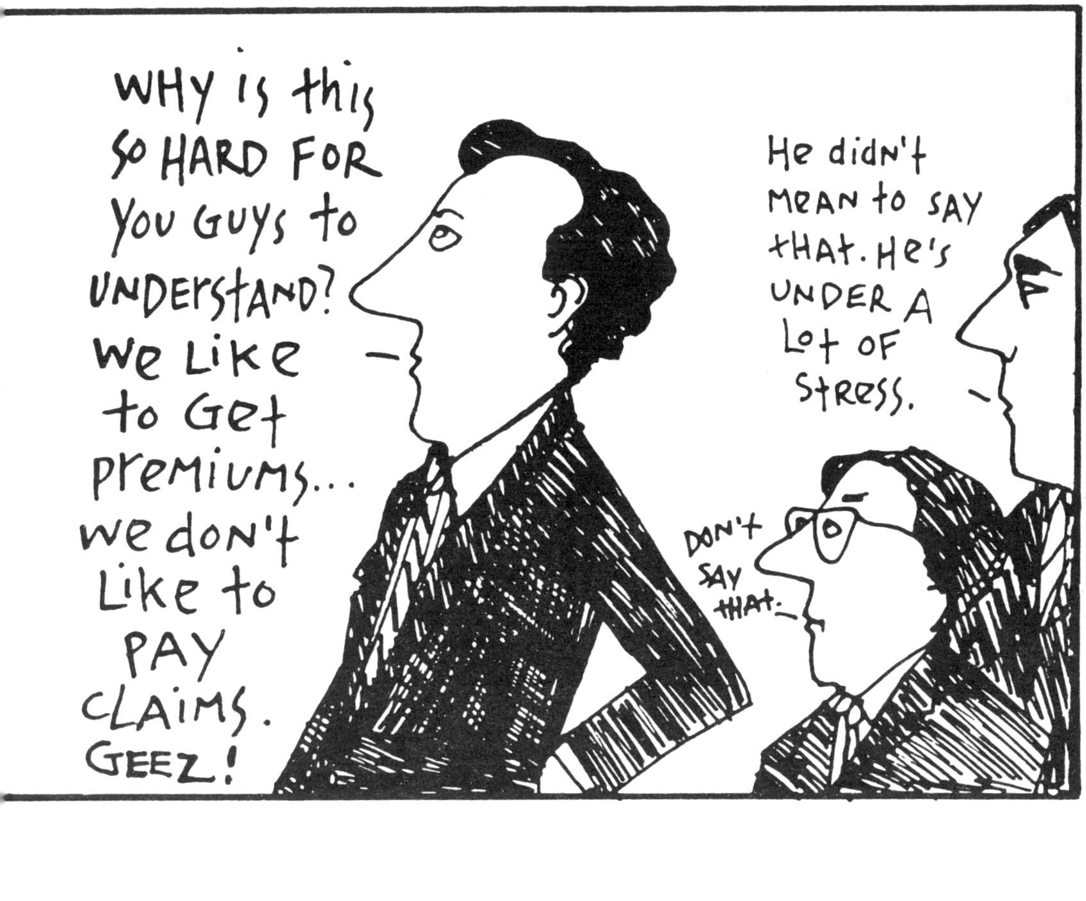
Why is this so hard for you guys to understand? We like to get premiums... we don't like to pay claims. Geez!
He didn't mean to say that. He's under a lot of stress.
Don't say that.

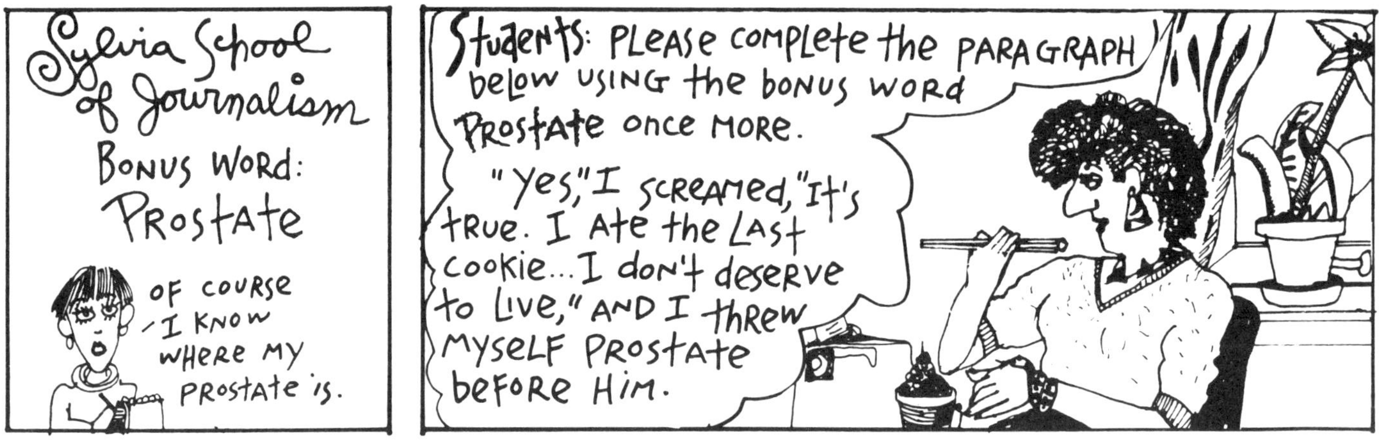
Sylvia School of Journalism
Bonus Word: Prostate
Of course I know where my prostate is.
Students: Please complete the paragraph below using the bonus word Prostate once more.
"Yes," I screamed, "It's true. I ate the last cookie... I don't deserve to live," and I threw myself prostate before him.

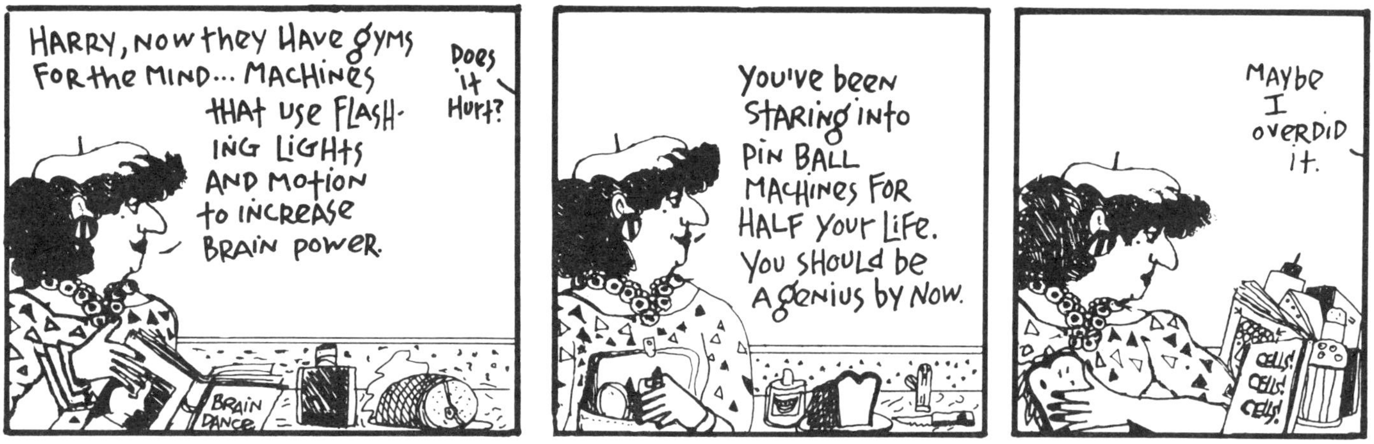
Harry, now they have gyms for the mind... machines that use flashing lights and motion to increase brain power.
Does it hurt?
You've been staring into pin ball machines for half your life. You should be a genius by now.
Maybe I overdid it.
Brain Dance

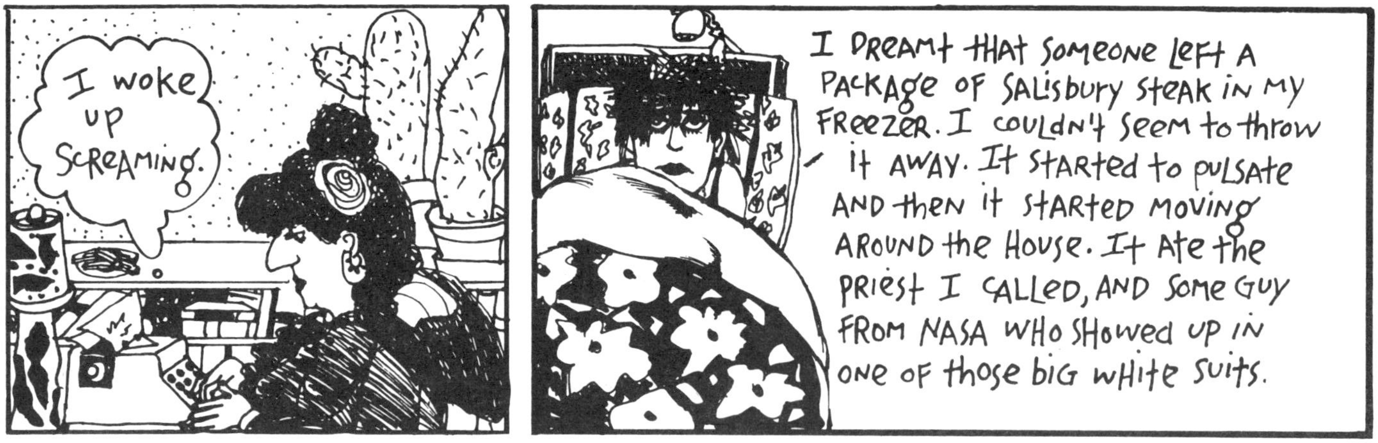
I woke up screaming.
I dreamt that someone left a package of Salisbury steak in my freezer. I couldn't seem to throw it away. It started to pulsate and then it started moving around the house. It ate the priest I called, and some guy from NASA who showed up in one of those big white suits.

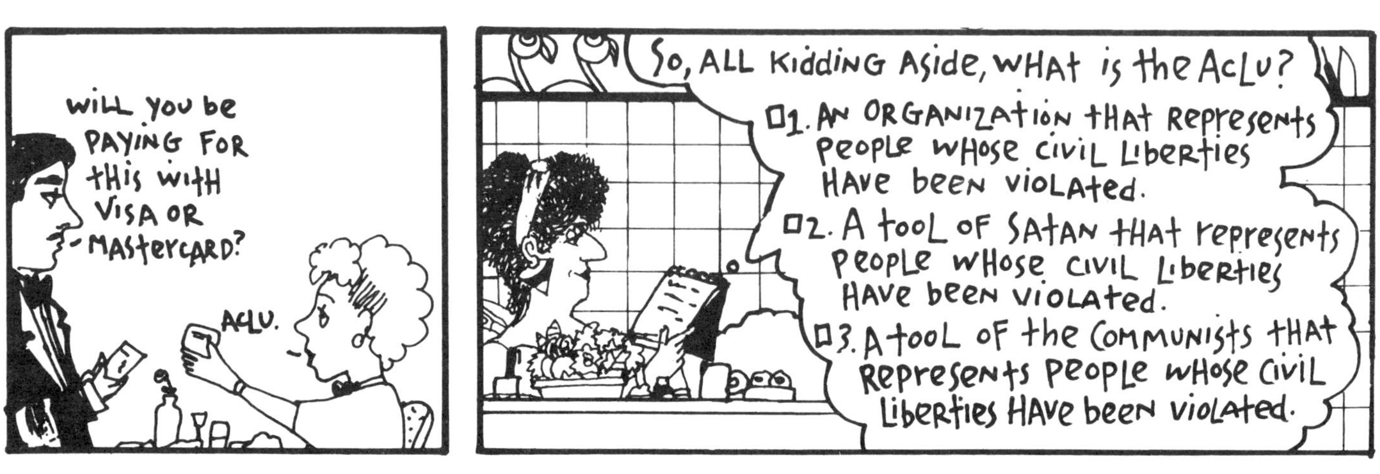
Will you be paying for this with Visa or Mastercard?
ACLU.
So, all kidding aside, what is the ACLU?
☐1. An organization that represents people whose civil liberties have been violated.
☐2. A tool of Satan that represents people whose civil liberties have been violated.
☐3. A tool of the Communists that represents people whose civil liberties have been violated.

THE HAM STORY

When I finally connected with United Parcel Service and opened the cardboard box that had been languishing at their depot for a week, I saw a ham. A Christmas gift from, I am sure, some ordinarily well-meaning people. This ham was not packed in dry ice, but rattling around in a simple cardboard box. True, the ham was sealed in plastic, but so what? Just looking at a ham that had been sent unprotected through the mail could be fatal.

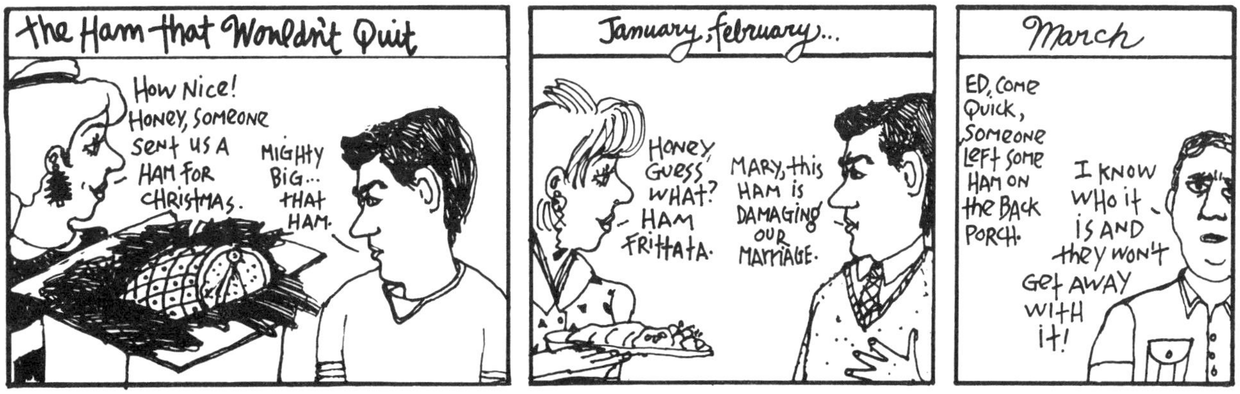
the Ham that Wouldn't Quit
How Nice! Honey, Someone sent us a Ham for Christmas.
Mighty Big... that Ham.
January, february...
Honey Guess what? Ham Frittata.
Mary, this Ham is damaging our marriage.
March
Ed, come quick, someone left some Ham on the Back Porch.
I know who it is and they won't get away with it!

I called UPS and asked them how cool the ham had been during the week it was under their care. They said that it had been at their warehouse, which is kept, they thought, pretty cool. I looked closely at the ham. It had been smoked at a butcher's in Michigan. I telephoned. I would have telephoned Europe. I spoke to the butcher's daughter. She said no one had ever called them to ask if it was all right to eat a vacuum sealed ham that had sat around in a UPS warehouse that was pretty cool. She thought I should talk to her dad. I knew he would make me feel stupid, and that in itself would be reassuring.

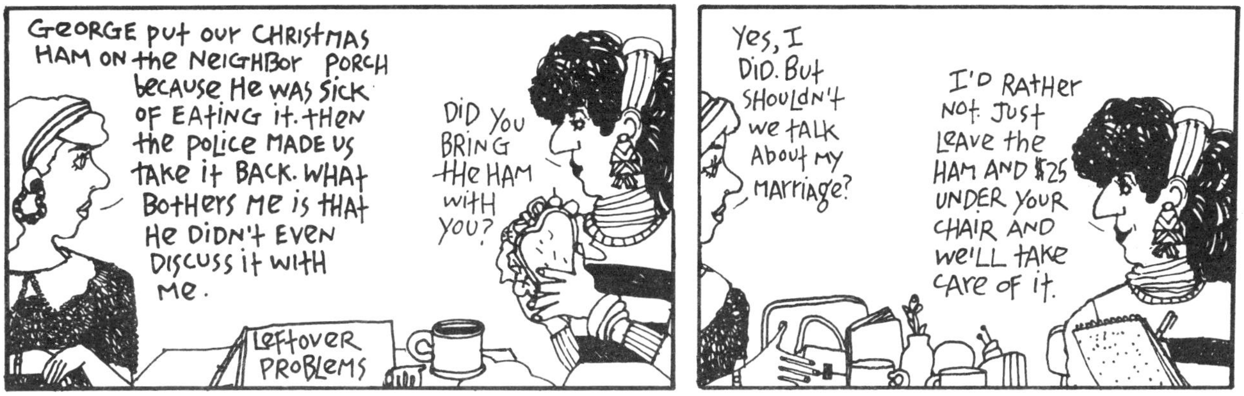
George put our Christmas Ham on the neighbor porch because he was sick of eating it. Then the police made us take it back. What bothers me is that he didn't even discuss it with me.
Did you bring the Ham with you?
Leftover Problems
Yes, I did. But shouldn't we talk about my marriage?
I'd rather not. Just leave the Ham and $25 under your chair and we'll take care of it.

He was unpleasant enough, but it didn't help as much as I'd hoped.

When faced with a problem like: "Should I eat a poisoned ham?," there are no unbiased parties. You pretty much get the answer you know you're going to get. I knew my mother would say, "Throw it out." So I called my sister who said, "I'm sure it's fine." I decided to go with that.

I ate a very tiny piece of the ham and waited twenty-four hours. I felt okay. I decided I could feed it to other people. The ham was large. The ham could have fed fifty or sixty people. I served it to everyone I could. I gave some to my sister to take home. I gave it to friends. I threw parties. I used it as the subject for two cartoons. It never seemed to diminish in size. For all I know it's still hanging around somewhere.

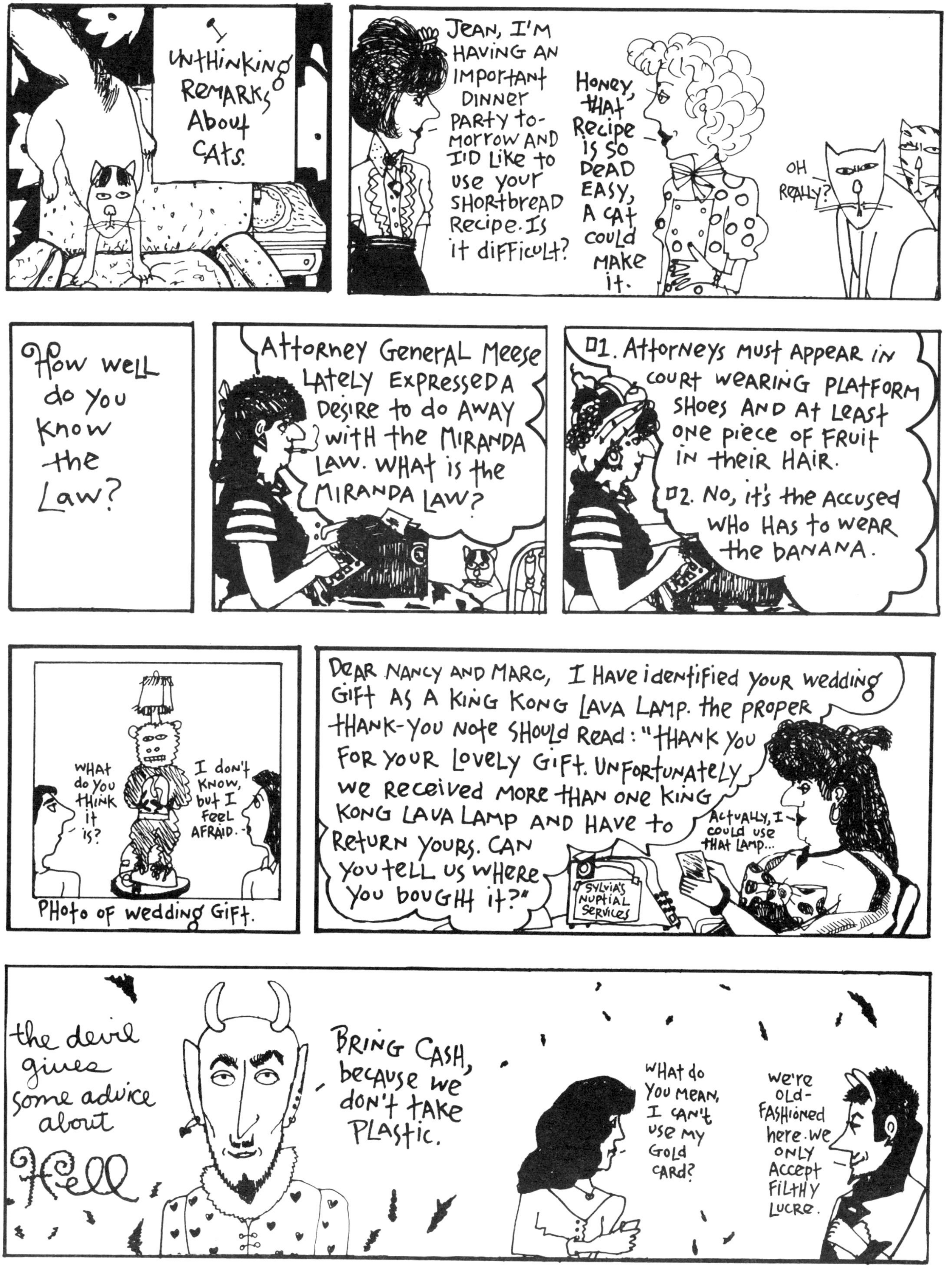
UNTHINKING REMARKS ABOUT CATS.
JEAN, I'M HAVING AN IMPORTANT DINNER PARTY TOMORROW AND I'D LIKE TO USE YOUR SHORTBREAD RECIPE. IS IT DIFFICULT?
HONEY, THAT RECIPE IS SO DEAD EASY, A CAT COULD MAKE IT.
OH REALLY?
How well do you know the Law?
ATTORNEY GENERAL MEESE LATELY EXPRESSED A DESIRE TO DO AWAY WITH THE MIRANDA LAW. WHAT IS THE MIRANDA LAW?
□1. ATTORNEYS MUST APPEAR IN COURT WEARING PLATFORM SHOES AND AT LEAST ONE PIECE OF FRUIT IN THEIR HAIR.
□2. NO, IT'S THE ACCUSED WHO HAS TO WEAR THE BANANA.
WHAT DO YOU THINK IT IS?
I DON'T KNOW, BUT I FEEL AFRAID.
PHOTO OF WEDDING GIFT.
DEAR NANCY AND MARC, I HAVE IDENTIFIED YOUR WEDDING GIFT AS A KING KONG LAVA LAMP. THE PROPER THANK-YOU NOTE SHOULD READ: "THANK YOU FOR YOUR LOVELY GIFT. UNFORTUNATELY WE RECEIVED MORE THAN ONE KING KONG LAVA LAMP AND HAVE TO RETURN YOURS. CAN YOU TELL US WHERE YOU BOUGHT IT?"
ACTUALLY, I COULD USE THAT LAMP...
SYLVIA'S NUPTIAL SERVICES
the devil gives some advice about Hell
BRING CASH, BECAUSE WE DON'T TAKE PLASTIC.
WHAT DO YOU MEAN, I CAN'T USE MY GOLD CARD?
WE'RE OLD-FASHIONED HERE. WE ONLY ACCEPT FILTHY LUCRE.

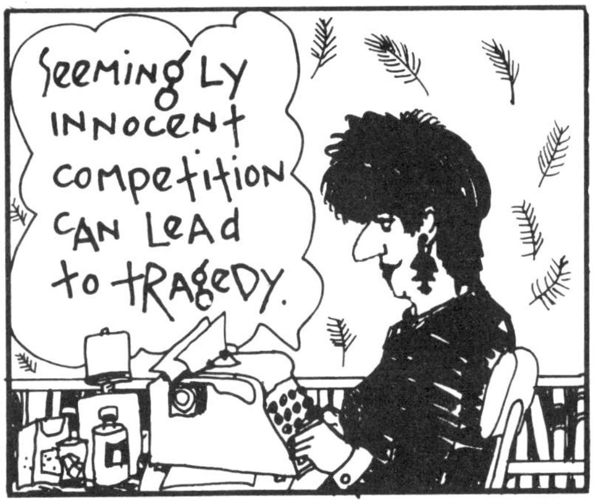
Seemingly innocent competition can lead to tragedy.

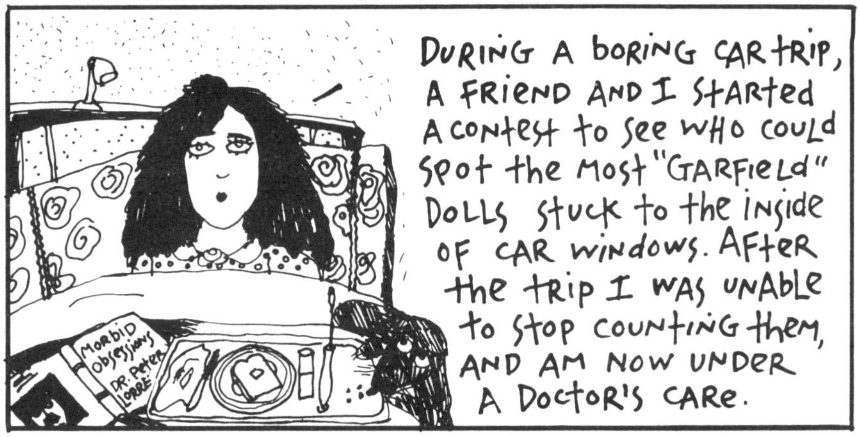
During a boring car trip, a friend and I started a contest to see who could spot the most "Garfield" dolls stuck to the inside of car windows. After the trip I was unable to stop counting them, and am now under a doctor's care.
Morbid Obsessions
Dr. Peter Lorre

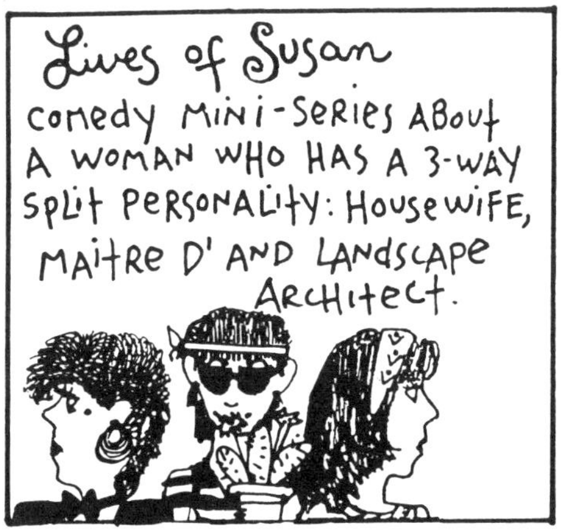
Lives of Susan
comedy mini-series about a woman who has a 3-way split personality: housewife, maitre d' and landscape architect.

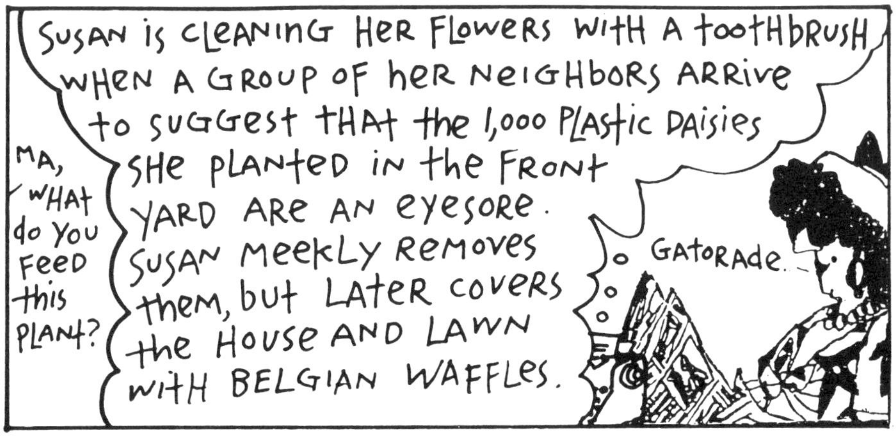
Susan is cleaning her flowers with a toothbrush when a group of her neighbors arrive to suggest that the 1,000 plastic daisies she planted in the front yard are an eyesore. Susan meekly removes them, but later covers the house and lawn with Belgian waffles.
Ma, what do you feed this plant?
Gatorade.

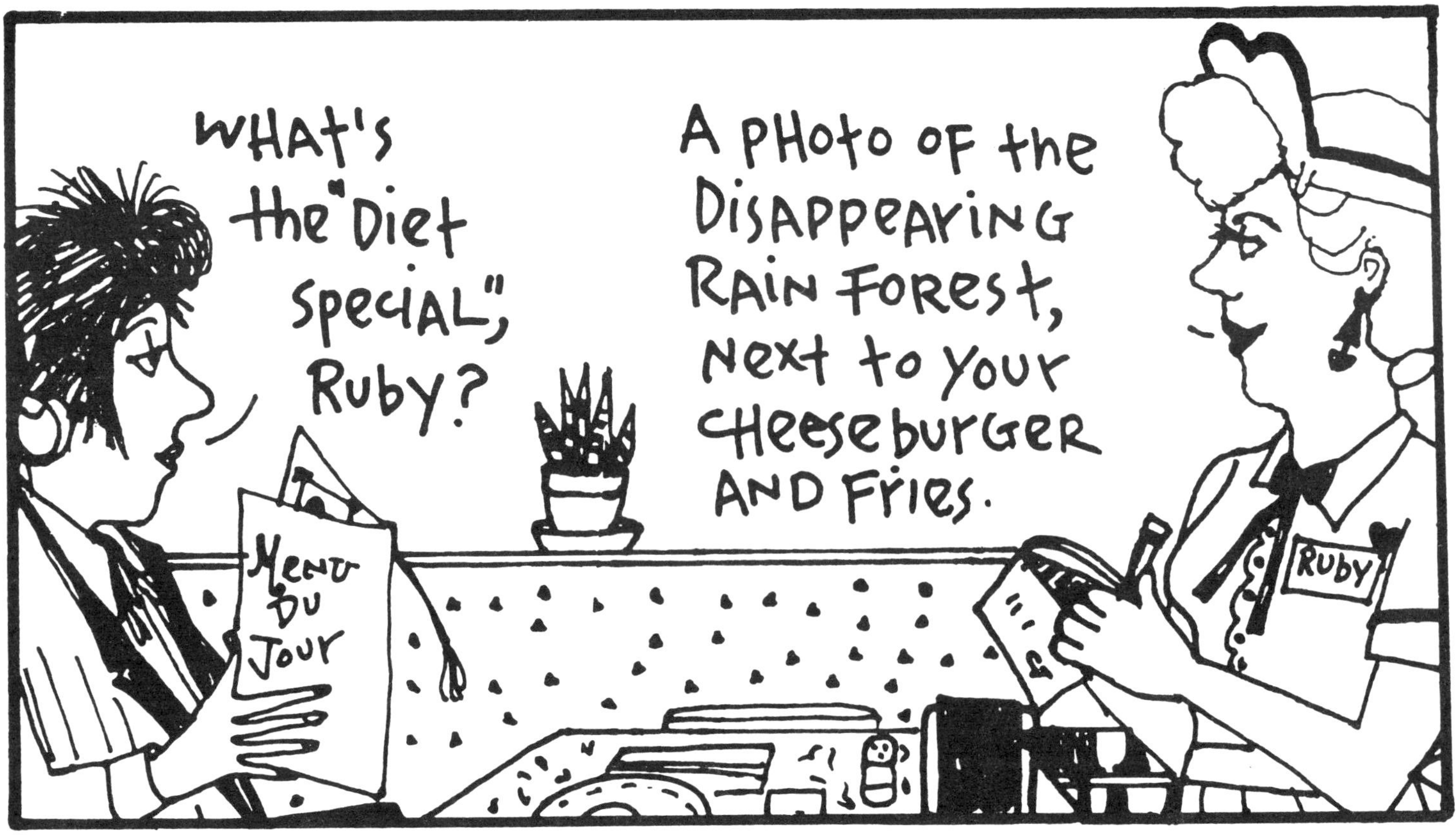
What's the "Diet Special", Ruby?
A photo of the disappearing rain forest, next to your cheeseburger and fries.
Menu du Jour
Ruby

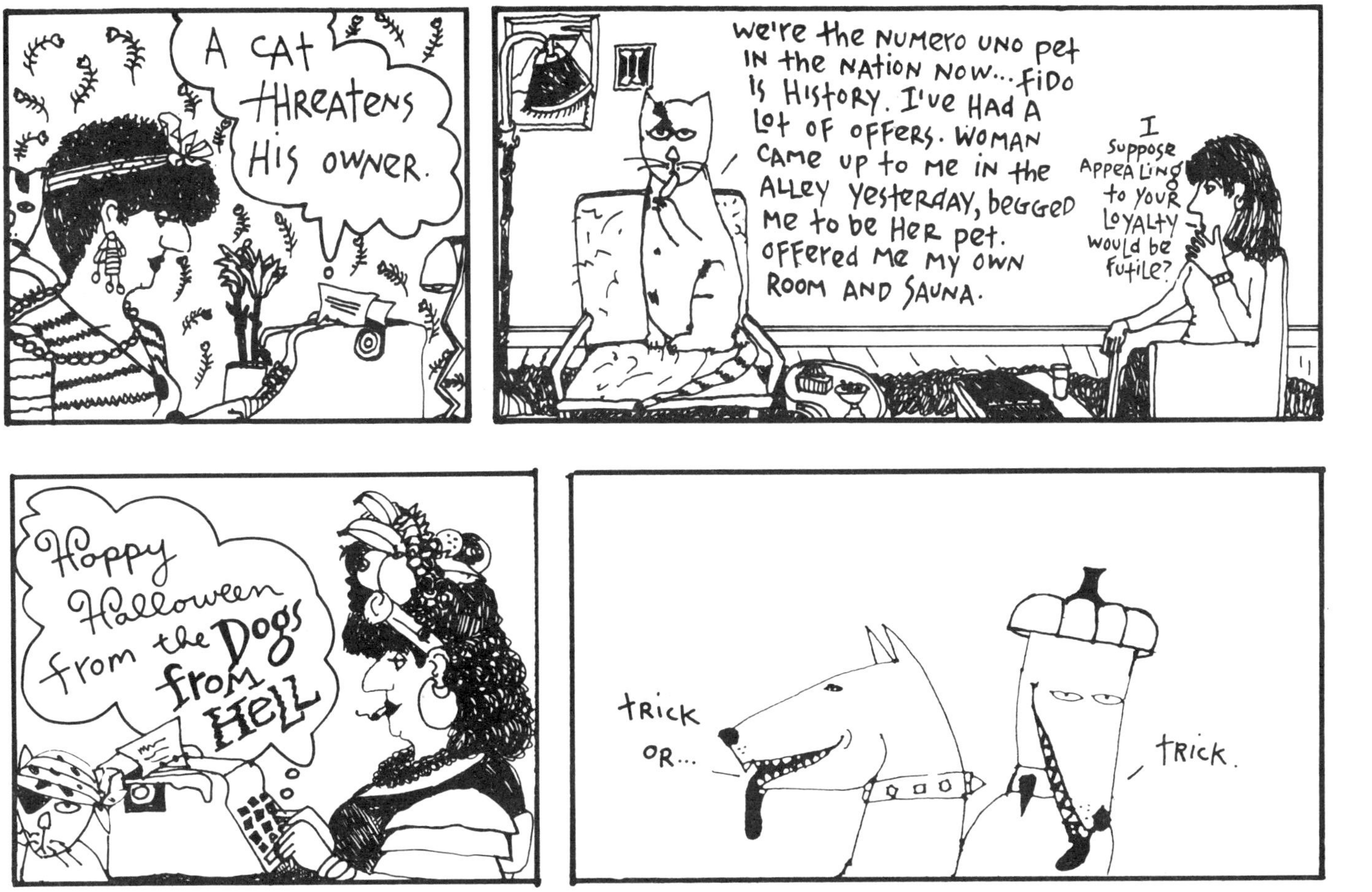
A CAT THREATENS HIS OWNER.
WE'RE THE NUMERO UNO PET IN THE NATION NOW... FIDO IS HISTORY. I'VE HAD A LOT OF OFFERS. WOMAN CAME UP TO ME IN THE ALLEY YESTERDAY, BEGGED ME TO BE HER PET. OFFERED ME MY OWN ROOM AND SAUNA.
I SUPPOSE APPEALING TO YOUR LOYALTY WOULD BE FUTILE?
Happy Halloween from the Dogs from HELL
TRICK OR...
TRICK.

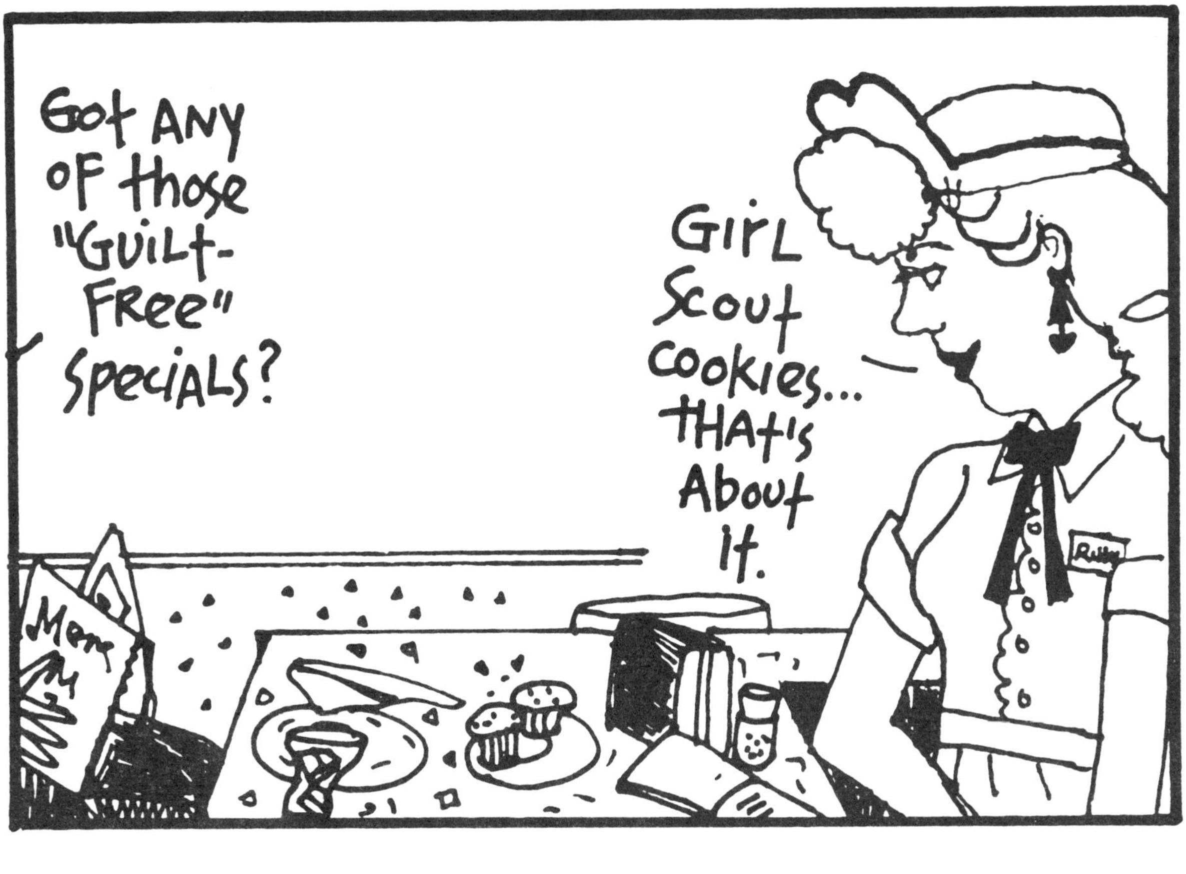
Got ANY of those "GUILT-FREE" SPECIALS?
GIRL SCOUT COOKIES... THAT'S ABOUT IT.

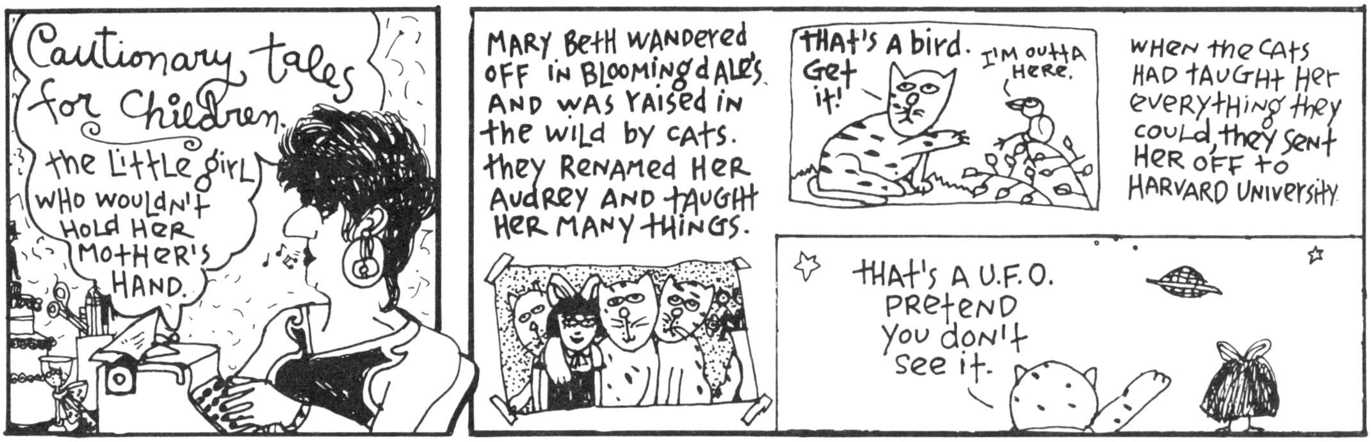
Cautionary tales for Children.
the Little girl WHO WOULDN'T HOLD HER MOTHER'S HAND.
MARY BETH WANDERED OFF IN BLOOMINGDALE'S AND WAS RAISED IN the WILD by CATS. they RENAMED HER Audrey AND TAUGHT HER MANY THINGS.
THAT'S A bird. Get it!
I'M OUTTA HERE.
WHEN the CATS HAD TAUGHT Her everything they could, they sent Her OFF to HARVARD UNIVERSITY.
THAT'S A U.F.O. pretend you don't see it.

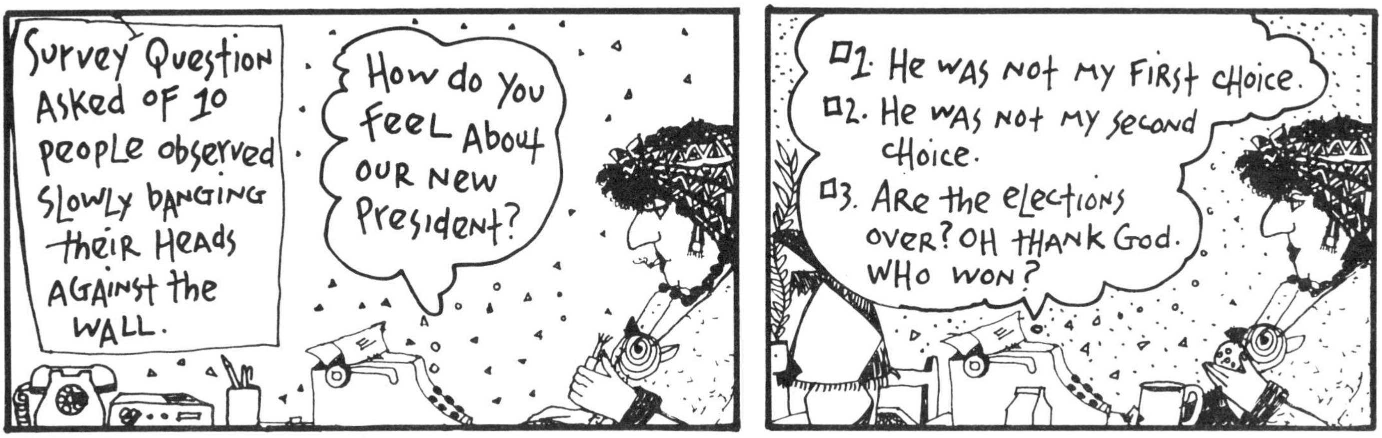
Survey Question Asked of 10 people observed SLOWLY BANGING their Heads AGAINST the WALL.
How do you feel About our new President?
1. He was not my first choice.
2. He was not my second choice.
3. Are the elections over? OH THANK God. WHO WON?

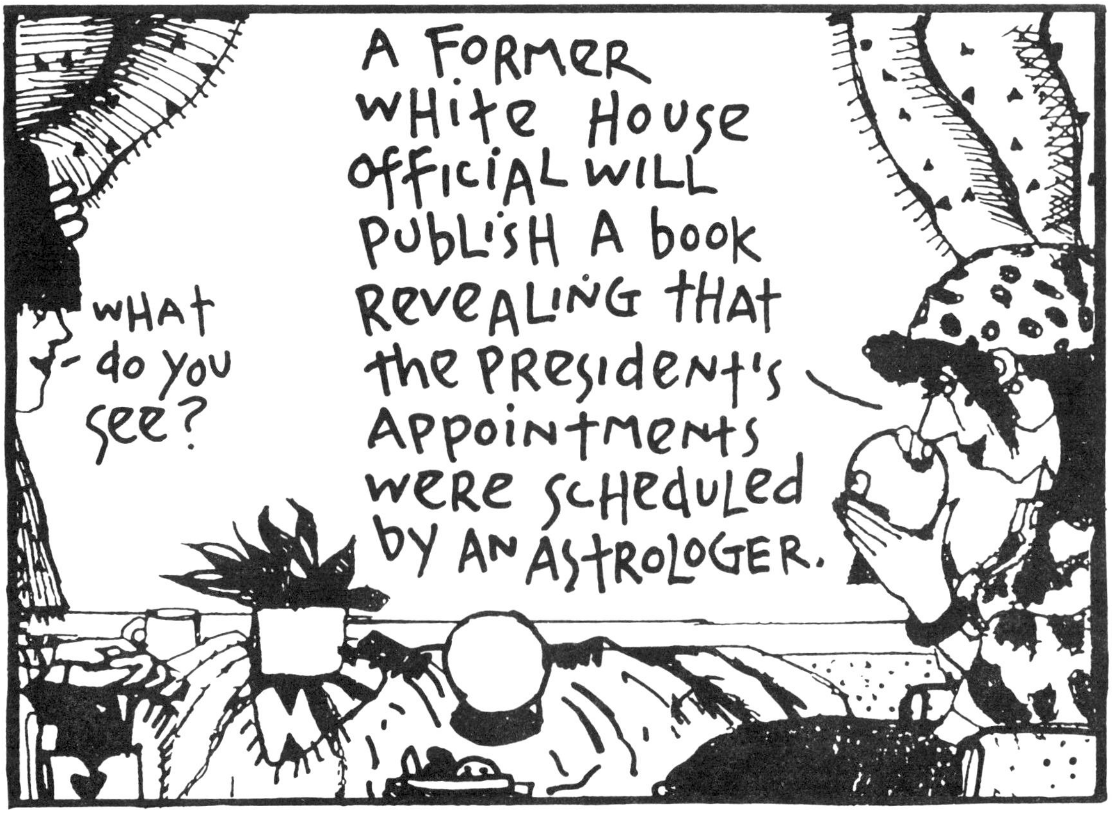
WHAT do you see?
A FORMER WHITE HOUSE OFFICIAL WILL PUBLISH A book REVEALING THAT the PRESIDENT'S APPOINTMENTS WERE SCHEDULED BY AN ASTROLOGER.

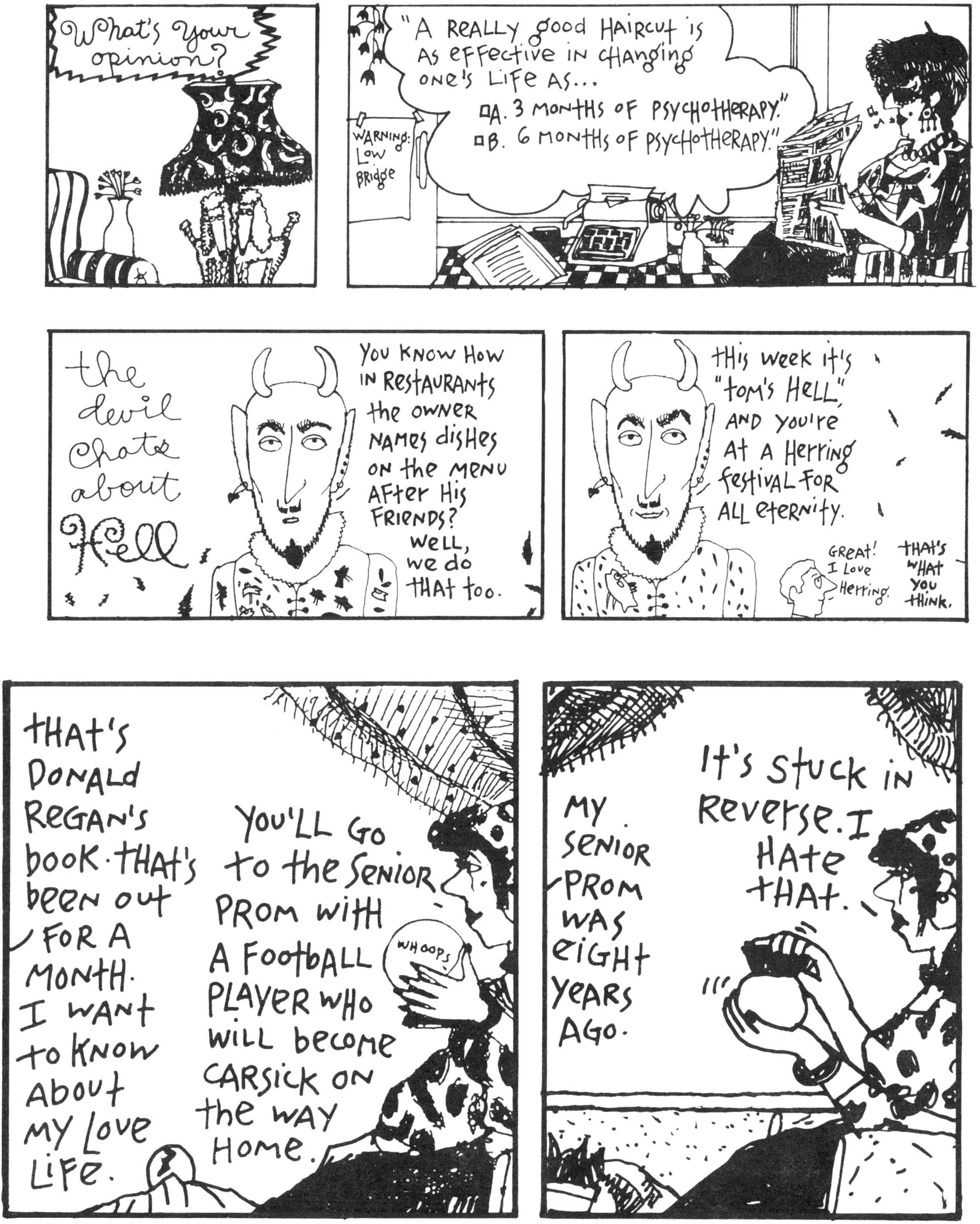
What's your opinion?
"A REALLY good HAIRcut is AS effective IN changing one's LIFE AS...
A. 3 MONTHS OF PSYCHOTHERAPY."
B. 6 MONTHS OF PSYCHOTHERAPY."
WARNING: LOW BRIDGE
the devil chats about Hell
YOU KNOW HOW IN RESTAURANTS the OWNER NAMES dishes ON the MENU AFTER HIS FRIENDS?
WELL, we do THAT too.
THIS week it's "tom's HELL," AND YOU'RE At A Herring festival FOR ALL eternity.
GREAT! I Love Herring.
THAT'S WHAT YOU THINK.
THAT'S DONALD REGAN'S book. THAT'S been out FOR A MONTH. I WANT to KNOW About MY Love LIFE.
YOU'LL GO to the SENIOR PROM with A FootbALL PLAYER WHO WILL become CARSICK ON the WAY HOME.
WHOOPS
MY SENIOR PROM WAS EIGHT YEARS AGO.
It's Stuck IN Reverse. I HATE THAT.

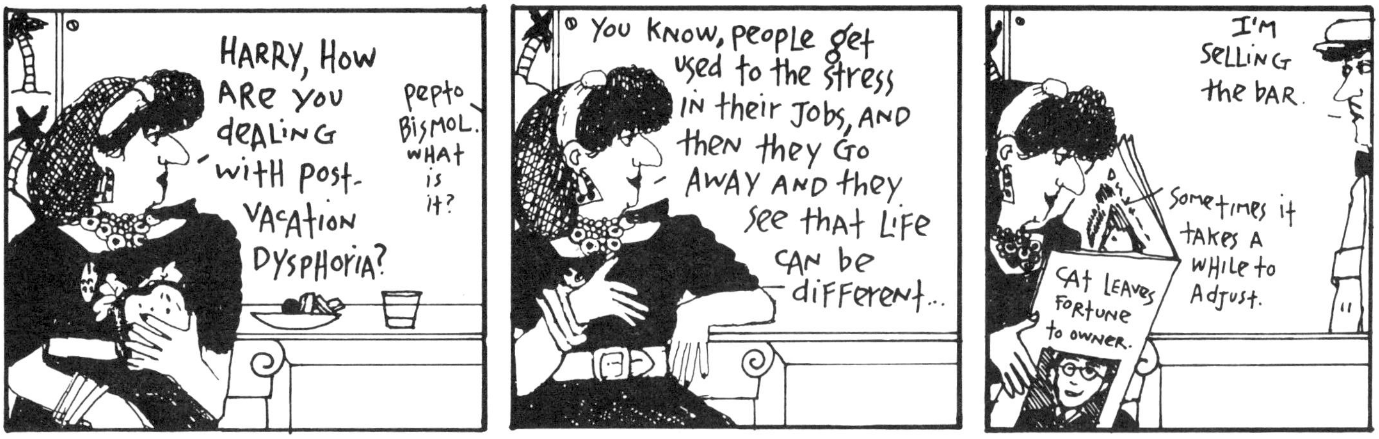
HARRY, HOW ARE YOU DEALING WITH POST-VACATION DYSPHORIA?
PEPTO BISMOL. WHAT IS IT?
YOU KNOW, PEOPLE GET USED TO THE STRESS IN THEIR JOBS, AND THEN THEY GO AWAY AND THEY SEE THAT LIFE CAN BE DIFFERENT...
I'M SELLING THE BAR.
SOMETIMES IT TAKES A WHILE TO ADJUST.
CAT LEAVES FORTUNE TO OWNER.

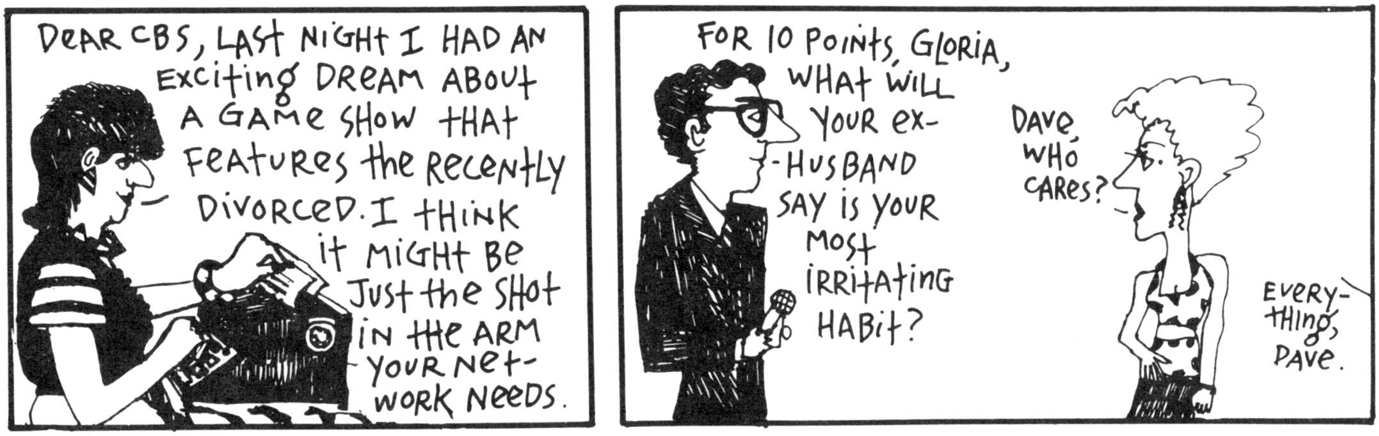
DEAR CBS, LAST NIGHT I HAD AN EXCITING DREAM ABOUT A GAME SHOW THAT FEATURES THE RECENTLY DIVORCED. I THINK IT MIGHT BE JUST THE SHOT IN THE ARM YOUR NETWORK NEEDS.
FOR 10 POINTS, GLORIA, WHAT WILL YOUR EX-HUSBAND SAY IS YOUR MOST IRRITATING HABIT?
DAVE, WHO CARES?
EVERYTHING, DAVE.

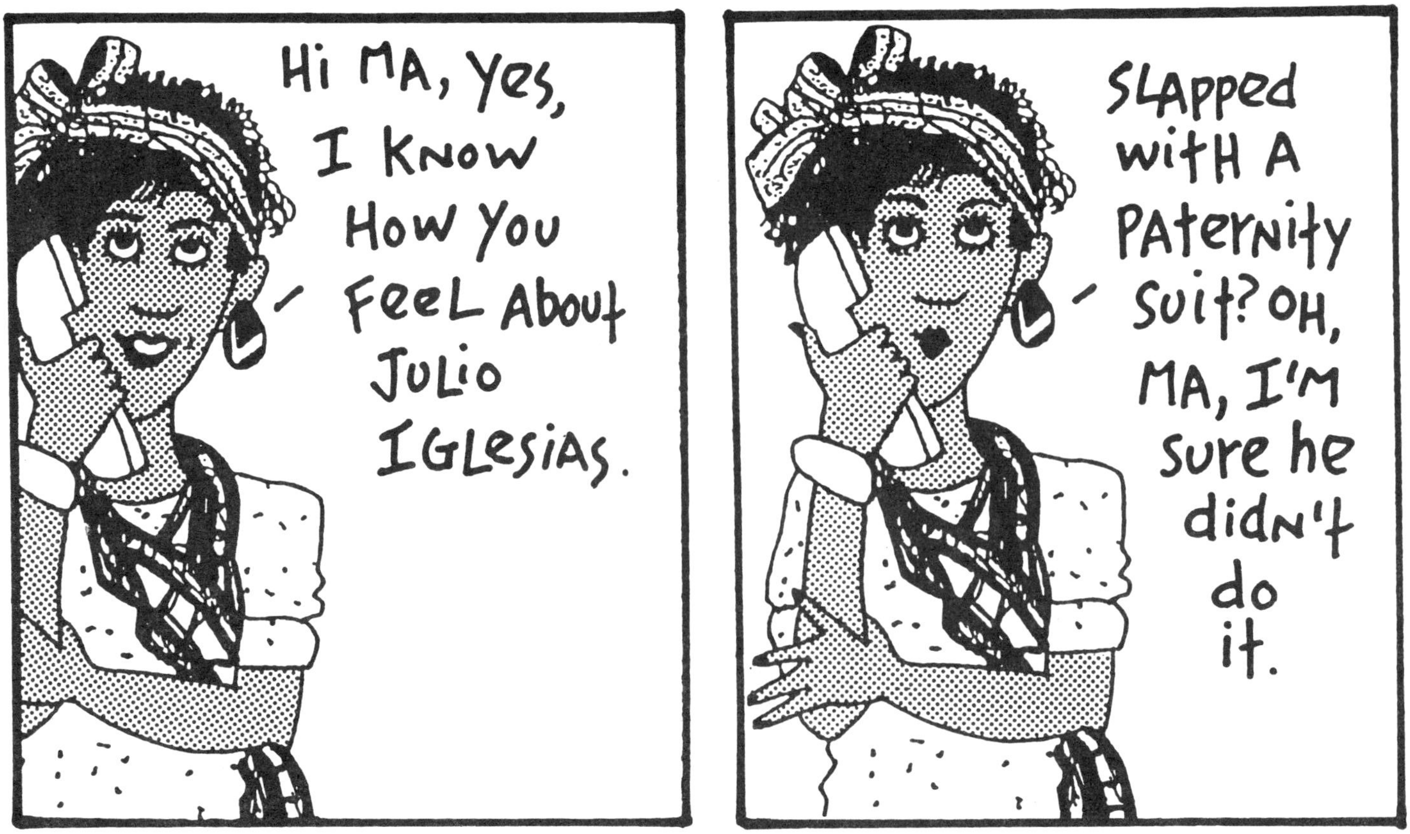
HI MA, YES, I KNOW HOW YOU FEEL ABOUT JULIO IGLESIAS.
SLAPPED WITH A PATERNITY SUIT? OH, MA, I'M SURE HE DIDN'T DO IT.

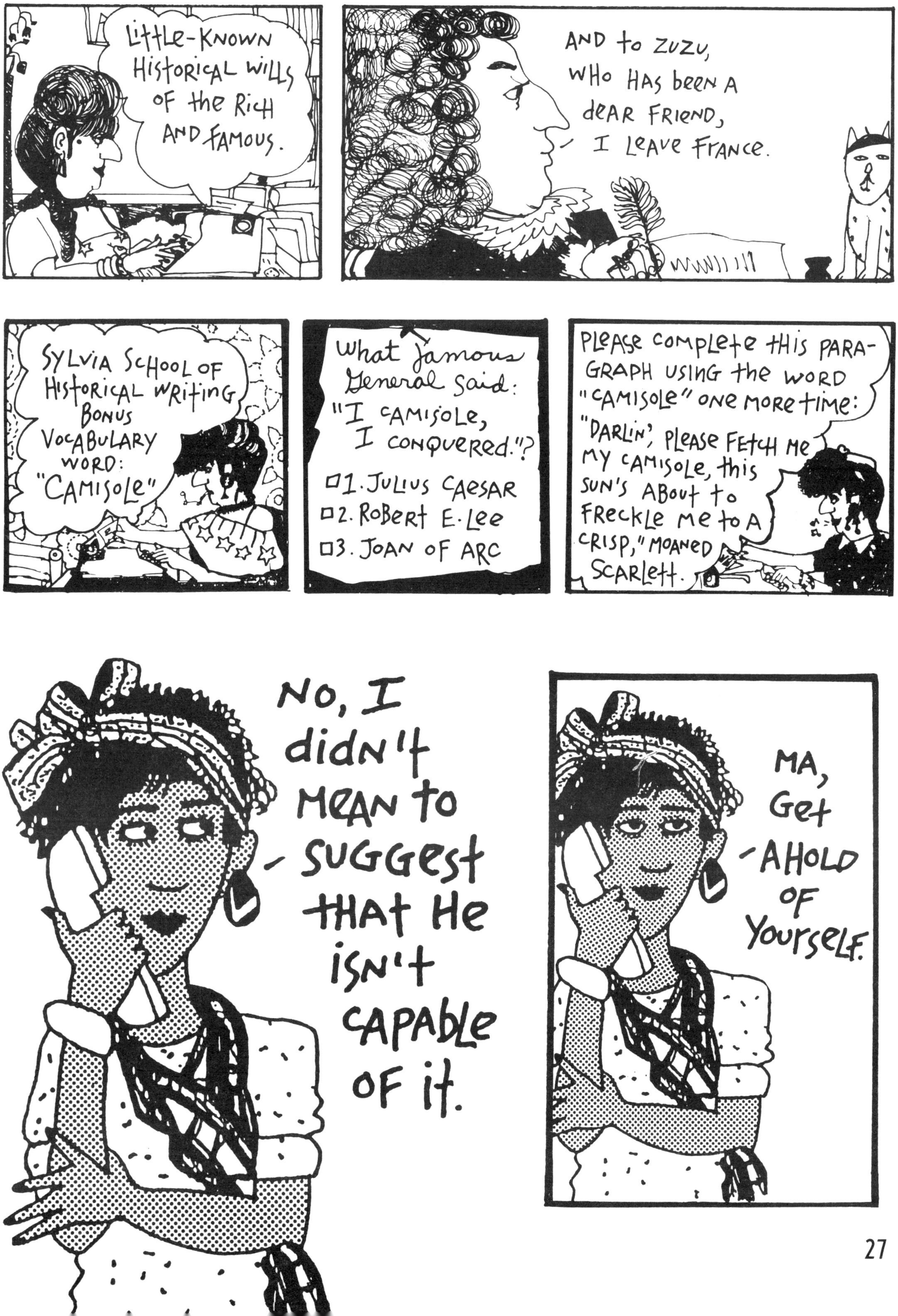

Little-Known Historical Wills of the Rich and Famous.
And to Zuzu, who has been a dear friend, I leave France.
Sylvia School of Historical Writing Bonus Vocabulary Word: "Camisole"
What famous General said: "I camisole, I conquered."?
☐1. Julius Caesar
☐2. Robert E. Lee
☐3. Joan of Arc
Please complete this paragraph using the word "camisole" one more time: "Darlin', please fetch me my camisole, this sun's about to freckle me to a crisp," moaned Scarlett.
No, I didn't mean to suggest that he isn't capable of it.
Ma, get a hold of yourself.

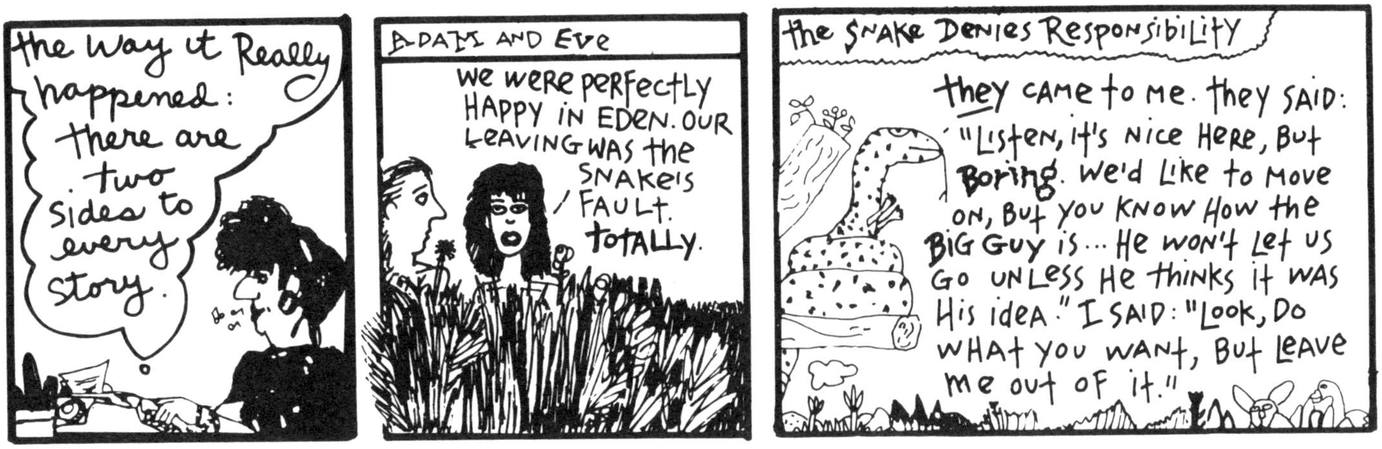

the Way it Really happened: there are two sides to every story.
ADAM AND EVE
we were perfectly HAPPY IN EDEN. OUR LEAVING WAS the SNAKE'S FAULT. TOTALLY.
the SNAKE DENIES RESPONSIBILITY
they came to me. they said: "Listen, it's Nice Here, But Boring. We'd Like to Move on, But you Know How the BIG GUY is... He won't Let us Go unless He thinks it was His idea." I SAID: "Look, Do what you want, But leave me out of it."

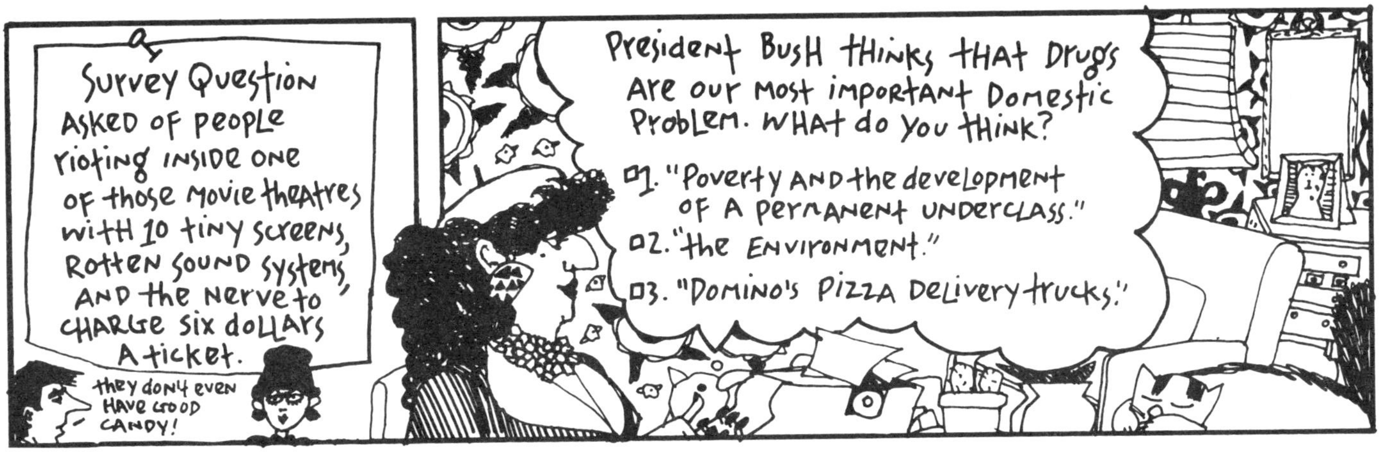

Survey Question Asked of people rioting inside one of those Movie theatres with 10 tiny screens, Rotten sound systems, And the Nerve to CHARGE six dollars A ticket.
they don't even Have GOOD CANDY!
President Bush thinks that Drugs Are our most important Domestic Problem. WHAT do you think?
☐1. "Poverty And the development of A permanent underclass."
☐2. "the Environment."
☐3. "Domino's Pizza Delivery trucks."

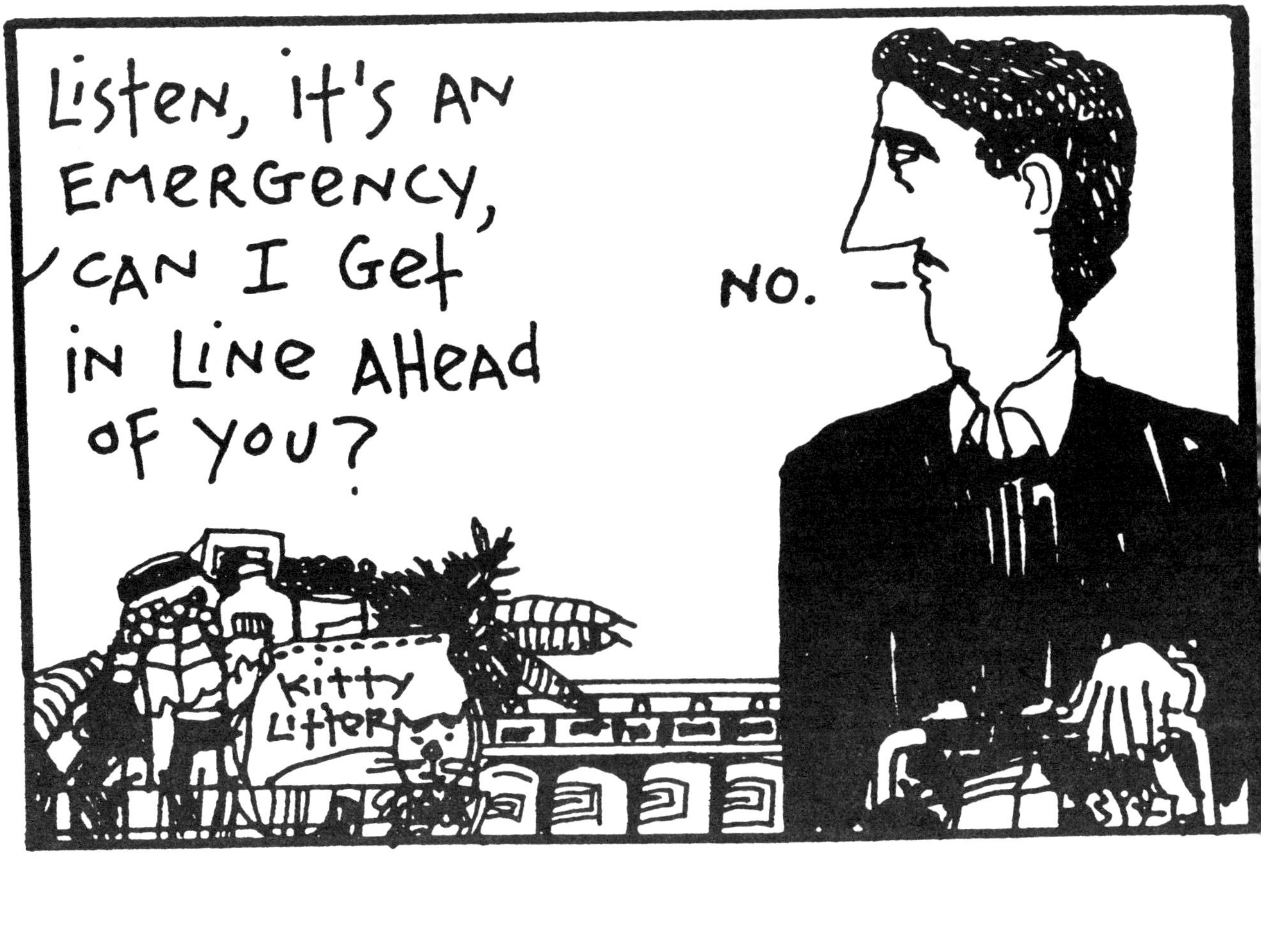

Listen, it's AN EMERGENCY, CAN I Get in Line AHead of You?
NO.
kitty Litter

How Well do you know your genders?

-HUH? -HUH?

PLEASE MATCH the statements below with the sex most likely to say them.

F M
☐ ☐ 1. "GOSH, I've got to get over to the dinosaur display at the museum. I've always wanted to see dinosaurs actual size."

F M
☐ ☐ 2. "MY HIPS ARE the SIZE of dinosaurs."

I'M AFRAID I HAVE SHORT TERM MEMORY LOSS.

Let's-be reasonable-therapy

the specter of Alzheimer's Disease makes all of us overly sensitive to normal forgetfulness.

So you're sure it isn't anything to worry about?

WHAT ISN'T?

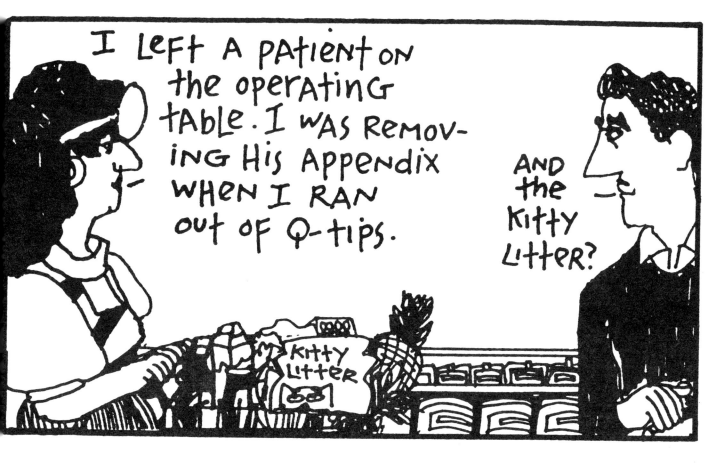

I LEFT A PATIENT ON the operating table. I WAS REMOVING HIS Appendix WHEN I RAN out of Q-tips.

AND the Kitty Litter?

Kitty Litter

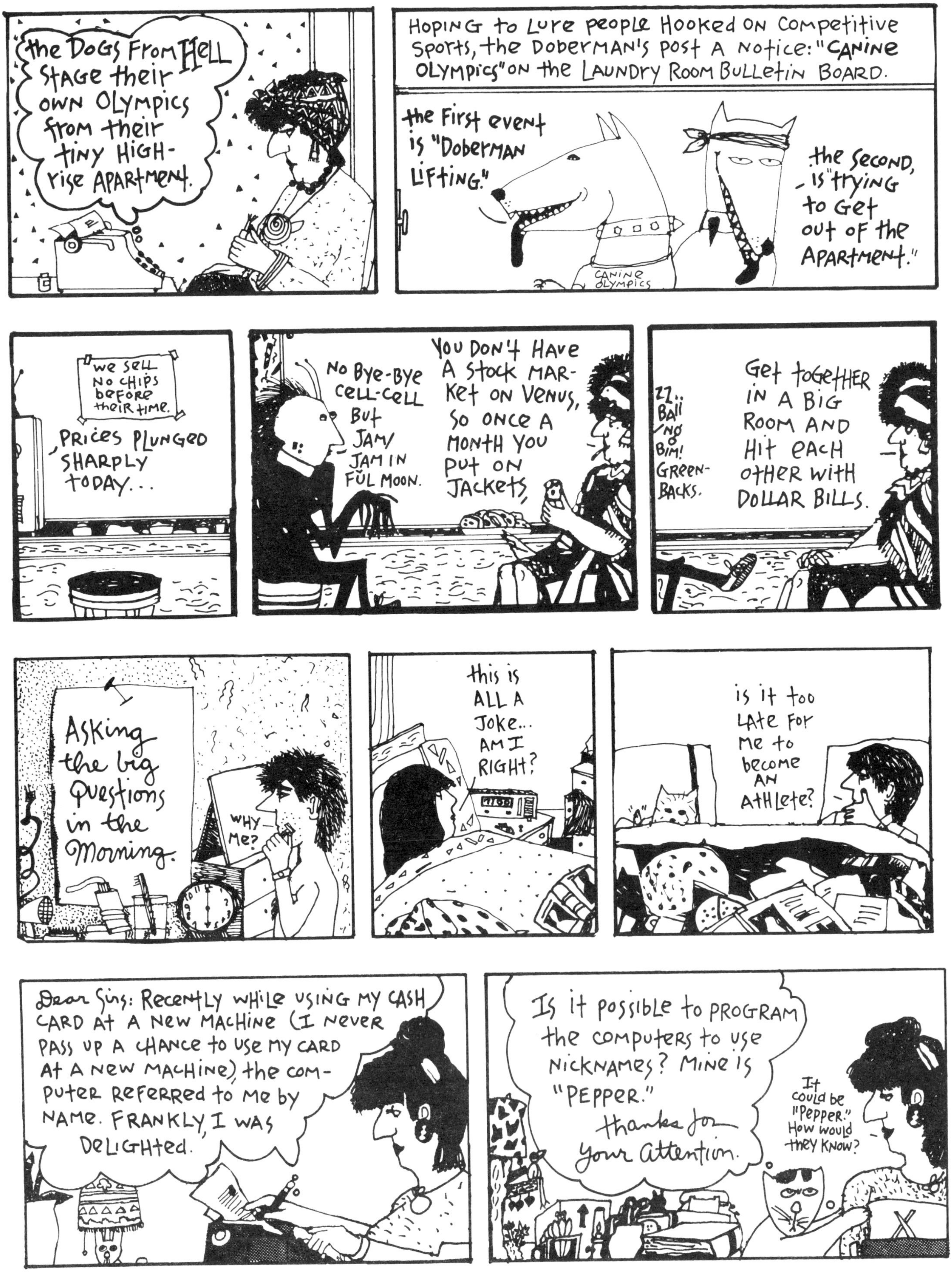
the Dogs From Hell stage their own Olympics from their tiny high-rise Apartment.
Hoping to lure people hooked on competitive sports, the Doberman's post a notice: "Canine Olympics" on the Laundry Room Bulletin Board.
the First event is "Doberman Lifting."
the second, is "trying to get out of the Apartment."
CANINE OLYMPICS
we sell no chips before their time.
Prices plunged sharply today...
No Bye-Bye Cell-Cell But Jam/Jam in Ful Moon.
You don't have a stock market on Venus, so once a month you put on jackets,
ZZ.. BAI /NO BIM! GREEN-BACKS.
Get together in a big room and hit each other with dollar bills.
Asking the big Questions in the Morning.
WHY ME?
this is ALL A Joke... AM I RIGHT?
is it too late for me to become an athlete?
Dear Sirs: Recently while using my cash card at a new machine (I never pass up a chance to use my card at a new machine) the computer referred to me by name. Frankly, I was delighted.
Is it possible to program the computers to use nicknames? Mine is "Pepper." thanks for your attention.
It could be "Pepper." How would they know?

UFOs

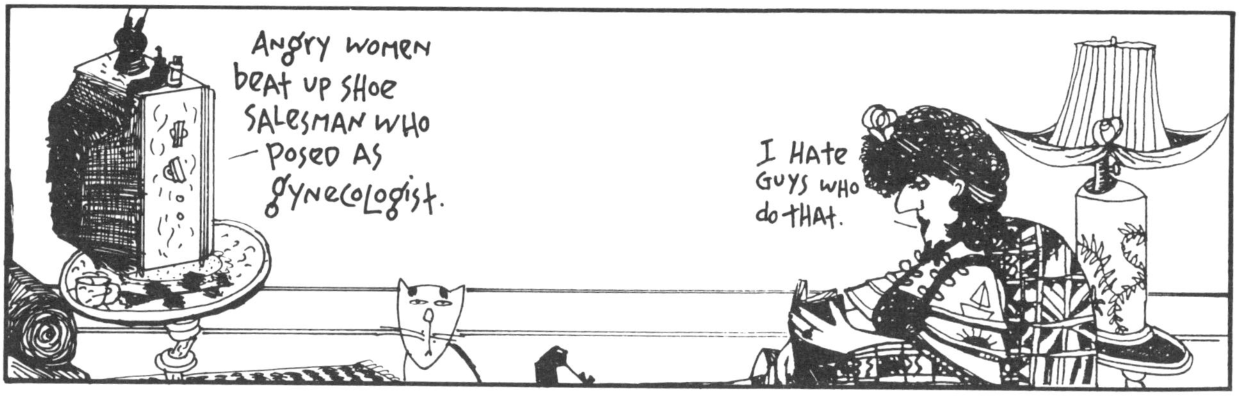
Angry women beat up shoe salesman who posed as gynecologist.
I hate guys who do that.

I used to feel it was dishonorable to get an idea from a tabloid newspaper and not buy the newspaper. I've relaxed my standards. I look at them while I'm in the checkout line. It isn't possible to remember those headlines. They have to be written out immediately. I think I'll remember them, the images are so vivid, but then I get distracted by a speck of dust and they're gone, so now I write them down on the back of deposit slips in my checkbook.

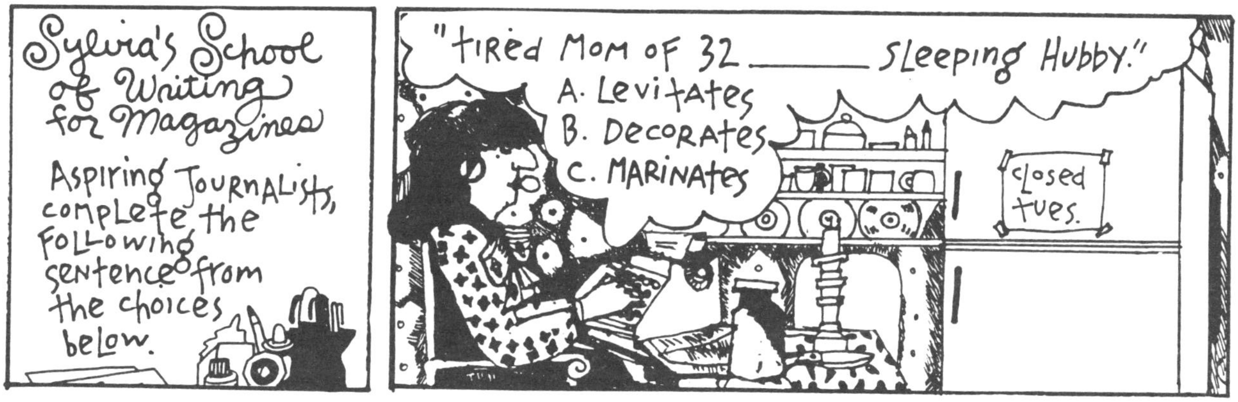
Sylvia's School of Writing for Magazines
Aspiring journalists, complete the following sentence from the choices below.
"Tired Mom of 32 ______ Sleeping Hubby."
A. Levitates
B. Decorates
C. Marinates
Closed Tues.

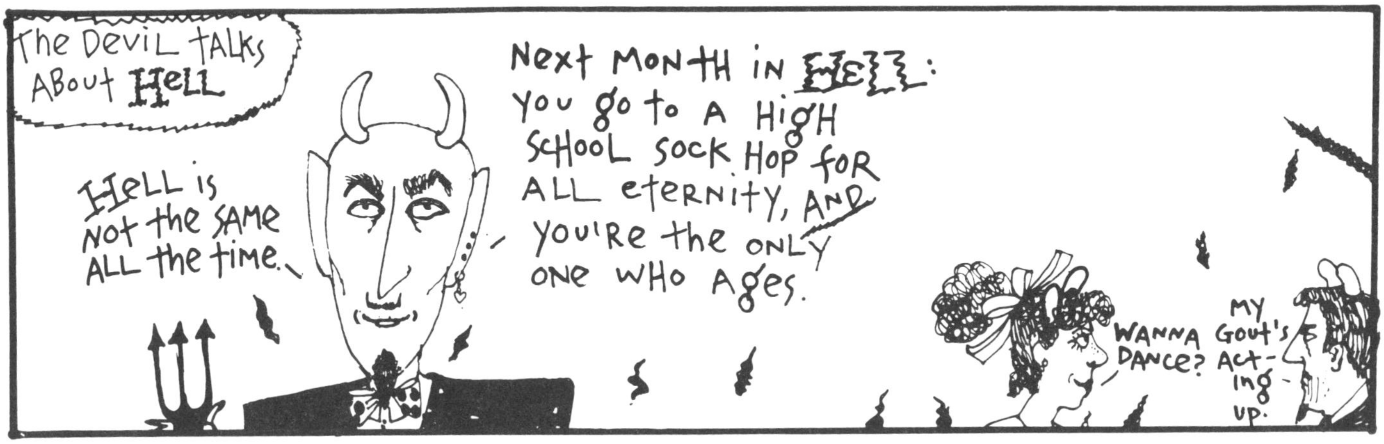
The Devil talks About Hell
Hell is not the same all the time.
Next month in Hell: you go to a high school sock hop for all eternity, and you're the only one who ages.
Wanna dance?
My gout's acting up.

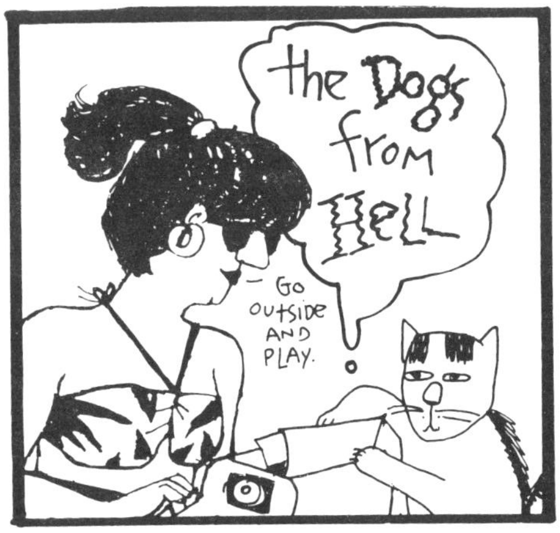
the Dogs from Hell
Go outside and play.

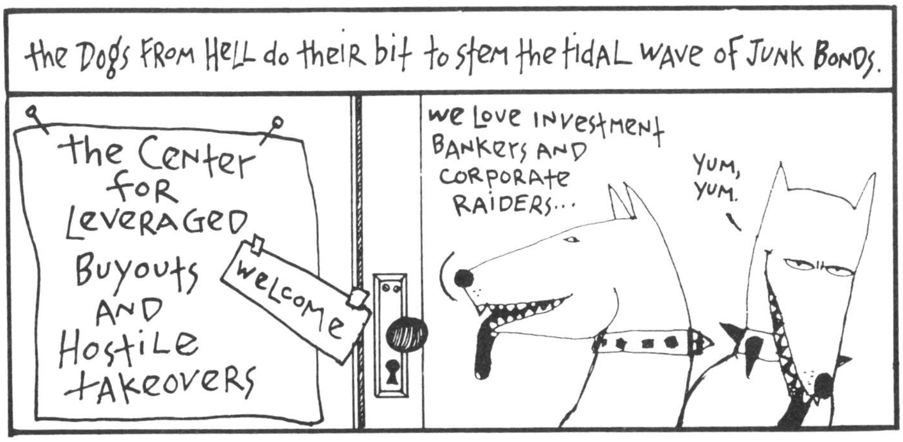
the Dogs from Hell do their bit to stem the tidal wave of junk bonds.
the Center for Leveraged Buyouts and Hostile takeovers
welcome
we love investment bankers and corporate raiders...
Yum, yum.

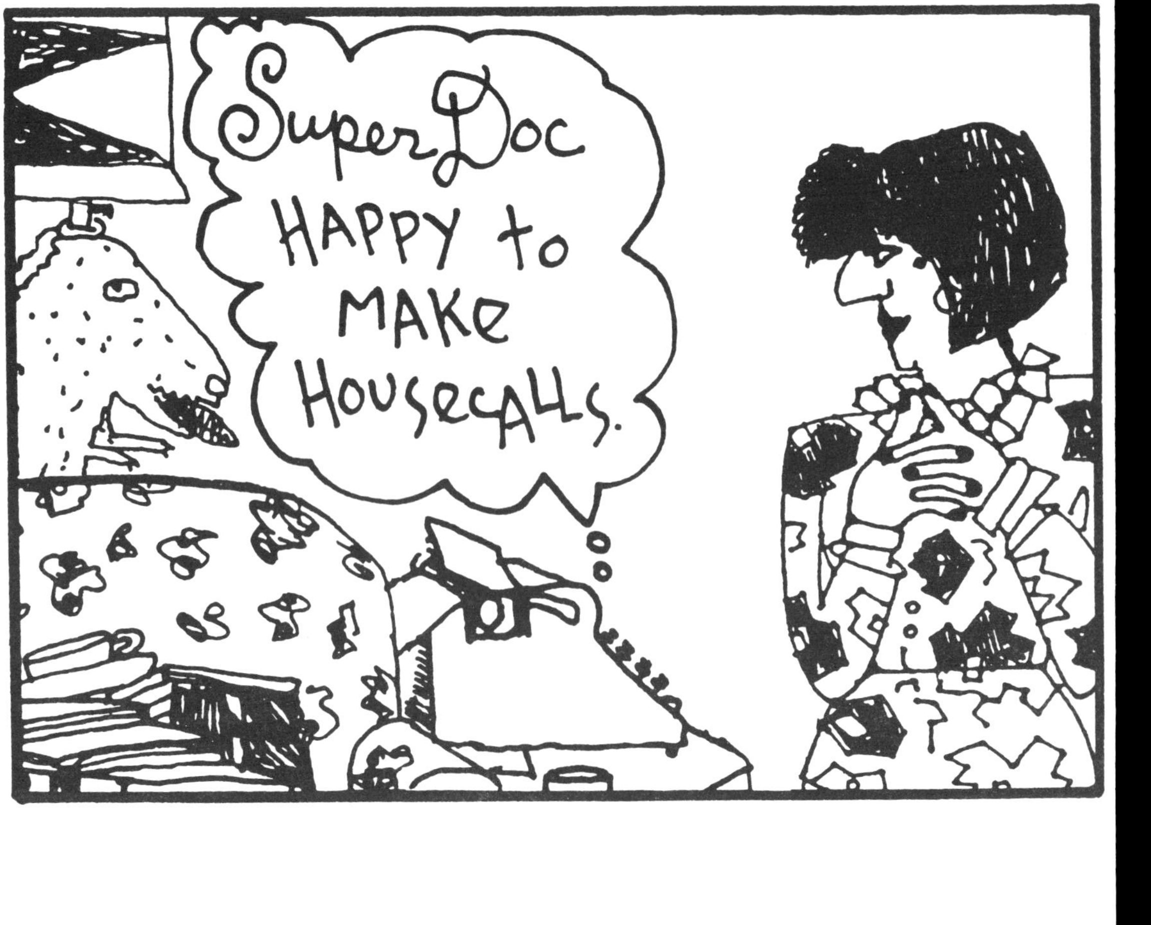
SuperDoc HAPPY to MAKE Housecalls.

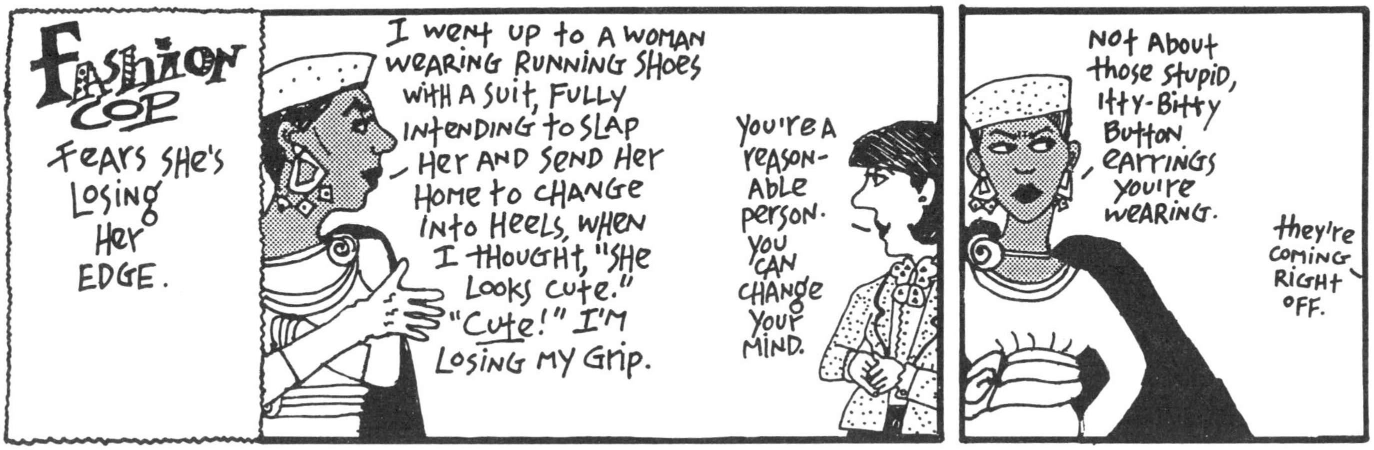
FASHION COP
Fears she's Losing Her EDGE.
I went up to a woman wearing running shoes with a suit, fully intending to slap her and send her home to change into heels, when I thought, "She looks cute." "Cute!" I'm losing my grip.
You're a reasonable person. You can change your mind.
Not about those stupid, itty-bitty button earrings you're wearing.
they're coming right off.

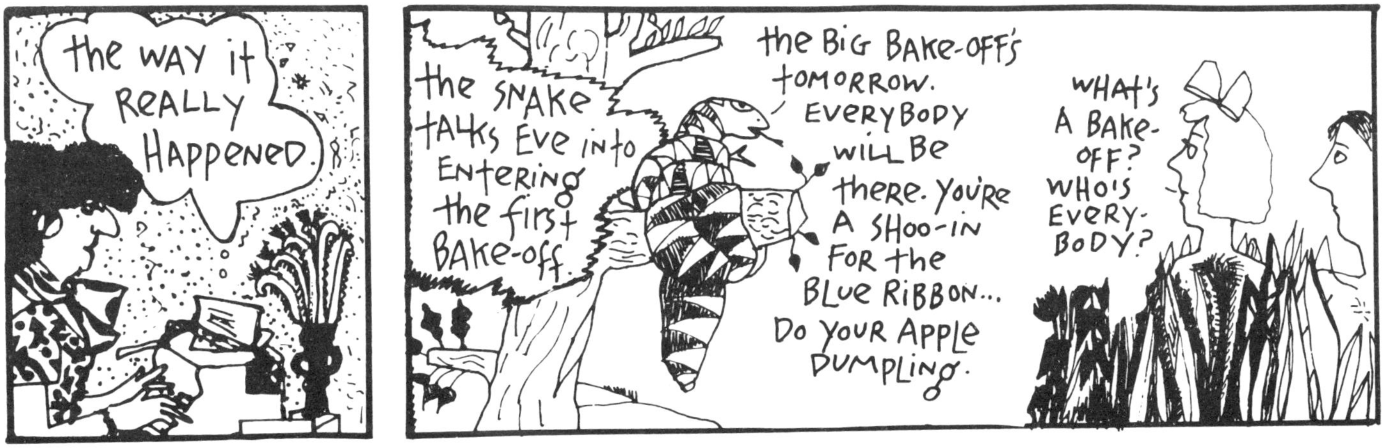
the way it really happened.
the snake talks Eve into entering the first bake-off
the Big Bake-off's tomorrow. Everybody will be there. You're a shoo-in for the blue ribbon... Do your apple dumpling.
What's a bake-off? Who's everybody?

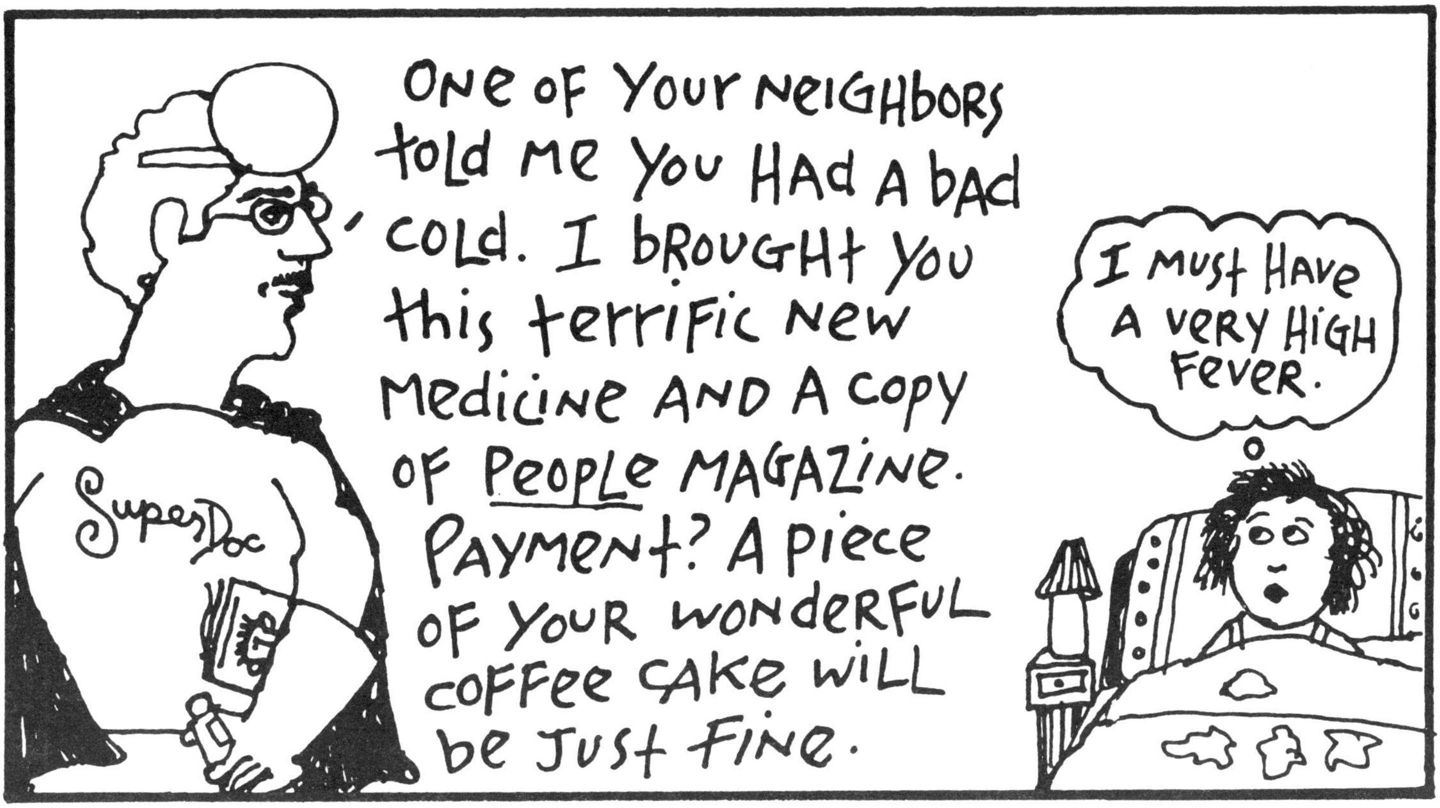
One of your neighbors told me you had a bad cold. I brought you this terrific new medicine and a copy of People magazine. Payment? A piece of your wonderful coffee cake will be just fine.
SuperDoc
I must have a very high fever.

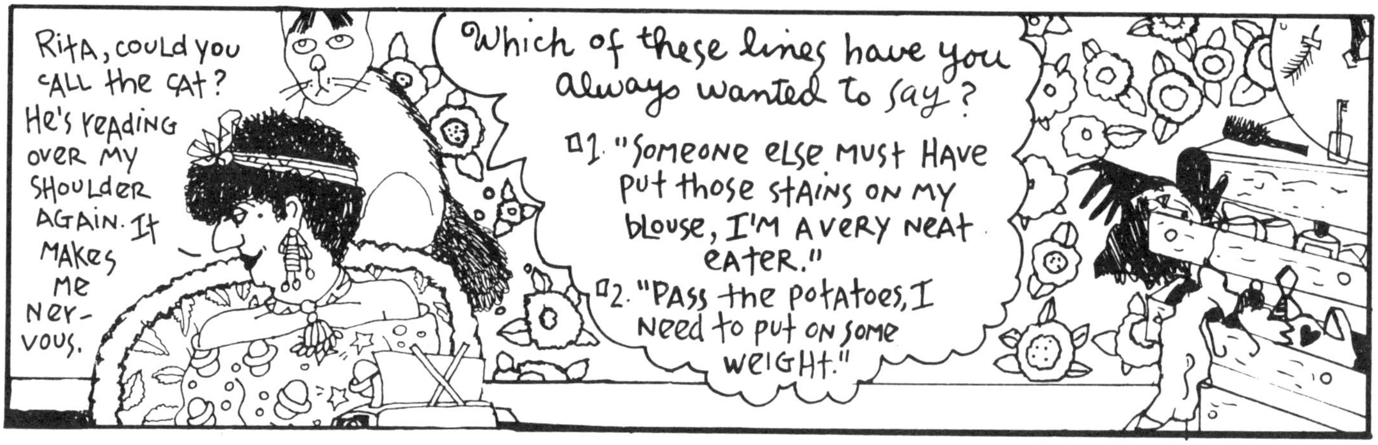
Rita, could you call the cat? He's reading over my shoulder again. It makes me ner-vous.
Which of these lines have you always wanted to say?
□1. "Someone else must have put those stains on my blouse, I'm a very neat eater."
□2. "Pass the potatoes, I need to put on some weight."

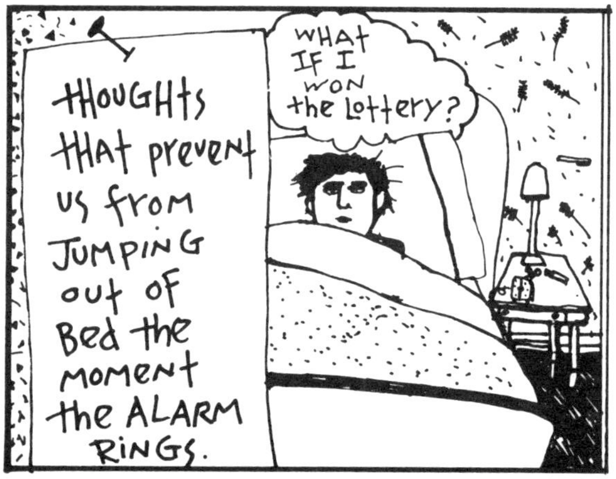
thoughts that prevent us from jumping out of bed the moment the alarm rings.
What if I won the lottery?

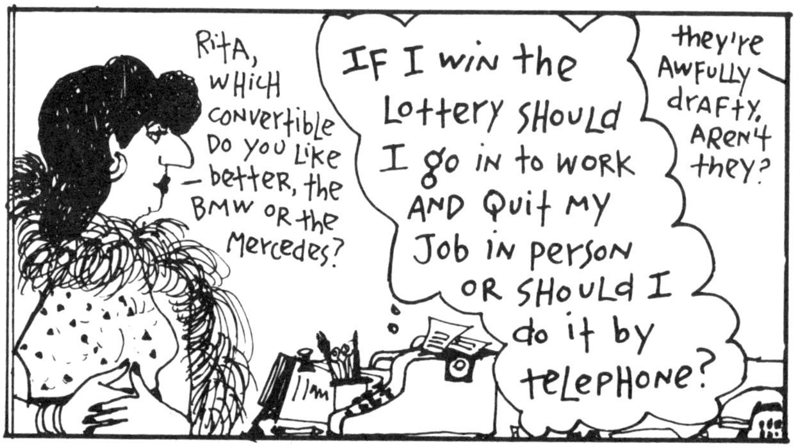
Rita, which convertible do you like better, the BMW or the Mercedes?
If I win the lottery should I go in to work and quit my job in person or should I do it by telephone?
they're awfully drafty, aren't they?

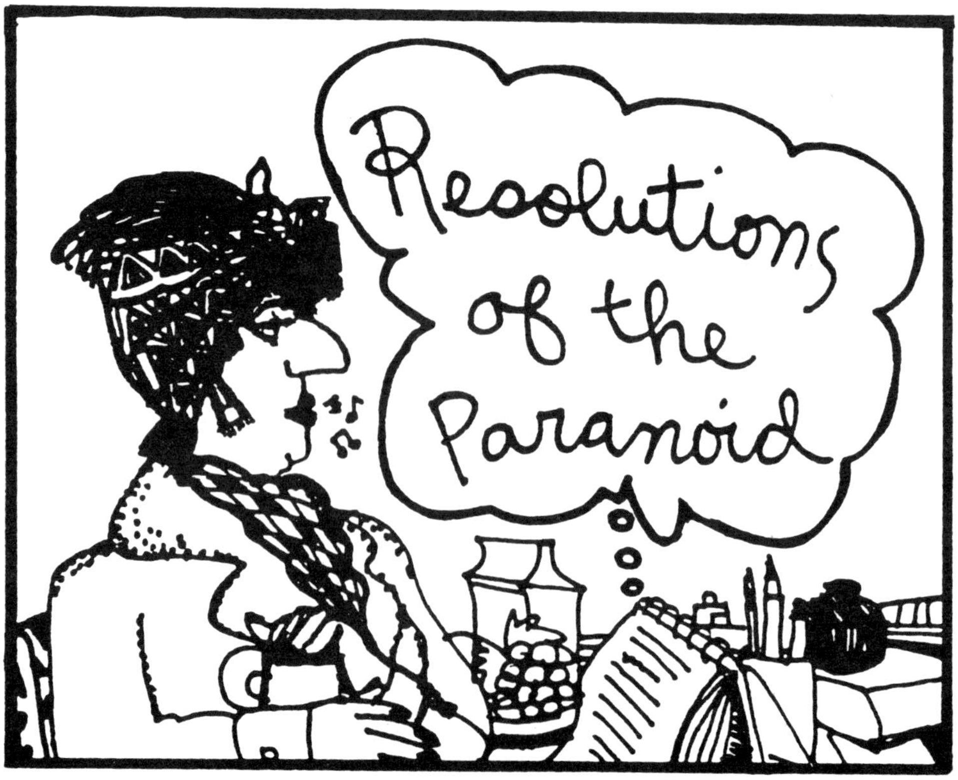
Resolutions of the Paranoid

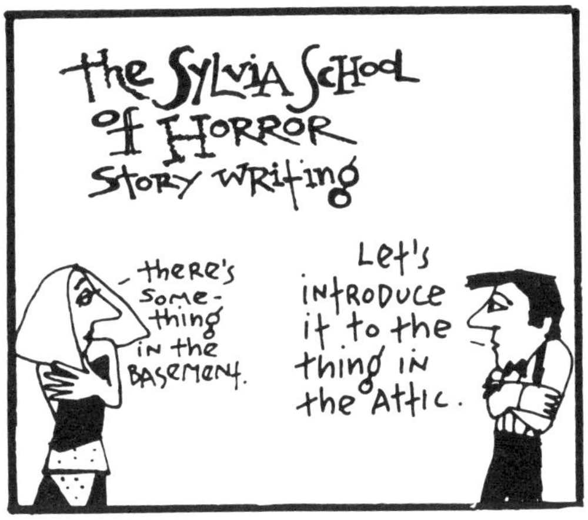

the Sylvia School of Horror Story Writing
there's some-thing in the Basement.
Let's introduce it to the thing in the Attic.

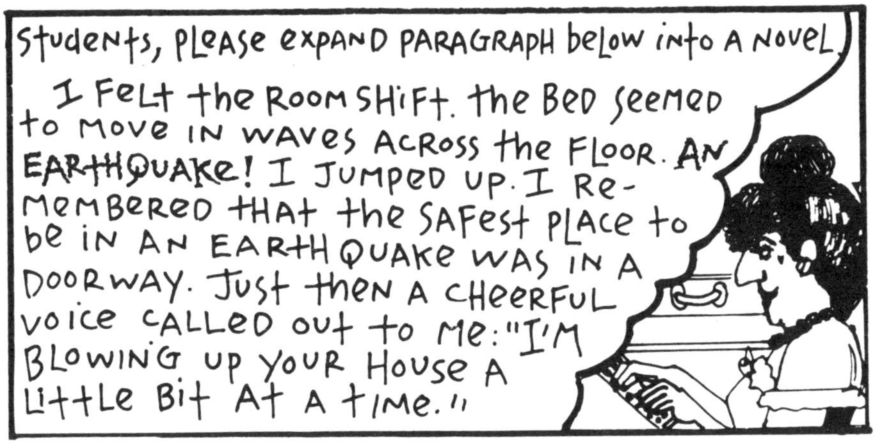

Students, please expand paragraph below into a novel.
I felt the room shift. the bed seemed to move in waves across the floor. An EARTHQUAKE! I jumped up. I remembered that the safest place to be in an earthquake was in a doorway. Just then a cheerful voice called out to me: "I'M BLOWING UP YOUR HOUSE A Little Bit At a time."

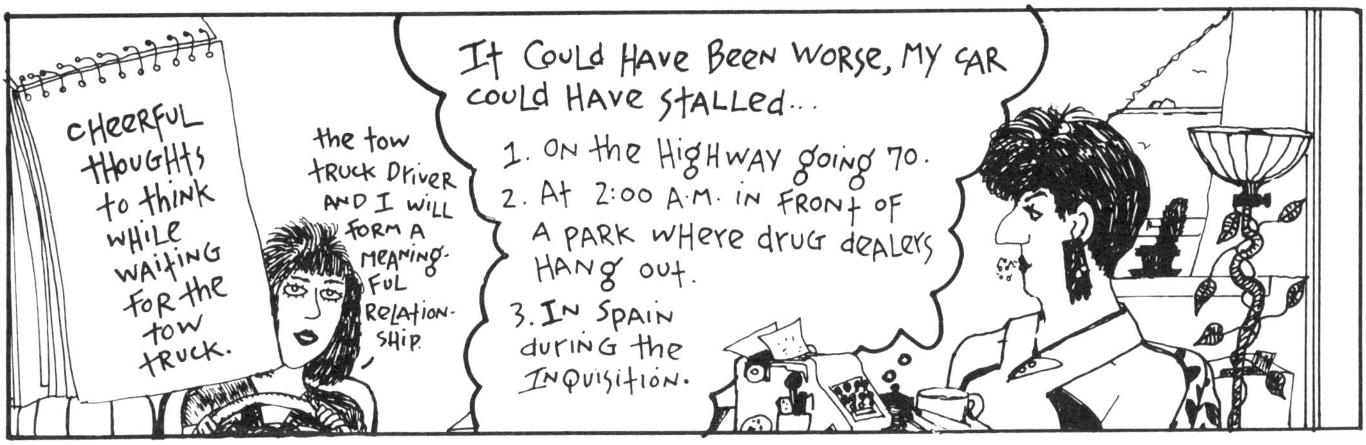

Cheerful thoughts to think while waiting for the tow truck.
the tow truck driver and I will form a meaning-ful relation-ship.
It Could Have Been Worse, My car could have stalled...
1. On the Highway going 70.
2. At 2:00 A.M. in front of a park where drug dealers hang out.
3. In Spain during the Inquisition.

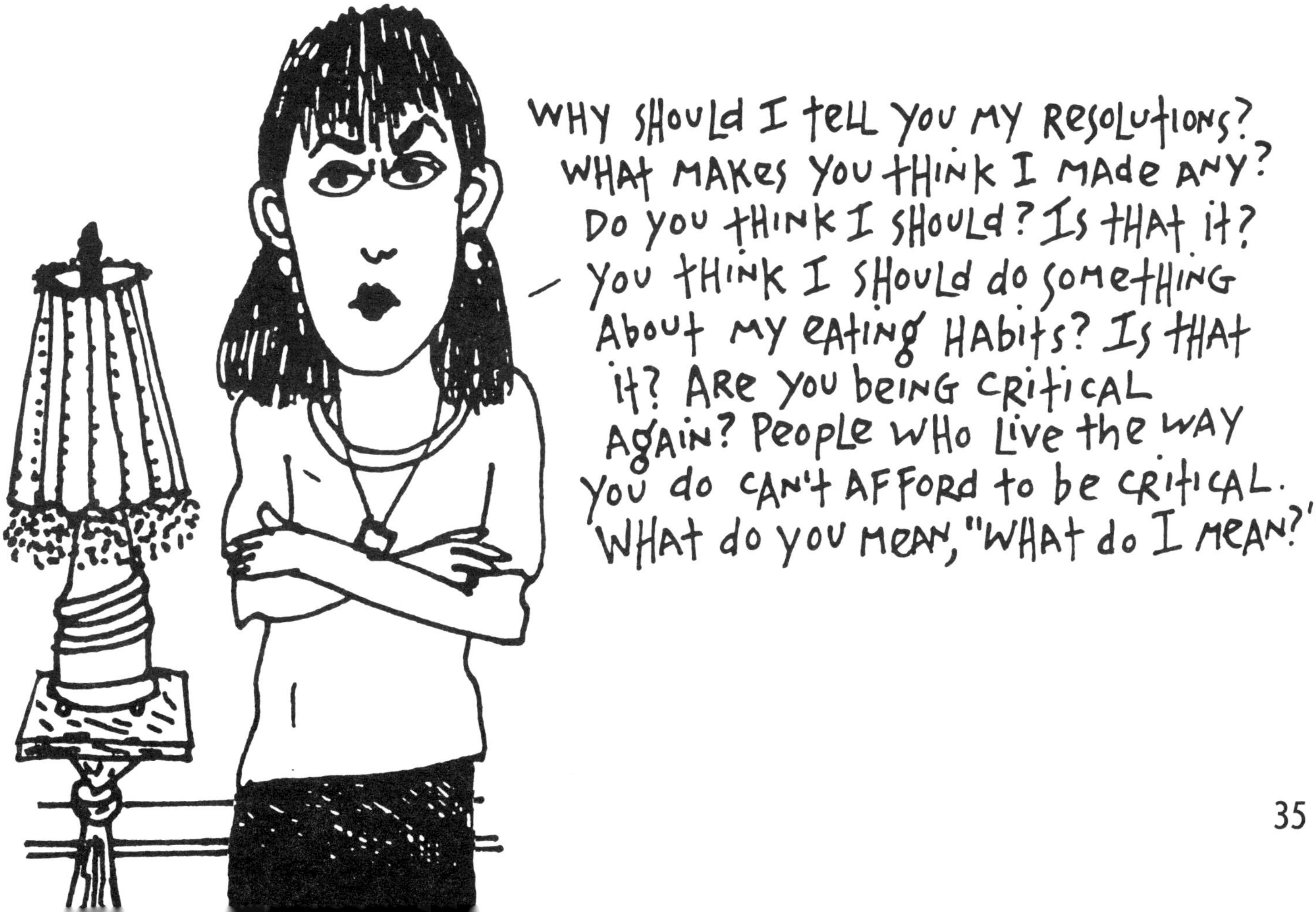

Why should I tell you my resolutions? What makes you think I made any? Do you think I should? Is that it? You think I should do something about my eating habits? Is that it? Are you being critical again? People who live the way you do can't afford to be critical. What do you mean, "What do I mean?"

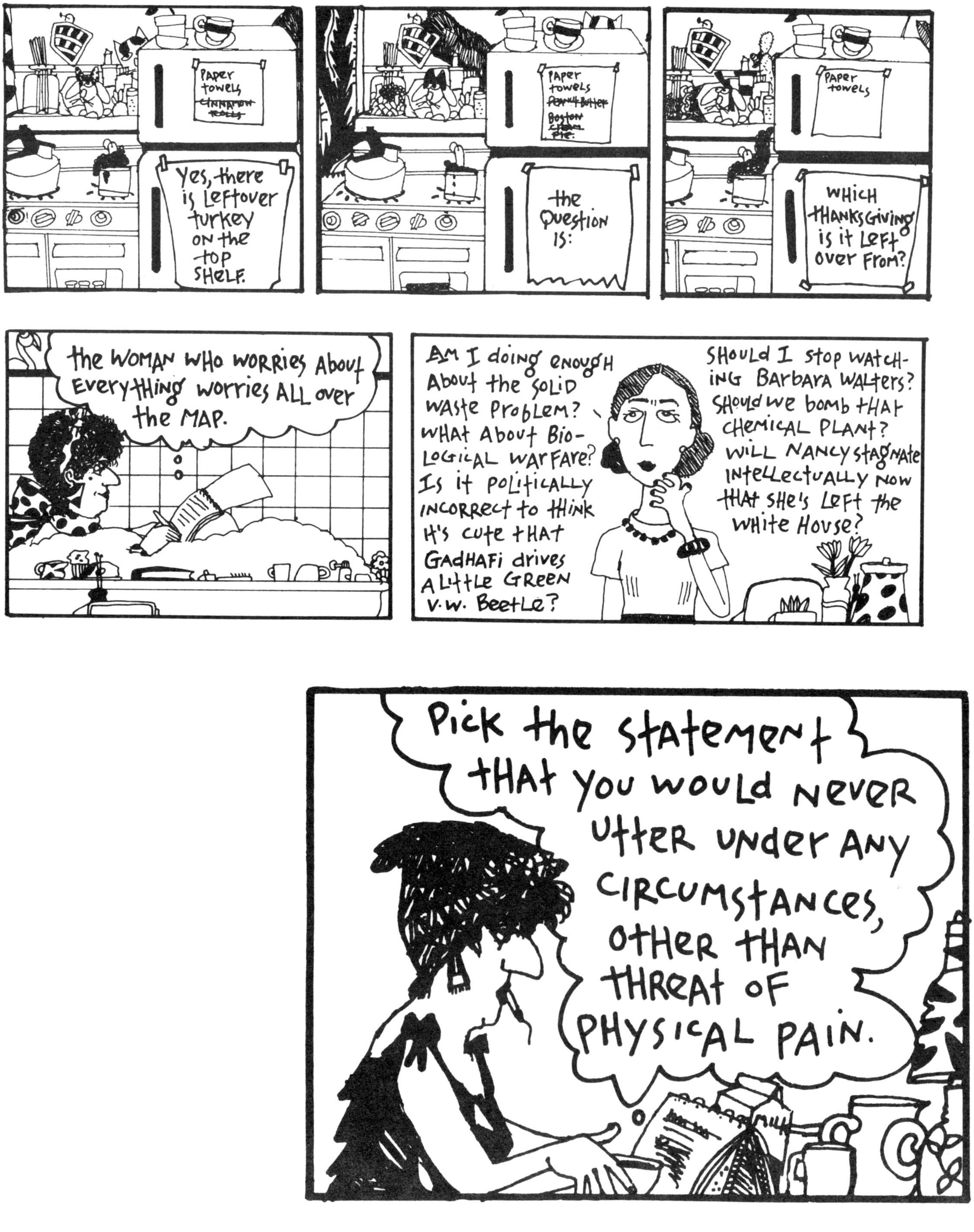

Paper towels
Yes, there is leftover turkey on the top shelf.
Paper towels
Peanut Butter
Boston Cream Pie
the Question is:
Paper towels
WHICH THANKSGIVING is it LEFT over From?
the WOMAN WHO WORRIES About Everything worries ALL over the MAP.
AM I doing enough About the solid waste Problem? WHAT About Biological warfare? Is it politically incorrect to think it's cute that Gadhafi drives A little Green V.W. Beetle?
SHOULD I stop watching Barbara Walters? Should we bomb that chemical plant? Will Nancy stagnate intellectually now that she's left the White House?
Pick the statement that you would never utter under any circumstances, other than threat of physical pain.

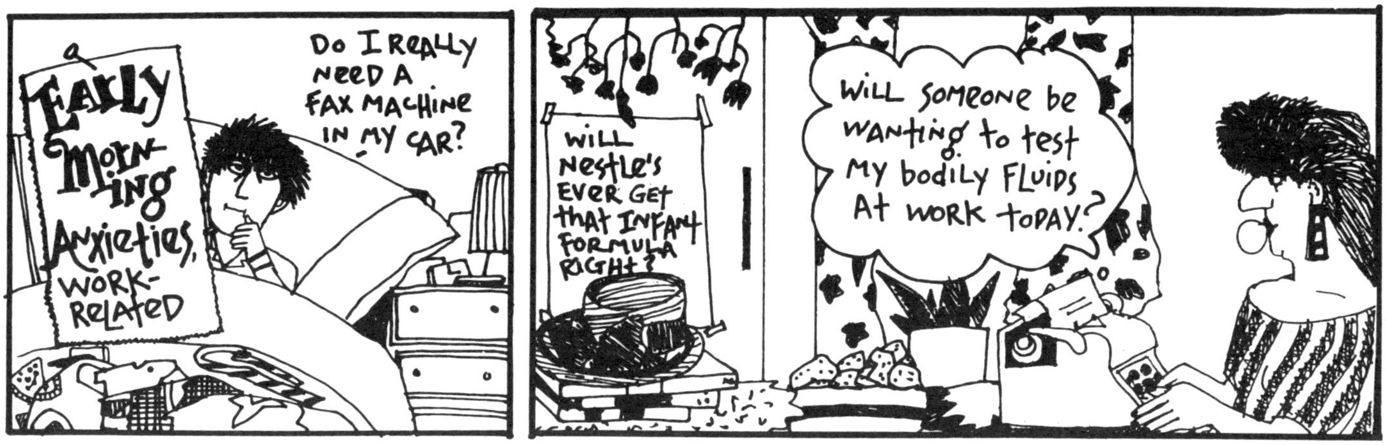
Early Morning Anxieties, Work-Related
Do I really need a fax machine in my car?
Will Nestle's ever get that infant formula right?
Will someone be wanting to test my bodily fluids at work today?

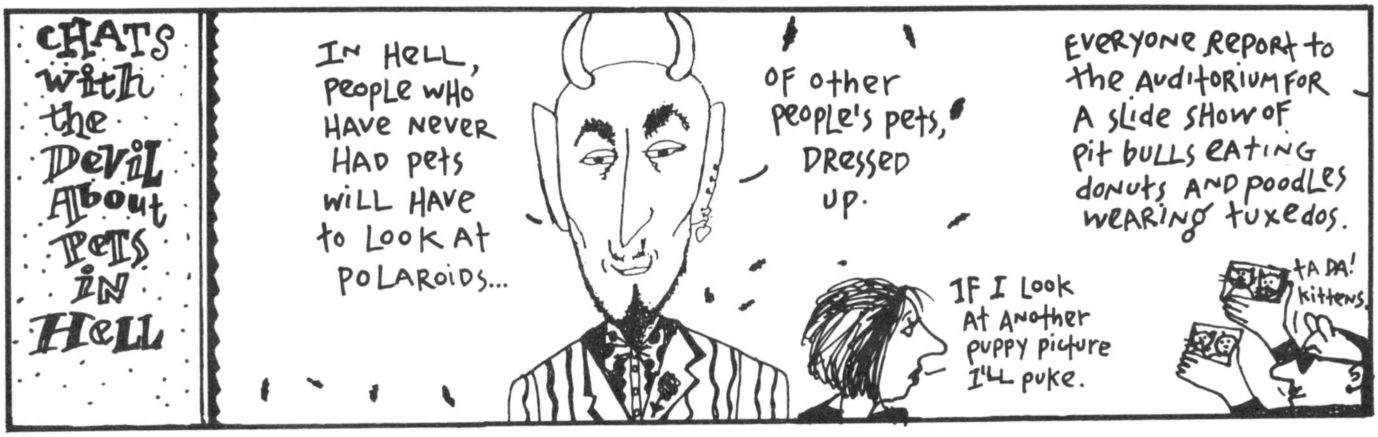
Chats with the Devil About Pets in Hell
In Hell, people who have never had pets will have to look at polaroids...
of other people's pets, dressed up.
Everyone report to the auditorium for a slide show of pit bulls eating donuts and poodles wearing tuxedos.
If I look at another puppy picture I'll puke.
ta da! kittens.

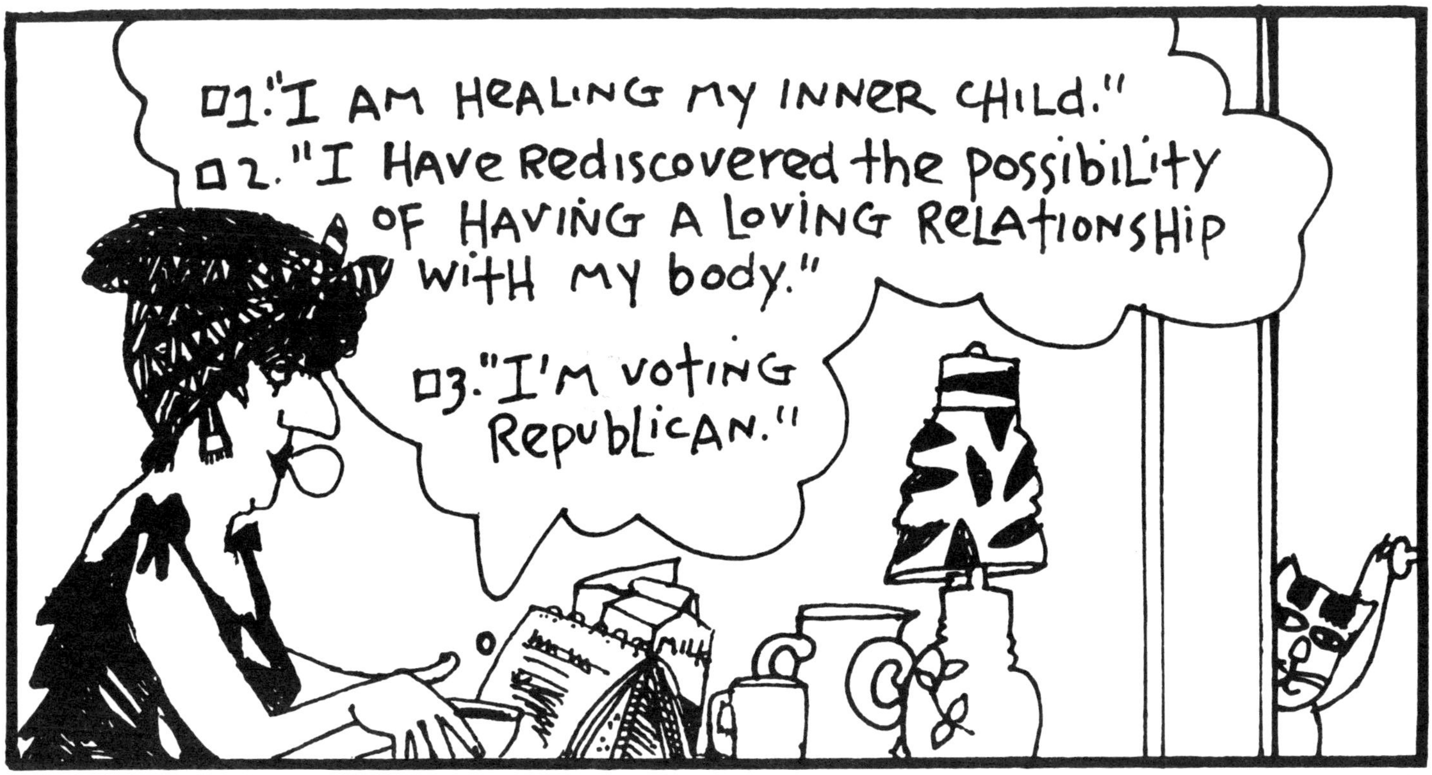
☐1. "I am healing my inner child."
☐2. "I have rediscovered the possibility of having a loving relationship with my body."
☐3. "I'm voting Republican."
milk

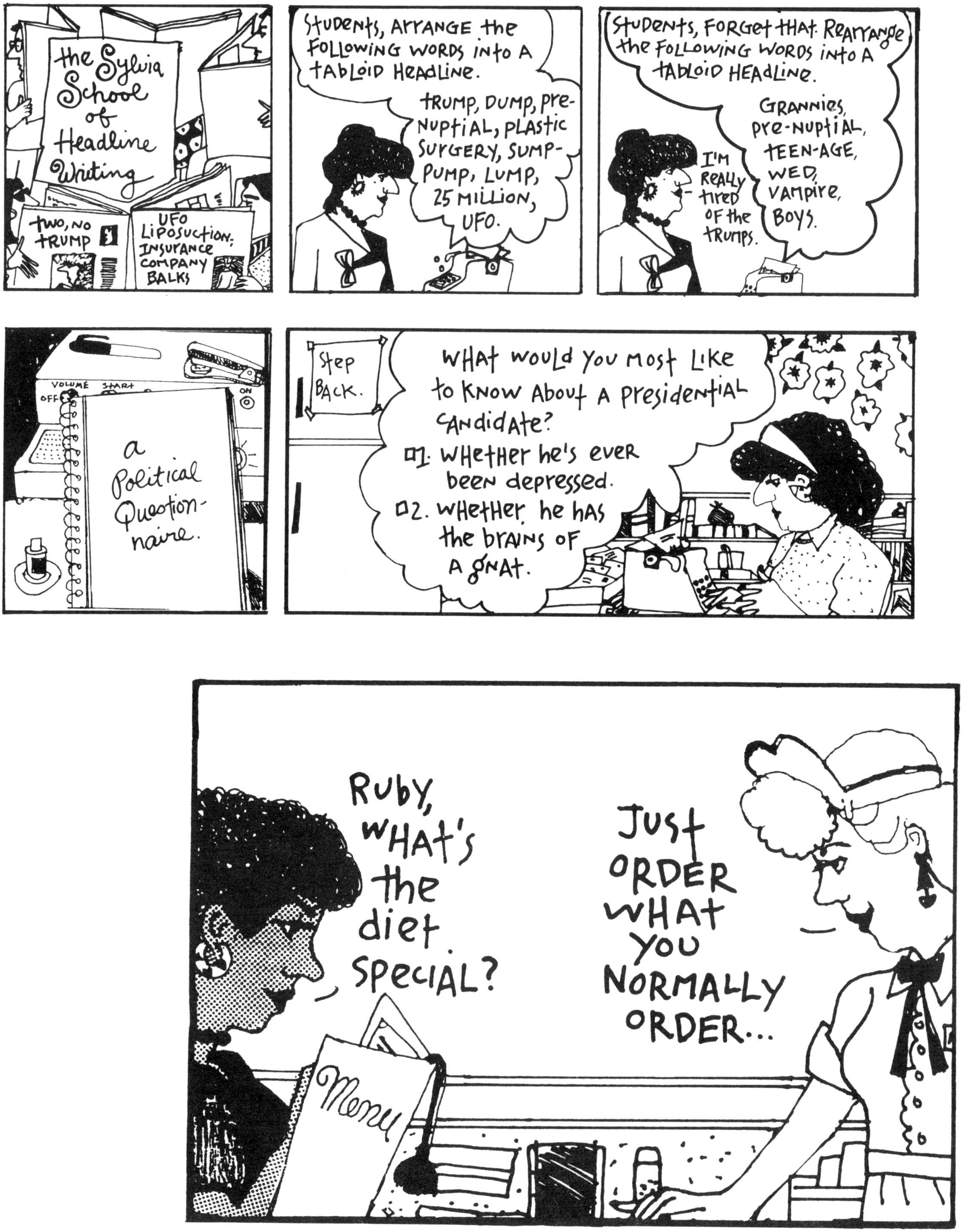

the Sylvia School of Headline Writing
TWO, NO TRUMP
UFO LIPOSUCTION: INSURANCE COMPANY BALKS
STUDENTS, ARRANGE THE FOLLOWING WORDS INTO A TABLOID HEADLINE.
TRUMP, DUMP, PRE-NUPTIAL, PLASTIC SURGERY, SUMP-PUMP, LUMP, 25 MILLION, UFO.
STUDENTS, FORGET THAT. REARRANGE THE FOLLOWING WORDS INTO A TABLOID HEADLINE.
I'M REALLY TIRED OF THE TRUMPS.
GRANNIES, PRE-NUPTIAL, TEEN-AGE, WED, VAMPIRE, BOYS.
VOLUME
START
OFF
ON
a Political Question-naire.
Step BACK.
WHAT WOULD YOU MOST LIKE TO KNOW ABOUT A PRESIDENTIAL CANDIDATE?
1. WHETHER HE'S EVER BEEN DEPRESSED.
2. WHETHER HE HAS THE BRAINS OF A GNAT.
RUBY, WHAT'S THE DIET SPECIAL?
JUST ORDER WHAT YOU NORMALLY ORDER...
Menu

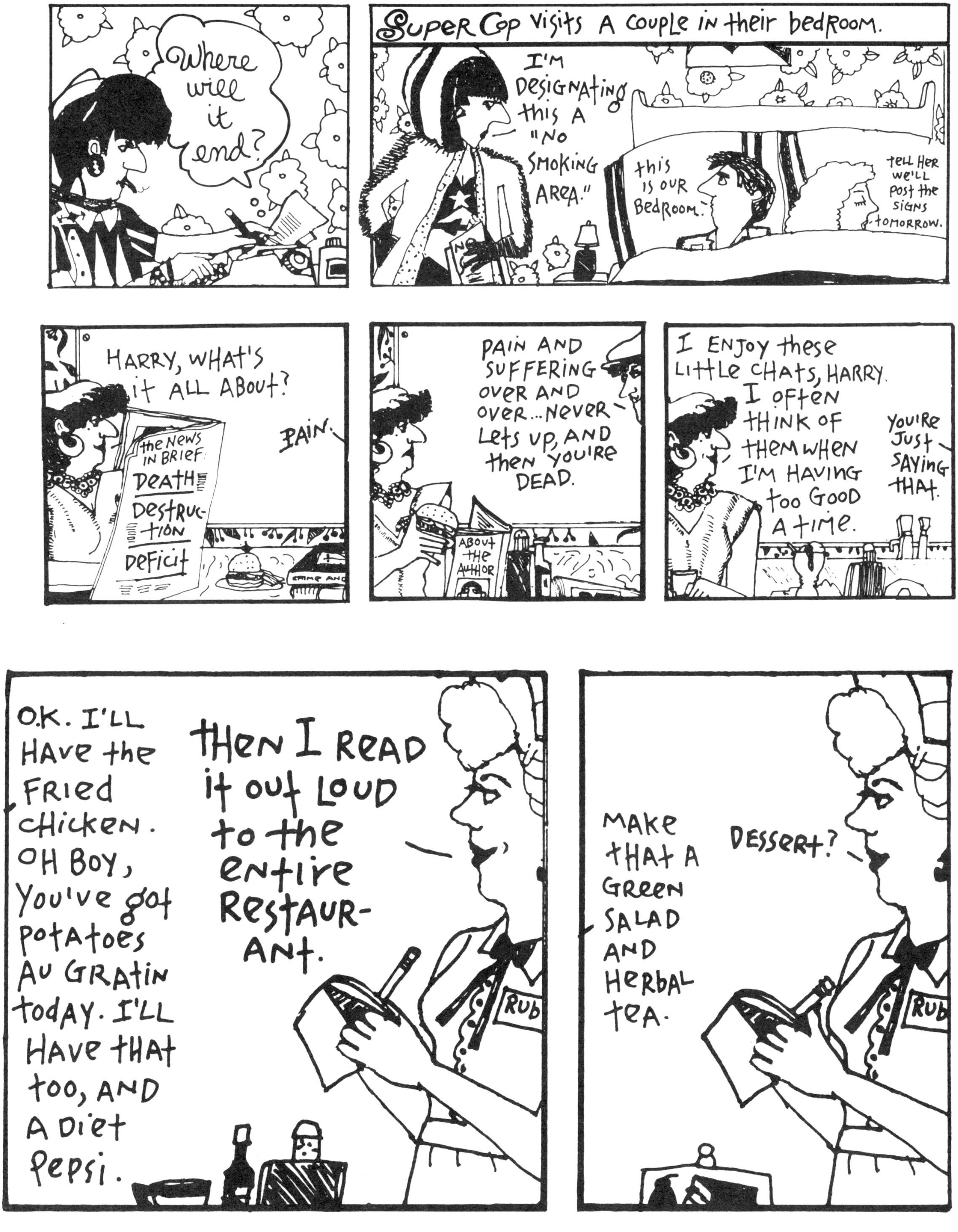
Where will it end?
Super Cop visits a couple in their bedroom.
I'M DESIGNATING this A "NO SMOKING AREA."
this is our Bedroom.
tell Her we'll post the signs tomorrow.
HARRY, WHAT'S it ALL About?
the News in Brief: Death Destruction Deficit
PAIN.
PAIN AND SUFFERING OVER AND OVER...NEVER Lets up, AND then you're DEAD.
About the Author
I ENJOY these Little CHATS, HARRY. I often think of them when I'm HAVING too Good A time.
You're Just saying that.
O.K. I'LL HAVE the Fried chicken. OH Boy, You've got potatoes Au Gratin today. I'LL HAVE that too, AND A Diet Pepsi.
then I read it out loud to the entire Restaurant.
Rub
DESSERT?
MAKE THAT A GREEN SALAD AND HERBAL tea.
Rub

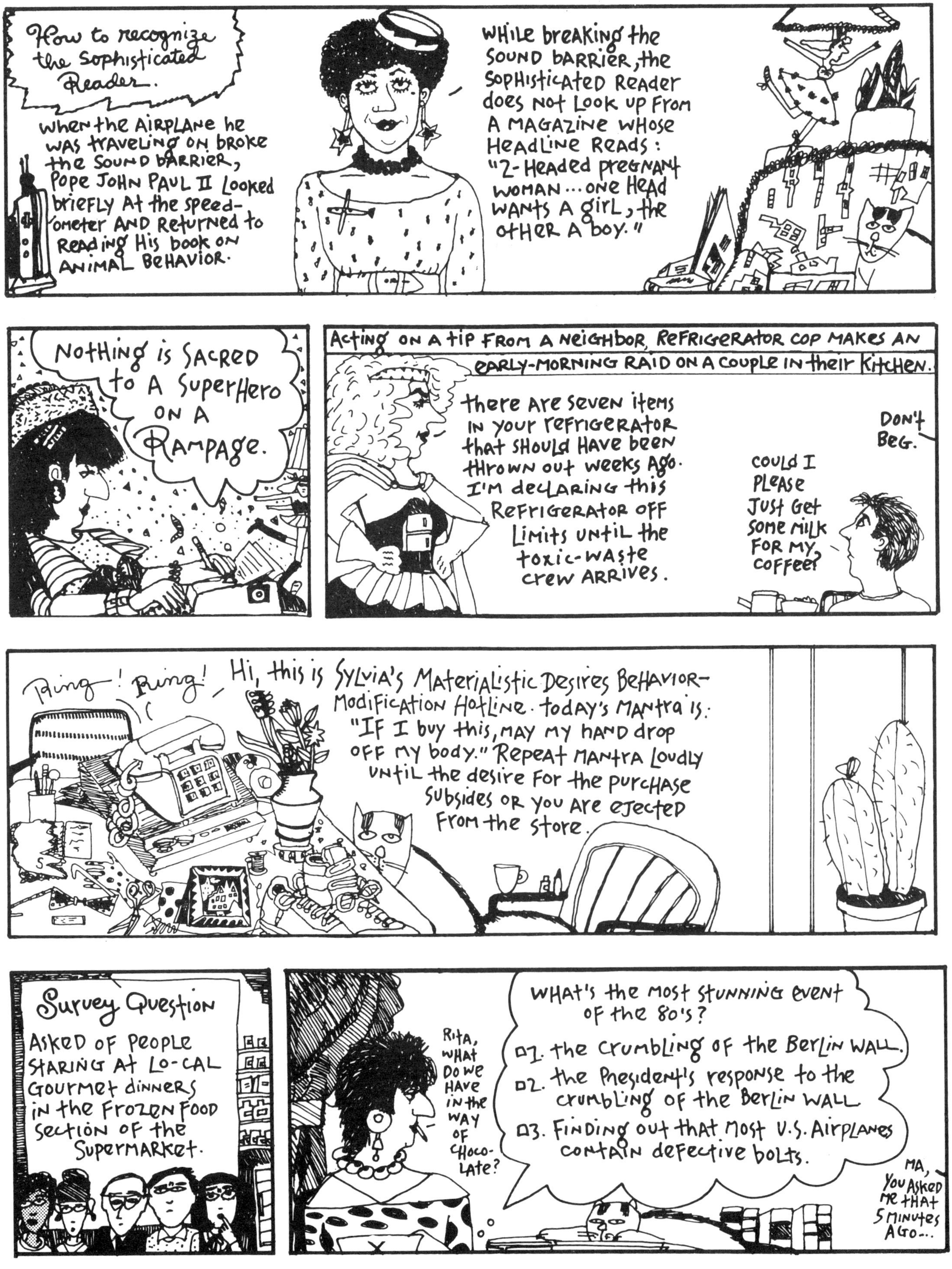
How to recognize the Sophisticated Reader.
when the AirPlane he was traveling on broke the sound barrier, Pope JOHN PAUL II Looked briefly At the speed-ometer AND Returned to Reading His book on ANIMAL BeHAVIOR.
WHILE breaking the SOUND BARRIER, the Sophisticated Reader does not Look up From A MAGAZINE WHOSE HEADLINE Reads: "2-Headed pregnant woman... one Head wants a girl, the other a boy."
Nothing is Sacred to A SuperHero ON A Rampage.
Acting on a tip from a neighbor, Refrigerator cop makes an early-morning raid on a couple in their kitchen.
there are seven items in your refrigerator that should have been thrown out weeks Ago. I'M declaring this Refrigerator off Limits until the toxic-waste crew Arrives.
Could I please just get some milk for my coffee?
Don't Beg.
Ring! Ring!
Hi, this is Sylvia's Materialistic Desires Behavior-Modification Hotline. today's Mantra is: "If I buy this, may my hand drop off my body." Repeat mantra loudly until the desire for the purchase subsides or you are ejected from the store.
Survey Question
Asked of people staring at Lo-Cal Gourmet dinners in the Frozen Food section of the Supermarket.
Rita, what do we have in the way of chocolate?
WHAT'S the most stunning event of the 80's?
1. the crumbling of the Berlin WALL.
2. the President's response to the crumbling of the Berlin WALL
3. Finding out that most U.S. Airplanes contain defective bolts.
MA, You Asked me that 5 minutes ago...

POLITICS

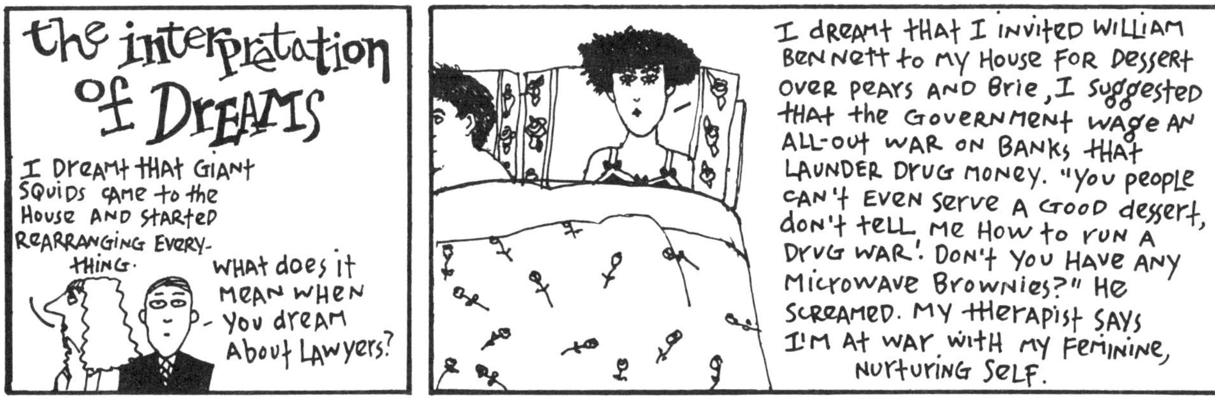
the interpretation of DREAMS
I DreAmt tHAt GiANt SQUiDS CAME to the House AND StARtED REARRANGING EVERY-tHING.
WHAt does it MEAN WHEN you dreAm About LAwyers?
I dreAmt tHAt I INVitED WILLIAM BENNETT to My House FOR DESSERT over PEARS AND Brie, I suggested tHAt the GOVERNMENT wage AN ALL-out WAR ON BANKS tHAt LAUNDER Drug MONEY. "You people CAN'T EVEN serve A GOOD dessert, don't tell me How to run A DRUG WAR! DON'T You HAVE ANY MicroWAVE Brownies?" He SCREAMED. My therapist SAYS I'M At WAR WItH My Feminine, NurturiNG SELF.

Since I am four weeks ahead in my strip, I can only deal with political issues that I'm confident will be around for four weeks. You'd be surprised how many disappear after three. My view of events is more self-centered than I think is proper. I have spent anxious mornings hoping someone in the center of a scandal would not be fired until after everyone read the morning paper.

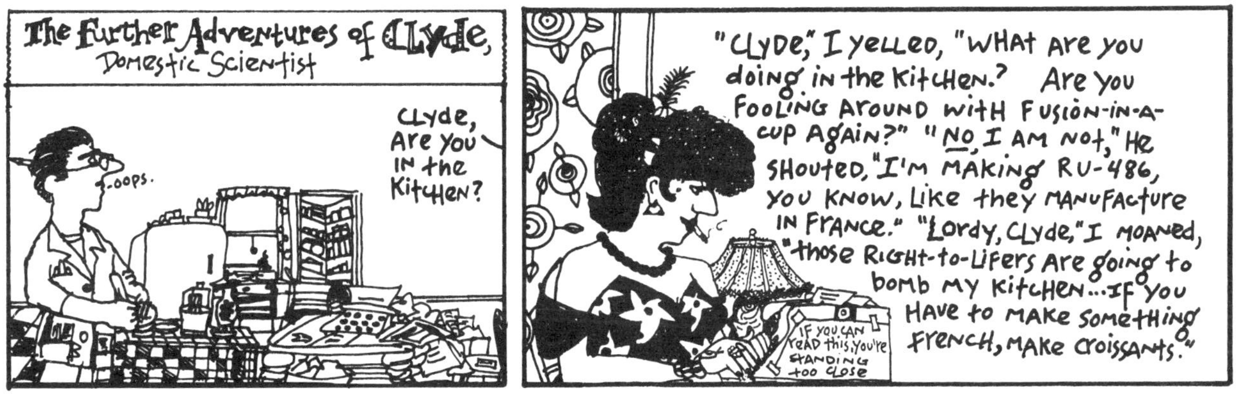
The Further Adventures of Clyde, Domestic Scientist
-oops.
Clyde, Are you IN the Kitchen?
"Clyde," I yelled, "WHAt Are you doing in the kitchen? Are you FOOLING AROUND WITH Fusion-in-A-cup Again?" "NO, I AM not," He SHOUTED, "I'M MAKING RU-486, you KNOW, Like they MANUFActure IN France." "Lordy, Clyde," I MOANED, "those Right-to-Lifers Are going to bomb my kitchen...If you HAVE to MAKE something French, MAKE croissants."
IF YOU CAN READ this, you're STANDING too close

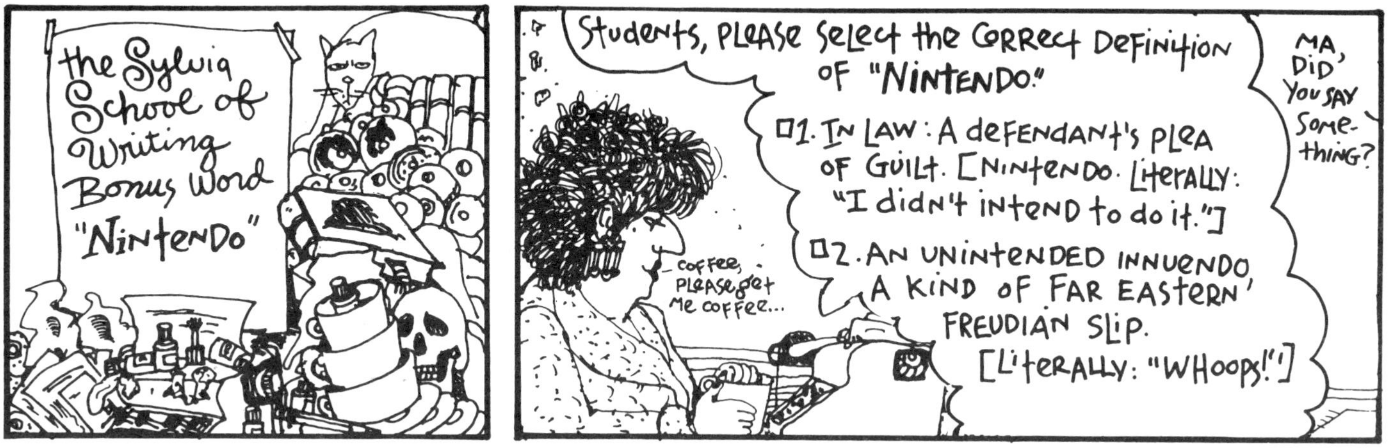
the Sylvia School of Writing Bonus Word "Nintendo"
Students, please select the correct definition of "NINTENDO."
☐1. In Law: A defendant's plea of guilt. [Nintendo. Literally: "I didn't intend to do it."]
☐2. An unintended innuendo, a kind of Far Eastern Freudian slip. [Literally: "Whoops!"]
coffee, please get me coffee...
MA, DID YOU SAY SOME-THING?

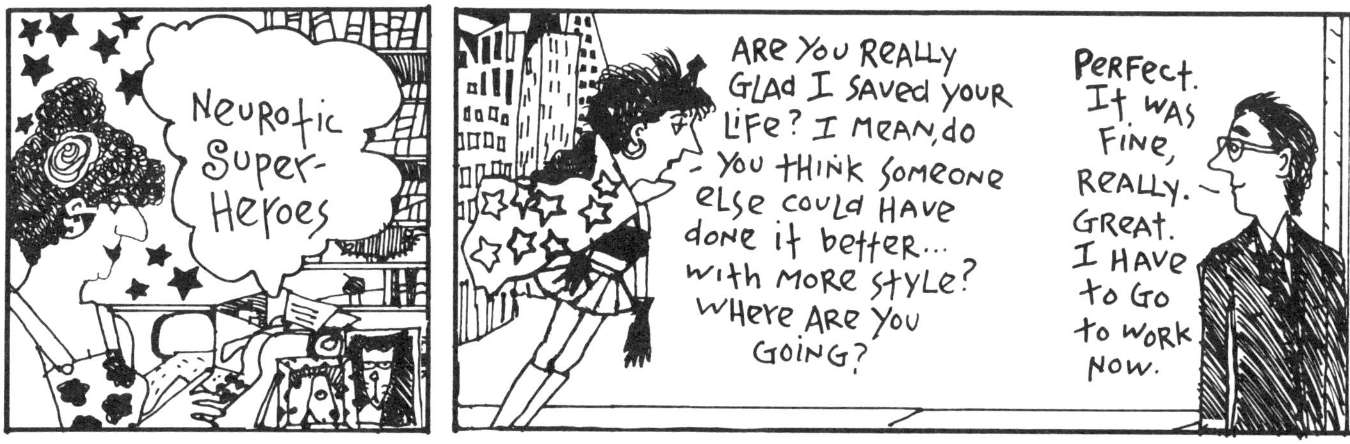
Neurotic Super-Heroes
Are you really glad I saved your life? I mean, do you think someone else could have done it better... with more style? Where are you going?
Perfect. It was fine, really. Great. I have to go to work now.

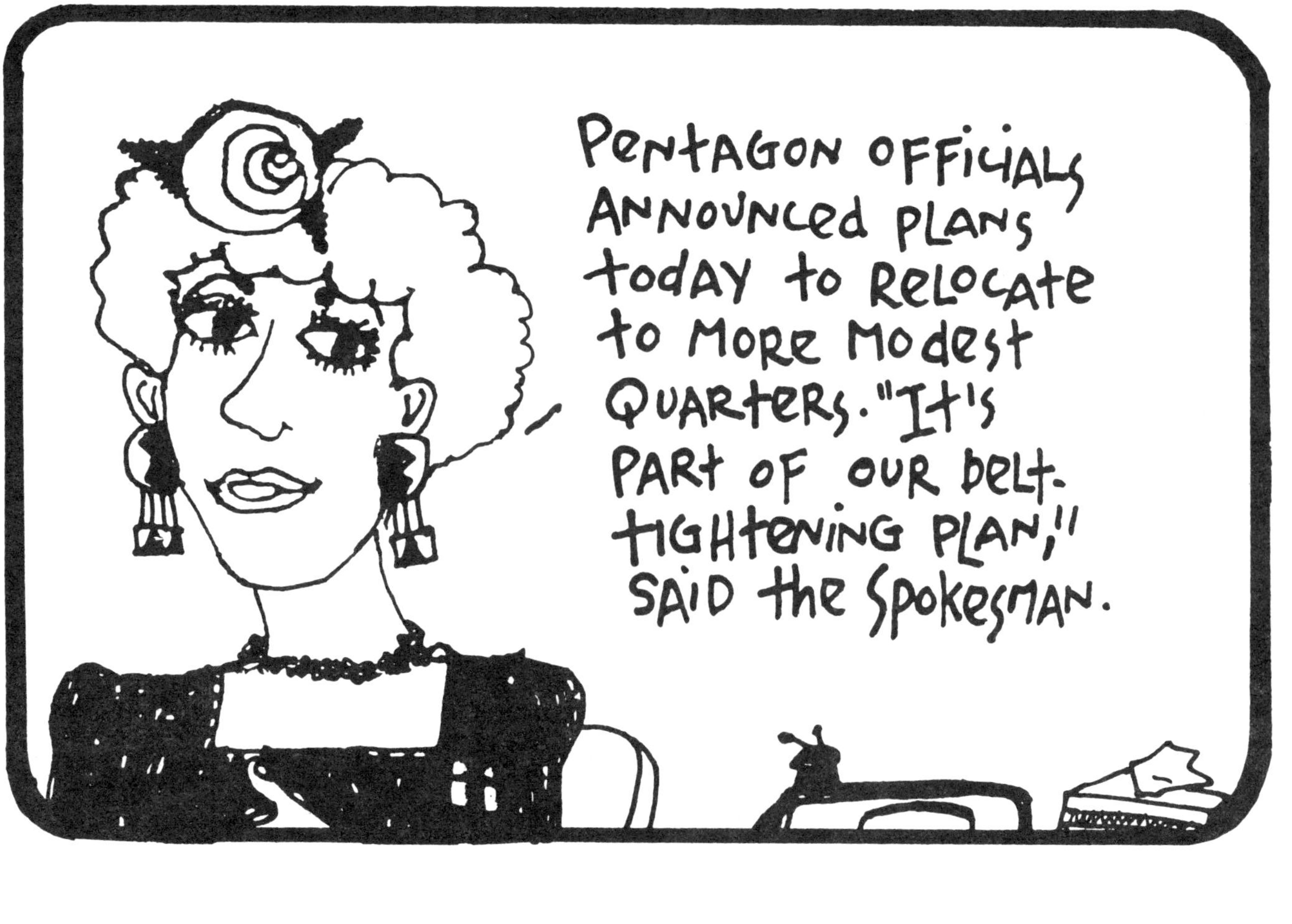
Pentagon officials announced plans today to relocate to more modest quarters. "It's part of our belt-tightening plan," said the spokesman.

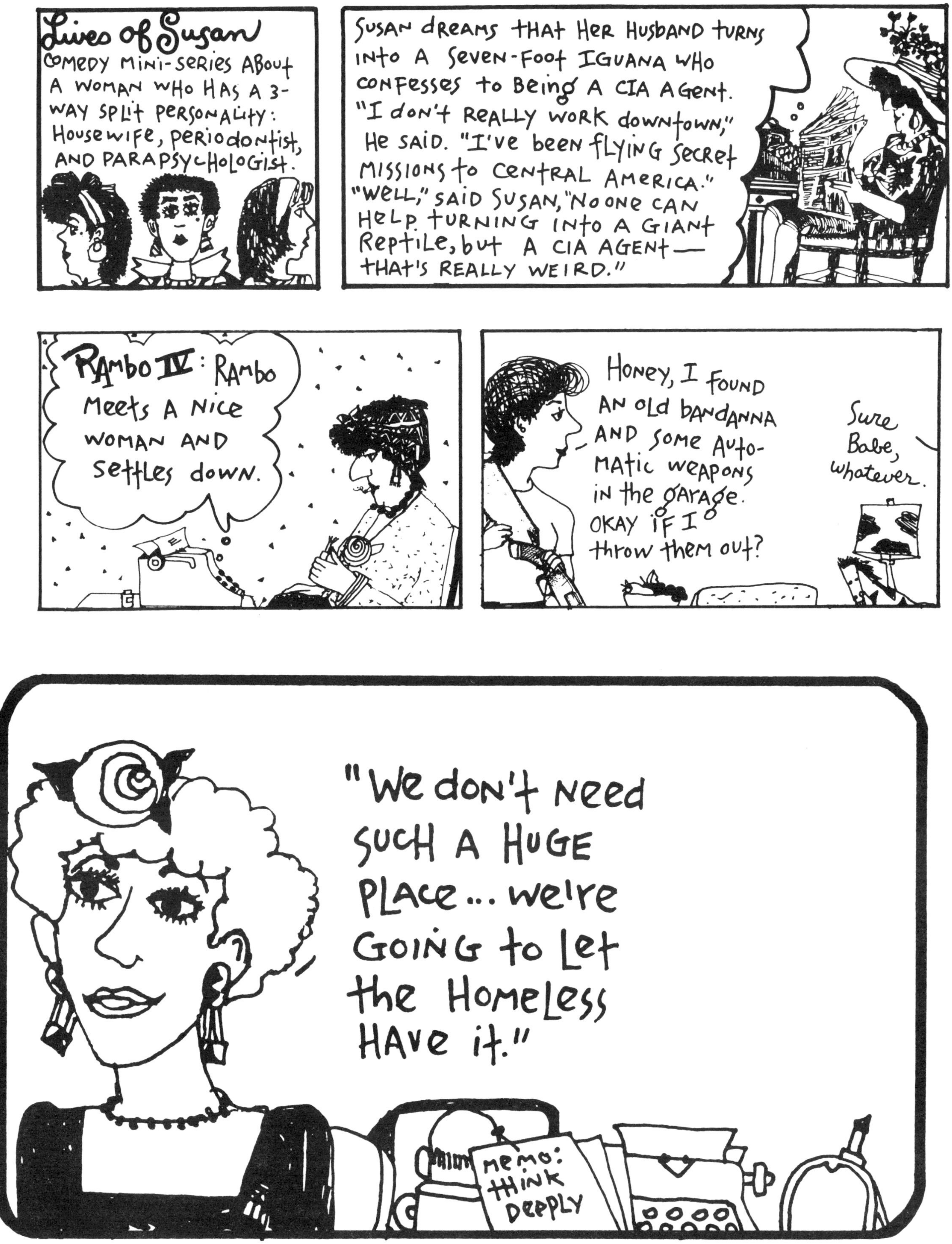
Lives of Susan
COMEDY MINI-SERIES ABOUT A WOMAN WHO HAS A 3-WAY SPLIT PERSONALITY: HOUSEWIFE, PERIODONTIST, AND PARAPSYCHOLOGIST.
SUSAN DREAMS THAT HER HUSBAND TURNS INTO A SEVEN-FOOT IGUANA WHO CONFESSES TO BEING A CIA AGENT. "I DON'T REALLY WORK DOWNTOWN," HE SAID. "I'VE BEEN FLYING SECRET MISSIONS TO CENTRAL AMERICA." "WELL," SAID SUSAN, "NO ONE CAN HELP TURNING INTO A GIANT REPTILE, BUT A CIA AGENT— THAT'S REALLY WEIRD."
RAMBO IV: RAMBO MEETS A NICE WOMAN AND SETTLES DOWN.
Honey, I FOUND AN OLD BANDANNA AND SOME AUTO-MATIC WEAPONS IN THE GARAGE. OKAY IF I THROW THEM OUT?
Sure Babe, whatever.
"WE DON'T NEED SUCH A HUGE PLACE... WE'RE GOING TO LET THE HOMELESS HAVE IT."
MEMO: THINK DEEPLY

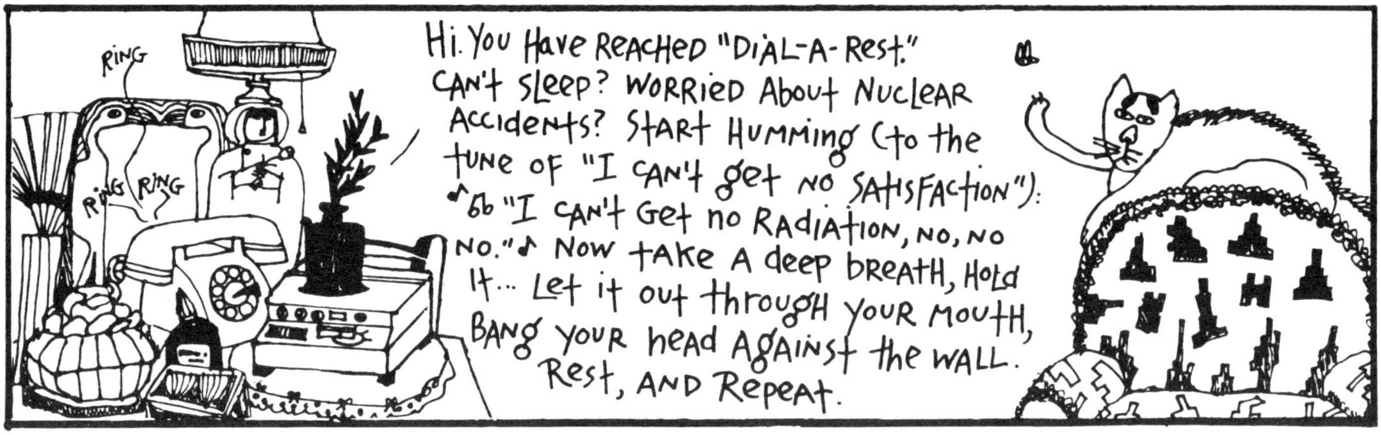
RING
RING RING
Hi. You have reached "Dial-a-Rest." Can't sleep? Worried about nuclear accidents? Start humming (to the tune of "I can't get no satisfaction"): ♪ "I can't get no radiation, no, no no." ♪ Now take a deep breath, hold it... Let it out through your mouth, bang your head against the wall. Rest, and repeat.

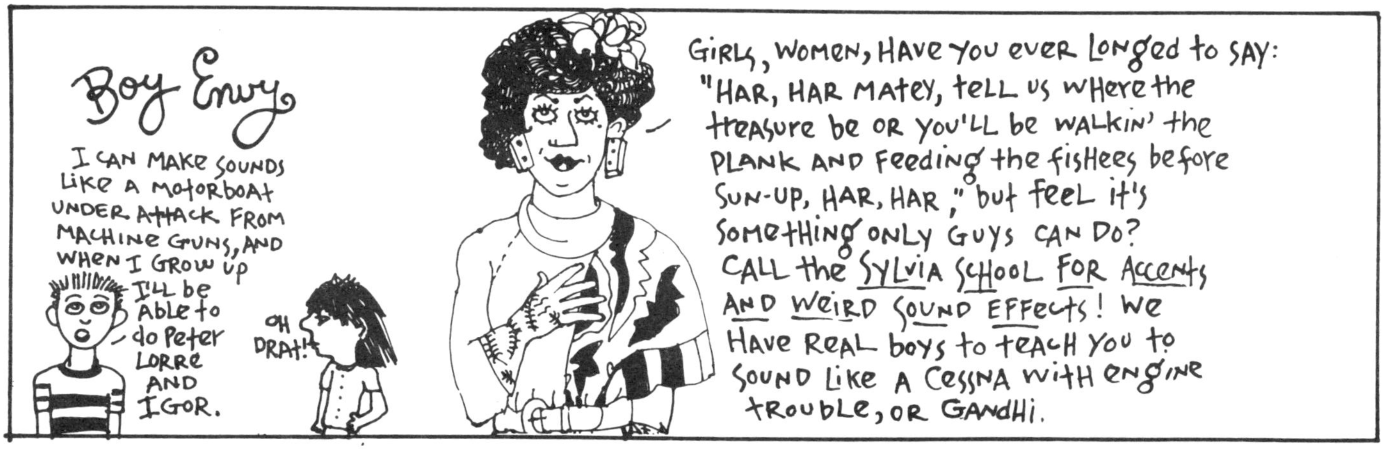
Boy Envy
I can make sounds like a motorboat under attack from machine guns, and when I grow up I'll be able to do Peter Lorre and Igor.
Oh drat!
Girls, women, have you ever longed to say: "Har, har matey, tell us where the treasure be or you'll be walkin' the plank and feeding the fishees before sun-up, har, har," but feel it's something only guys can do? Call the Sylvia School for Accents and Weird Sound Effects! We have real boys to teach you to sound like a Cessna with engine trouble, or Gandhi.

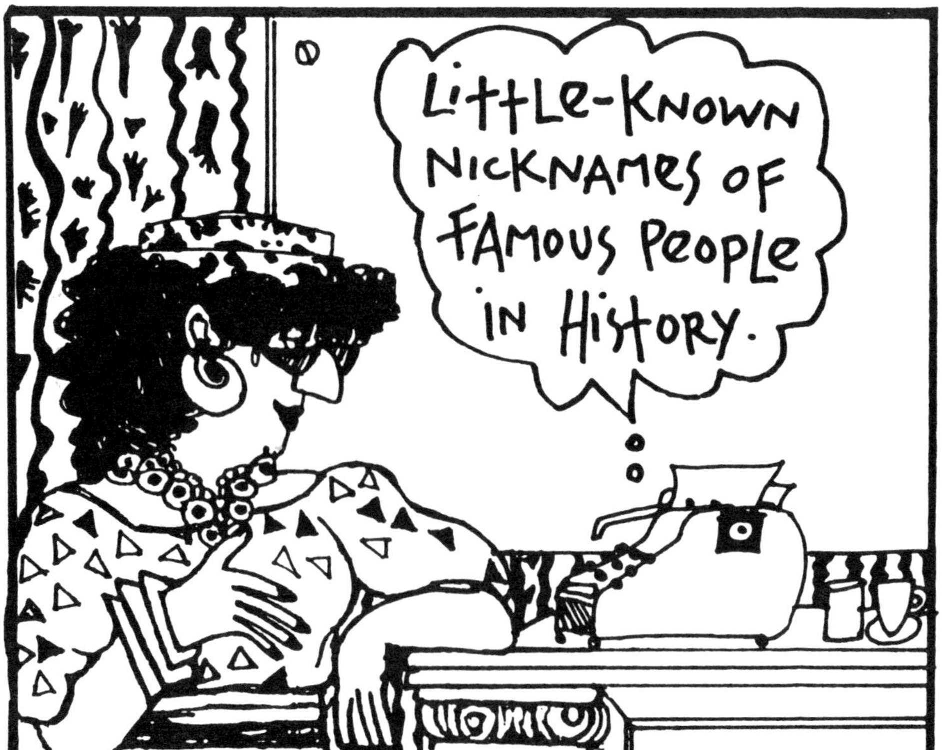
Little-Known Nicknames of Famous People in History.

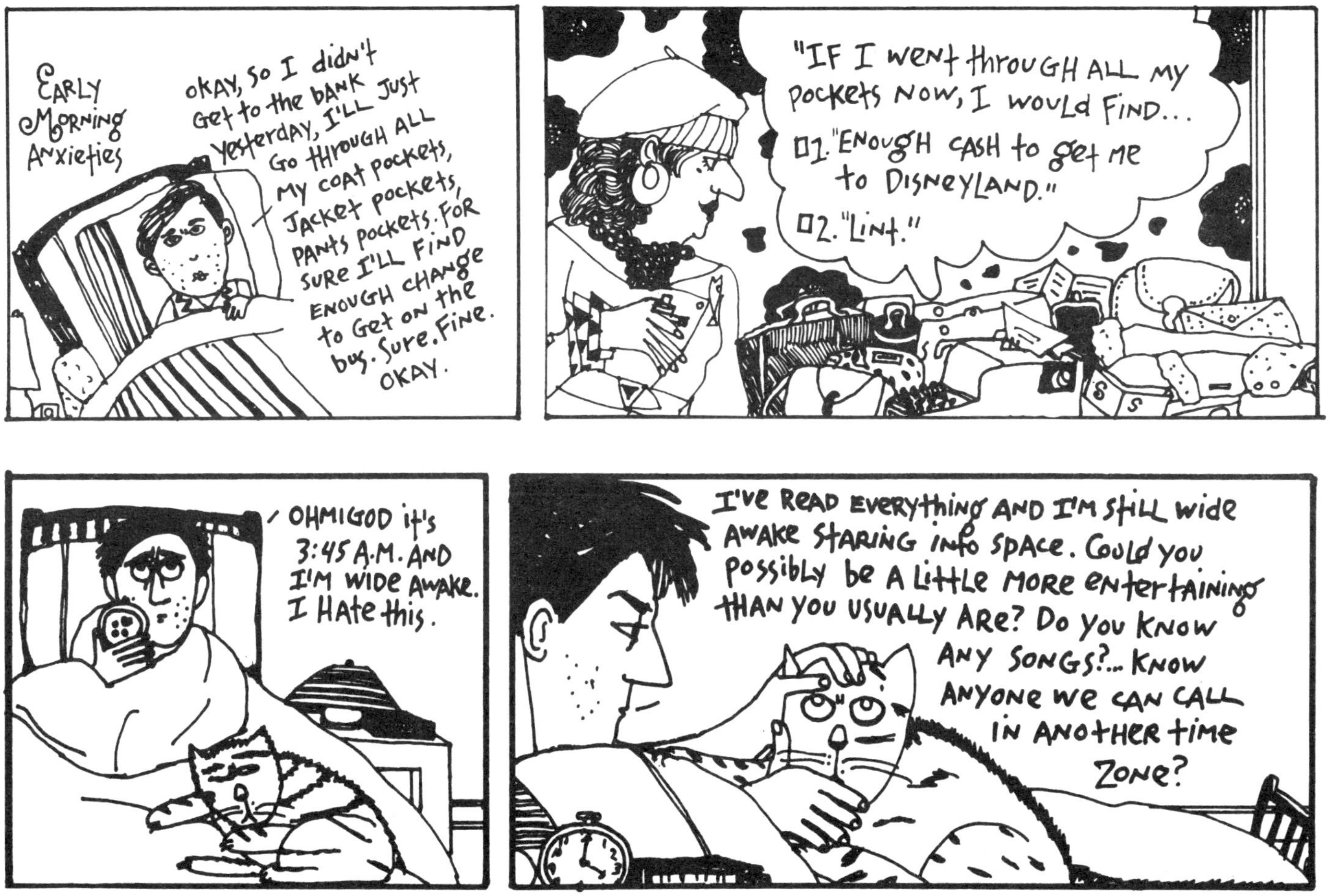
EARLY MORNING ANXIETIES
OKAY, SO I DIDN'T GET TO THE BANK YESTERDAY, I'LL JUST GO THROUGH ALL MY COAT POCKETS, JACKET POCKETS, PANTS POCKETS. FOR SURE I'LL FIND ENOUGH CHANGE TO GET ON THE BUS. SURE. FINE. OKAY.
"IF I WENT THROUGH ALL MY POCKETS NOW, I WOULD FIND...
□1. "ENOUGH CASH TO GET ME TO DISNEYLAND."
□2. "LINT."
OHMIGOD IT'S 3:45 A.M. AND I'M WIDE AWAKE. I HATE THIS.
I'VE READ EVERYTHING AND I'M STILL WIDE AWAKE STARING INTO SPACE. COULD YOU POSSIBLY BE A LITTLE MORE ENTERTAINING THAN YOU USUALLY ARE? DO YOU KNOW ANY SONGS?... KNOW ANYONE WE CAN CALL IN ANOTHER TIME ZONE?

Lucretia Borgia's Mom tries to talk some sense into her.

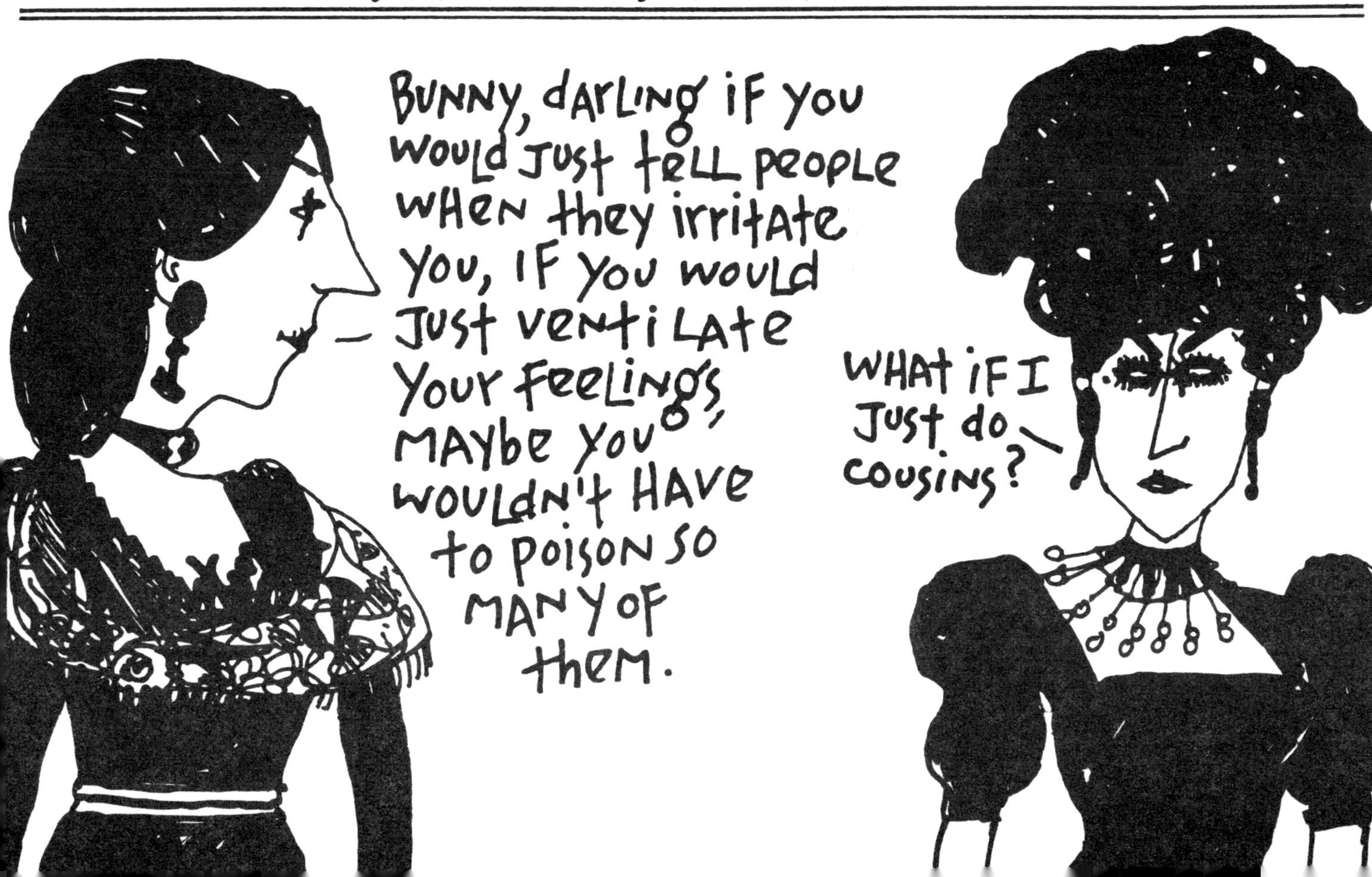
BUNNY, DARLING IF YOU WOULD JUST TELL PEOPLE WHEN THEY IRRITATE YOU, IF YOU WOULD JUST VENTILATE YOUR FEELINGS, MAYBE YOU WOULDN'T HAVE TO POISON SO MANY OF THEM.
WHAT IF I JUST DO COUSINS?

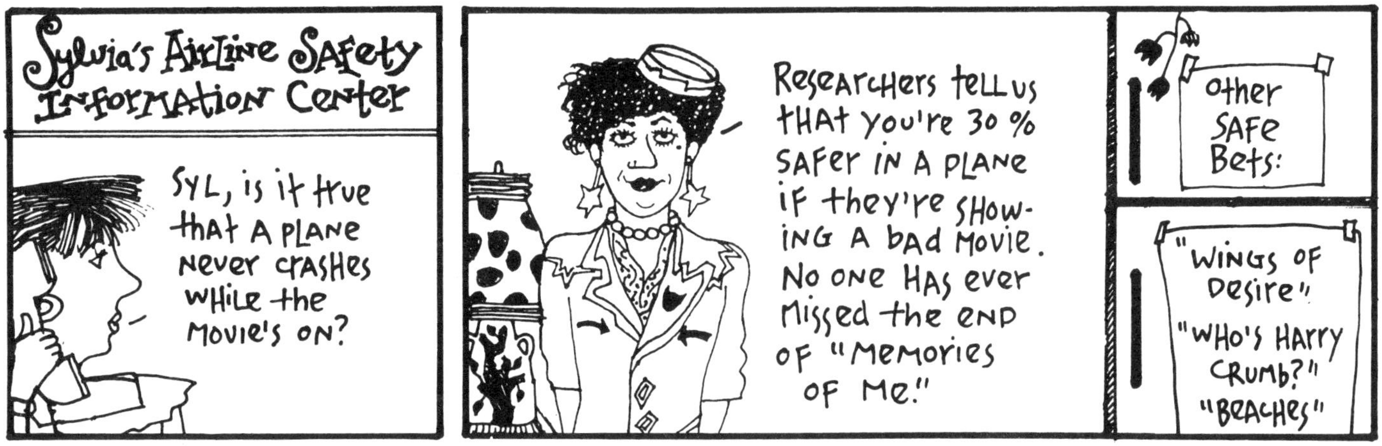
Sylvia's Airline Safety Information Center
Syl, is it true that a plane never crashes while the movie's on?
Researchers tell us that you're 30% safer in a plane if they're showing a bad movie. No one has ever missed the end of "Memories of Me."
Other Safe Bets:
"Wings of Desire"
"Who's Harry Crumb?"
"Beaches"

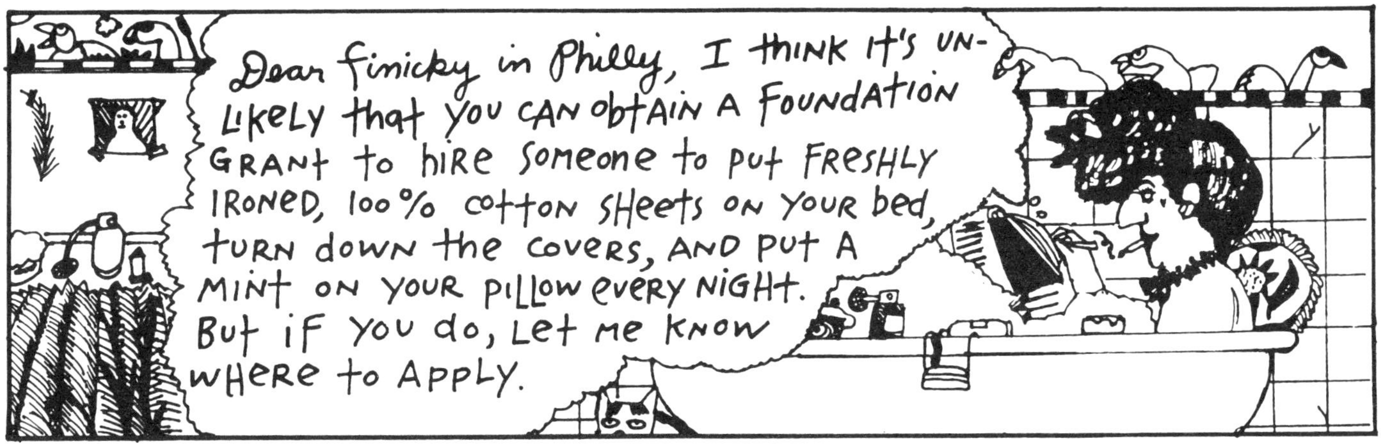
Dear Finicky in Philly, I think it's unlikely that you can obtain a foundation grant to hire someone to put freshly ironed, 100% cotton sheets on your bed, turn down the covers, and put a mint on your pillow every night. But if you do, let me know where to apply.

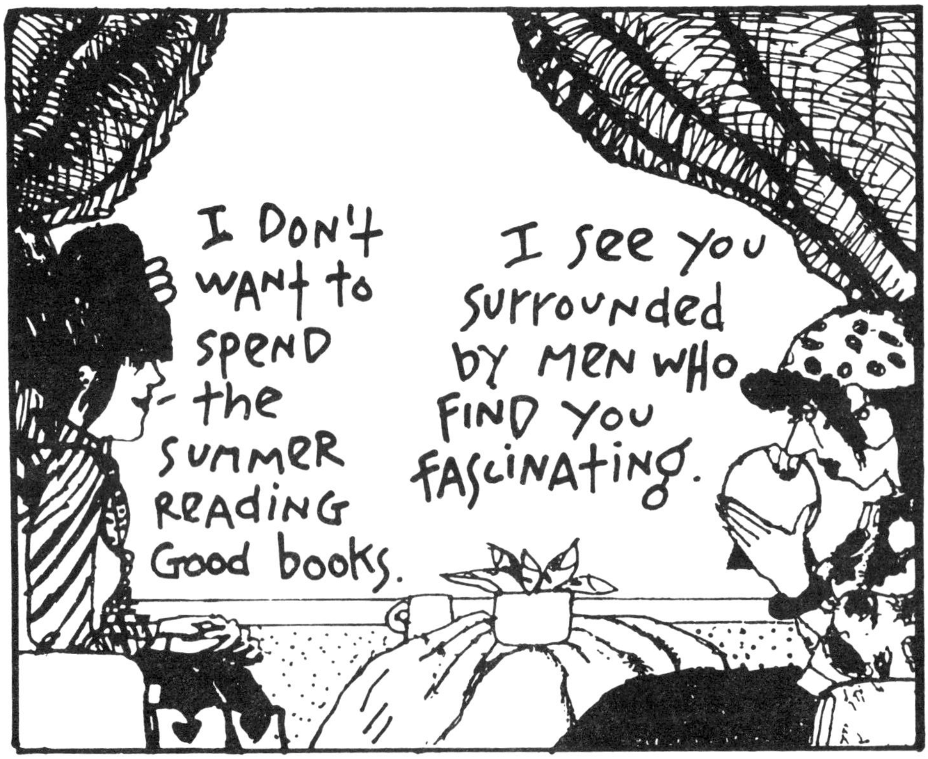
I don't want to spend the summer reading good books.
I see you surrounded by men who find you fascinating.

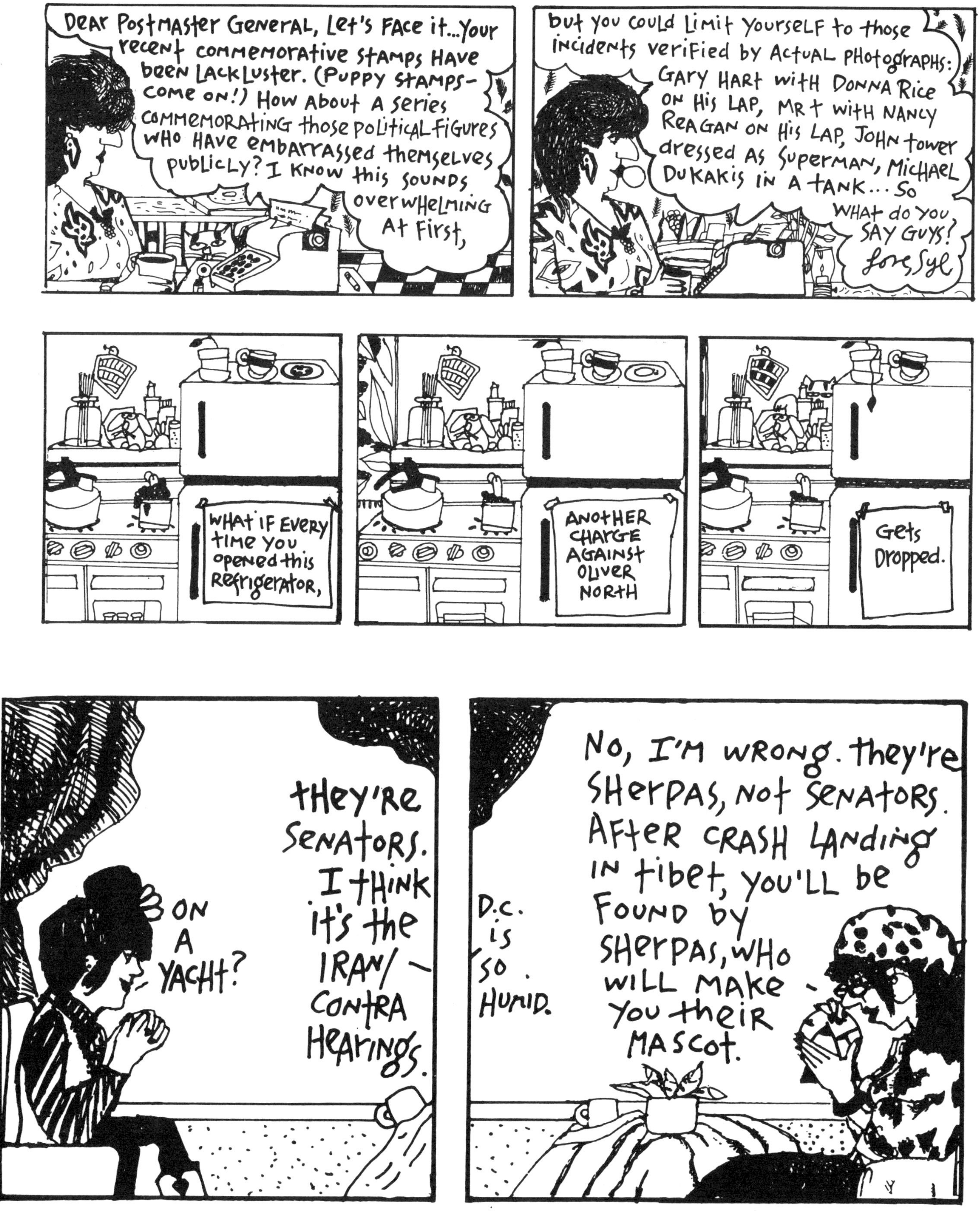

Dear Postmaster General, Let's Face it...Your recent commemorative stamps Have been LackLuster. (Puppy stamps– come on!) How About A series commemorating those political figures who have embarrassed themselves publicly? I know this sounds overwhelming At First,
but you could Limit yourself to those incidents verified by Actual photographs: Gary Hart with Donna Rice on His Lap, Mr T with Nancy Reagan on His Lap, John tower dressed As Superman, Michael Dukakis in A tank... So what do you say Guys? Love, Syl
WHAT IF EVERY time you opened this Refrigerator,
ANOTHER CHARGE AGAINST OLIVER NORTH
Gets Dropped.
ON A YACHT?
they're Senators. I think it's the IRAN/CONTRA Hearings.
D.C. is so Humid.
No, I'm wrong. they're SHerpas, not Senators. After crash landing in tibet, you'll be Found by SHerpas, who will make you their MASCOT.

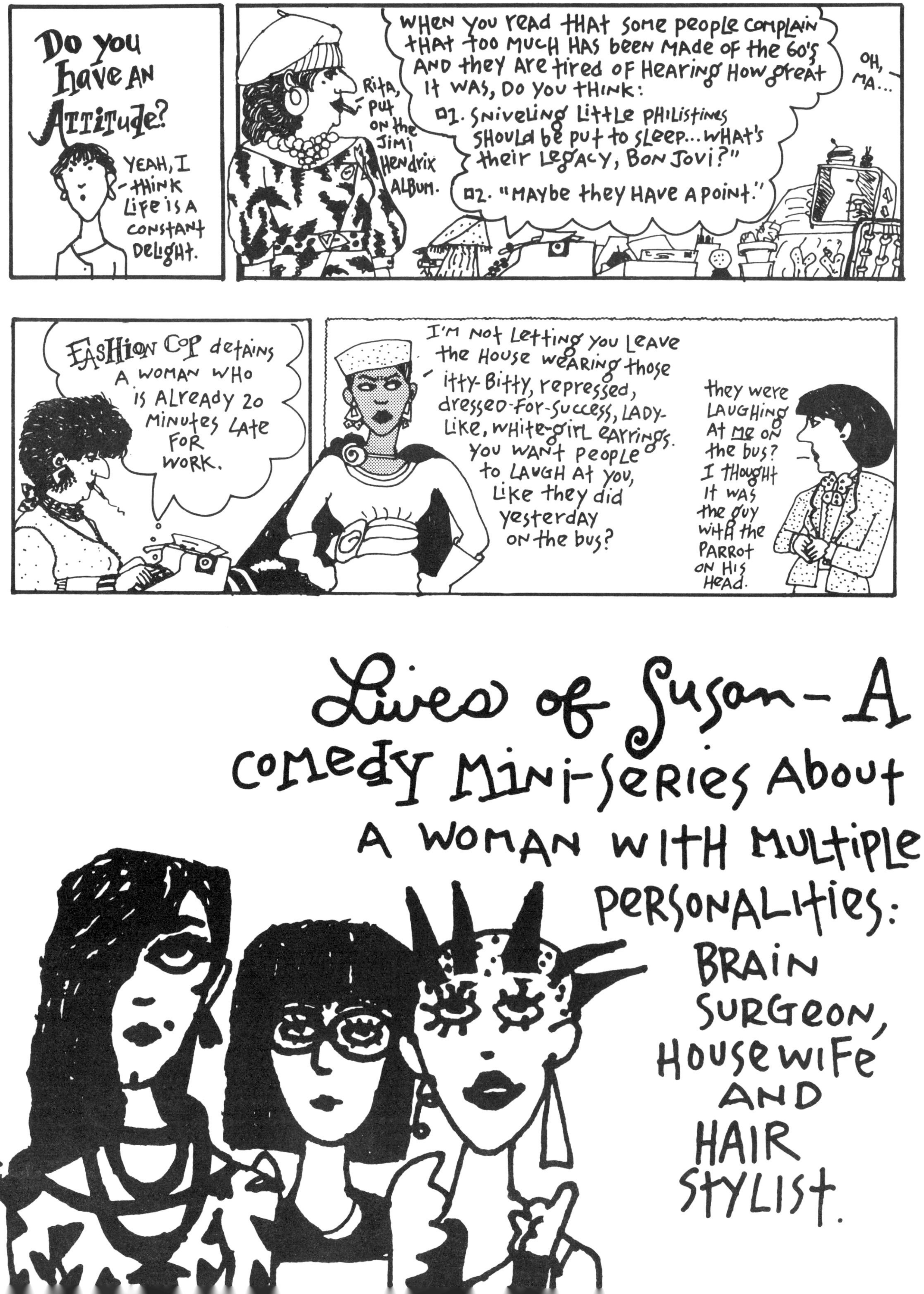
Do you have AN ATTITUDE?
YEAH, I THINK LIFE IS A CONSTANT DELIGHT.
RITA, PUT ON THE JIMI HENDRIX ALBUM.
WHEN YOU READ THAT SOME PEOPLE COMPLAIN THAT TOO MUCH HAS BEEN MADE OF THE 60'S AND THEY ARE TIRED OF HEARING HOW GREAT IT WAS, DO YOU THINK:
□1. SNIVELING LITTLE PHILISTINES SHOULD BE PUT TO SLEEP... WHAT'S THEIR LEGACY, BON JOVI?"
□2. "MAYBE THEY HAVE A POINT."
OH, MA...
FASHION COP DETAINS A WOMAN WHO IS ALREADY 20 MINUTES LATE FOR WORK.
I'M NOT LETTING YOU LEAVE THE HOUSE WEARING THOSE ITTY-BITTY, REPRESSED, DRESSED-FOR-SUCCESS, LADY-LIKE, WHITE-GIRL EARRINGS. YOU WANT PEOPLE TO LAUGH AT YOU, LIKE THEY DID YESTERDAY ON THE BUS?
THEY WERE LAUGHING AT ME ON THE BUS? I THOUGHT IT WAS THE GUY WITH THE PARROT ON HIS HEAD.
Lives of Susan – A COMEDY MINI-SERIES ABOUT A WOMAN WITH MULTIPLE PERSONALITIES: BRAIN SURGEON, HOUSEWIFE AND HAIR STYLIST.

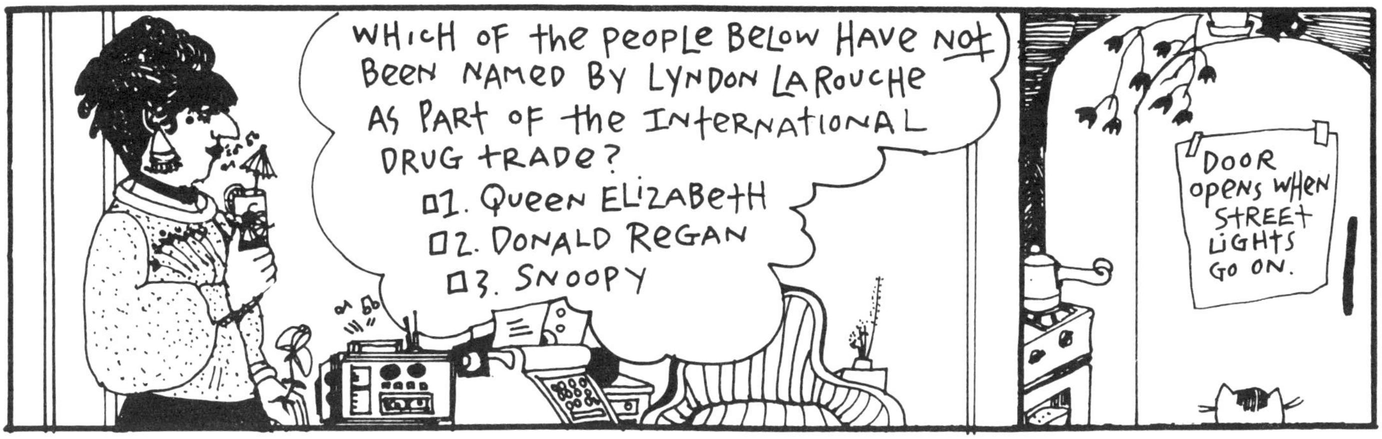
WHICH OF THE PEOPLE BELOW HAVE NOT BEEN NAMED BY LYNDON LAROUCHE AS PART OF THE INTERNATIONAL DRUG TRADE?
□1. QUEEN ELIZABETH
□2. DONALD REGAN
□3. SNOOPY
DOOR OPENS WHEN STREET LIGHTS GO ON.

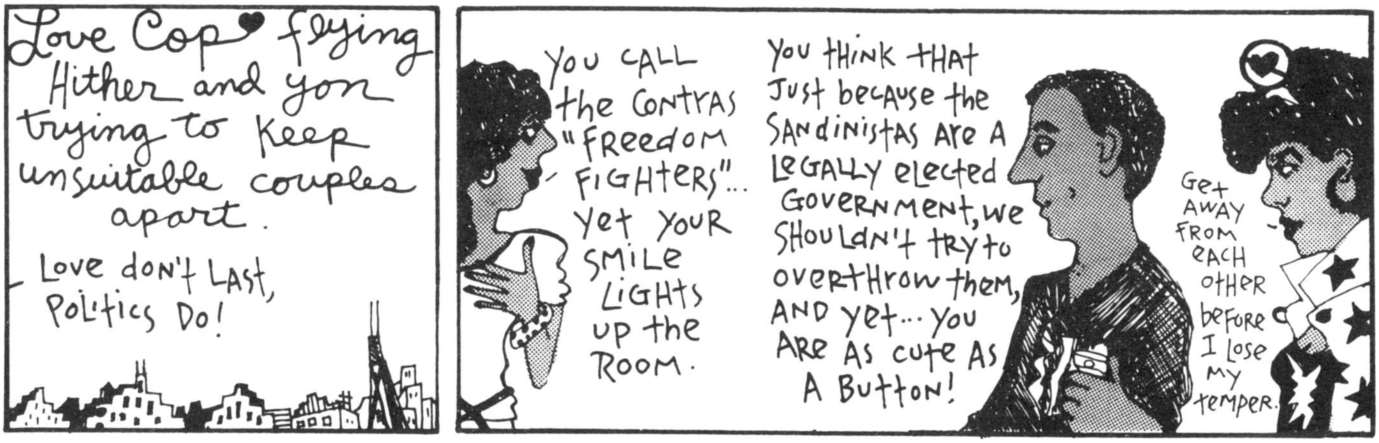
Love Cop flying Hither and yon trying to keep unsuitable couples apart.
Love don't Last, Politics Do!
YOU CALL THE CONTRAS "FREEDOM FIGHTERS"... YET YOUR SMILE LIGHTS UP THE ROOM.
YOU THINK THAT JUST BECAUSE THE SANDINISTAS ARE A LEGALLY ELECTED GOVERNMENT, WE SHOULDN'T TRY TO OVERTHROW THEM, AND YET... YOU ARE AS CUTE AS A BUTTON!
GET AWAY FROM EACH OTHER BEFORE I LOSE MY TEMPER.

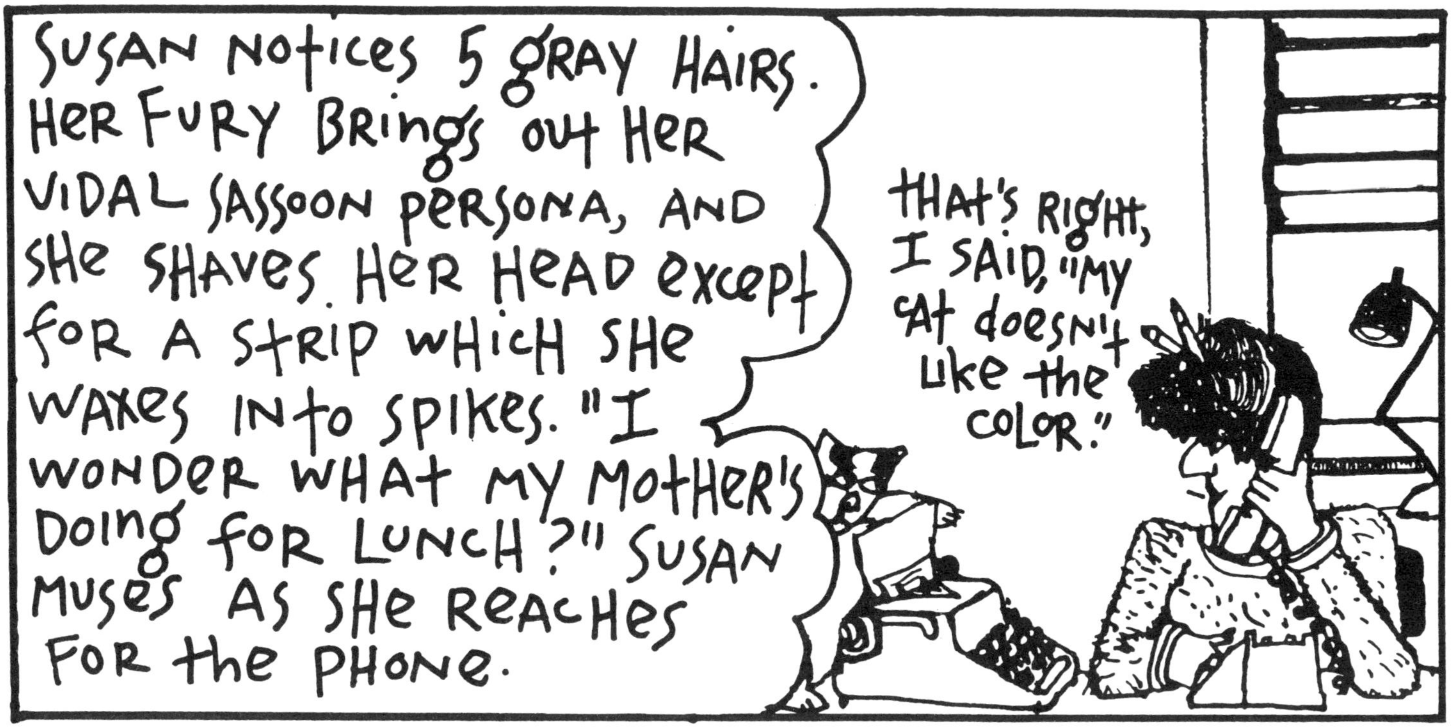
SUSAN NOTICES 5 GRAY HAIRS. HER FURY BRINGS OUT HER VIDAL SASSOON PERSONA, AND SHE SHAVES HER HEAD EXCEPT FOR A STRIP WHICH SHE WAXES INTO SPIKES. "I WONDER WHAT MY MOTHER'S DOING FOR LUNCH?" SUSAN MUSES AS SHE REACHES FOR THE PHONE.
THAT'S RIGHT, I SAID, "MY CAT DOESN'T LIKE THE COLOR."

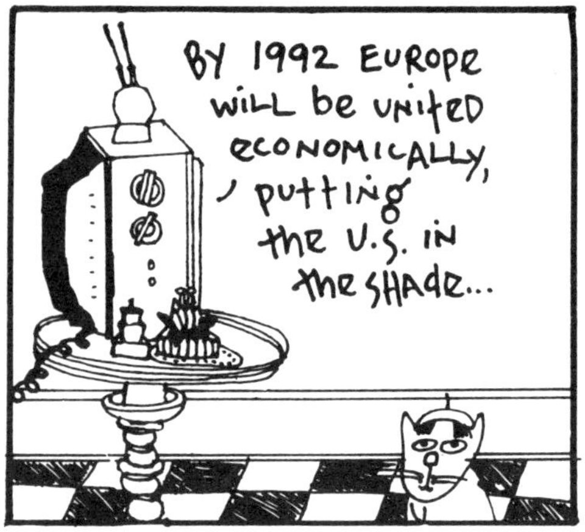
BY 1992 EUROPE WILL be UNITED ECONOMICALLY, PUTTING the U.S. IN the SHAde...

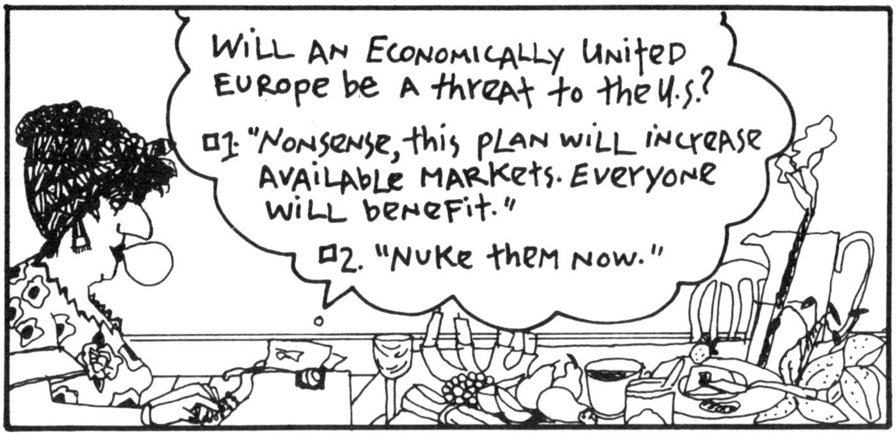
WILL AN ECONOMICALLY UNITED EUROPE be A threat to the U.S.?
□1. "Nonsense, this PLAN WILL increase AVAILABLE MARKETS. EVERYONE WILL beNEFIT."
□2. "NUKE them NOW."

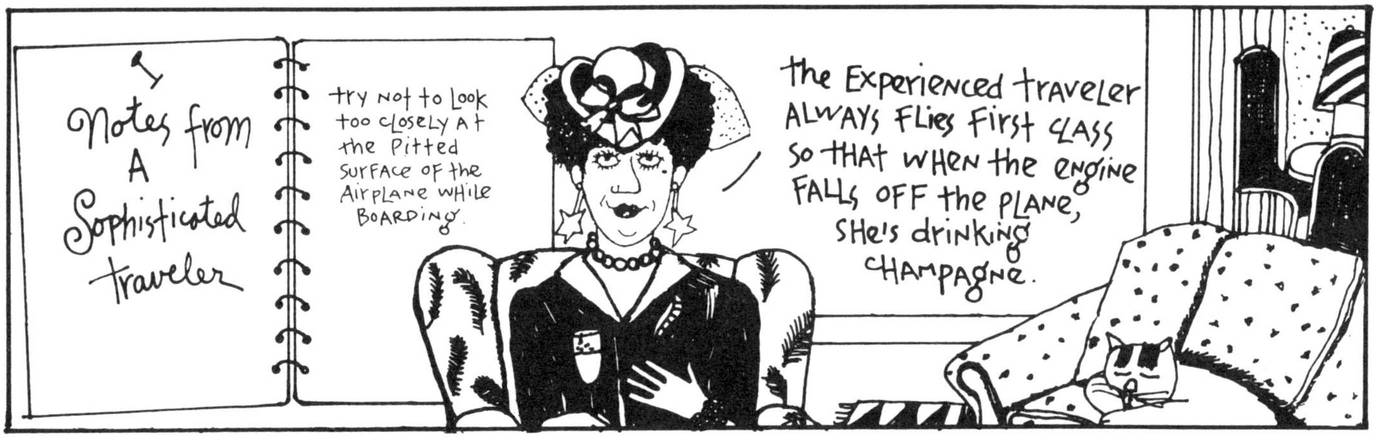
I
Notes from A Sophisticated traveler
try not to Look too closeLy At the Pitted surface of the Airplane while boarding.
the Experienced traveler ALWAYS Flies First CLASS so that when the engine FALLS OFF the PLANE, SHe's drinking CHAMPAGNE.

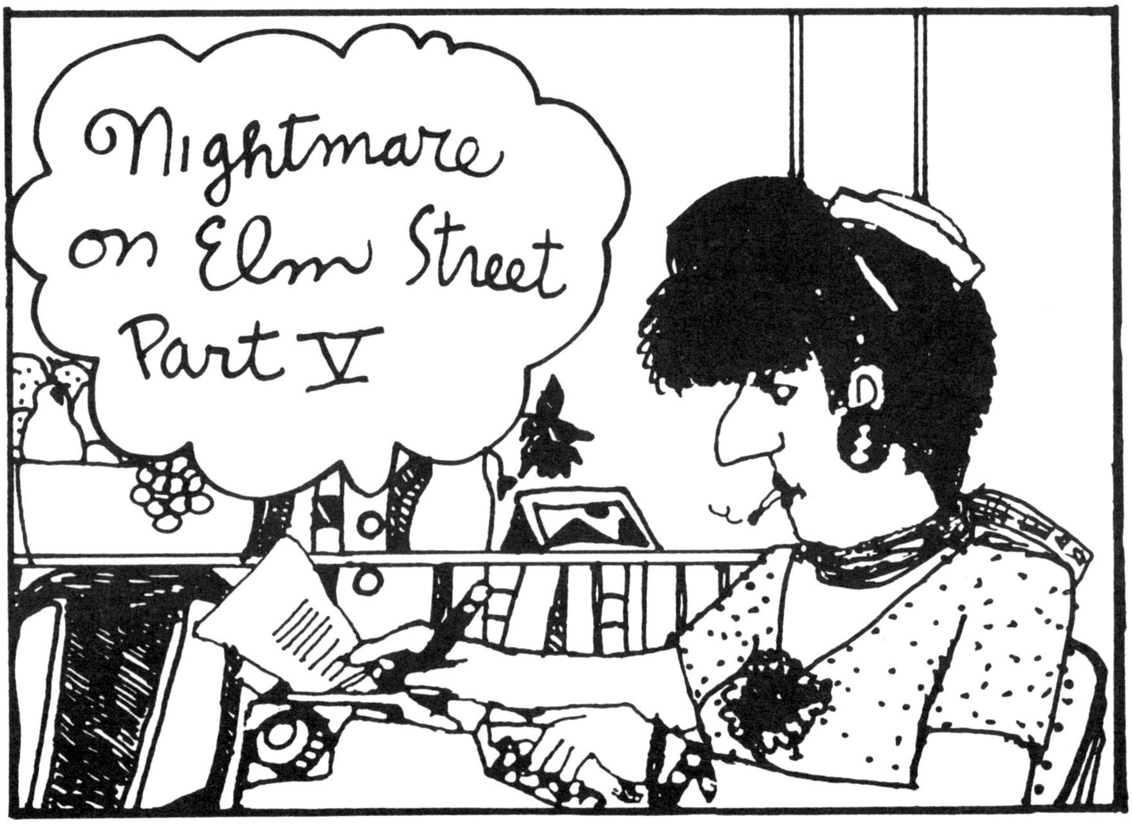
Nightmare on Elm Street Part V

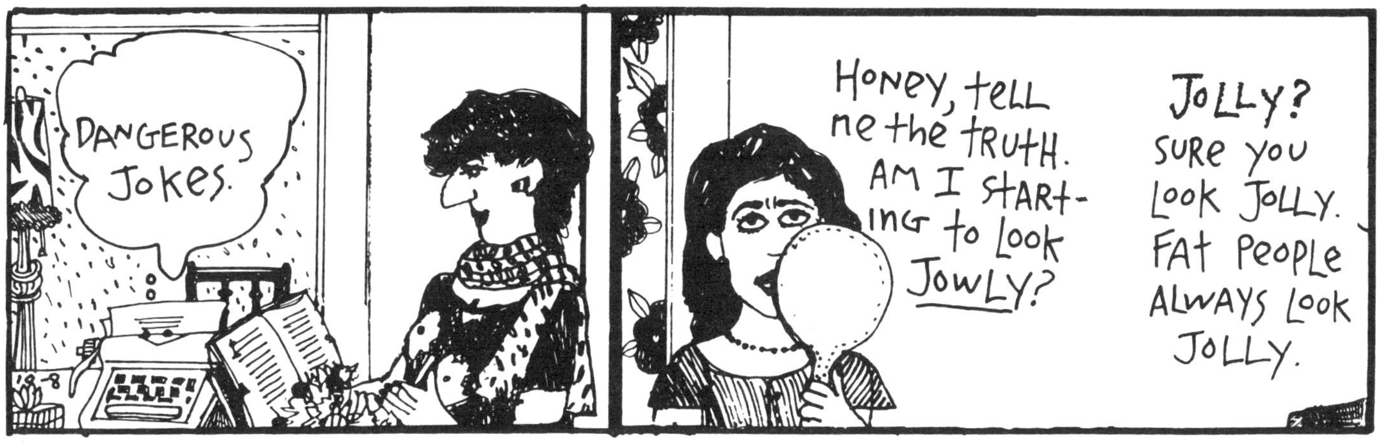
DANGEROUS JOKES.
Honey, tell me the truth. AM I START-ING to Look JOWLY?
JOLLY? SURE you Look JOLLY. FAT PeopLe ALWAYS Look JOLLY.

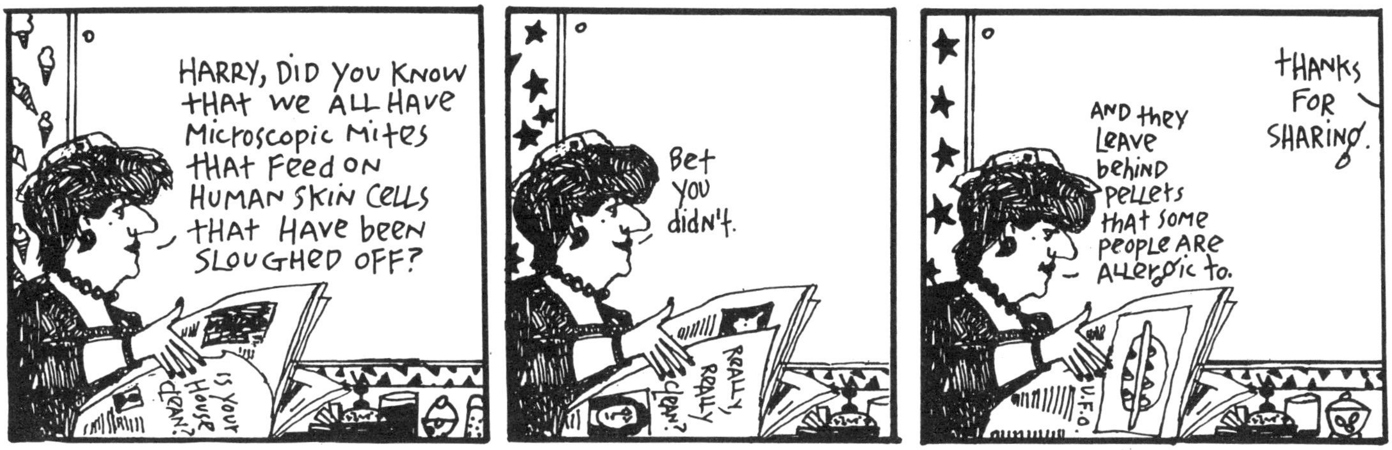
HARRY, DID YOU KNOW THAT WE ALL HAVE Microscopic Mites THAT Feed ON HUMAN SKIN CELLS THAT HAVE been SLOUGHED OFF?
IS YOUR HOUSE CLEAN?
Bet You didn't.
REALLY, REALLY CLEAN?
AND they Leave behind pellets that some people ARE ALLERGIC to.
THANKS FOR SHARING.
U.F.O.

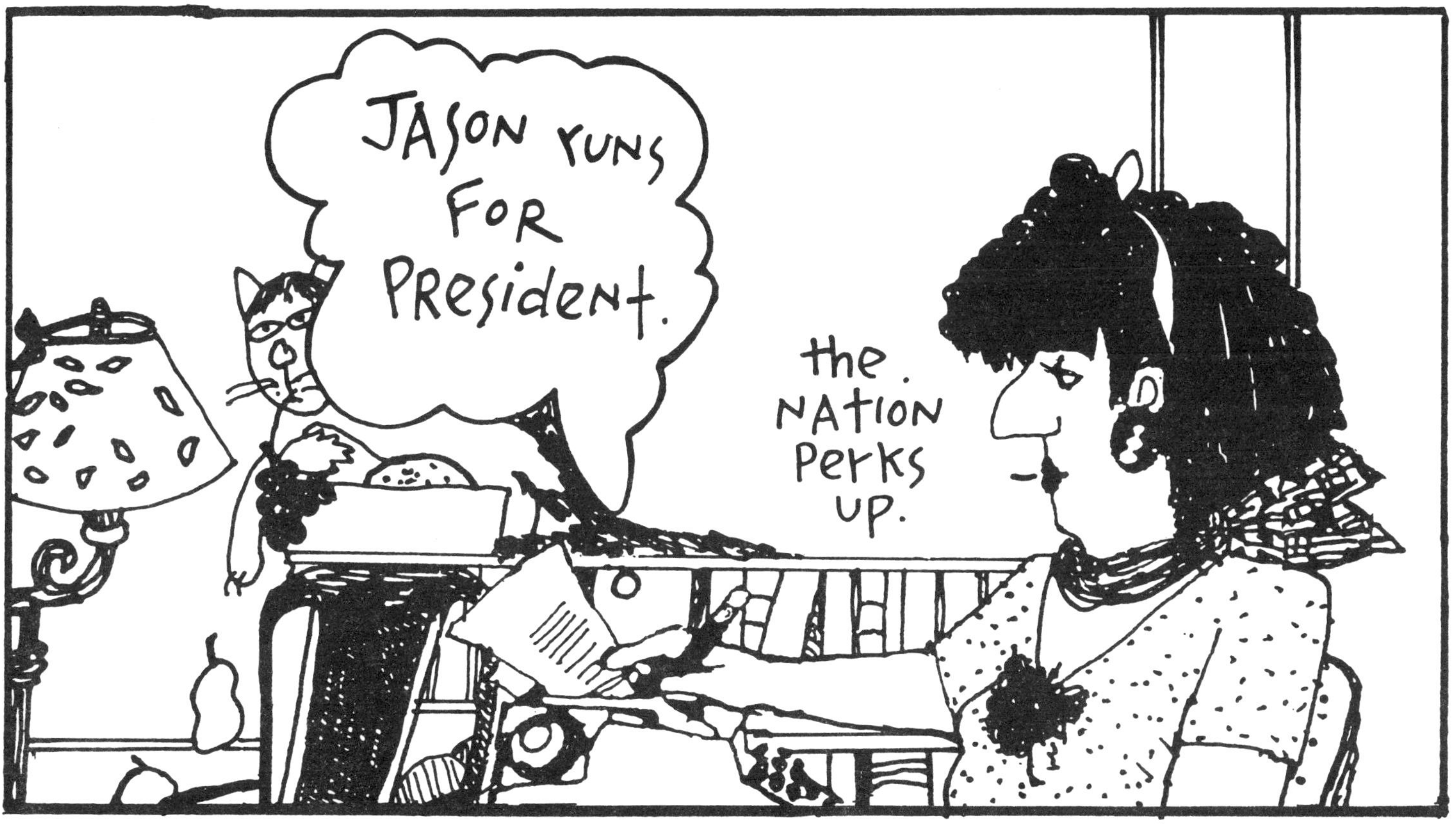
JASON runs FOR President.
the NATION Perks up.

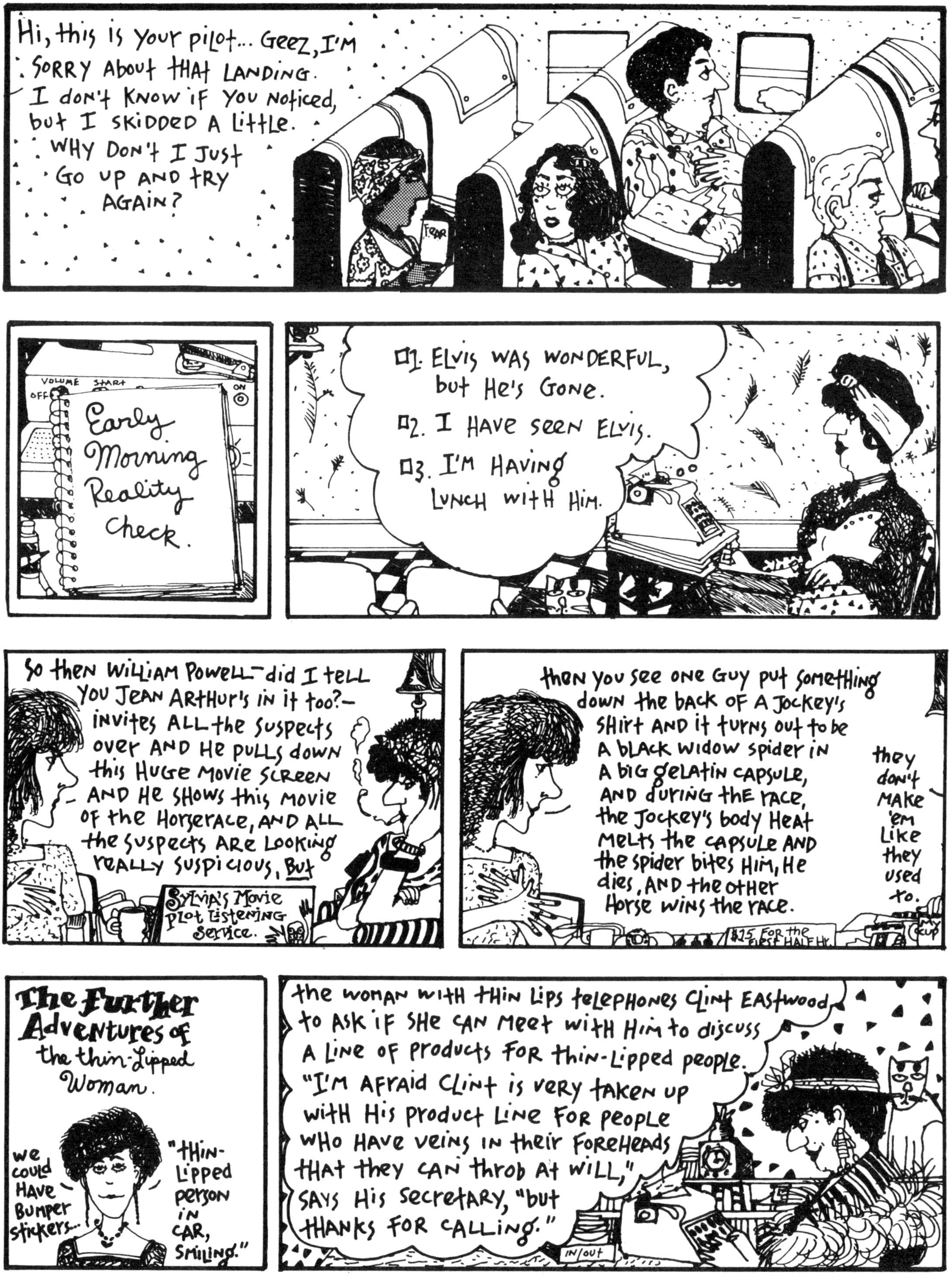
Hi, this is your pilot... Geez, I'M SORRY About that LANDING. I don't Know if you noticed, but I skidded A little. WHY Don't I JUST Go up AND try AGAIN?
Early Morning Reality Check.
VOLUME
START
OFF
ON
☐1. Elvis was wonderful, but He's Gone.
☐2. I have seen Elvis.
☐3. I'M HAVING Lunch with Him.
So then William Powell—did I tell you Jean Arthur's in it too?—invites all the suspects over and he pulls down this huge movie screen and he shows this movie of the horserace, and all the suspects are looking really suspicious, but
Sylvia's Movie Plot Listening Service.
then you see one guy put something down the back of a jockey's shirt and it turns out to be a black widow spider in a big gelatin capsule, and during the race, the jockey's body heat melts the capsule and the spider bites him, he dies, and the other horse wins the race.
they don't make 'em like they used to.
$25 for the first half hr.
MY CUP
The Further Adventures of the thin-Lipped Woman.
we could have bumper stickers...
"thin-lipped person in car, smiling."
the woman with thin lips telephones Clint Eastwood to ask if she can meet with him to discuss a line of products for thin-lipped people. "I'm afraid Clint is very taken up with his product line for people who have veins in their foreheads that they can throb at will," says his secretary, "but thanks for calling."
IN/OUT

IN THE BASEMENT

"Something bad has happened in the basement. Something very Stephen Kingish has happened in my basement," I yelled from the kitchen. "Indeed," said my weekend houseguests, bounding down the basement steps, "what fun. We thought we would be bored out here with nothing to do but walk on the beach and visit the mall."

"It looks like the basement floor is covered with raw sewage," said Lynda and Ira, smiling sweetly at me. "Oh," I said, "that explains the hideous insects that are swarming over the surface of the washer and dryer."

"I've got an idea," I said, "let's go get a few drinks and call for help from a bar." "No," said Ira, looking at his watch. "What we'll do is go buy some garbage bags and shovel this disgusting muck into them and get it out of the basement. If we start right now, we'll be done in an hour."

"I think this is the worst thing that has ever happened to me this year," I moaned. "Think of it as an interesting experience," they said. "I think I may have had one too many interesting experiences and have injured myself permanently," I replied. "But if my guests want to shovel unspeakable things out of the basement in shorts and sandals, then we'll do it."

Later I got some wonderful guys from Gene's Sewer and Septic to come out and disinfect the basement and kill the bugs, and then *much* later, I did this cartoon.

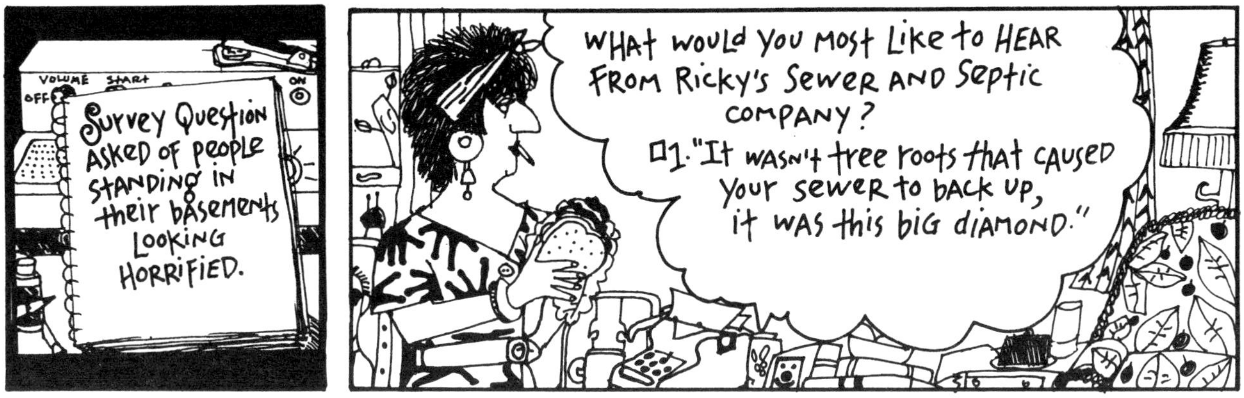
VOLUME
START
OFF
ON
Survey Question ASKED of people STANDING IN their basements LOOKING HORRIFIED.
WHAT would you most Like to HEAR FROM Ricky's Sewer AND Septic COMPANY?
□1. "It WASN'T tree roots that CAUSED your sewer to BACK UP, it WAS this big diamond."

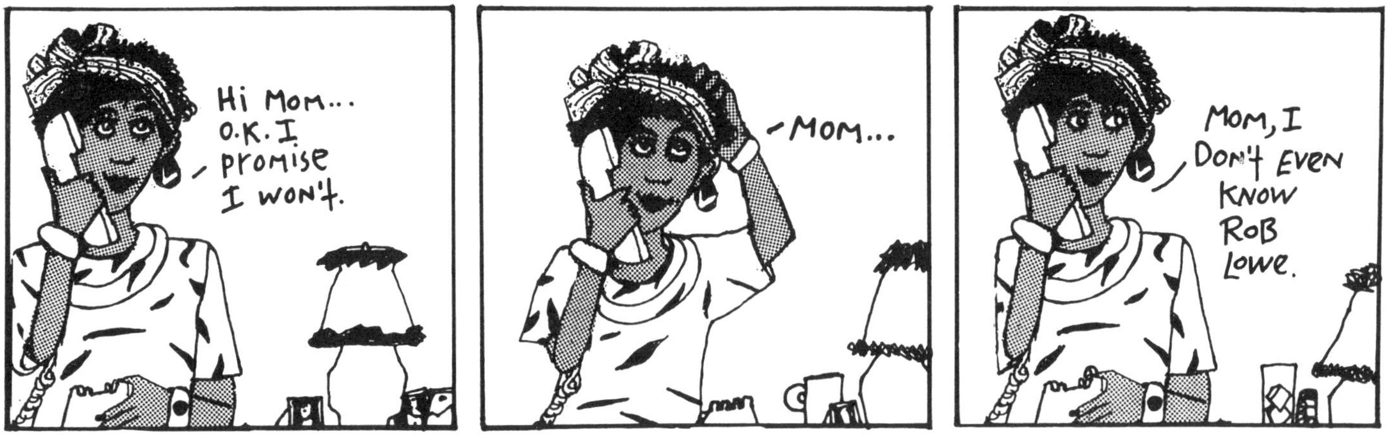
Hi Mom... O.K. I promise I won't.
-Mom...
Mom, I Don't even know Rob Lowe.

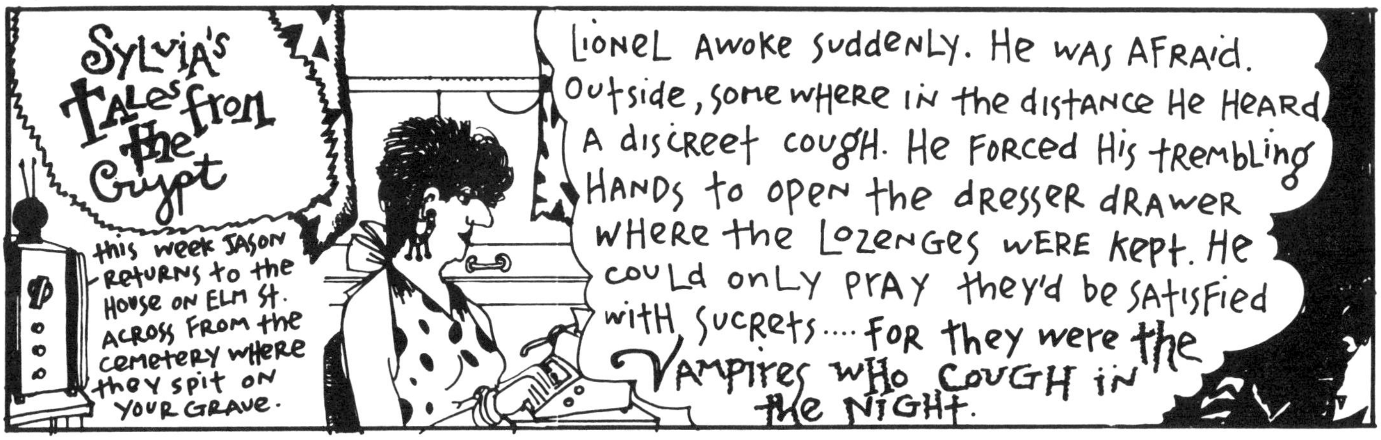
Sylvia's Tales from the Crypt
this week Jason returns to the House on Elm St. across from the cemetery where they spit on your grave.
Lionel awoke suddenly. He was afraid. Outside, somewhere in the distance he heard a discreet cough. He forced his trembling hands to open the dresser drawer where the lozenges were kept. He could only pray they'd be satisfied with Sucrets.... For they were the Vampires who cough in the night.

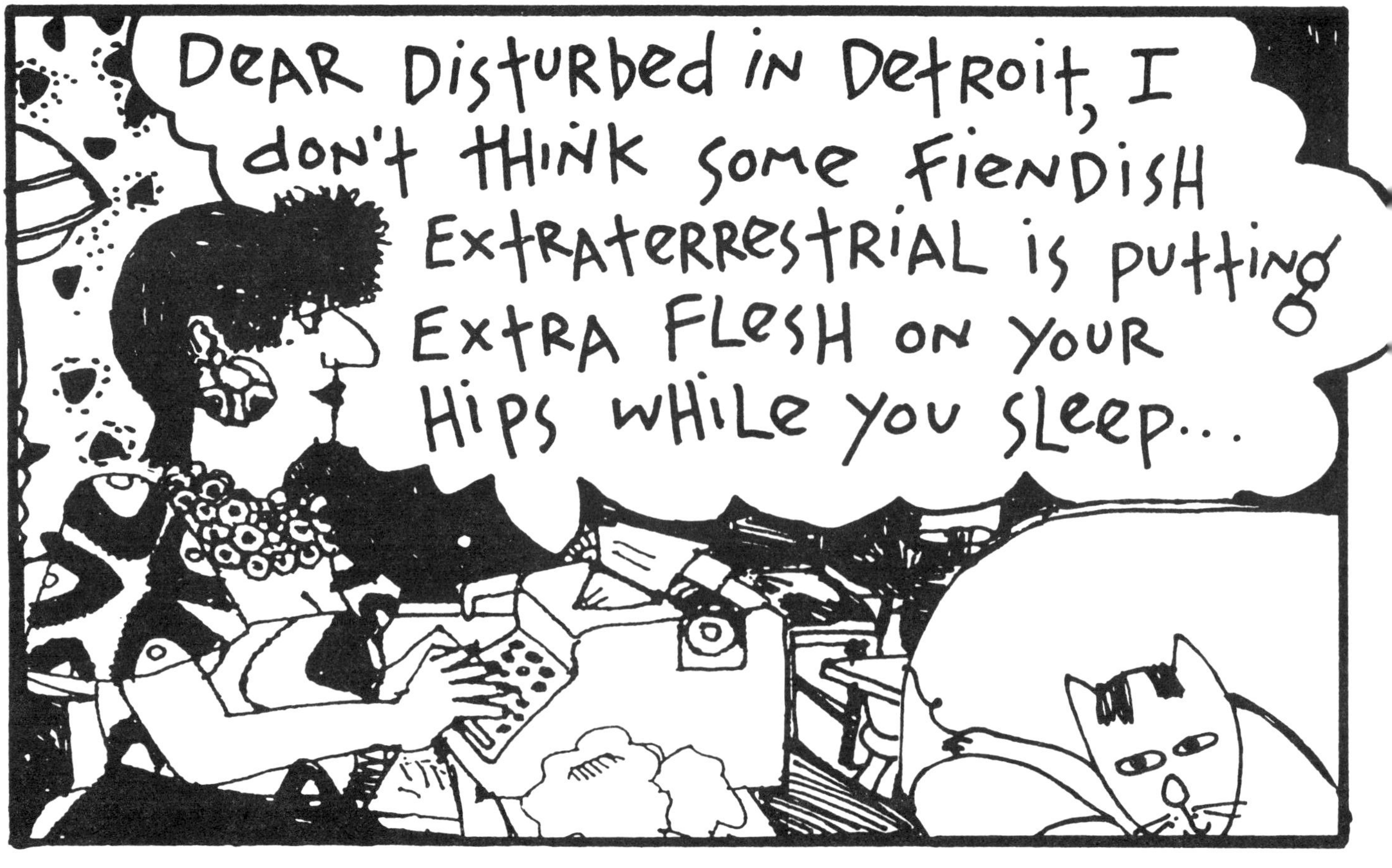
Dear Disturbed in Detroit, I don't think some fiendish extraterrestrial is putting extra flesh on your hips while you sleep...

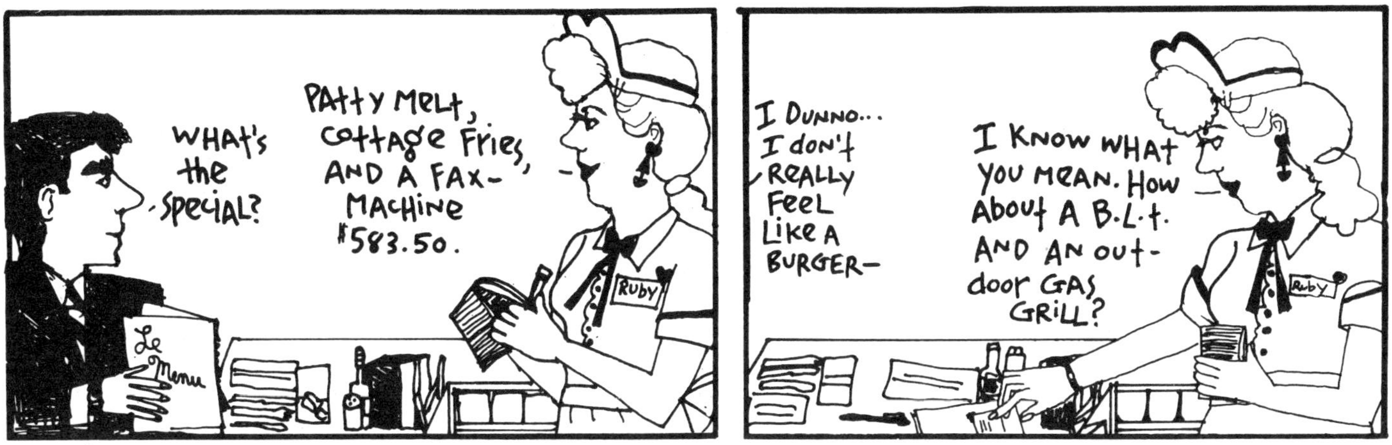
WHAT's the Special?
PAtty Melt, cottage Fries, AND A FAX-MACHINE #583.50.
Le Menu
Ruby
I DUNNO... I don't REALLY FeeL Like A BURGER-
I KNOW WHAT YOU MEAN. HOW About A B.L.T. AND AN out-door GAS GRILL?
Ruby

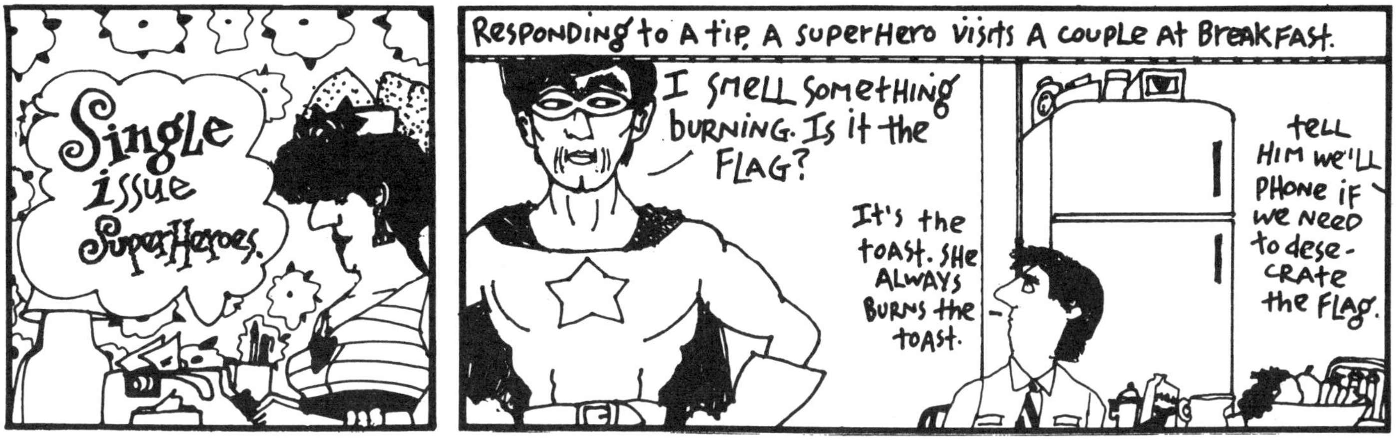
Single issue SuperHeroes.
ResponDING to A tip, A superHero visits A couple At BreakFAst.
I SMELL SomeTHING BURNING. Is it the FLAG?
It's the toAst. SHE ALWAYS BURNS the toAst.
tell HIM we'll PHONE if we NEED to dese-crate the FLAG.

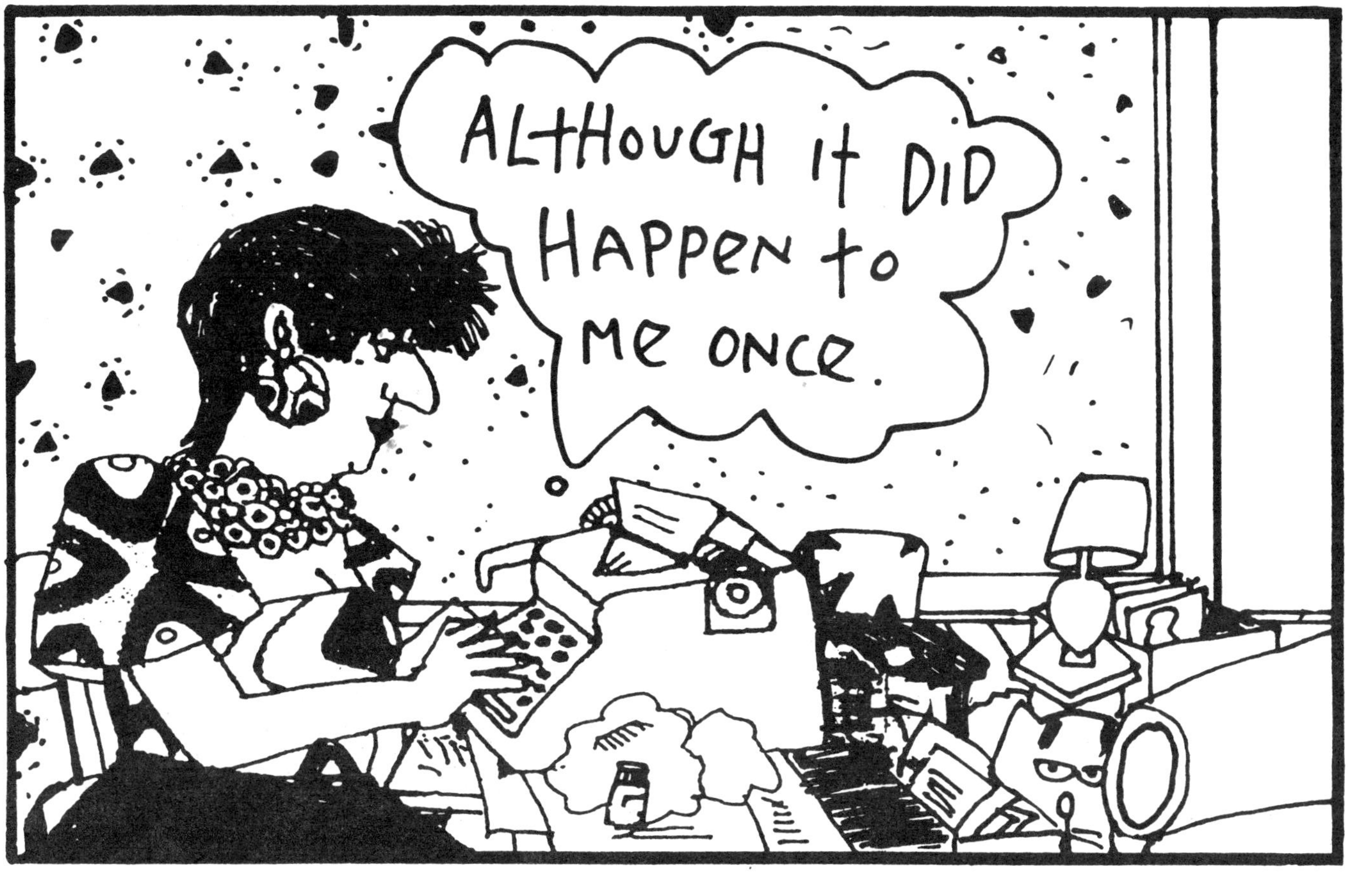
ALTHOUGH it DID HAPPEN to ME ONCE.

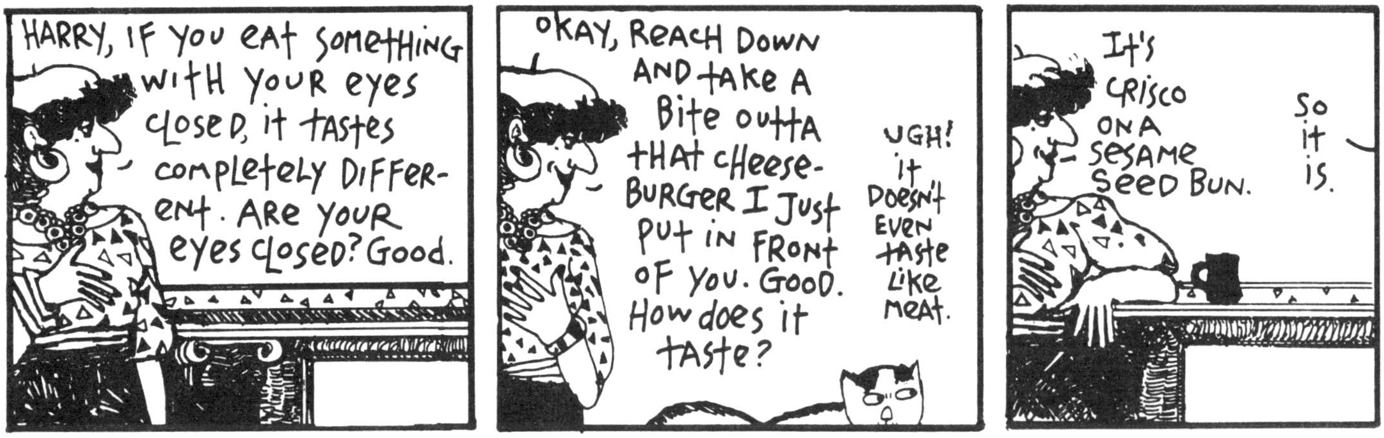
HARRY, IF YOU EAT SOMETHING WITH YOUR EYES CLOSED, IT TASTES COMPLETELY DIFFERENT. ARE YOUR EYES CLOSED? GOOD.
OKAY, REACH DOWN AND TAKE A BITE OUTTA THAT CHEESEBURGER I JUST PUT IN FRONT OF YOU. GOOD. HOW DOES IT TASTE?
UGH! IT DOESN'T EVEN TASTE LIKE MEAT.
IT'S CRISCO ON A SESAME SEED BUN.
SO IT IS.

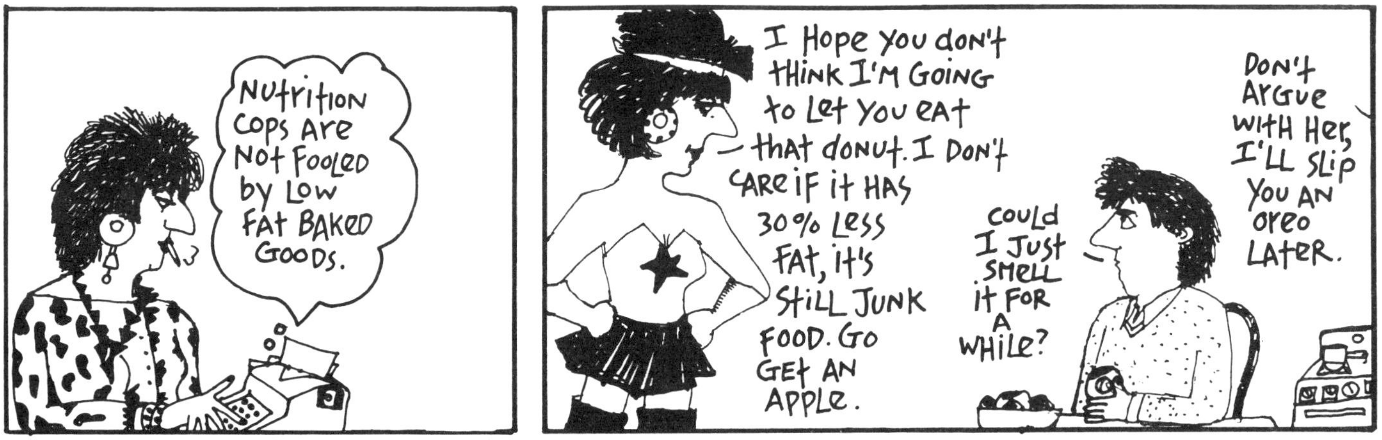
NUTRITION COPS ARE NOT FOOLED BY LOW FAT BAKED GOODS.
I HOPE YOU DON'T THINK I'M GOING TO LET YOU EAT THAT DONUT. I DON'T CARE IF IT HAS 30% LESS FAT, IT'S STILL JUNK FOOD. GO GET AN APPLE.
COULD I JUST SMELL IT FOR A WHILE?
DON'T ARGUE WITH HER, I'LL SLIP YOU AN OREO LATER.

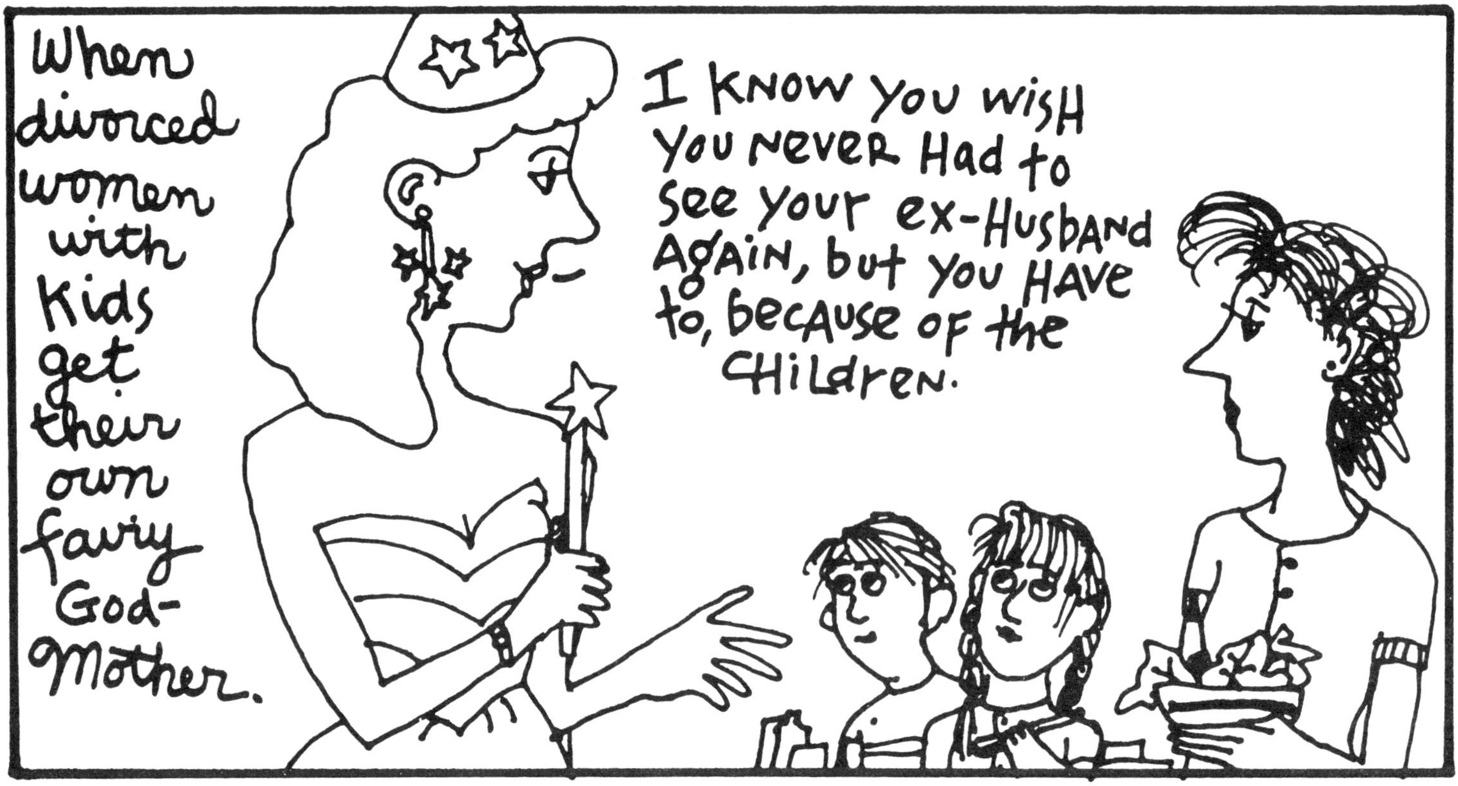
When divorced women with kids get their own fairy God-mother.
I KNOW YOU WISH YOU NEVER HAD TO SEE YOUR EX-HUSBAND AGAIN, BUT YOU HAVE TO, BECAUSE OF THE CHILDREN.

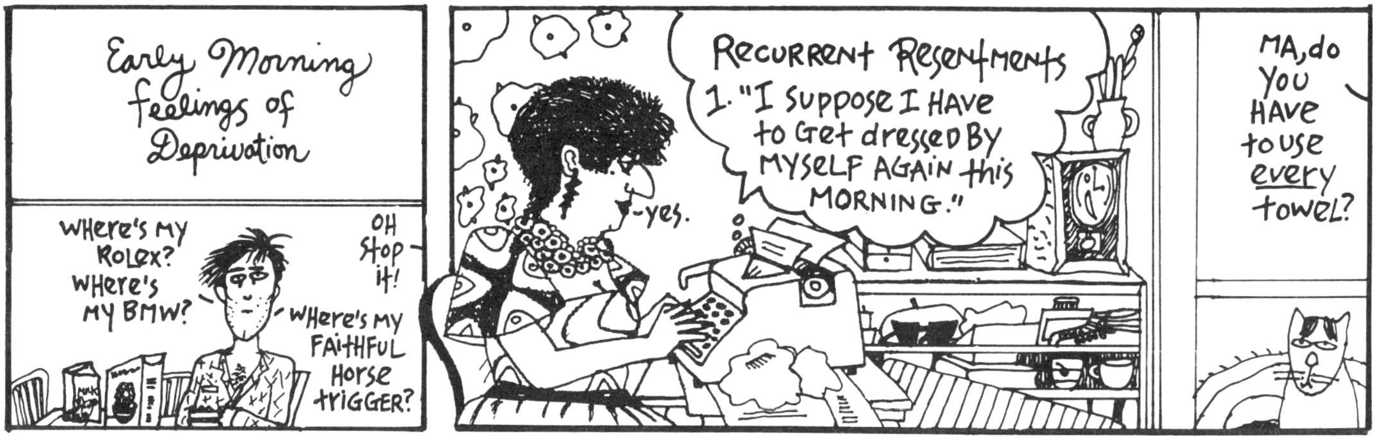
Early Morning feelings of Deprivation
WHERE'S MY ROLEX? WHERE'S MY BMW?
WHERE'S MY FAITHFUL HORSE TRIGGER?
OH STOP IT!
RECURRENT RESENTMENTS
1. "I SUPPOSE I HAVE TO GET DRESSED BY MYSELF AGAIN THIS MORNING."
-YES.
MA, DO YOU HAVE TO USE EVERY TOWEL?

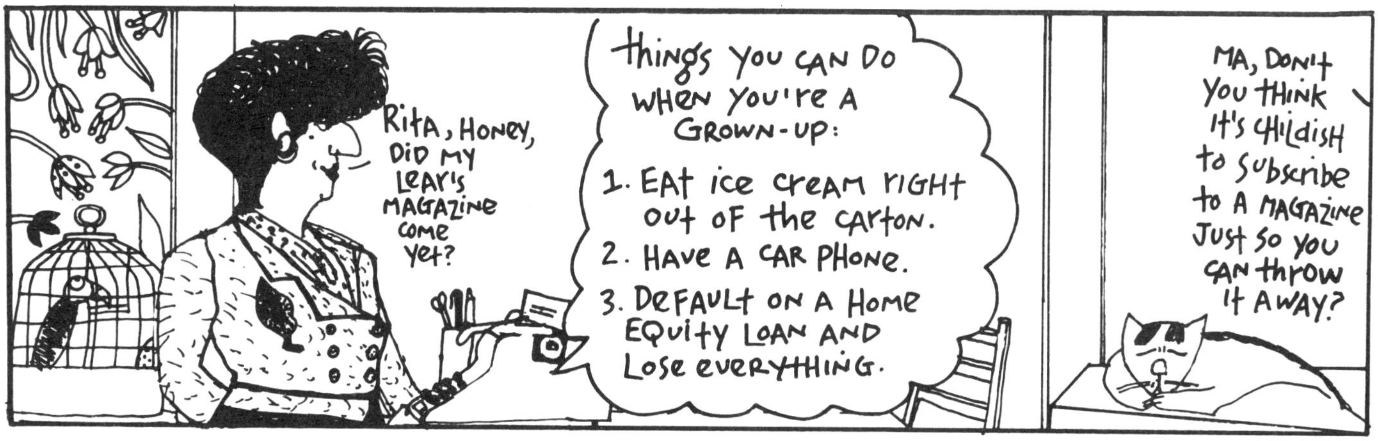
RITA, HONEY, DID MY LEAR'S MAGAZINE COME YET?
THINGS YOU CAN DO WHEN YOU'RE A GROWN-UP:
1. EAT ICE CREAM RIGHT OUT OF THE CARTON.
2. HAVE A CAR PHONE.
3. DEFAULT ON A HOME EQUITY LOAN AND LOSE EVERYTHING.
MA, DON'T YOU THINK IT'S CHILDISH TO SUBSCRIBE TO A MAGAZINE JUST SO YOU CAN THROW IT AWAY?

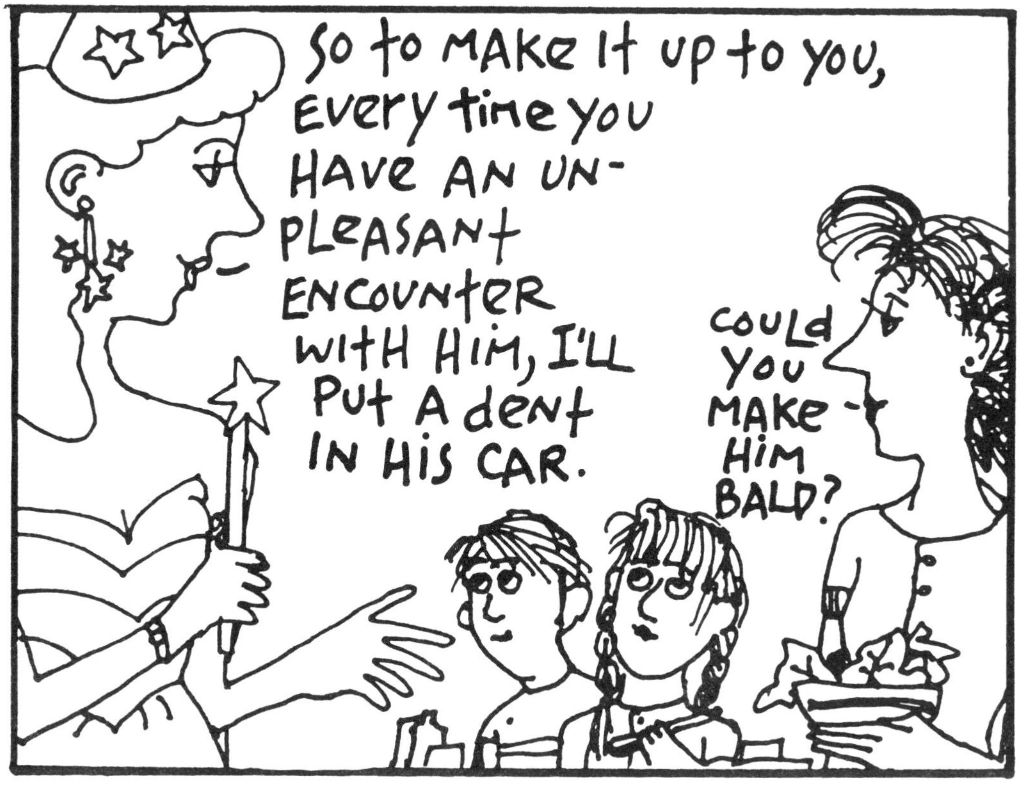
SO TO MAKE IT UP TO YOU, EVERY TIME YOU HAVE AN UN-PLEASANT ENCOUNTER WITH HIM, I'LL PUT A DENT IN HIS CAR.
COULD YOU MAKE HIM BALD?

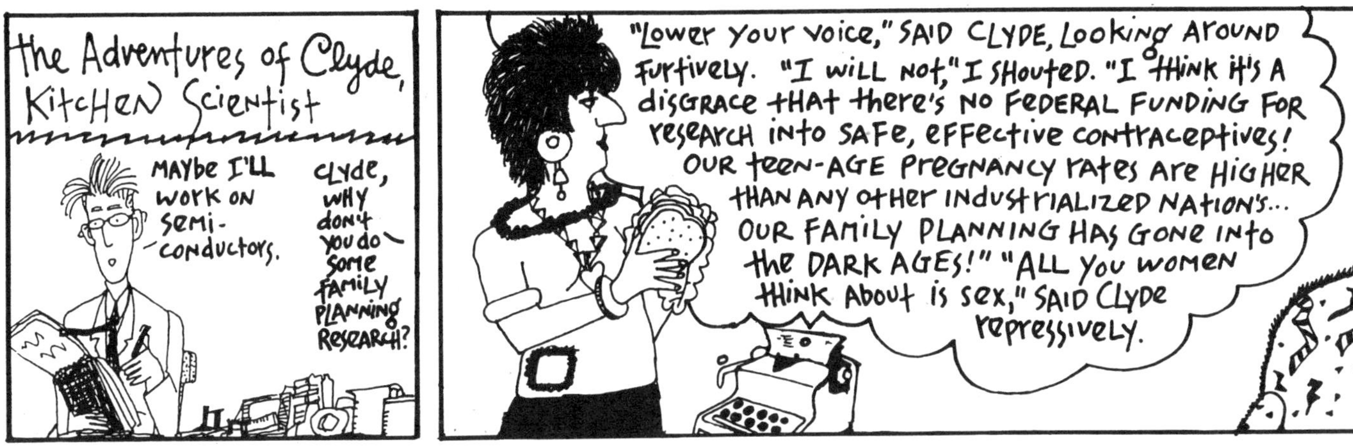
the Adventures of Clyde, Kitchen Scientist
MAYbe I'LL work on semi-conductors.
clyde, why don't you do some family planning research?
"Lower your voice," SAID CLYDE, Looking AROUND furtively. "I will not," I shouted. "I think it's A disgrace that there's NO FEDERAL FUNDING FOR research into SAFE, effective contraceptives! OUR teen-AGE PREGNANCY rates ARE HIGHER THAN ANY OTHER INDUSTRIALIZED NATION'S... OUR FAMILY PLANNING HAS GONE INTO the DARK AGES!" "ALL you women think About is sex," SAID CLYDE repressively.

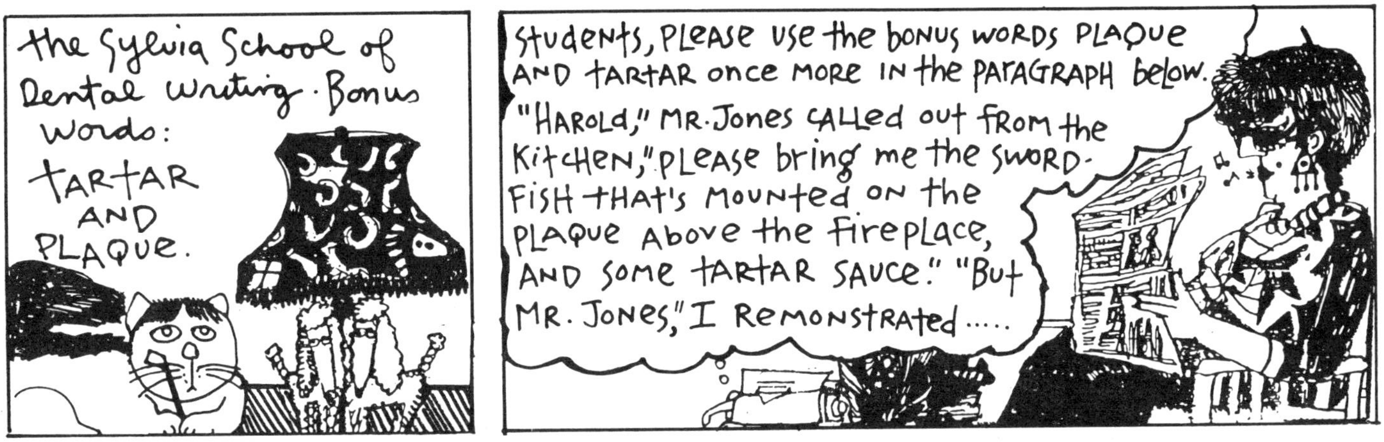
the Sylvia School of Dental Writing. Bonus words:
TARTAR AND PLAQUE.
Students, PLEASE use the bonus words PLAQUE AND TARTAR once MORE IN the PARAGRAPH below.
"HAROLD," MR. Jones called out from the Kitchen, "please bring me the sword-fish that's mounted on the plaque above the fireplace, AND some TARTAR SAUCE." "But MR. JONES," I Remonstrated.....

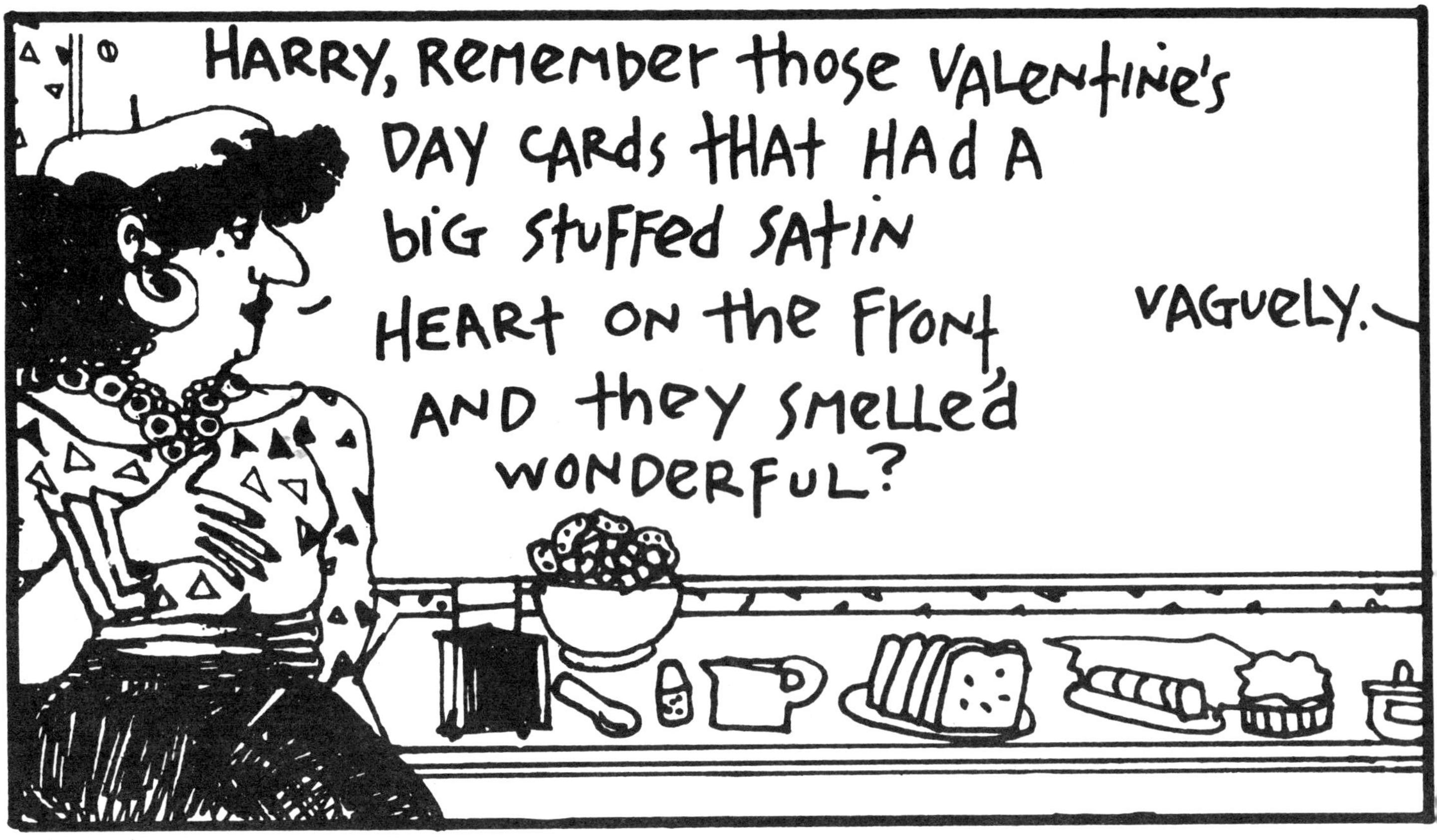
HARRY, Remember those VALentine's DAY cards that HAd A big stuffed satin HEART ON the Front AND they smelled WONDERFUL?
VAGUELY.

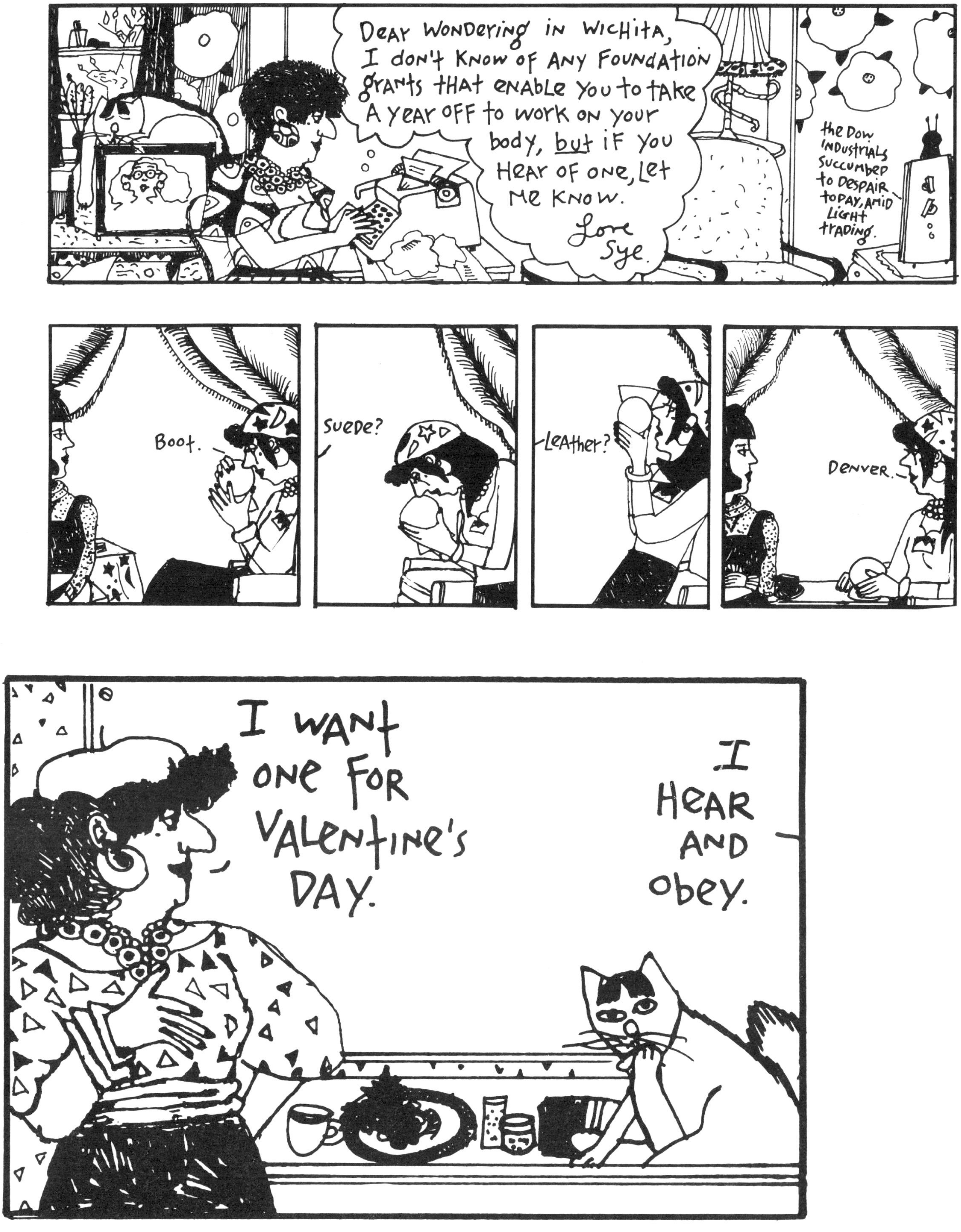
Dear Wondering in Wichita,
I don't know of any foundation grants that enable you to take a year off to work on your body, but if you hear of one, let me know.
Love
Sye.
the Dow industrials succumbed to despair today, amid light trading.
Boot.
Suede?
Leather?
Denver.
I want one for Valentine's Day.
I hear and obey.

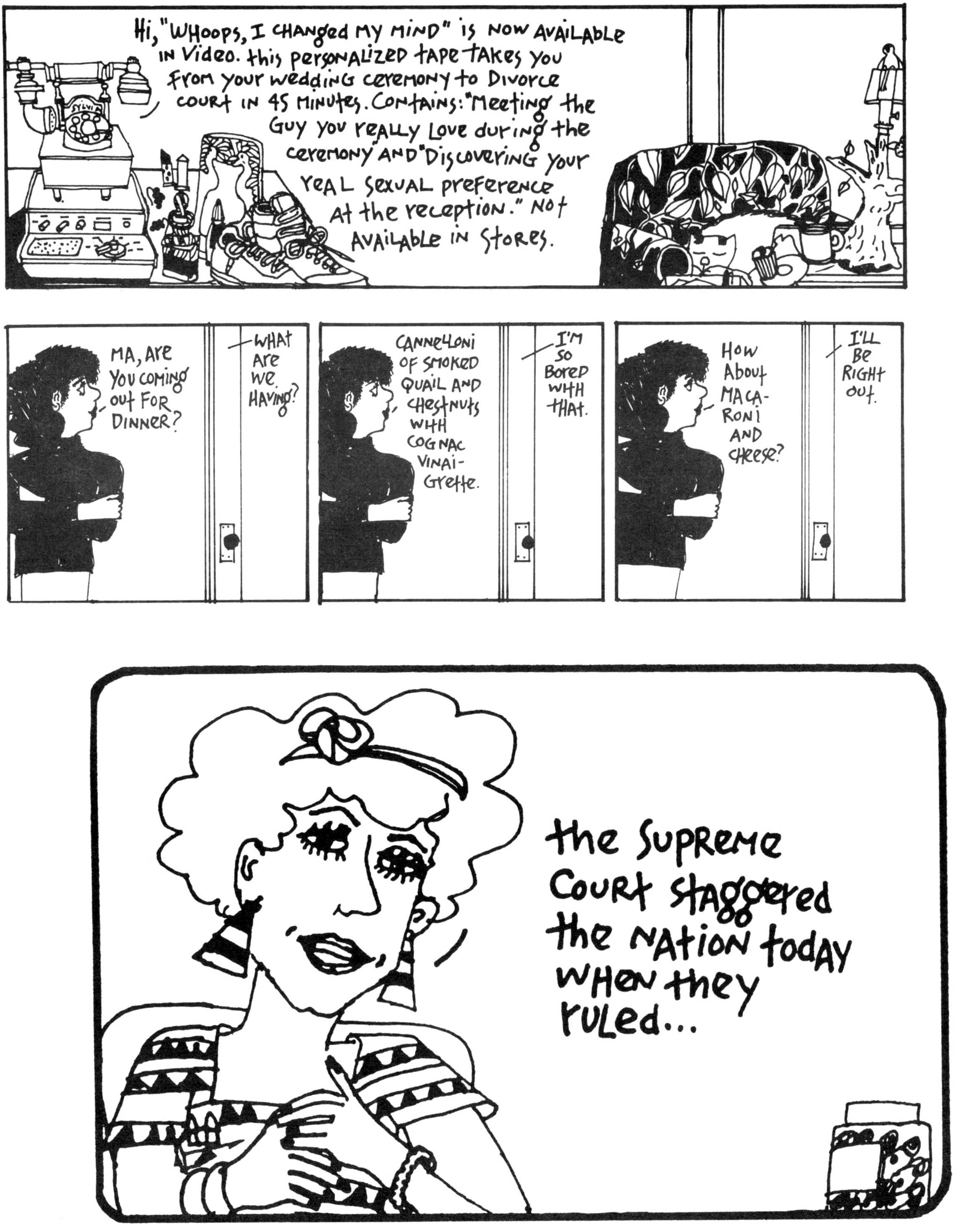
Hi, "Whoops, I changed my mind" is now available in Video. this personalized tape takes you from your wedding ceremony to Divorce court in 45 minutes. Contains: "Meeting the Guy you really Love during the ceremony" and "Discovering your real sexual preference at the reception." Not available in Stores.
Ma, are you coming out for dinner?
What are we having?
Cannelloni of smoked quail and chestnuts with cognac vinaigrette.
I'm so bored with that.
How about macaroni and cheese?
I'll be right out.
the Supreme Court staggered the nation today when they ruled...

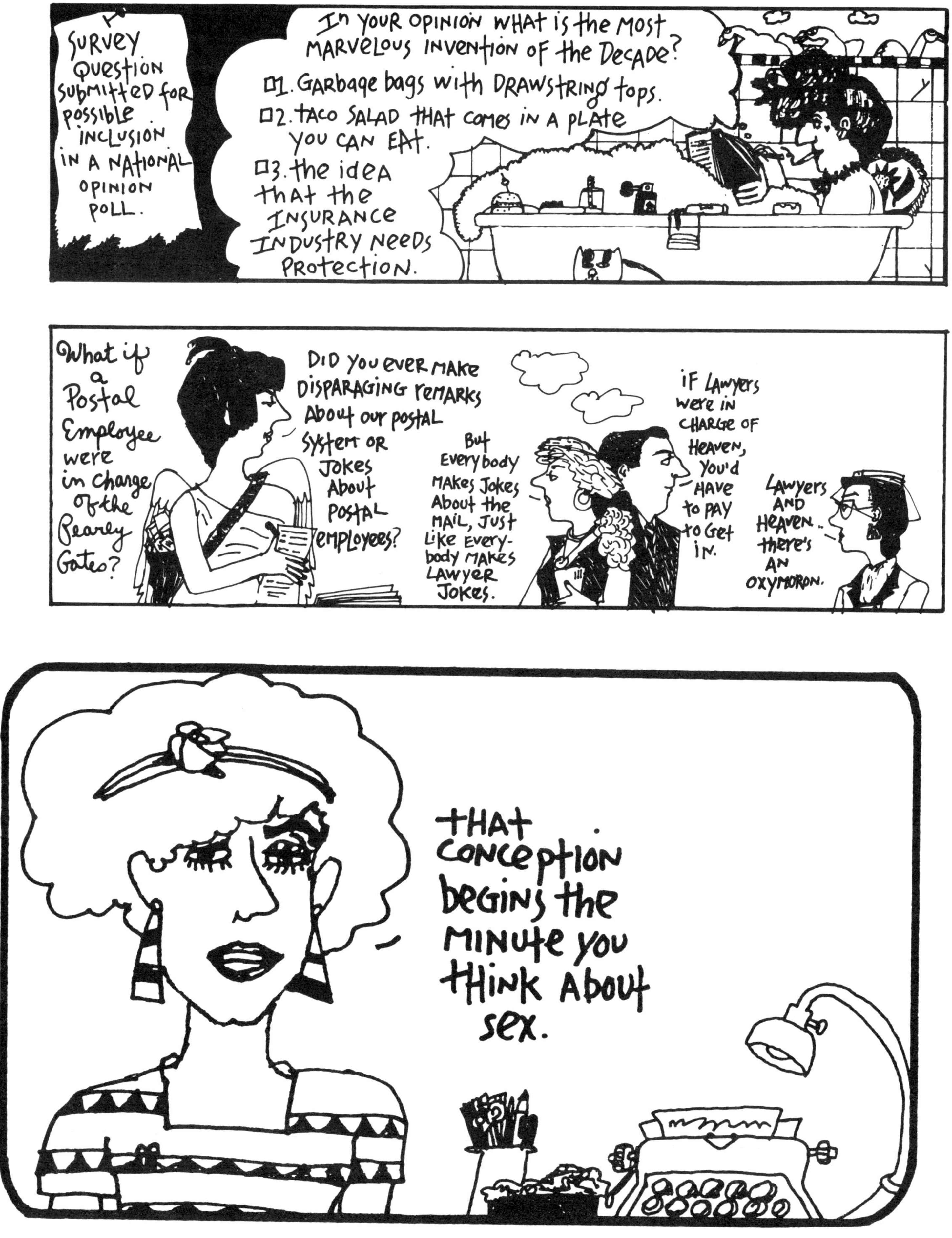
Survey question submitted for possible inclusion in a national opinion poll.
In your opinion what is the most marvelous invention of the decade?
□1. Garbage bags with drawstring tops.
□2. Taco salad that comes in a plate you can eat.
□3. The idea that the insurance industry needs protection.
What if a Postal Employee were in charge of the Pearly Gates?
Did you ever make disparaging remarks about our postal system or jokes about postal employees?
But everybody makes jokes about the mail, just like everybody makes lawyer jokes.
If lawyers were in charge of heaven, you'd have to pay to get in.
Lawyers and heaven.. there's an oxymoron.
That conception begins the minute you think about sex.

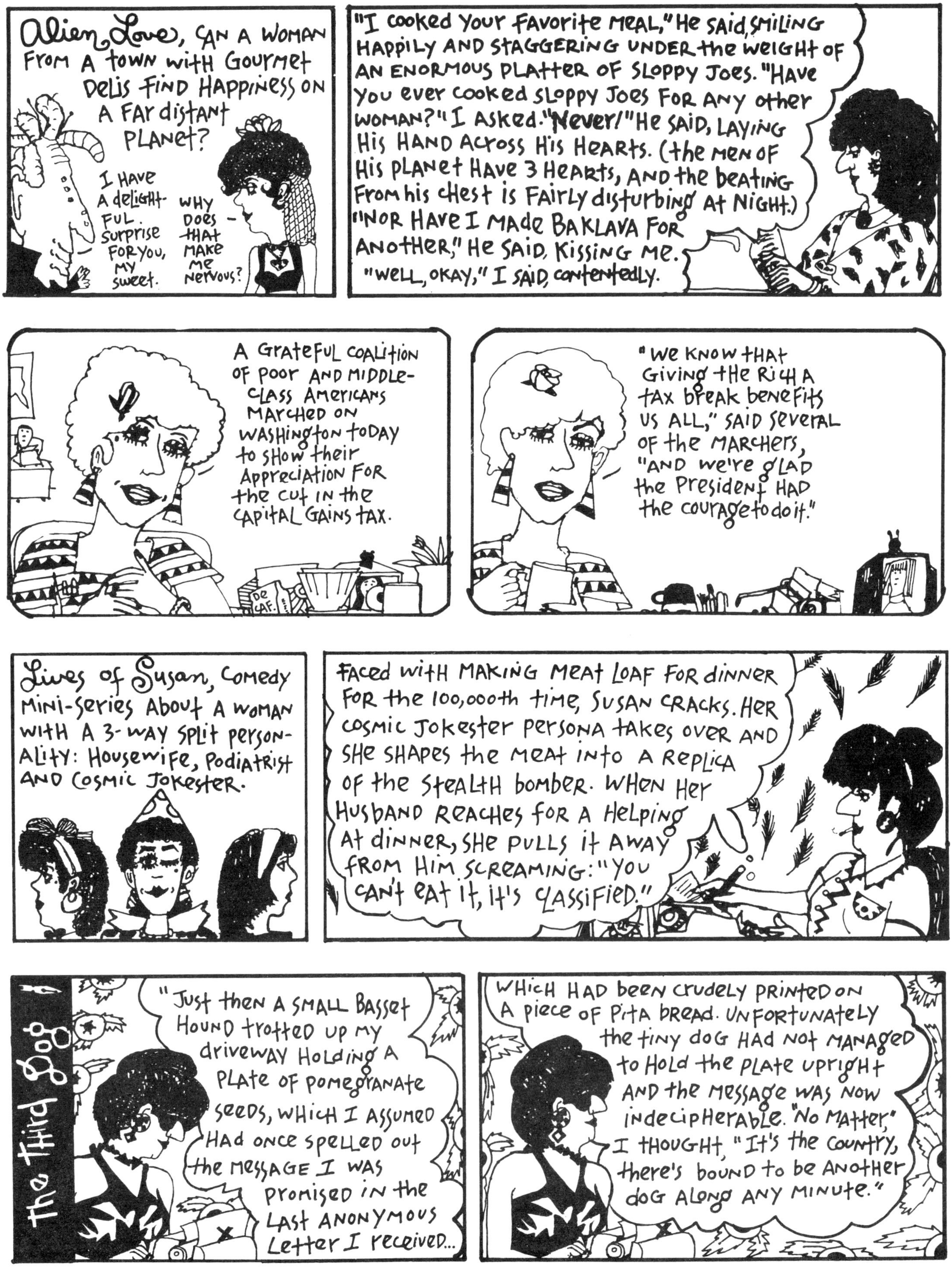
Alien Love, CAN A WOMAN FROM A town with Gourmet Delis FIND HAPPINESS ON A FAR distant PLANET?
I HAVE A delightful surprise FOR you, MY sweet.
WHY DOES THAT MAKE ME NERVOUS?
"I cooked your favorite meal," He said, smiling happily and staggering under the weight of an enormous platter of sloppy Joes. "Have you ever cooked sloppy Joes for any other woman?" I asked. "Never!" He said, laying His hand across His Hearts. (the men of His planet Have 3 Hearts, and the beating from his chest is fairly disturbing at night.) "Nor Have I made Baklava for another," He said, kissing me. "Well, okay," I said, contentedly.
A Grateful coalition of poor and middle-class Americans marched on Washington today to show their appreciation for the cut in the capital gains tax.
DE CAF.
"We know that giving the rich a tax break benefits us all," said several of the marchers, "and we're glad the President had the courage to do it."
Lives of Susan, Comedy Mini-series About a woman with a 3-way split personality: Housewife, Podiatrist and Cosmic Jokester.
Faced with making meat loaf for dinner for the 100,000th time, Susan cracks. Her cosmic Jokester persona takes over and she shapes the meat into a replica of the stealth bomber. When her husband reaches for a helping at dinner, she pulls it away from him screaming: "You can't eat it, it's classified."
The Third Dog!
"Just then a small Basset Hound trotted up my driveway holding a plate of pomegranate seeds, which I assumed had once spelled out the message I was promised in the last anonymous letter I received...
which had been crudely printed on a piece of pita bread. Unfortunately the tiny dog had not managed to hold the plate upright and the message was now indecipherable. "No matter," I thought, "It's the country, there's bound to be another dog along any minute."

PAVLAR & THE BIG-BONED BLONDE

My character Pavlar is sleazier and not as bright as my favorite fictional detective, Lew Archer.

Archer, the creation of Ross MacDonald, is compassionate, painstaking, loyal and intelligent. Pavlar writes an interplanetary gossip column, and his moral code is not rigorous, but they are both vulnerable loners, trusting in spite of their experience, embroiled in mysteries that have their roots in the murky (demented?) libidos of past generations.

The Adventures of Pavlar first appeared in a color Sunday strip, where I had the space to complete an entire story each week. I have since tried doing Pavlar stories in my daily strip, continuing the plot over several days, but I always have more copy than I can fit into a cartoon format, and besides I'd rather write about Pavlar than draw him.

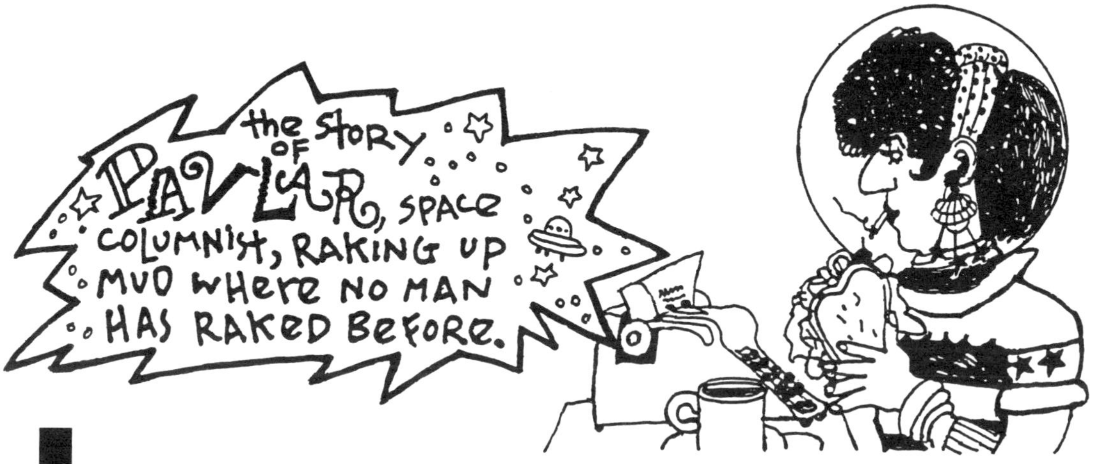
the STORY OF PAVLAR, SPACE COLUMNIST, RAKING UP MUD WHERE NO MAN HAS RAKED BEFORE.

I was hiding out on one of the warmer planets working on my tan and avoiding a few neurotics I'd mentioned in my column who felt I'd ruined their lives, when I got a message to call Stella Le Roy. Stella was big, she was beautiful, she was an old mah jongg buddy of my mother's. I hadn't heard from her for years, but then not many people called me. My family's been writing gossip columns for seven generations...inter-married so often, hardly any of us can stand upright or speak the truth for longer than a minute. We've been thrown out of every place worth writing about. By the time I was born we had worn out our welcome on the big planet and I was forced to make my living on the distant worlds...to go where no columnist had gone before, raking up mud and dishing the dirt.

Business was good....Everybody likes a little gossip, why fight the feeling? Stella Le Roy liked it more than most. Rumor had it she was writing an autobiography that would cause a large rip in the fragile fabric of our society. I was curious. I was jealous. I called her.

"Who the hell is this?" that unmistakable voice asked—Stella's voice was pitched almost too high for the human ear, irritating to most women, irresistible to men.

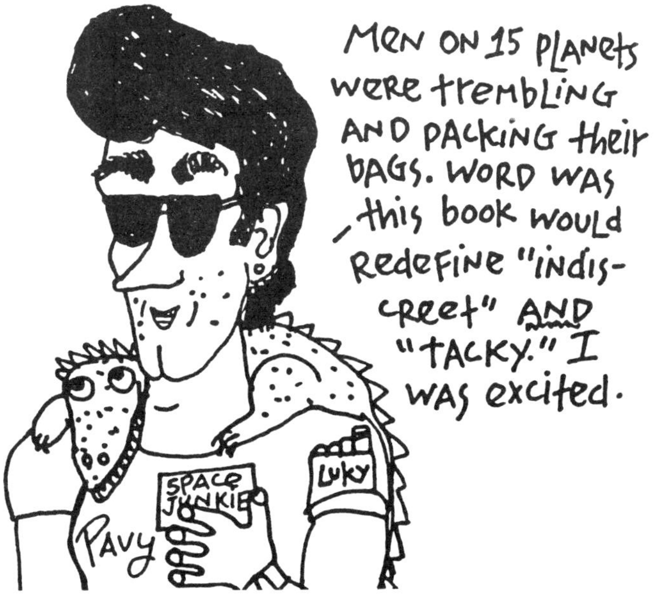
MEN ON 15 PLANETS WERE TREMBLING AND PACKING THEIR BAGS. WORD WAS THIS BOOK WOULD REDEFINE "INDISCREET" AND "TACKY." I WAS EXCITED.
SPACE JUNKIE
LUKY
PAVY

"It's me, Pavy, I got your message," I said nervously. I was always nervous on the phone, a handicap for gossip columnists. I had spent years in therapy with the result that I sometimes stuttered.

"Oh, Pav, you little ferret," she said, using the family nickname. "I'm ever so glad you called, I'm in terrible trouble and even a fuck-up like you can't make it any worse. Get over here as fast as you can."

"I'm being blackmailed," she said, as she led me into her tiny apartment. Stella was a big, big woman. Her apartment made her seem even larger. It was like a cave, filled with the tiniest furniture I'd ever seen. I loved coming here when I was a kid. The furniture was exactly my size and she always made me the center of her lavish attention, fixing her huge eyes on me until I felt like a deer frozen in the headlights of a truck, but nice. Now, as always, a tray appeared, with bite-size lemon meringue cakes and in deference to my adult status, tiny martinis, twelve for each of us.

"Bottoms up, mon petit ferret," she said, chucking her empty martini glass in the direction of the maid. "I have written my memoirs. People are trembling in anticipation of juicy revelations. There will be no reviews. The books will be sent to every bookstore in the universe at once. Word will mysteriously leak out....The pathetic and the wealthy will be camped in line for days in front of the stores, money clenched in their damp fists, fighting to be the first to be outraged."

PAVY, MON petit ferret, try and focus. I'm being BLACKMAILED.

"Sounds good to me," I said. "What's the hitch?"

"Vile Thirnicock," she hissed. I thought Vile Thirnicock was one of her ex-husbands, but I wasn't sure. "Thirnicock and his dim-witted twin are threatening to leak some of the more juicy passages of the book to the press." "Twins?" Right. She had married twins. It was quite a fad one summer.

"They're even threatening to spread it around that I'm your real mother—before the book is released—I won't have it. Double merde!" She kicked a tiny sofa across the room. "They want a lot of money to keep quiet and it chills me to the very bone to give those numbnuts even one red cent. I'd happily cut their huevos rancheros off and keep them in this little glass bowl. The Grand Duke gave me this, along with a stable of horses, remember, liebchen?"

"You're my mother?" I whispered, my heart beating wildly. "Lucy Belle wasn't my real mother?" I felt dizzy. "Wait a minute! If Lucy Belle wasn't my real

mother, is Gorgi my real father or what? Don't tell me it's one of the dukes? Not the squinty chauffeur? I couldn't bear it." A horrible thought occurred to me. "He wasn't one of those big Lizard guys, was he," I asked, "not that I'm prejudiced."

"Read my book," she snapped, and then, more kindly, "You had no father. It was an immaculate conception. Well, almost immaculate," she said, smiling sheepishly. "If Thirnicock blabs, no one

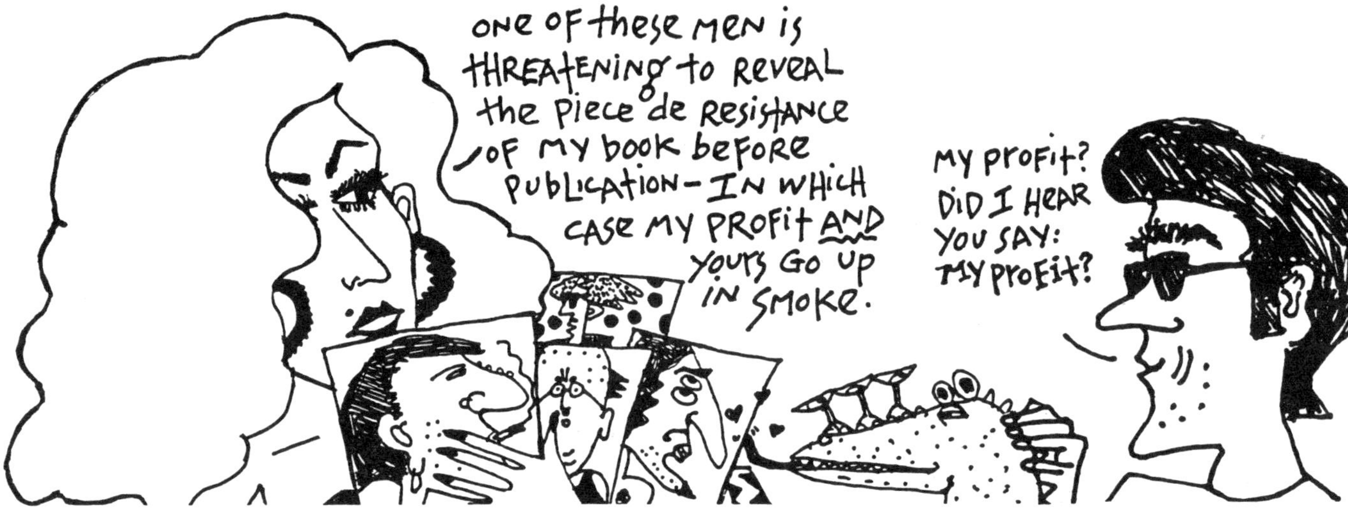
one of these men is threatening to reveal the piece de resistance of my book before publication—in which case my profit AND yours go up in smoke.
My profit? Did I hear you say: my profit?

will need to read the book. People will gasp, they'll be titillated for free," she hissed.

"I hate when that happens," I said, feeling the first stirrings of true outrage.

"And my dear ferret," Stella murmured, "all that money was to be yours. It was to be a legacy for my little unfertiliized egg," she said, tickling me under the chin. "Perhaps I should fill you in on the details."

I was reeling. I had a new mother, my father might be the Holy Ghost, and I was an heir—that and the twelve tiny martinis forced me to lie down on the floor and do some breathing exercises.

"Want to hear the plan? It's fabulous," she said, drinking more martinis and whirling around the room like a gigantic Loretta Young.

"The day the book hit the market I was going to stage my death. It would happen while you were interviewing me. I would be talking merrily about the revelations in my book—luxuriating in my wantonness—when suddenly I would notice the shock and horror in your face—seeing the disgust on that innocent face, I would realize how foul I had become. 'I can live no longer!' I would scream, tears running down my lovely cheeks. I would run from the room and into the sea. You would run after me, but it would be too late, because of the undertow and because you never learned to swim. You would be found sobbing, alone, on the beach. My book sales would go through the roof and we could spend the rest of our lives working on the perfect Bearnaise sauce." She knew my weaknesses.

"Wait a minute," I said, "How long have you been planning this?"

"Oh," she said, having the grace to pretend to be embarrassed, "I see you're remembering that the family discouraged you from learning to swim."

"Discouraged me," I yelled. "They told me that if my body was ever fully immersed in water, my arms would shrivel and fall off! Was that a lie?" I shouted. "I've never taken a shower in my whole life, I was afraid to. I take little wimpy sponge baths."

"Sponge baths are better for you anyway, I'm sure," she said, holding my hands and feeding me bits of meringue.

"As I was saying, after my tragic suicide, you would be found weeping at the edge of the sea, and I would be on a transporter heading for the Planet of the Seven Swiss Banks, where I have a charming cottage....Days later an unrecognizable corpse would be washed ashore, wearing my signature colors."

"Where would this corpse come from?" I asked, my voice trembling. "I hope it's no one I know." I was thinking of all those maids who'd fled Stella's house...leaving in the middle of the night, sick to death of dusting doll furniture. Maybe one of them hadn't run off to a better job. Maybe there were groups of them packed together in that pink freezer in the basement.

PLUS, they're threatening to tell everyone I'm your real mother! Step aside Pavy dear, —I'm about to start throwing furniture out the window.

"Don't be silly," she said, putting a bit of meringue on the end of my nose. "Procuring a corpse will be no problem. Your own dear mama, Lucy Belle, had many connections at the morgue, which I have assiduously cultivated." That was true, my mother had a lot of pals at the morgue. She often visited there, looking for an unidentified corpse that might turn out to be Elvis.

Suddenly Stella began pulling her hair and screaming: "The plan was perfect and those two dim witted, syphilitic oafs are going to ruin it. No! No! I won't let them." She was stamping her feet, turning red, and then deep burgundy. I could see how she had enslaved the crowned heads of the Old Euro Planet. She started whirling around, her full skirt knocking miniature cups and saucers in all directions. The maid and the dog ran howling from the room. "How satisfying to have tiny furniture," she yelled, lifting up a sofa and two fireside chairs and hurling them out the window.

"Now, I am calm again," she said, motioning me to sit at her feet. "I've been dreadfully selfish, mon petit. Tell me all about what you've been doing, and we won't talk of murder until I've heard your news."

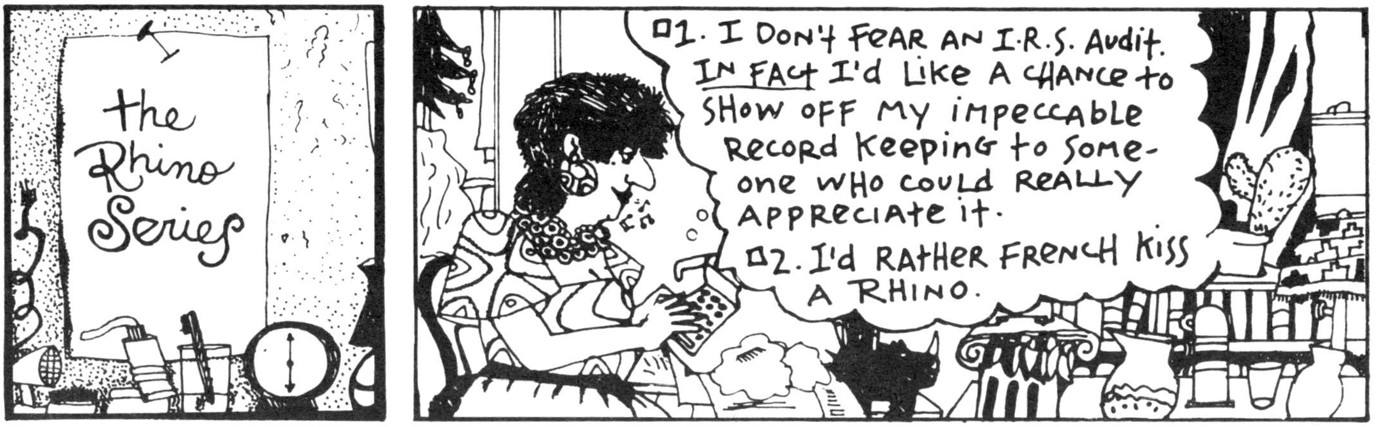
the Rhino Series
□1. I Don't FEAR AN I.R.S. Audit. IN FACT I'd Like A CHANCE to SHOW OFF MY impeccable Record Keeping to Someone WHO COULD REALLY APPRECIATE it.
□2. I'd RATHER FRENCH KISS A RHINO.

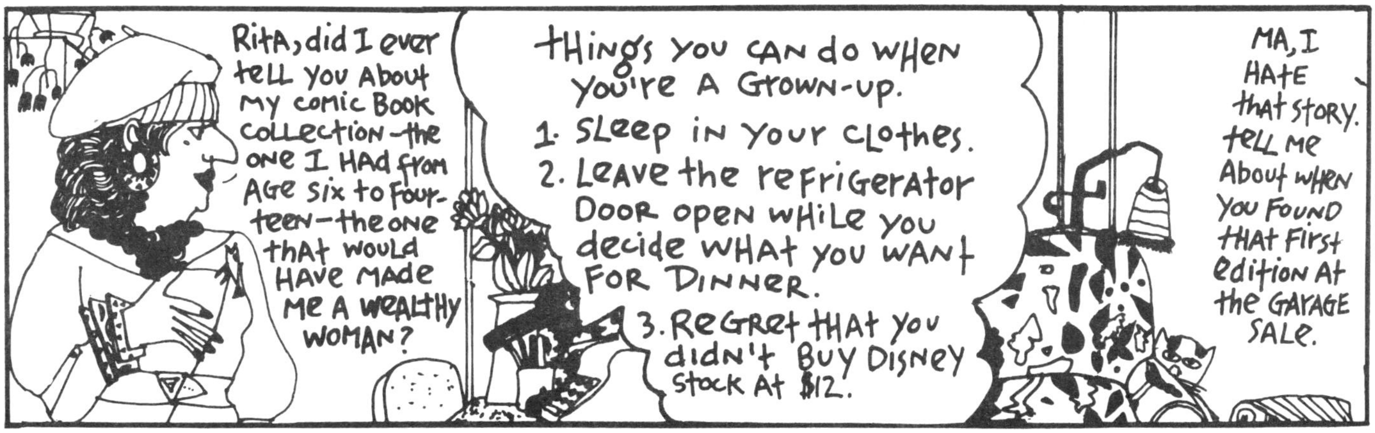
RitA, did I ever tell you About my comic Book collection—the one I HAd from Age six to Fourteen—the one that would Have made me A wealthy woman?
things you can do when you're A Grown-up.
1. Sleep in your clothes.
2. Leave the refrigerator Door open while you decide what you want For Dinner.
3. Regret that you didn't Buy Disney Stock At $12.
MA, I HATE that story. tell me About when you Found that First edition At the GARAGE SALE.

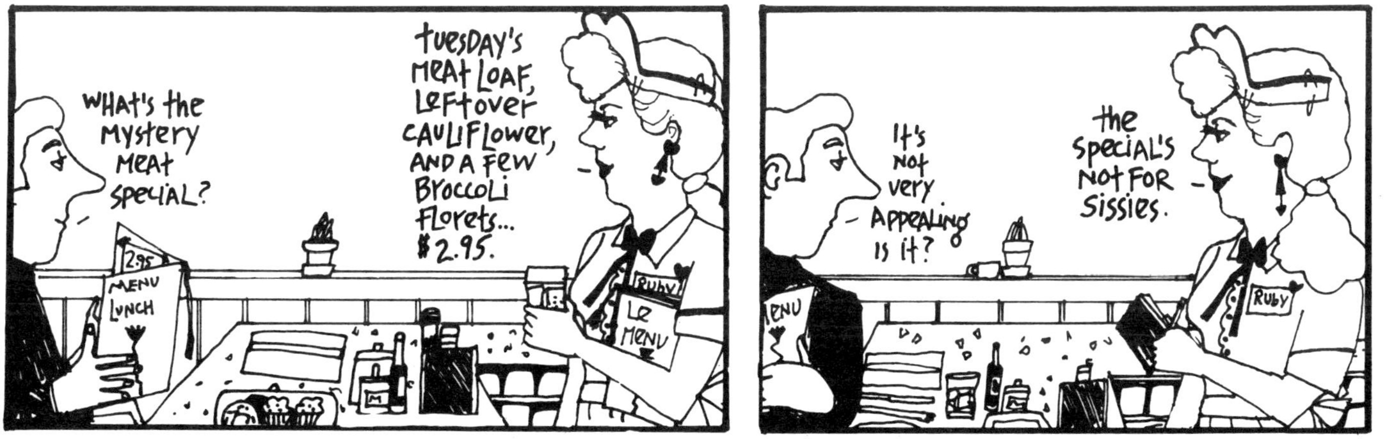
WHAT's the Mystery Meat Special?
tuesDAY's MeAt LoAF, Leftover CAULIFLower, AND A Few Broccoli Florets... $2.95.
2.95 MENU LUNCH
RUBY
LE MENU
It's not very Appealing is it?
the special's Not For Sissies.
Ruby

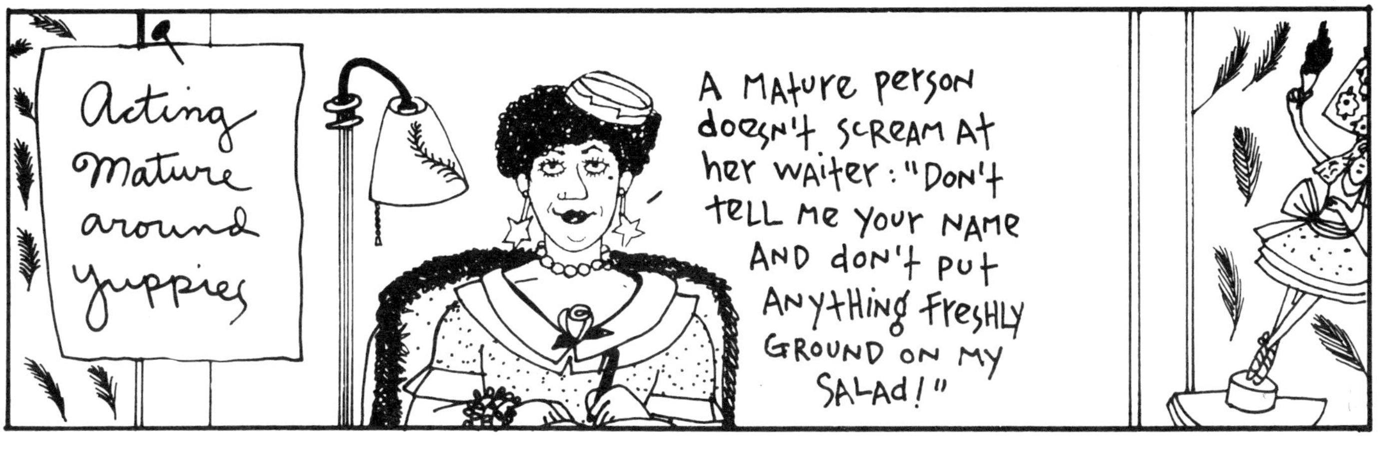
Acting Mature around Yuppies
A Mature person doesn't scream At her waiter: "Don't tell me your NAME AND don't put Anything Freshly GROUND ON MY SALAD!"

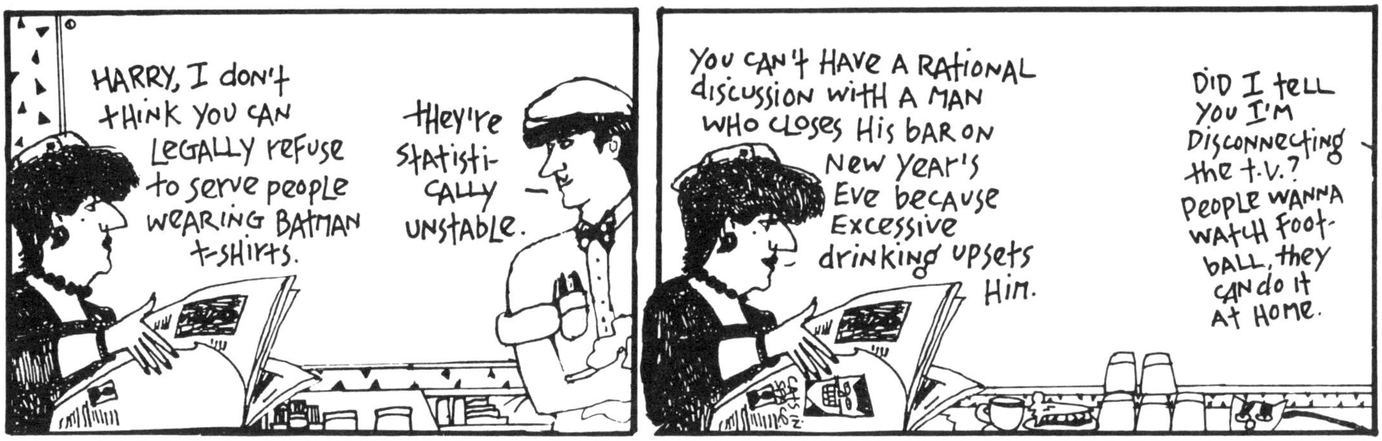
HARRY, I don't think you can legally refuse to serve people wearing BATMAN t-shirts.
They're statistically unstable.
You can't have a rational discussion with a man who closes his bar on New Year's Eve because excessive drinking upsets him.
Did I tell you I'm disconnecting the t.v.? People wanna watch football, they can do it at home.

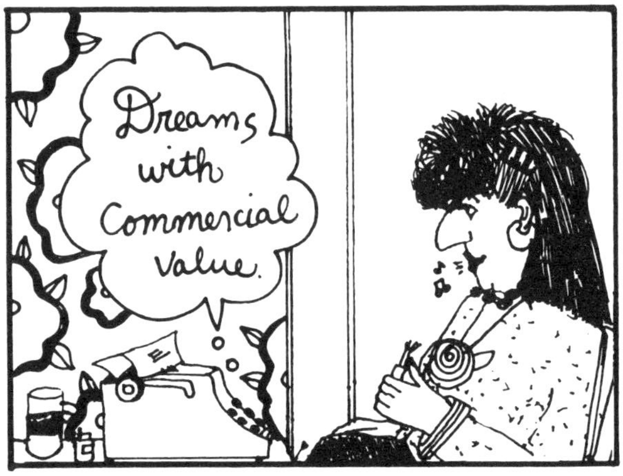
Dreams with Commercial Value.

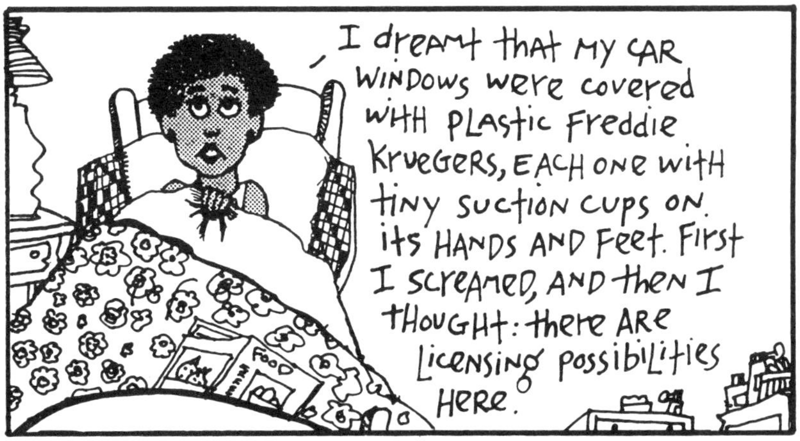
I dreamt that my car windows were covered with plastic Freddie Kruegers, each one with tiny suction cups on its hands and feet. First I screamed, and then I thought: there are licensing possibilities here.

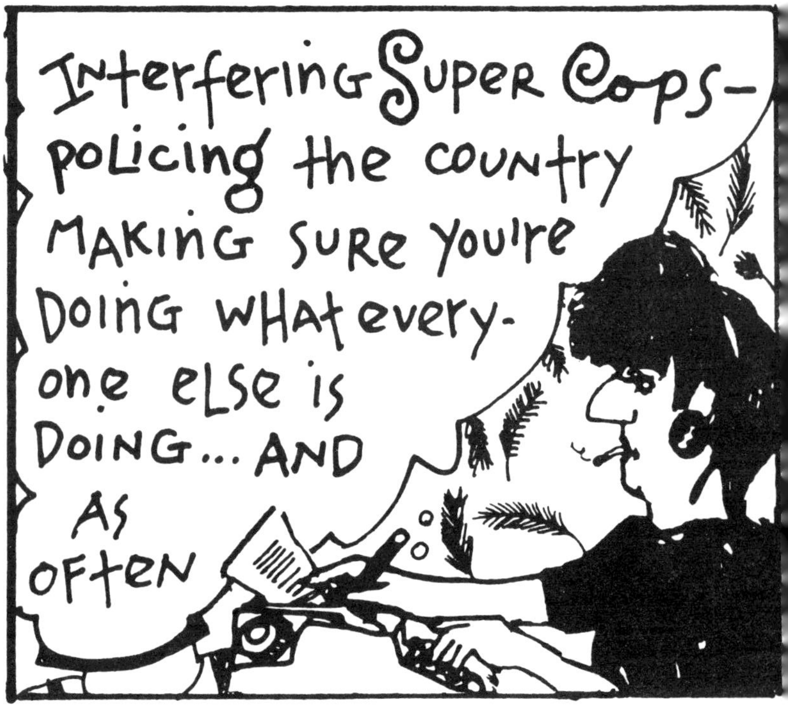
Interfering Super Cops— policing the country making sure you're doing what everyone else is doing... and as often

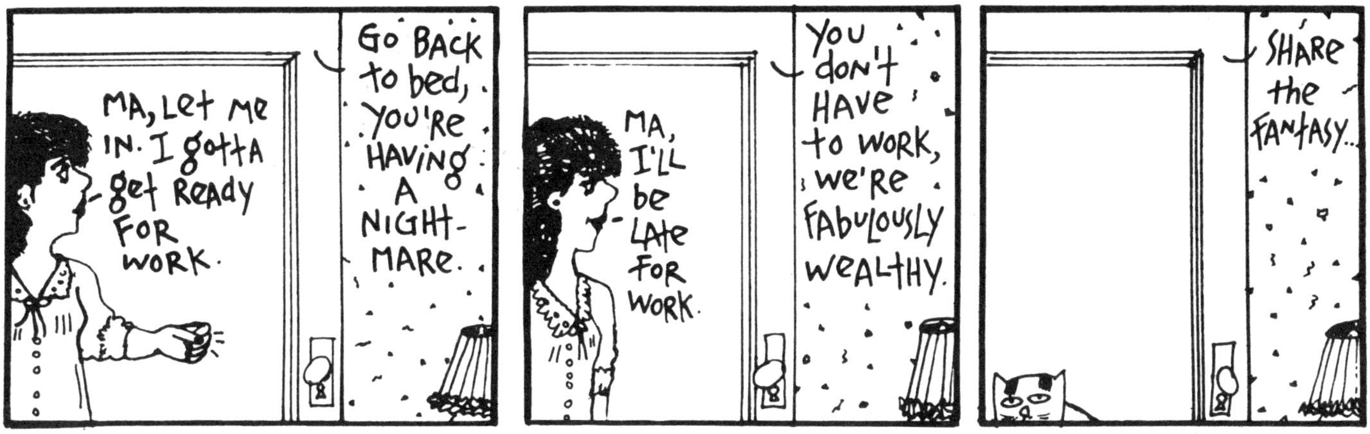
MA, LET ME IN. I gotta get Ready FOR WORK.
Go BACK to bed, YOU'RE HAVING A NIGHT-MARE.
MA, I'LL be LATE FOR WORK.
YOU don't HAVE to WORK, we're FABULOUSLY WEALTHY.
SHARE the FANTASY...

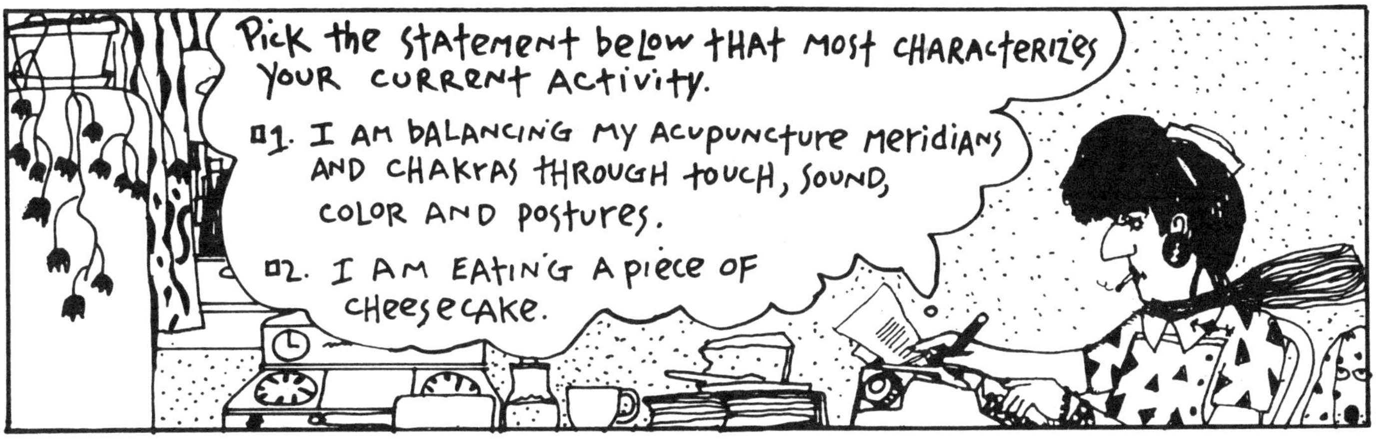
Pick the statement below that most characterizes your current activity.
1. I AM BALANCING MY ACUPUNCTURE MERIDIANS AND CHAKRAS THROUGH TOUCH, SOUND, COLOR AND POSTURES.
2. I AM EATING A piece OF CHEESECAKE.

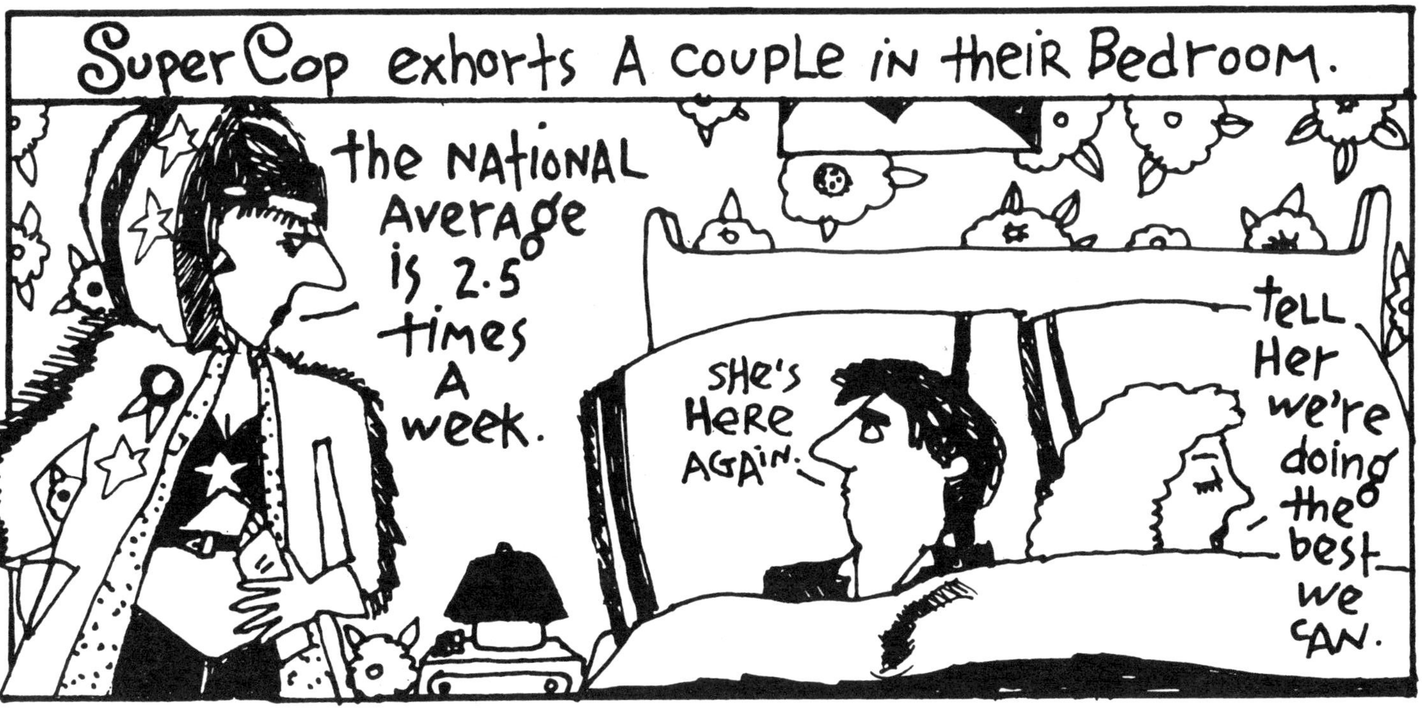
SuperCop exhorts A couple in their Bedroom.
the NATIONAL Average is 2.5 times A week.
SHE'S HERE AGAIN.
tell Her we're doing the best we CAN.

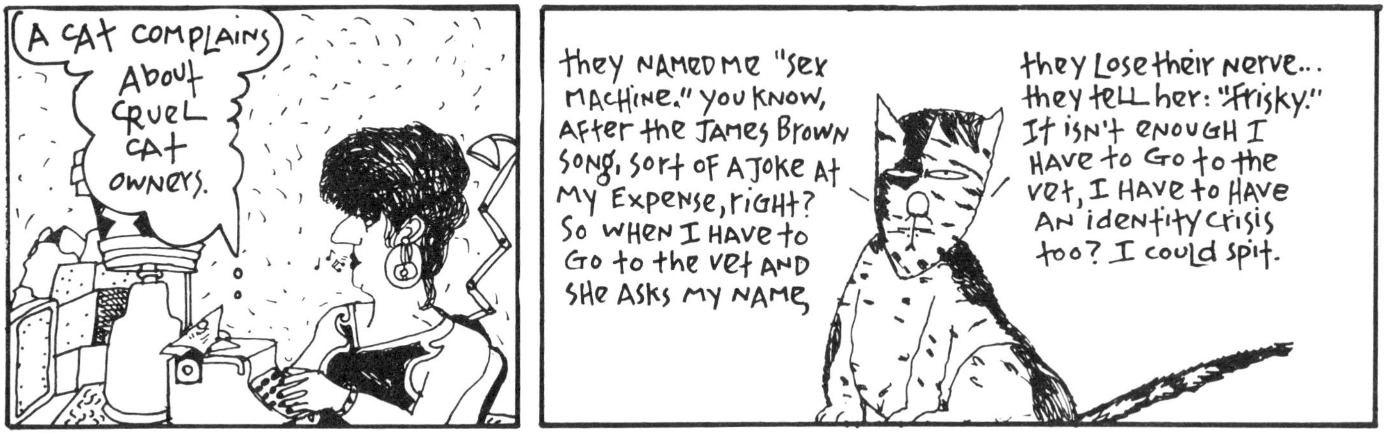
A CAT COMPLAINS About CRUEL CAT OWNERS.
they NAMED ME "sex MACHINE." you KNOW, After the James Brown song, sort of A joke At MY Expense, right? So WHEN I HAVE to Go to the vet AND SHE ASKS MY NAME,
they Lose their Nerve... they tell her: "Frisky." It isn't ENOUGH I HAVE to Go to the vet, I HAVE to HAVE AN identity crisis too? I could spit.

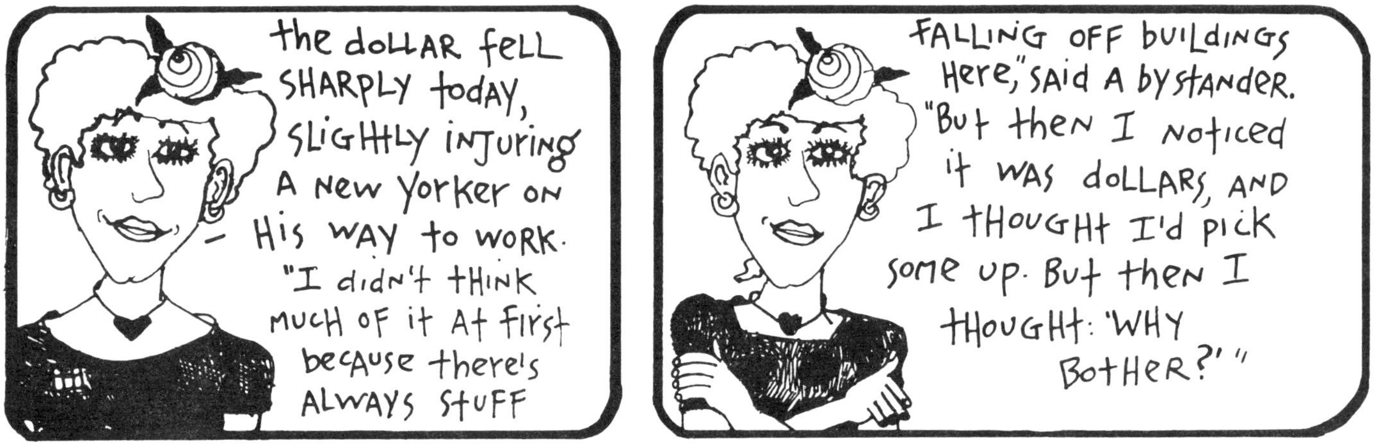
the dollar fell SHARPLY today, SLIGHTLY INJURING A New Yorker ON HIS WAY to WORK. "I didn't THINK MUCH OF it At first because there's ALWAYS STUFF
FALLING OFF buildings Here," SAID A bystander. "But then I Noticed it WAS dollars, AND I THOUGHT I'd pick some up. But then I THOUGHT: 'WHY Bother?'"

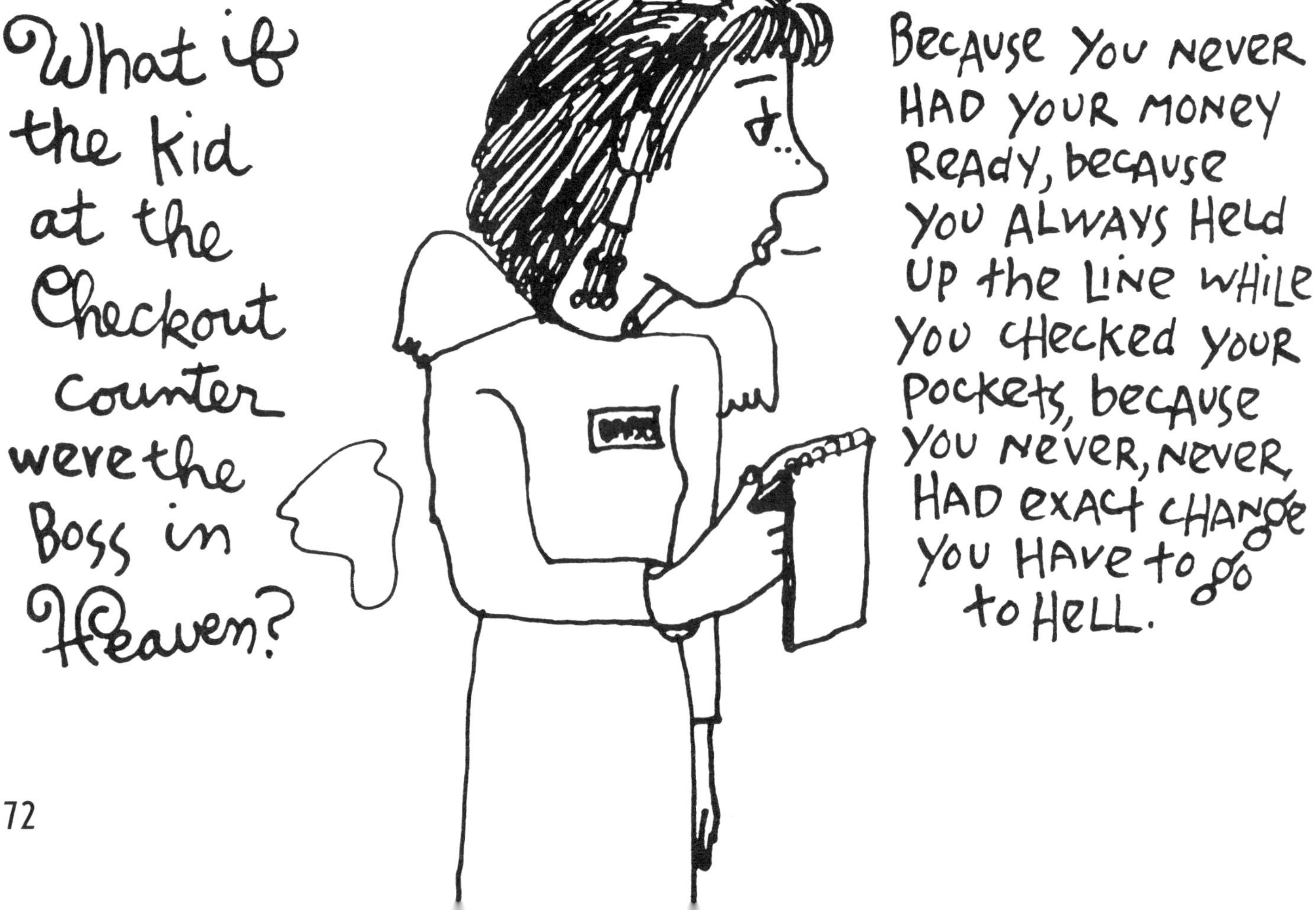
What if the kid at the Checkout counter were the Boss in Heaven?
Because You never HAD your MONEY Ready, because You ALWAYS Held UP the Line WHILE You checked your Pockets, because You Never, never, HAD exact change You HAVe to go to Hell.

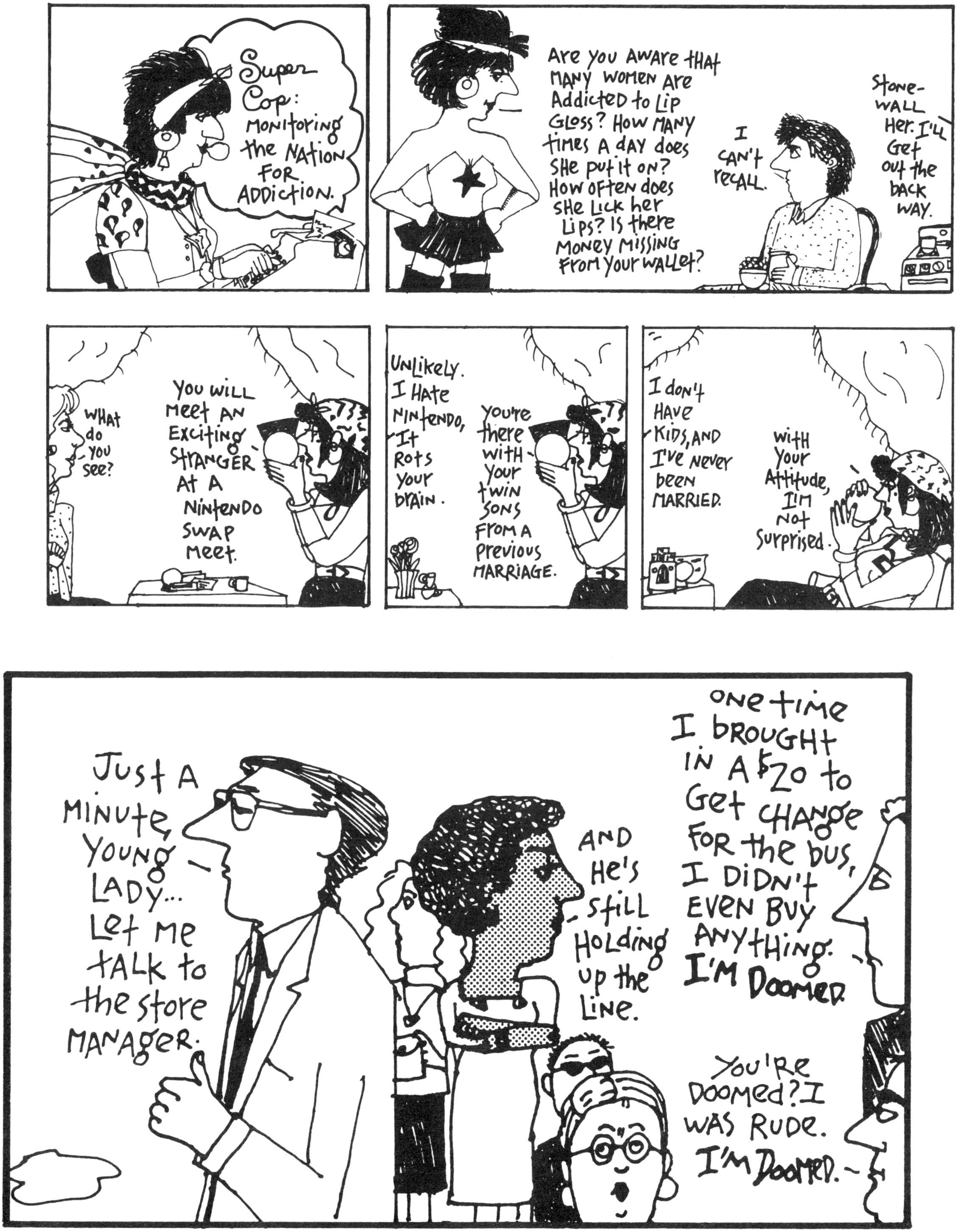

Super Cop: Monitoring the Nation for Addiction.
Are you aware that many women are addicted to lip gloss? How many times a day does she put it on? How often does she lick her lips? Is there money missing from your wallet?
I can't recall.
Stonewall her. I'll get out the back way.
What do you see?
You will meet an exciting stranger at a Nintendo swap meet.
Unlikely. I hate Nintendo. It rots your brain.
You're there with your twin sons from a previous marriage.
I don't have kids, and I've never been married.
With your attitude, I'm not surprised.
Just a minute, young lady... Let me talk to the store manager.
And he's still holding up the line.
One time I brought in a $20 to get change for the bus, I didn't even buy anything. I'M DOOMED.
You're doomed? I was rude. I'M DOOMED.

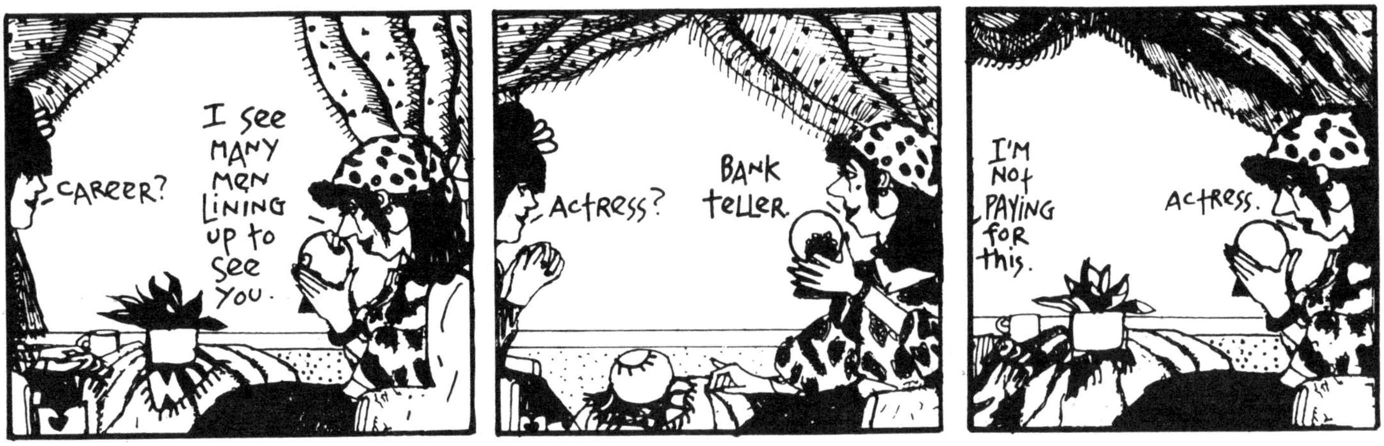
CAREER?
I see MANY MEN LINING up to see you.
Actress?
BANK teller.
I'M Not PAYING for this.
Actress.

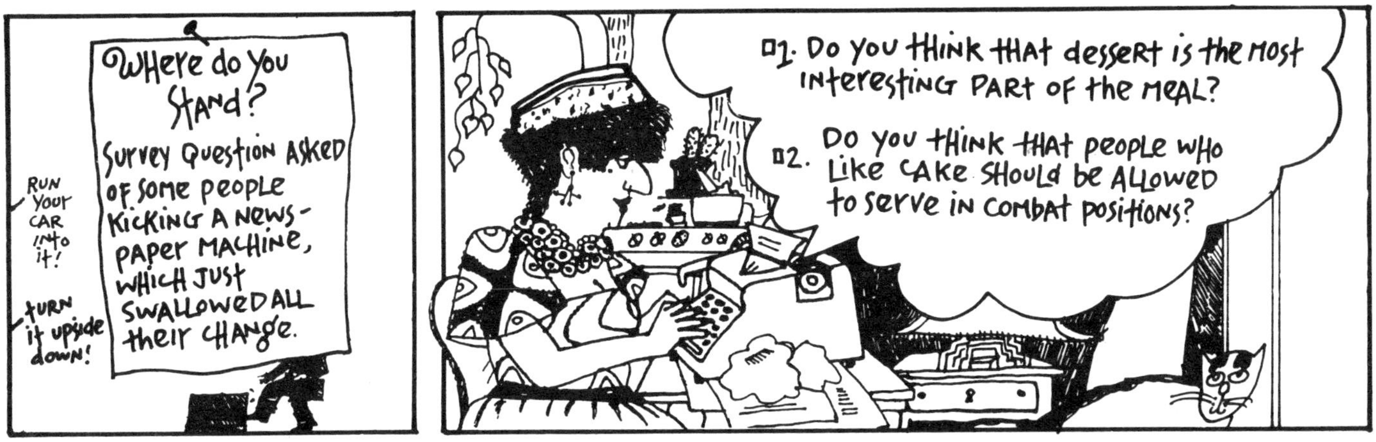
Where do you Stand?
Survey Question Asked of some people Kicking a news-paper machine, which just swallowed all their change.
RUN your CAR into it!
turn it upside down!
□1. Do you think that dessert is the most interesting part of the meal?
□2. Do you think that people who like cake should be allowed to serve in combat positions?

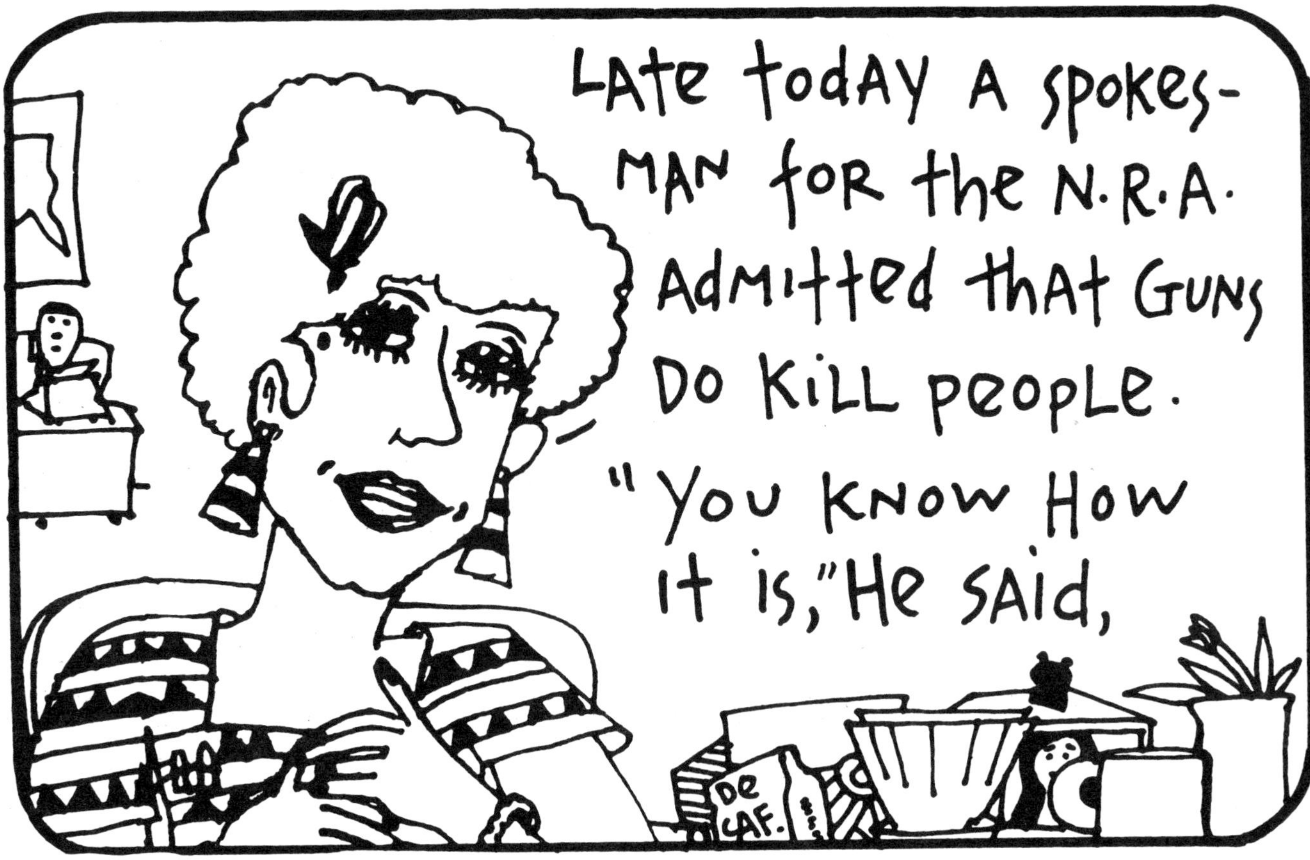
LATE today A spokes-MAN for the N.R.A. Admitted that GUNS DO KILL people. "You KNOW HOW it is," He said,
De CAF.

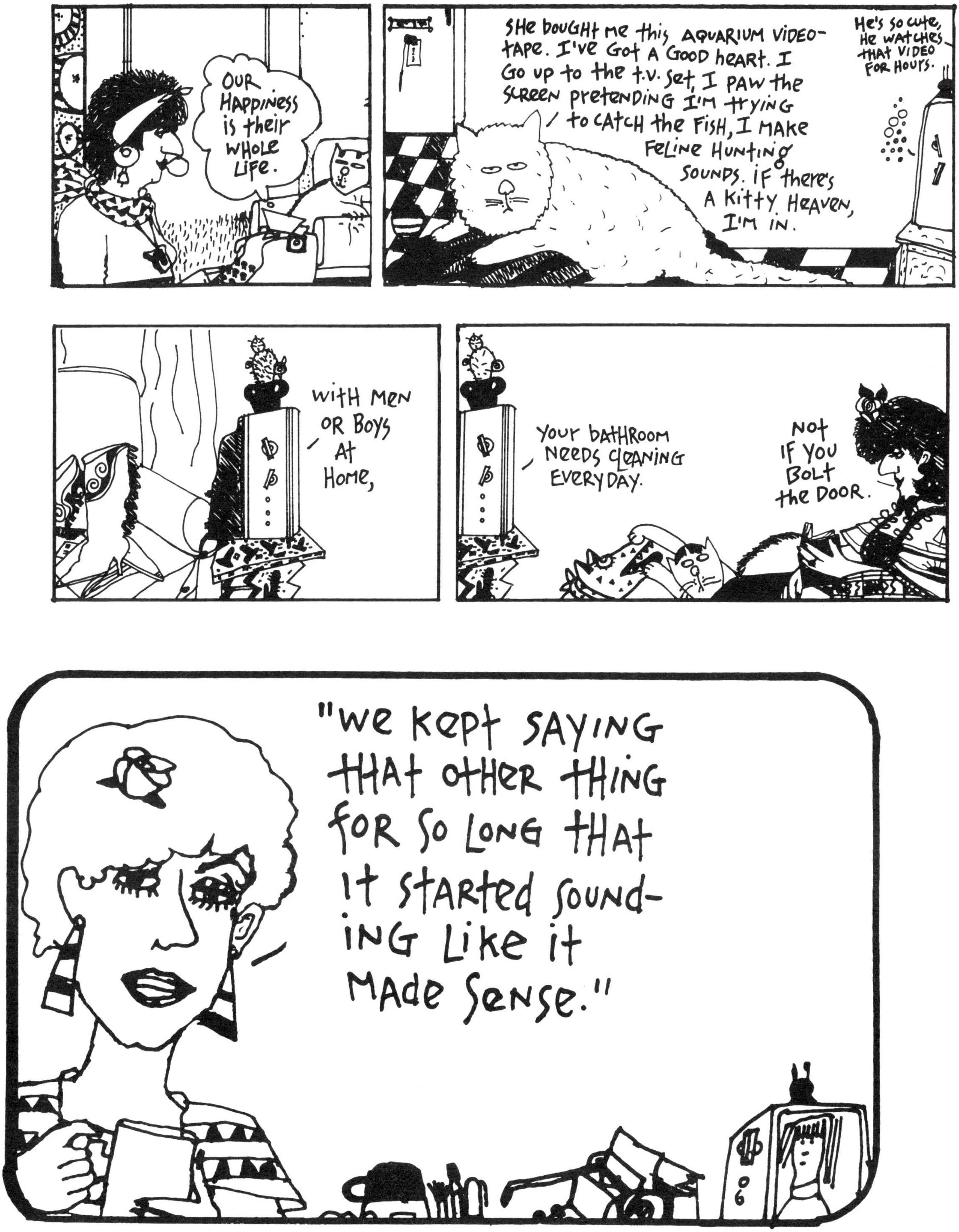
OUR HAPPINESS is their WHOLE Life.
SHe bouGHt me this AQUARIUM VIDEO-tape. I've Got A GOOD heart. I Go up to the t.v. set, I PAW the SCREEN pretenDING I'M trying to CATCH the FISH, I MAKE Feline Hunting sounDS. IF there's A Kitty HEAVEN, I'M IN.
He's so cute, He watches that video for Hours.
with Men or Boys At Home,
Your bathroom Needs cleaning everyday.
Not If you Bolt the Door.
"we kept saying that other thing for so long that it started sounding like it made sense."

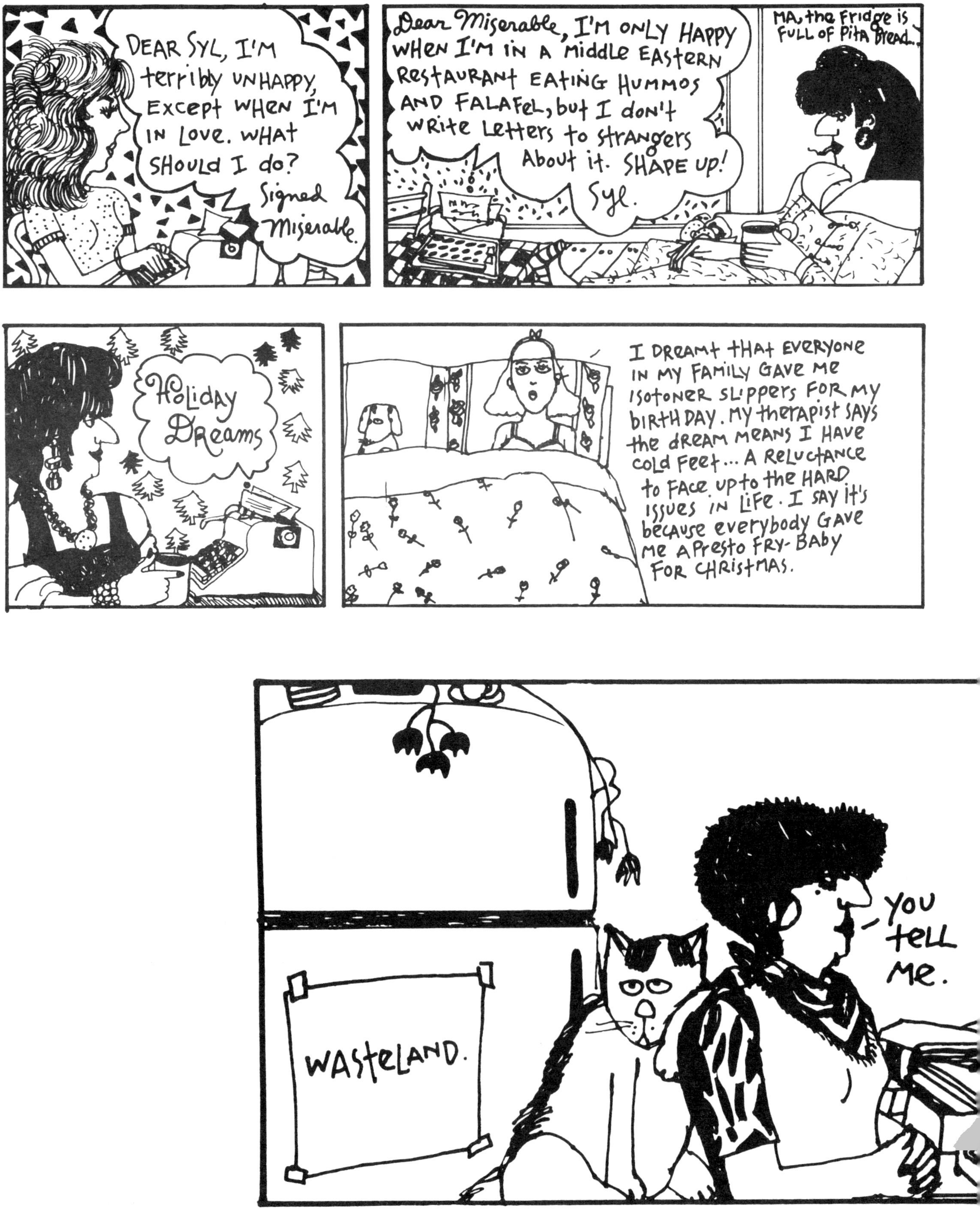
DEAR SYL, I'M terribly UNHAPPY, EXCEPT WHEN I'M IN LOVE. WHAT SHOULD I do? Signed Miserable.
Dear Miserable, I'M ONLY HAPPY WHEN I'M IN A MIDDLE EASTERN RESTAURANT EATING HUMMOS AND FALAFEL, but I don't write Letters to strangers About it. SHAPE UP! Syl.
MA, the Fridge is FULL OF Pita Bread...
Holiday Dreams
I DREAMT THAT EVERYONE IN MY FAMILY GAVE ME ISOTONER SLIPPERS FOR MY BIRTHDAY. MY THERAPIST SAYS THE DREAM MEANS I HAVE COLD FEET... A RELUCTANCE TO FACE UP TO THE HARD ISSUES IN LIFE. I SAY IT'S BECAUSE EVERYBODY GAVE ME A PRESTO FRY-BABY FOR CHRISTMAS.
WASTELAND.
YOU TELL ME.

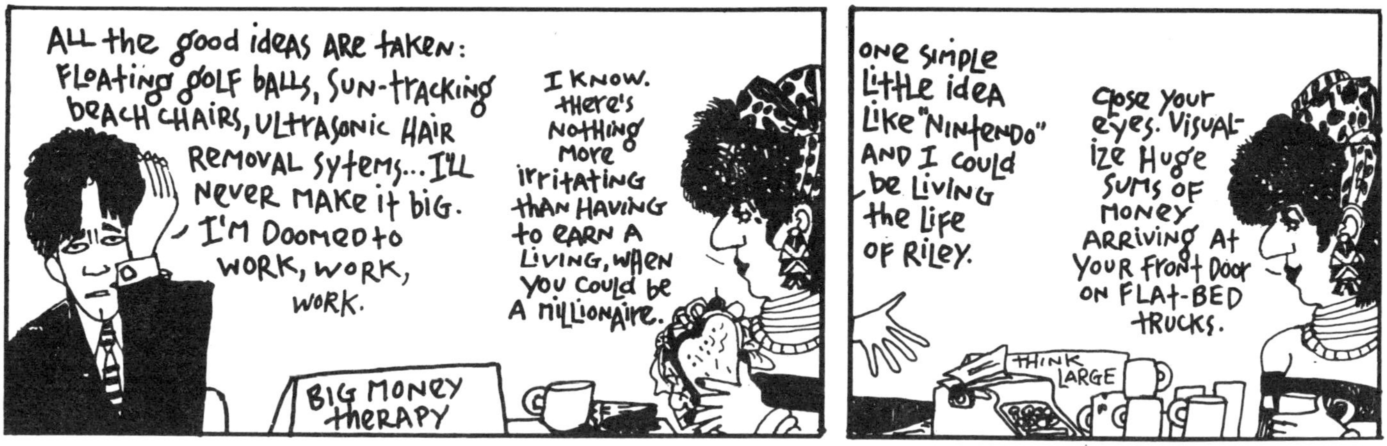
All the good ideas are taken: Floating golf balls, sun-tracking beach chairs, ultrasonic hair removal sytems... I'll never make it big. I'm doomed to work, work, work.
I know. There's nothing more irritating than having to earn a living, when you could be a millionaire.
BIG MONEY THERAPY
One simple little idea like "Nintendo" and I could be living the life of Riley.
Close your eyes. Visualize huge sums of money arriving at your front door on flat-bed trucks.
THINK LARGE

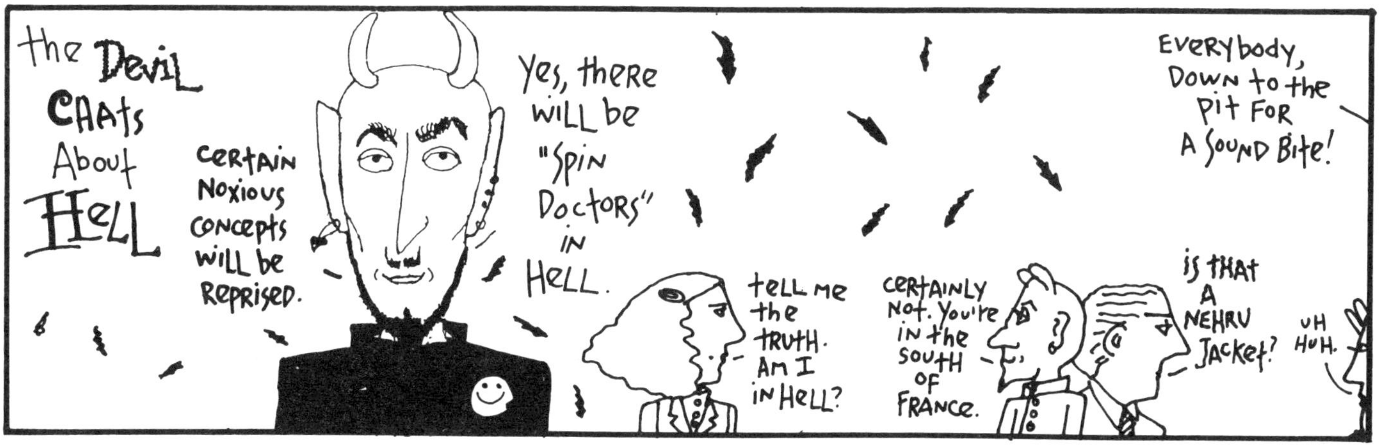
The Devil Chats About Hell
Certain noxious concepts will be reprised.
Yes, there will be "Spin Doctors" in Hell.
Everybody, down to the pit for a sound bite!
Tell me the truth. Am I in Hell?
Certainly not. You're in the South of France.
Is that a Nehru jacket?
Uh huh.

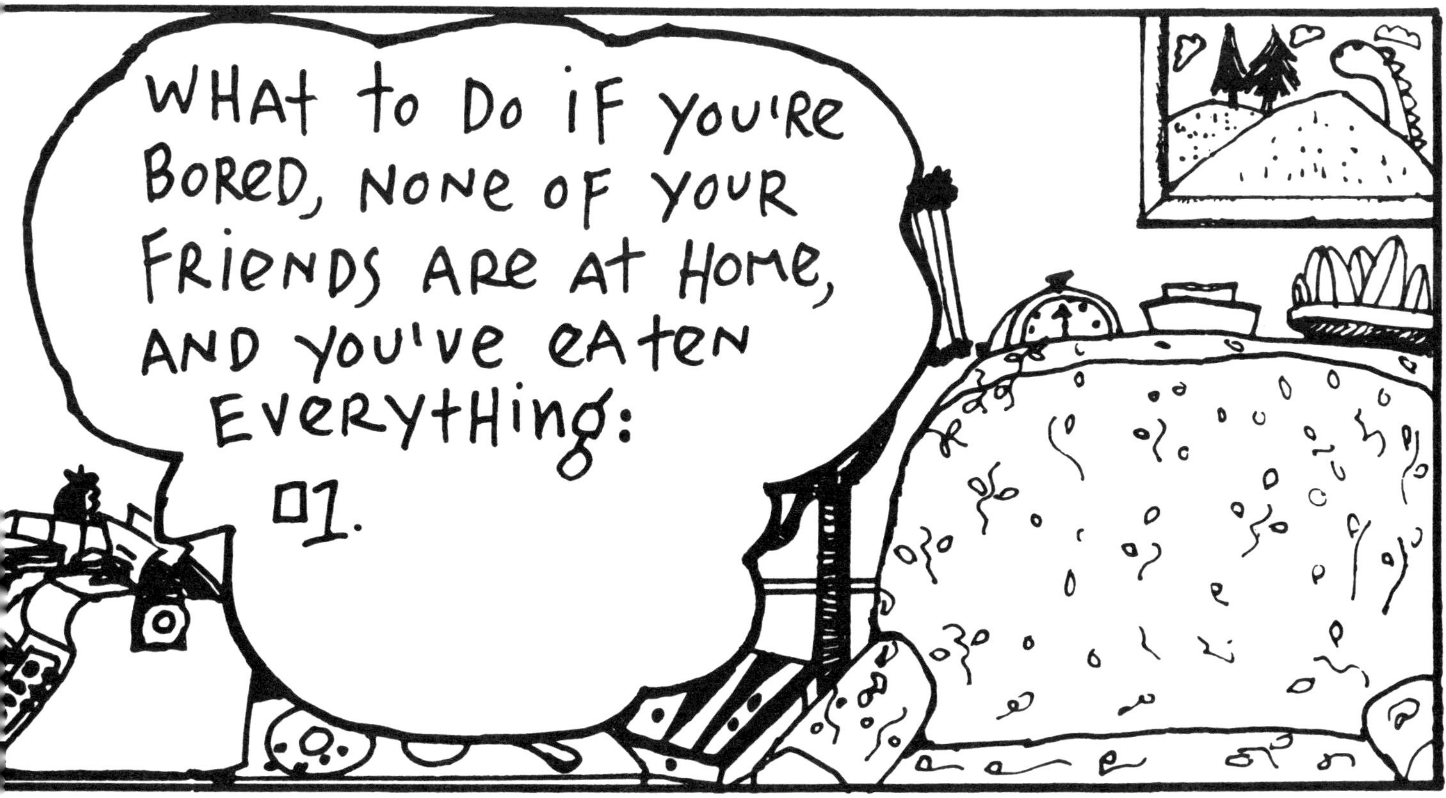
What to do if you're bored, none of your friends are at home, and you've eaten everything:
01.

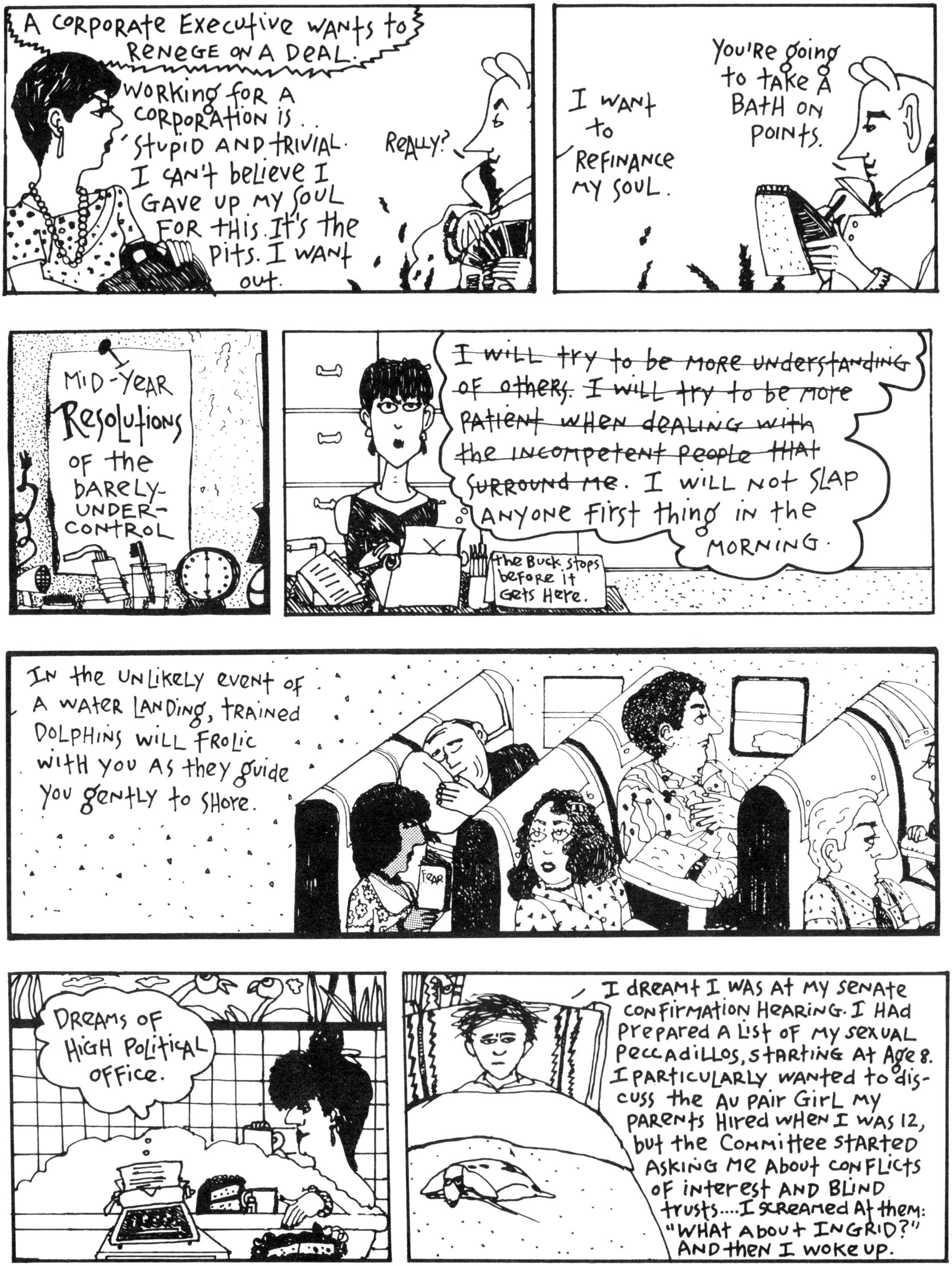
A CORPORATE EXECUTIVE WANTS TO RENEGE ON A DEAL.
WORKING FOR A CORPORATION IS STUPID AND TRIVIAL. I CAN'T BELIEVE I GAVE UP MY SOUL FOR THIS. IT'S THE PITS. I WANT OUT.
REALLY?
I WANT TO REFINANCE MY SOUL.
YOU'RE GOING TO TAKE A BATH ON POINTS.
MID-YEAR RESOLUTIONS OF THE BARELY-UNDER-CONTROL
~~I WILL TRY TO BE MORE UNDERSTANDING OF OTHERS. I WILL TRY TO BE MORE PATIENT WHEN DEALING WITH THE INCOMPETENT PEOPLE THAT SURROUND ME~~. I WILL NOT SLAP ANYONE FIRST THING IN THE MORNING.
THE BUCK STOPS BEFORE IT GETS HERE.
IN THE UNLIKELY EVENT OF A WATER LANDING, TRAINED DOLPHINS WILL FROLIC WITH YOU AS THEY GUIDE YOU GENTLY TO SHORE.
FEAR
DREAMS OF HIGH POLITICAL OFFICE.
I DREAMT I WAS AT MY SENATE CONFIRMATION HEARING. I HAD PREPARED A LIST OF MY SEXUAL PECCADILLOS, STARTING AT AGE 8. I PARTICULARLY WANTED TO DISCUSS THE AU PAIR GIRL MY PARENTS HIRED WHEN I WAS 12, BUT THE COMMITTEE STARTED ASKING ME ABOUT CONFLICTS OF INTEREST AND BLIND TRUSTS.... I SCREAMED AT THEM: "WHAT ABOUT INGRID?" AND THEN I WOKE UP.

YUPPIE BAITING

Yuppies in Hell
I'd like to leave the world in an upscale way. What kinda end you got me down for?
Natural causes, while watching wrestling on t.v., eating a Butter-Finger bar, wearing raggedy boxer shorts.
Yuck! I'd sell my soul for a more stylish end.
You're on! You've just been dancing the night away in some After-Hours club that very few people ever get admitted to, and you're driving home in your Volvo, watching a wrestling tape on your hand-held VCR, when you reach for a Butter-Finger bar and go over a cliff.

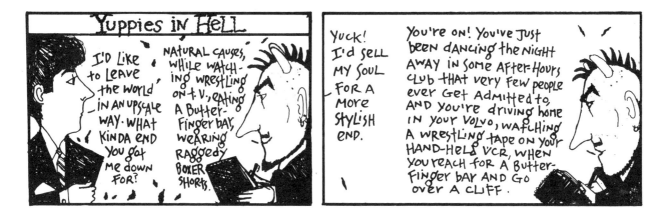

In the last scene of the movie *Internal Affairs,* Andy Garcia responds to Richard Gere's taunt, "You yuppie," by filling him full of lead. I've never heard anyone acknowledge being a yuppie, but I've never heard a violent response to the accusation either. I live in a yuppie neighborhood...good restaurants, many places to buy frocks. There are some advantages to living near those boring twits.

Harry, cats have replaced dogs as the nation's number one pet.
No. 1
No!
Yes, because of yuppies...
Woof woof bye bye
Cramped
Cat demands own room.
A yuppie shouldn't be allowed to own a pet...
You don't have to rush home from work to walk a cat.
Let 'em put stuffed animals on their beds.

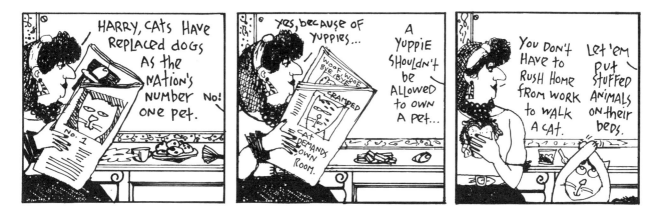

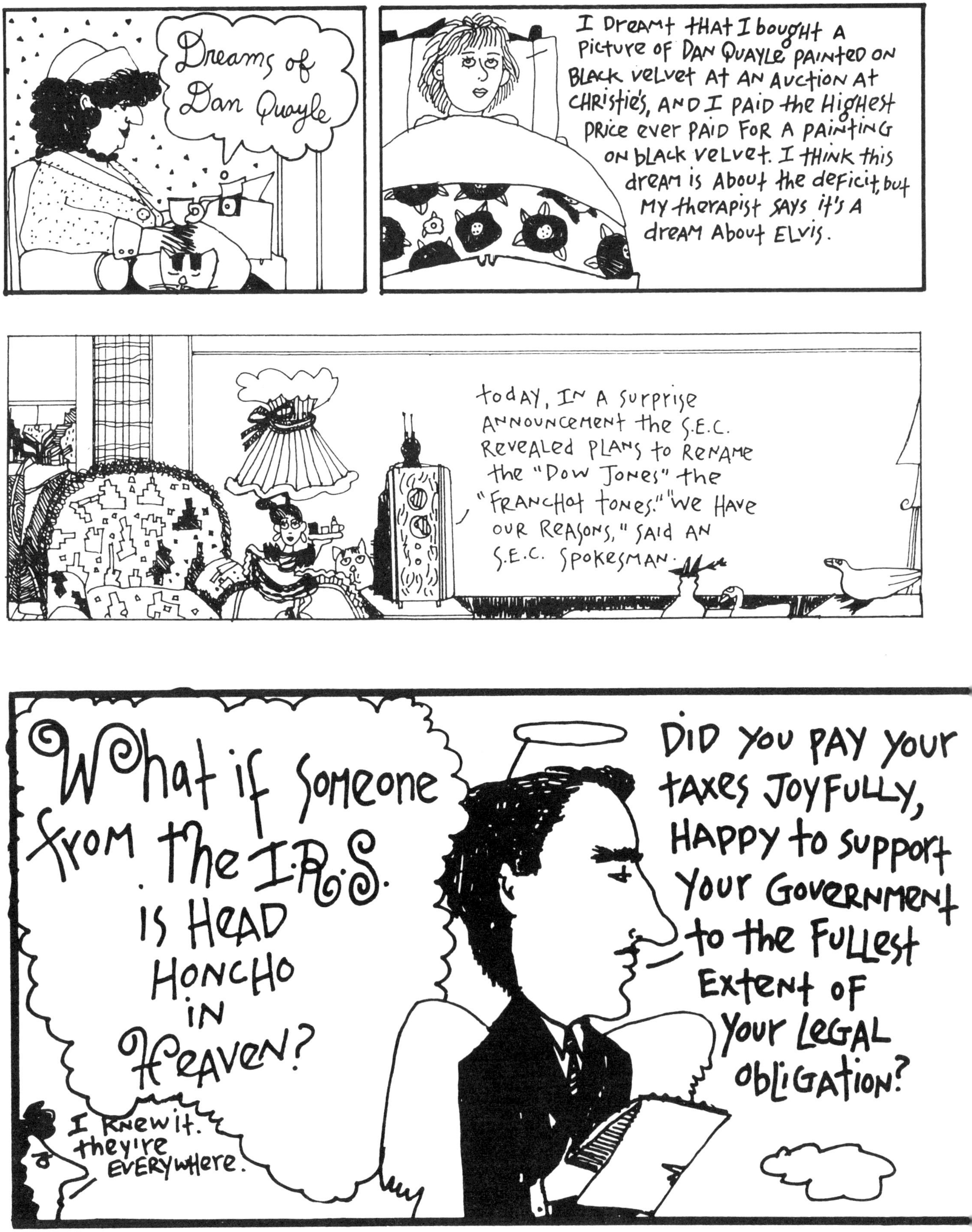

Dreams of Dan Quayle
I Dreamt that I bought a picture of Dan Quayle painted on black velvet at an auction at Christie's, and I paid the highest price ever paid for a painting on black velvet. I think this dream is about the deficit, but my therapist says it's a dream about Elvis.
today, in a surprise announcement the S.E.C. revealed plans to rename the "Dow Jones" the "Franchot tones." "We have our reasons," said an S.E.C. spokesman.
What if someone from the I.R.S. is head honcho in heaven?
Did you pay your taxes joyfully, happy to support your government to the fullest extent of your legal obligation?
I knew it. they're everywhere.

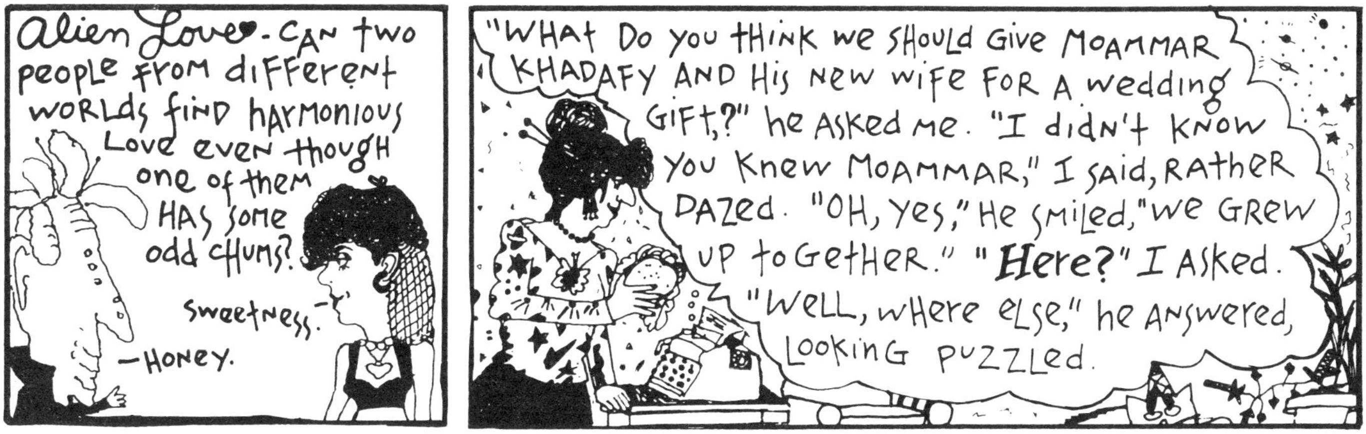
Alien Love - CAN two people from different worlds find harmonious Love even though one of them HAS some odd cHums?
Sweetness.
-Honey.
"WHAT Do you tHINK we sHOULd Give MOAMMAR KHADAFY AND His new wife FOR A wedding GIFT?" he Asked me. "I didn't know you Knew MOAMMAR," I said, RATHER DAZed. "OH, yes," He smiled, "we GREW up toGether." "Here?" I Asked. "WELL, where else," he answered, Looking puzzled.

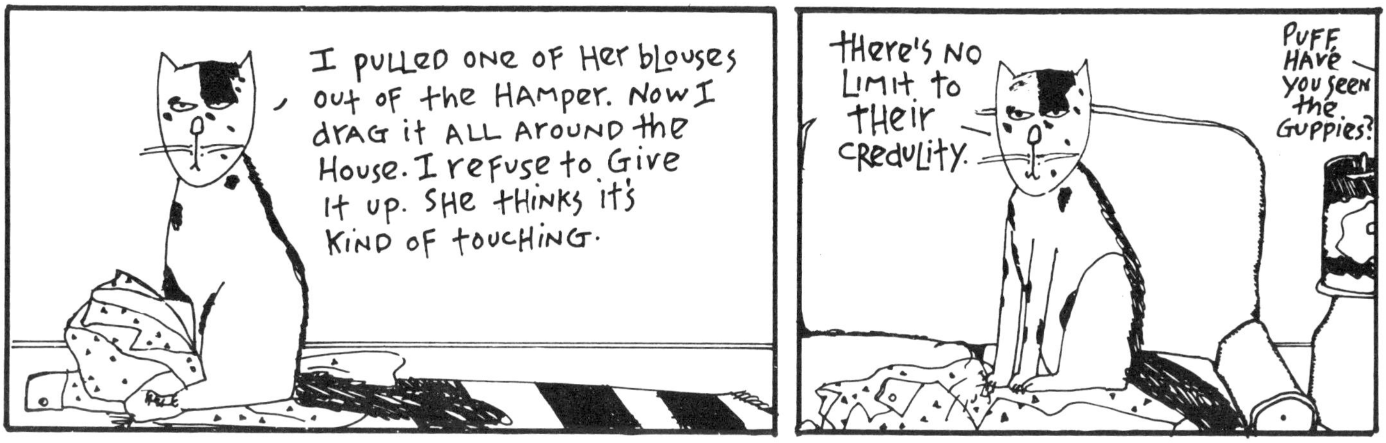
I pulled one of Her blouses out of the HAMPER. Now I drag it ALL AROUND the House. I refuse to Give it up. SHE tHINKS it's KIND OF touchING.
tHere's NO Limit to their credulity.
PUFF HAVE you seen the Guppies?

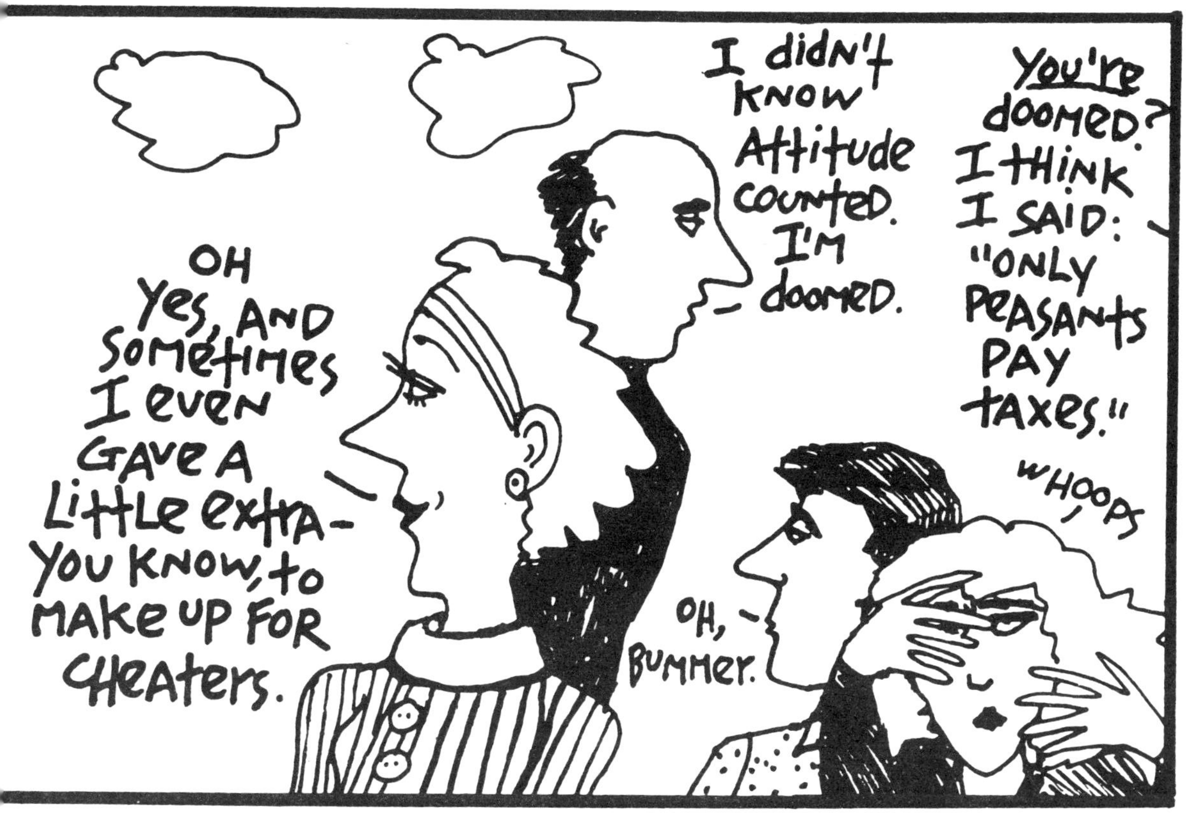
I didn't know Attitude counted. I'M doomed.
You're doomed? I THINK I SAID: "ONLY PEASANTS PAY taxes."
OH yes, AND sometimes I even GAVE A Little extra - you KNOW, to MAKE UP FOR cHeaters.
WHOOPS
OH, - Bummer.

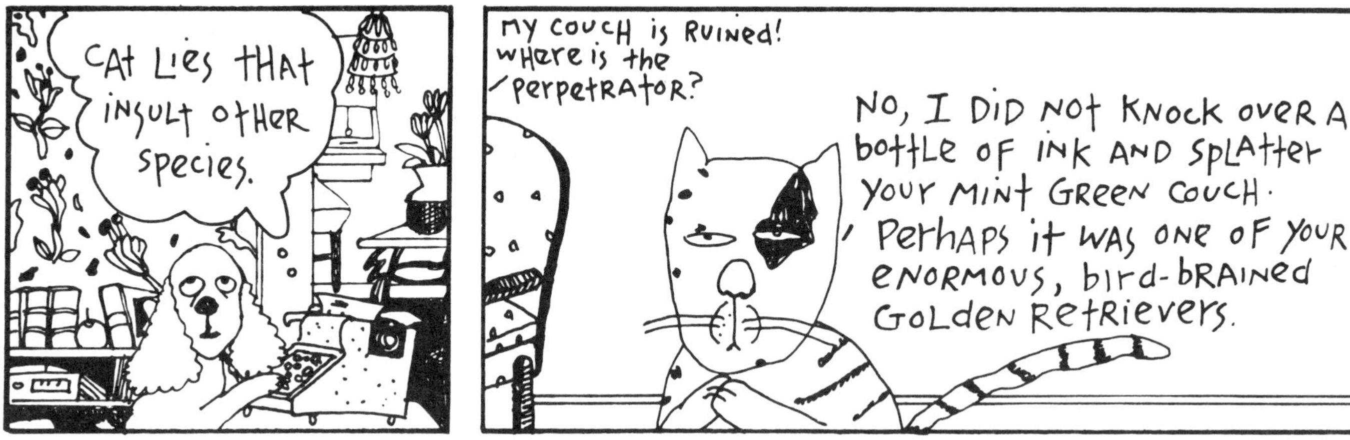
CAt Lies tHAt insuLt otHer species.
My couch is Ruined! where is the perpetrator?
No, I DID Not Knock over A bottle of ink AND spLatter your Mint Green couch. Perhaps it was one of your enormous, bird-brained Golden Retrievers.

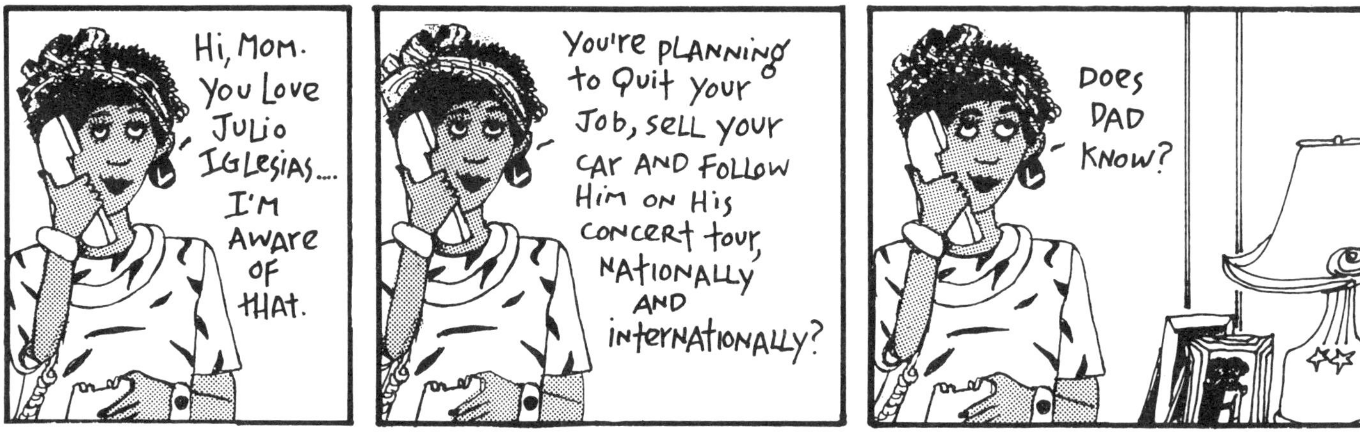
Hi, Mom. You Love Julio Iglesias.... I'M Aware of tHAt.
You're pLanning to Quit your Job, sell your car AND FoLLow Him on His concert tour, NATIONALLY AND internationally?
Does DAD Know?

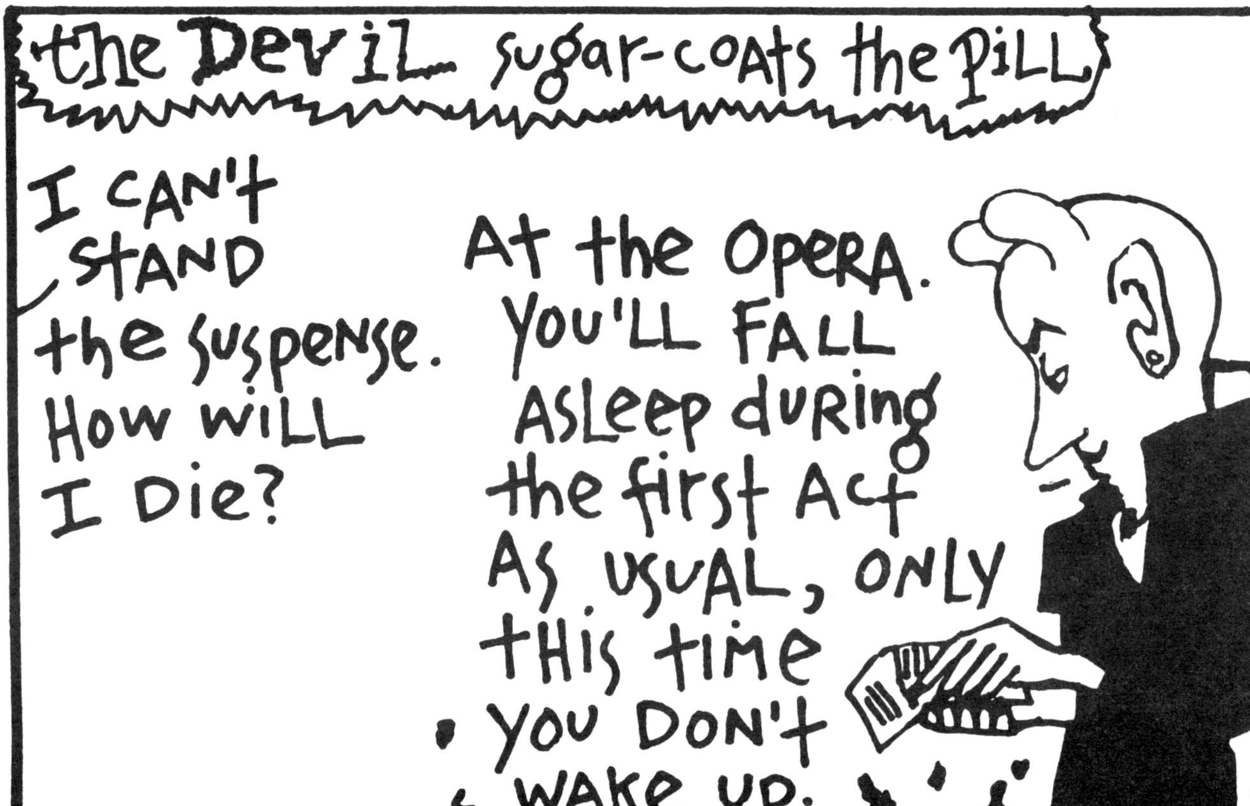
the Devil sugar-coats the PiLL
I CAN'T StAND the suspense. How wiLL I Die?
At the OPERA. You'LL FALL AsLeep during the first Act As usuAL, ONLY tHis time you DON'T WAKe up.

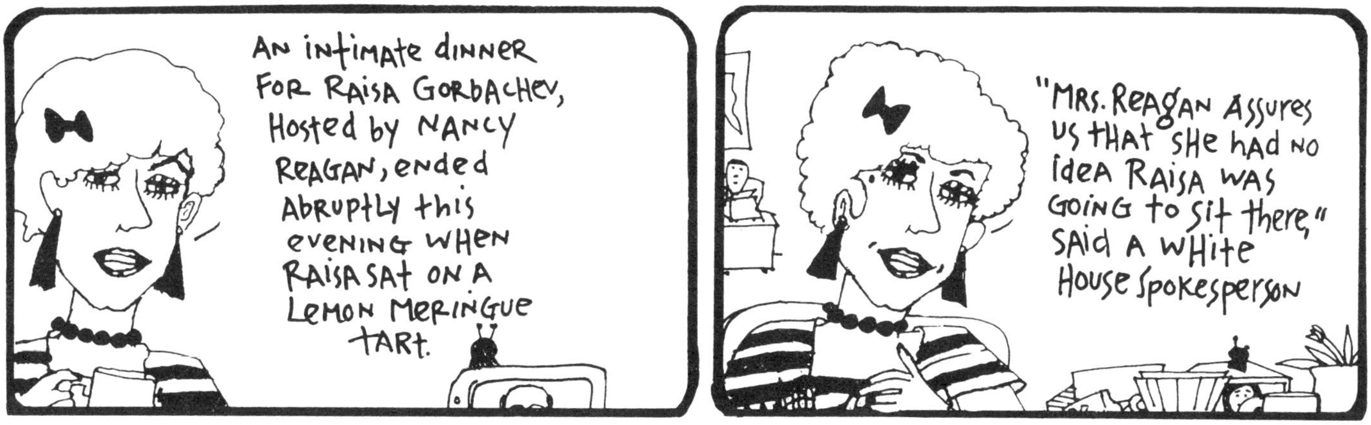
AN intimate dinner FOR RAISA GORBACHEV, Hosted by NANCY REAGAN, ended ABRUPTLY this evening WHEN RAISA SAT ON A LEMON MERINGUE TART.
"MRS. REAGAN ASSURES US THAT SHE had NO idea RAISA WAS GOING to Sit there," SAId A WHITE HOUSE Spokesperson

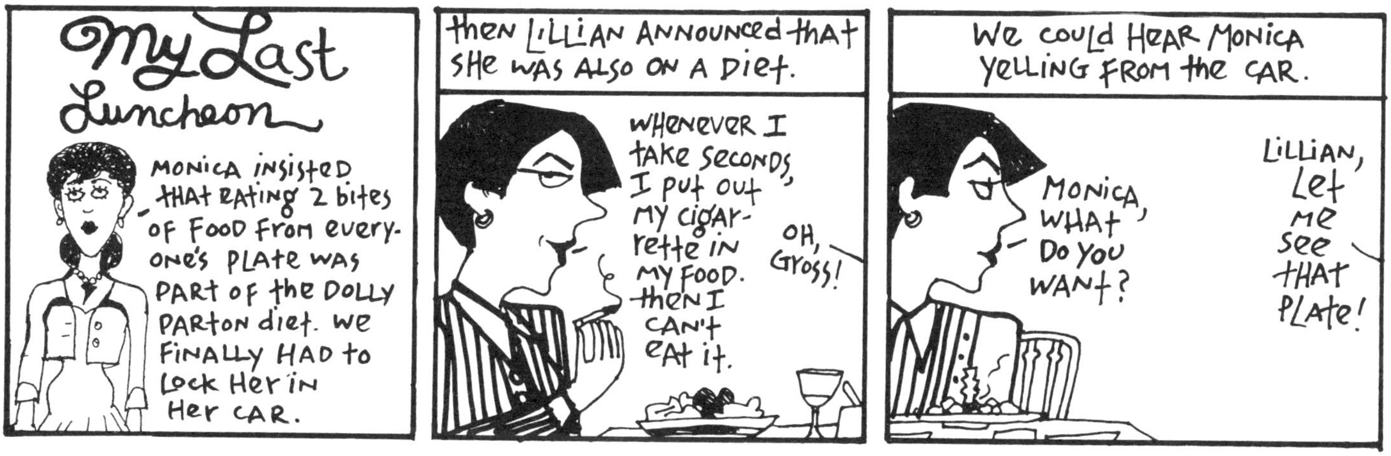
My Last Luncheon
MONICA insisted that eating 2 bites of Food From everyone's PLATE WAS PART OF the DOLLY PARTON diet. WE FINALLY HAD to Lock Her in Her CAR.
then LILLIAN ANNOUNCED that SHE WAS ALSO ON A Diet.
WHENEVER I take SECONDS, I put out MY cigarette in MY FOOD. then I CAN'T eat it.
OH, GROSS!
We could HEAR MONICA YELLING FROM the CAR.
MONICA, WHAT DO YOU WANT?
LILLIAN, Let me see THAT PLATE!

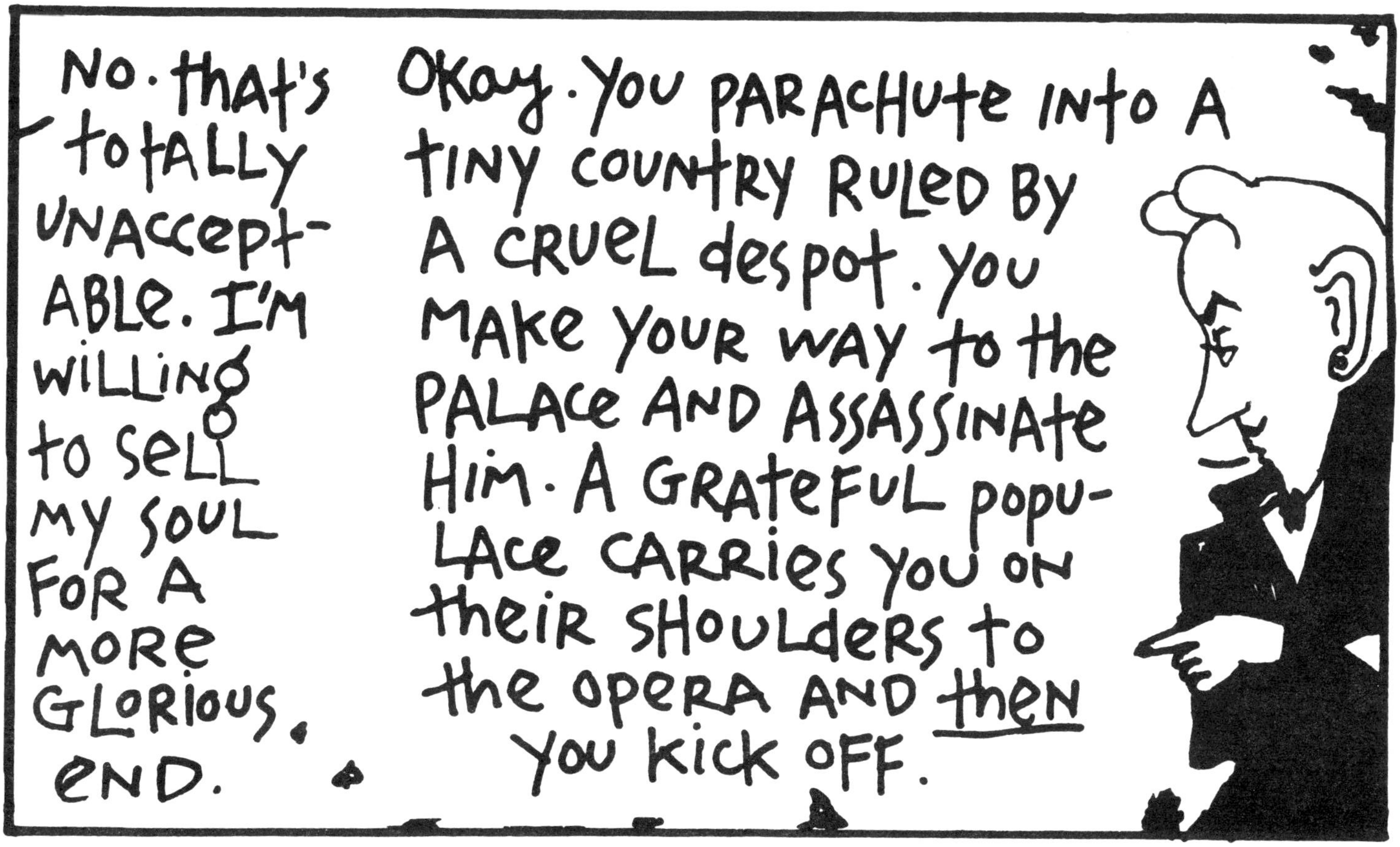
No. that's totally UNACCEPTABLE. I'M WILLING to SELL MY SOUL FOR A MORE GLORIOUS END.
Okay. You PARACHUTE INTO A TINY COUNTRY RULED BY A CRUEL despot. you MAKE YOUR WAY to the PALACE AND ASSASSINATE HIM. A GRATEFUL populace CARRIES YOU ON their SHOULDERS to the opera AND then you KICK OFF.

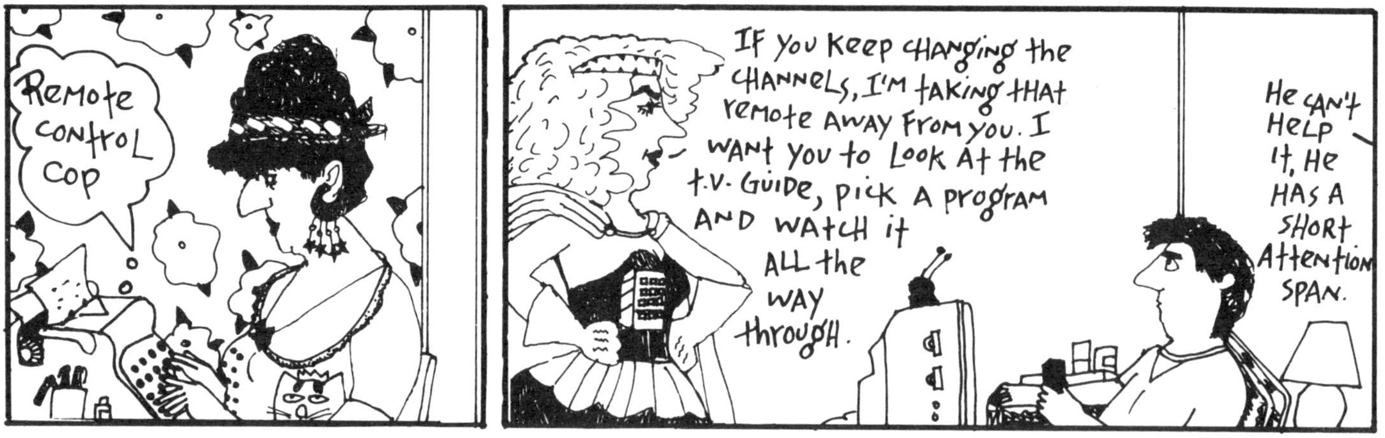
Remote control cop
If you keep changing the channels, I'm taking that remote away from you. I want you to look at the t.v. Guide, pick a program and watch it all the way through.
He can't help it, he has a short attention span.

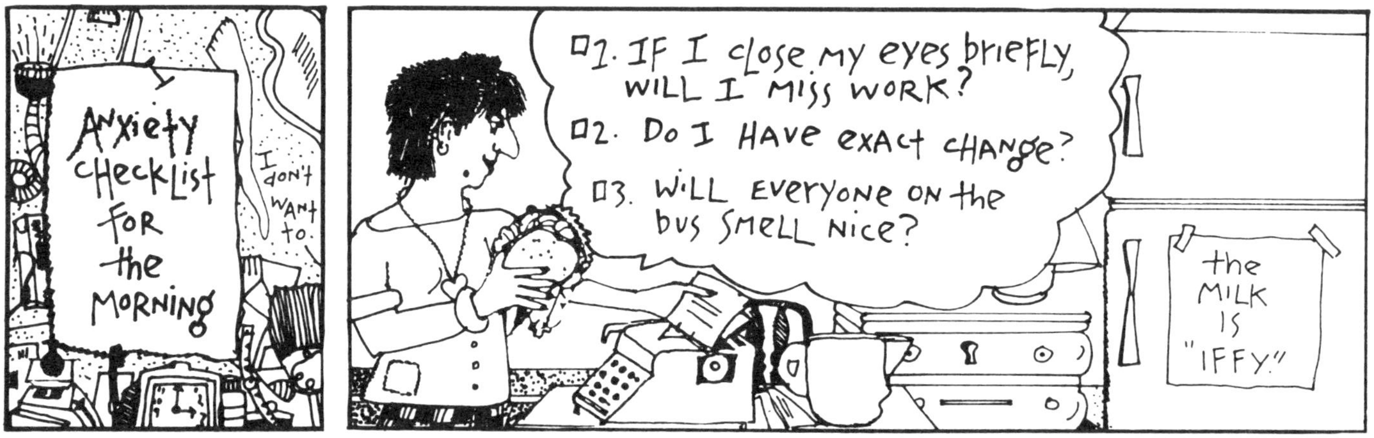
Anxiety checklist for the morning
I don't want to.
□1. If I close my eyes briefly, will I miss work?
□2. Do I have exact change?
□3. Will everyone on the bus smell nice?
the milk is "iffy."

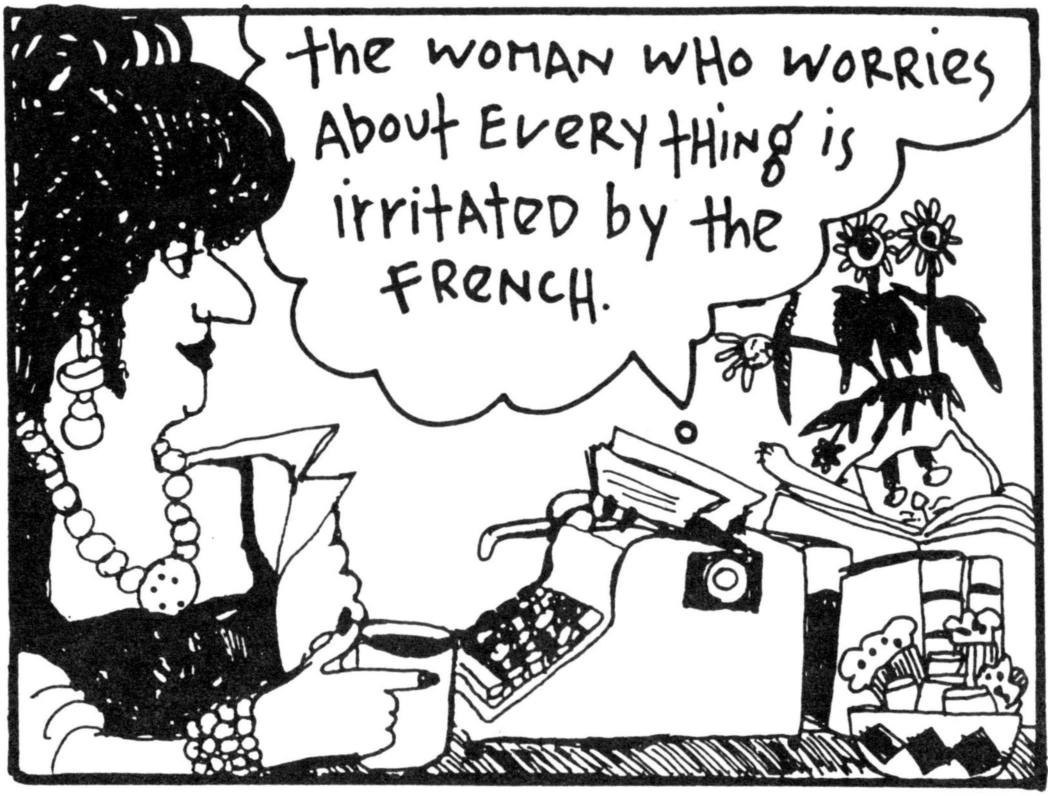
the woman who worries about everything is irritated by the French.

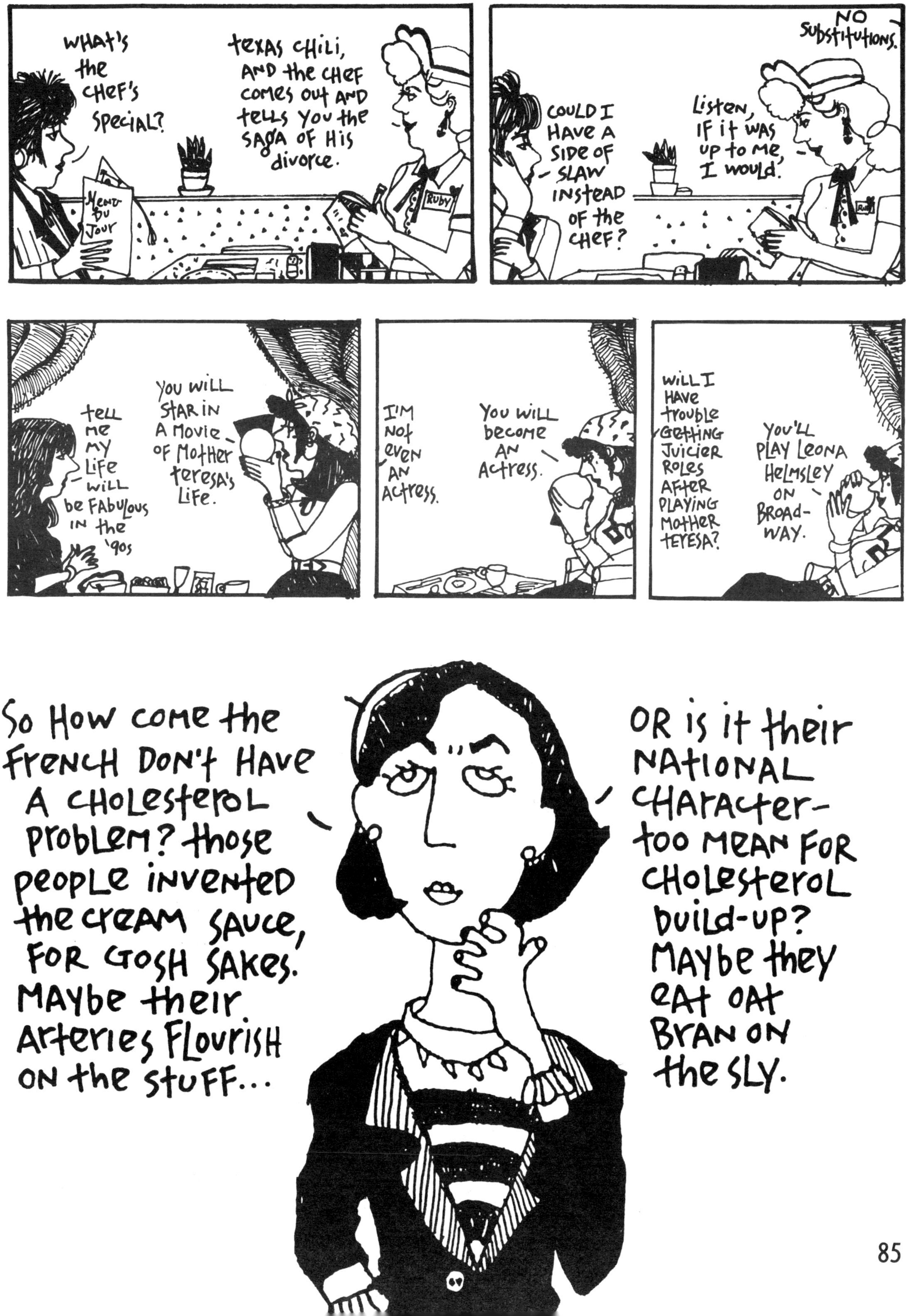
WHAT'S the CHEF'S SPECIAL?
MENU DU JOUR
TEXAS CHILI, AND the CHEF COMES OUT AND TELLS YOU the SAGA OF HIS DIVORCE.
RUBY
NO SUBSTITUTIONS.
COULD I HAVE A SIDE OF SLAW INSTEAD OF the CHEF?
LISTEN, IF IT WAS UP TO ME, I WOULD.
TELL ME MY LIFE WILL BE FABULOUS IN the '90s
YOU WILL STAR IN A MOVIE OF MOTHER TERESA'S LIFE.
I'M NOT EVEN AN ACTRESS.
YOU WILL BECOME AN ACTRESS.
WILL I HAVE TROUBLE GETTING JUICIER ROLES AFTER PLAYING MOTHER TERESA?
YOU'LL PLAY LEONA HELMSLEY ON BROADWAY.
SO HOW COME the FRENCH DON'T HAVE A CHOLESTEROL PROBLEM? THOSE PEOPLE INVENTED the CREAM SAUCE, FOR GOSH SAKES. MAYBE THEIR ARTERIES FLOURISH ON the STUFF...
OR IS IT THEIR NATIONAL CHARACTER-TOO MEAN FOR CHOLESTEROL BUILD-UP? MAYBE THEY EAT OAT BRAN ON the SLY.

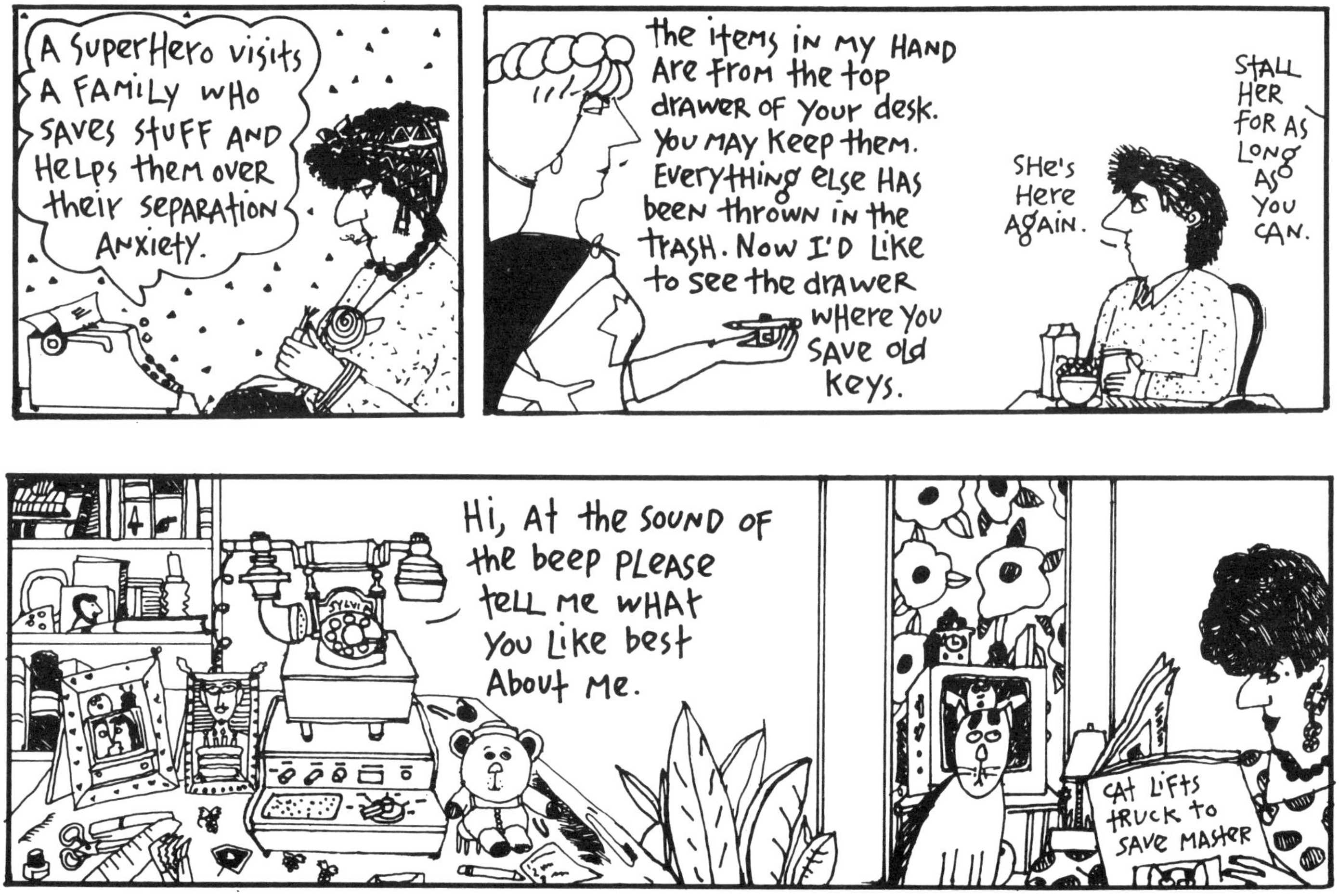
A SuperHero visits A FAMILY WHO SAVES STUFF AND HeLps them over their SEPARATION Anxiety.
the items in my HAND Are from the top drawer of your desk. You MAY keep them. Everything else HAS been thrown in the TRASH. Now I'D Like to see the drawer where you SAVE old keys.
SHe's Here AgAin.
STALL HER FOR AS LONG AS YOU CAN.
Hi, At the SOUND OF the beep PLEASE tell me WHAT You Like best About me.
CAT Lifts truck to SAVE MASTER

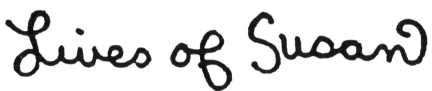

Lives of Susan

COMEDY MINI-SERIES ABOUT A WOMAN WITH A 3-WAY SPLIT PERSONALITY: HOUSEWIFE, ELECTRICIAN AND COMPULSIVE SHOPPER.

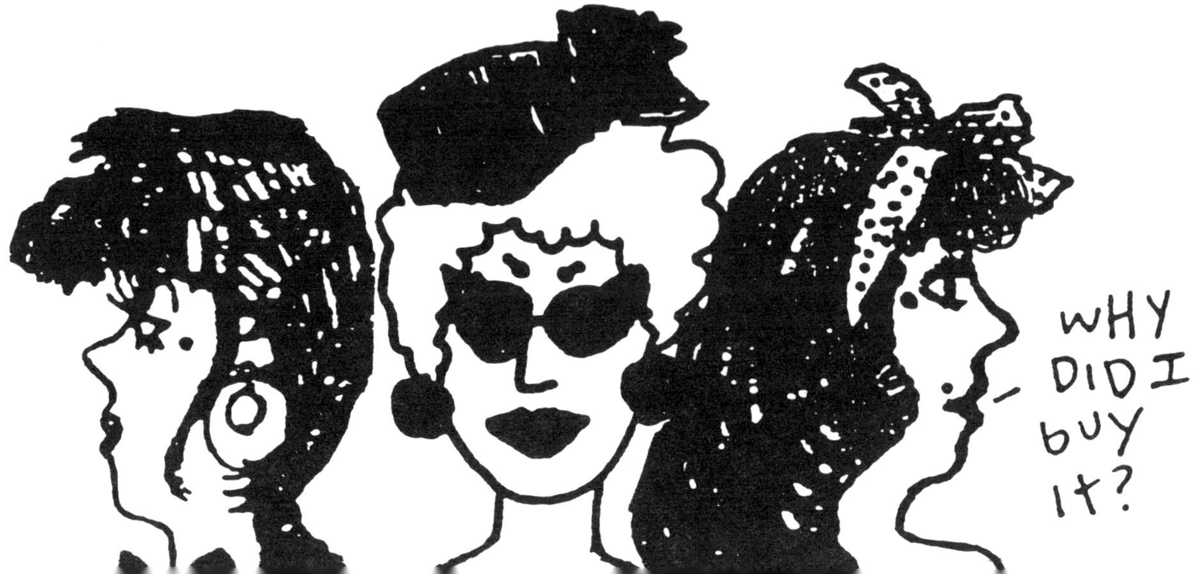
WHY DID I buy it?

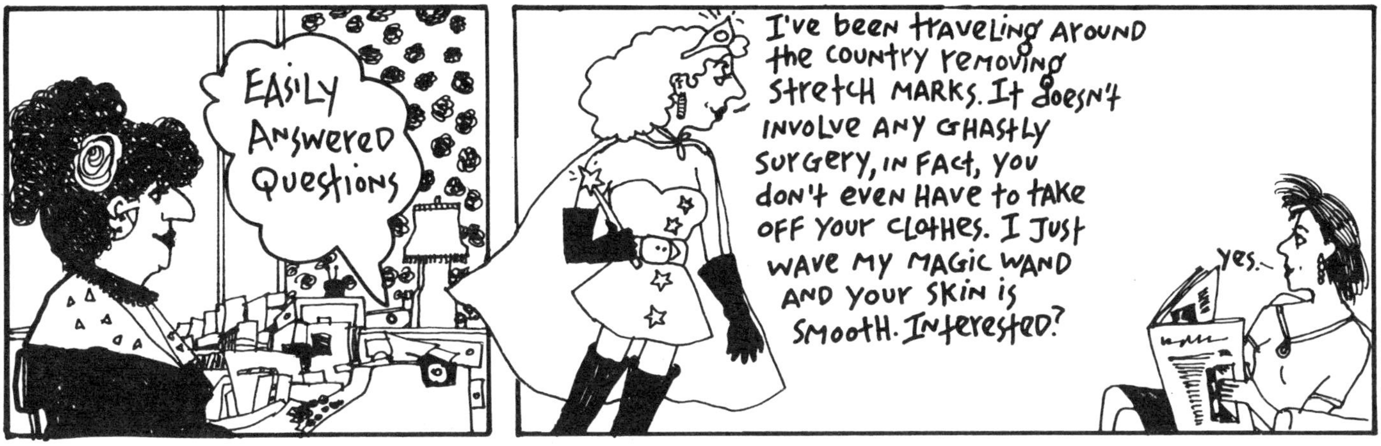
EASILY Answered Questions
I've been traveling around the country removing stretch marks. It doesn't involve any ghastly surgery, in fact, you don't even have to take off your clothes. I just wave my magic wand and your skin is smooth. Interested?
Yes.

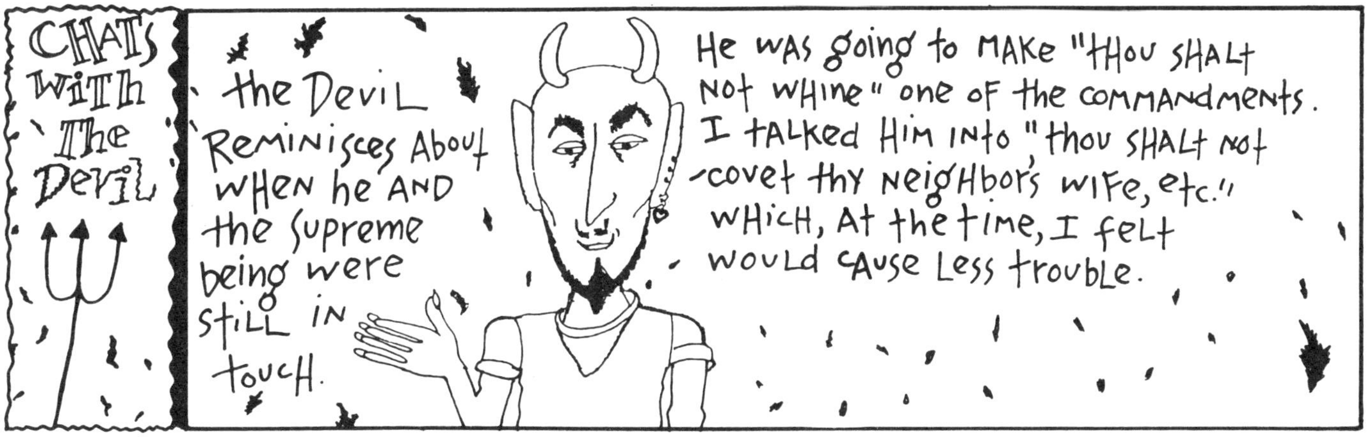
CHATS WITH THE DEVIL
the Devil Reminisces About when he and the supreme being were still in touch.
He was going to make "thou shalt not whine" one of the commandments. I talked Him into "thou shalt not covet thy neighbor's wife, etc." which, at the time, I felt would cause less trouble.

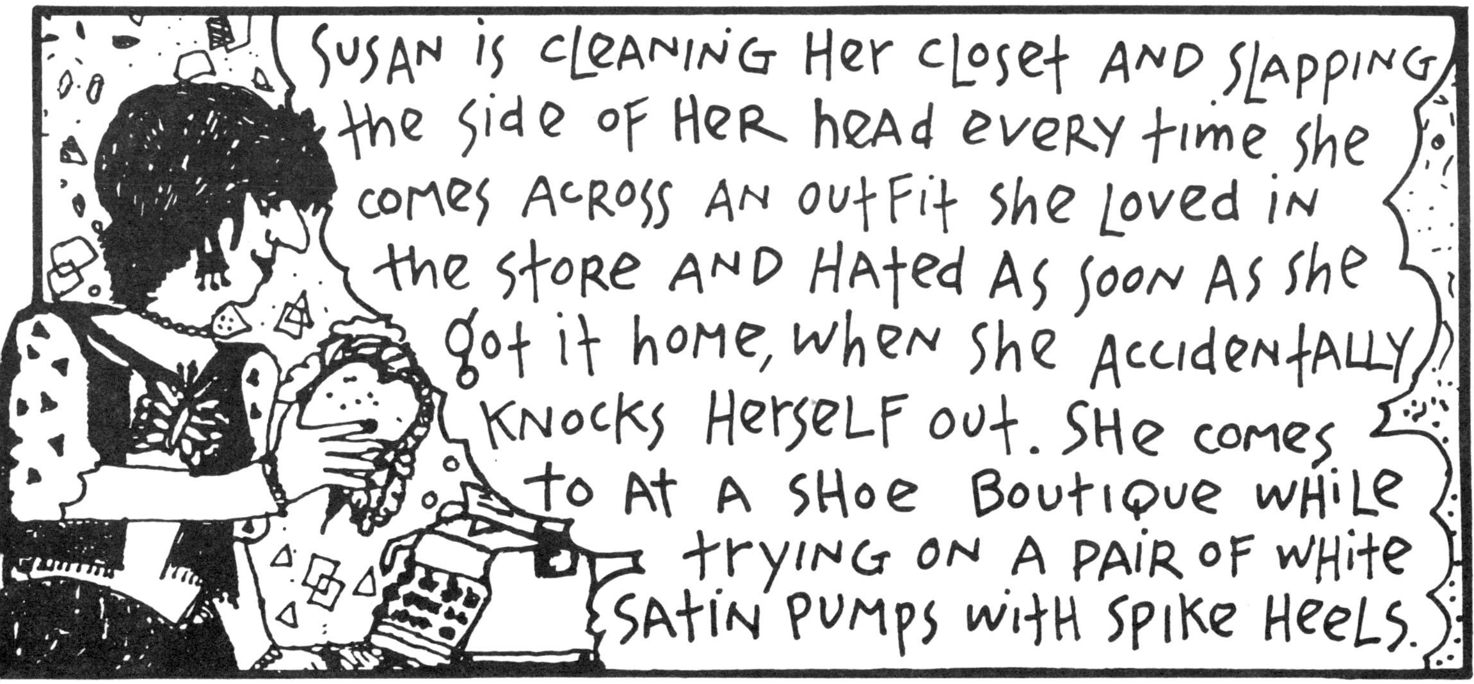
Susan is cleaning her closet and slapping the side of her head every time she comes across an outfit she loved in the store and hated as soon as she got it home, when she accidentally knocks herself out. She comes to at a shoe boutique while trying on a pair of white satin pumps with spike heels.

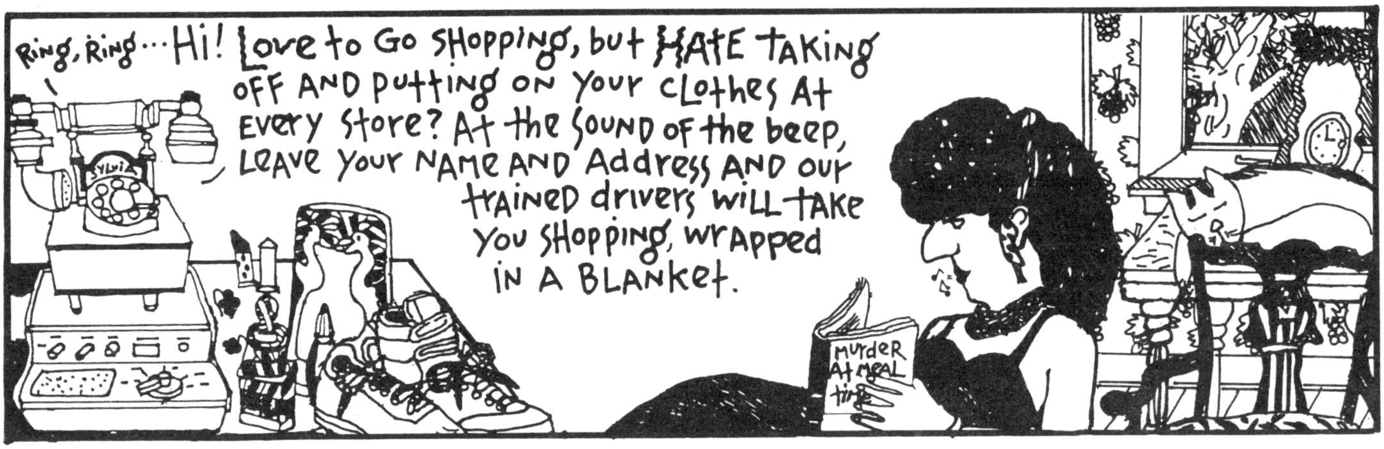
Ring, Ring ... Hi! Love to Go Shopping, but HATE taking off and putting on your clothes at every store? At the sound of the beep, leave your name and address and our trained drivers will take you shopping, wrapped in a blanket.
SYLVIA
MURDER AT MEAL TIME

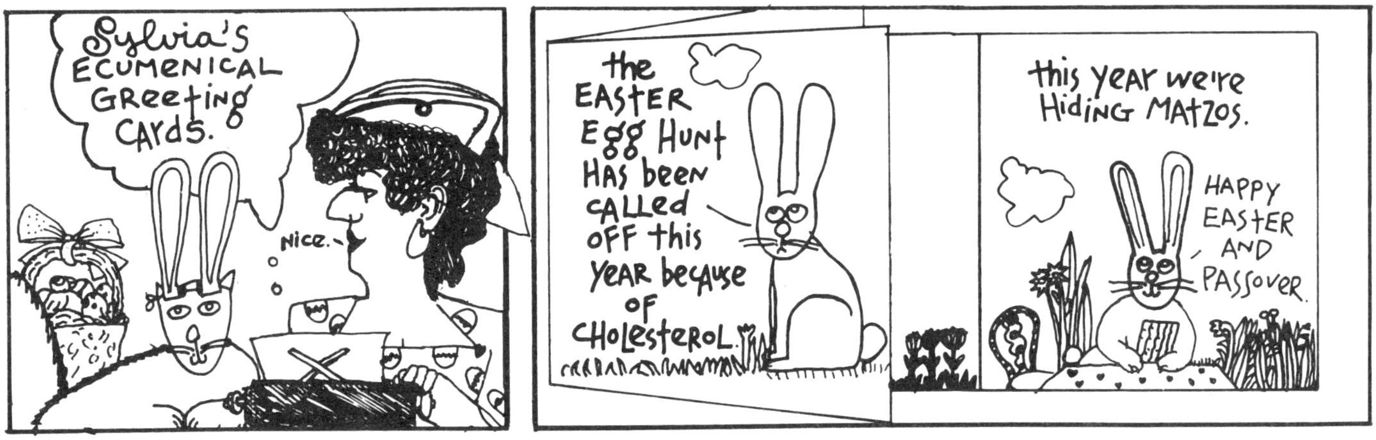
Sylvia's ECUMENICAL Greeting Cards.
Nice.
the EASTER Egg Hunt Has been called off this year because of CHOLESTEROL.
this year we're Hiding MATZOS.
HAPPY EASTER AND PASSOVER.

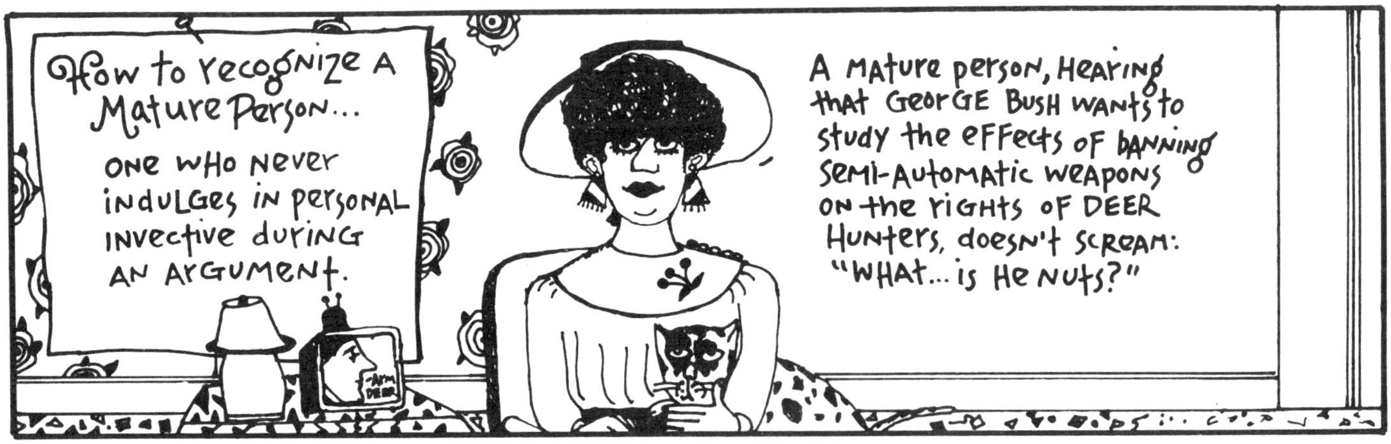
How to recognize a Mature Person...
one who never indulges in personal invective during an argument.
A mature person, hearing that George Bush wants to study the effects of banning semi-automatic weapons on the rights of deer hunters, doesn't scream: "WHAT... is he nuts?"

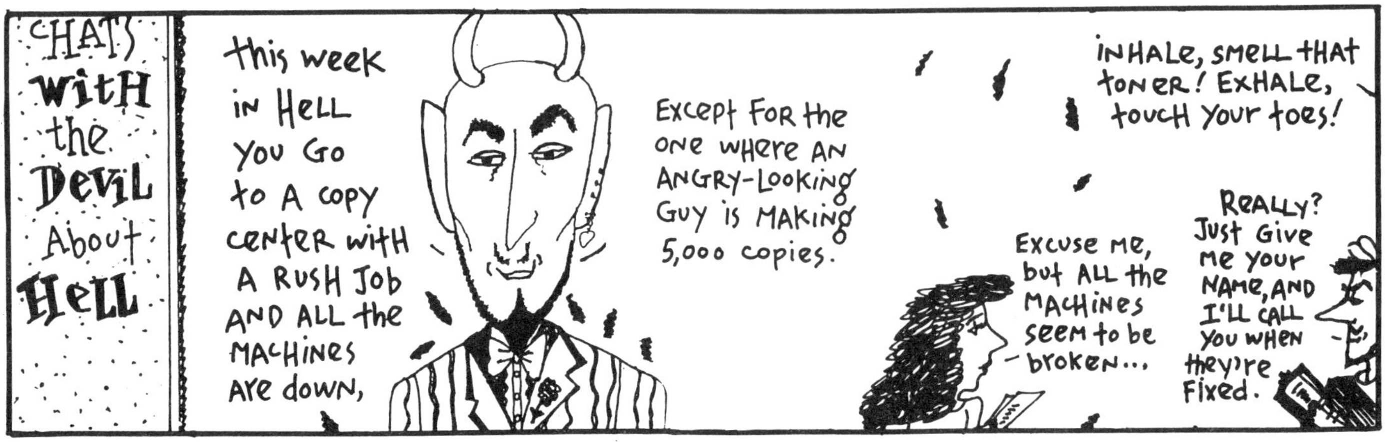
CHATS WITH the DEVIL About HELL
this week in Hell you go to a copy center with a rush job and all the machines are down,
Except for the one where an angry-looking guy is making 5,000 copies.
inhale, smell that toner! Exhale, touch your toes!
Excuse me, but all the machines seem to be broken...
Really? Just give me your name, and I'll call you when they're fixed.

MY LAST BRUNCH

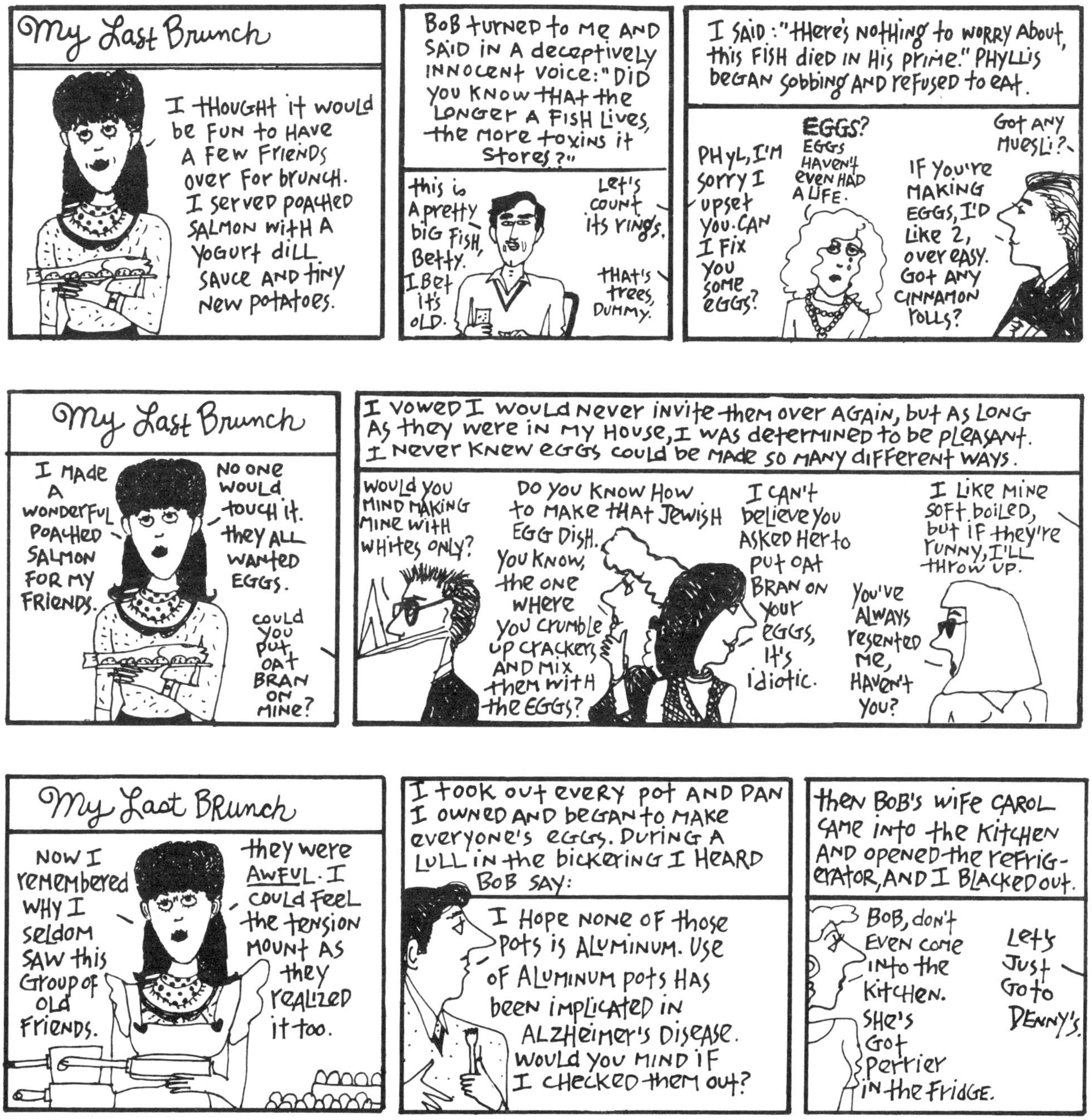
My Last Brunch
I thought it would be fun to have a few friends over for brunch. I served poached salmon with a yogurt dill sauce and tiny new potatoes.
Bob turned to me and said in a deceptively innocent voice: "Did you know that the longer a fish lives, the more toxins it stores?"
this is a pretty big fish, Betty. I bet it's old.
Let's count its rings.
that's trees, dummy.
I said: "there's nothing to worry about, this fish died in his prime." Phyllis began sobbing and refused to eat.
Phyl, I'm sorry I upset you. Can I fix you some eggs?
EGGS? Eggs haven't even had a life.
If you're making eggs, I'd like 2, over easy. Got any cinnamon rolls?
Got any muesli?
My Last Brunch
I made a wonderful poached salmon for my friends.
No one would touch it. they all wanted eggs.
could you put oat bran on mine?
I vowed I would never invite them over again, but as long as they were in my house, I was determined to be pleasant. I never knew eggs could be made so many different ways.
Would you mind making mine with whites only?
Do you know how to make that Jewish egg dish. You know, the one where you crumble up crackers and mix them with the eggs?
I can't believe you asked her to put oat bran on your eggs, it's idiotic.
You've always resented me, haven't you?
I like mine soft boiled, but if they're runny, I'll throw up.
My Last Brunch
Now I remembered why I seldom saw this group of old friends.
they were AWFUL. I could feel the tension mount as they realized it too.
I took out every pot and pan I owned and began to make everyone's eggs. During a lull in the bickering I heard Bob say:
I hope none of those pots is aluminum. Use of aluminum pots has been implicated in Alzheimer's disease. Would you mind if I checked them out?
then Bob's wife Carol came into the kitchen and opened the refrigerator, and I blacked out.
Bob, don't even come into the kitchen. She's got Perrier in the fridge.
Let's just go to Denny's.

When I was growing up, no one was afraid of food. I ate raw onion or banana sandwiches after school. Those were the only fresh vegetables or fruit I ever had at home. No one imagined that food could hurt you, and only milk was actually good for you. My mother didn't see any benefit in fresh fruit or vegetables. The ones we ate came out of cans. She liked cooking to be easy.

She made wonderful apple pies, but rarely, because we ate them too quickly. "It takes so long to make them and then people eat them," she would say, outraged.

In those days people ate everything. You didn't tell your hostess your dietary preferences. Why would she care? She wouldn't expect to hear your sexual preferences. That was a halcyon time.

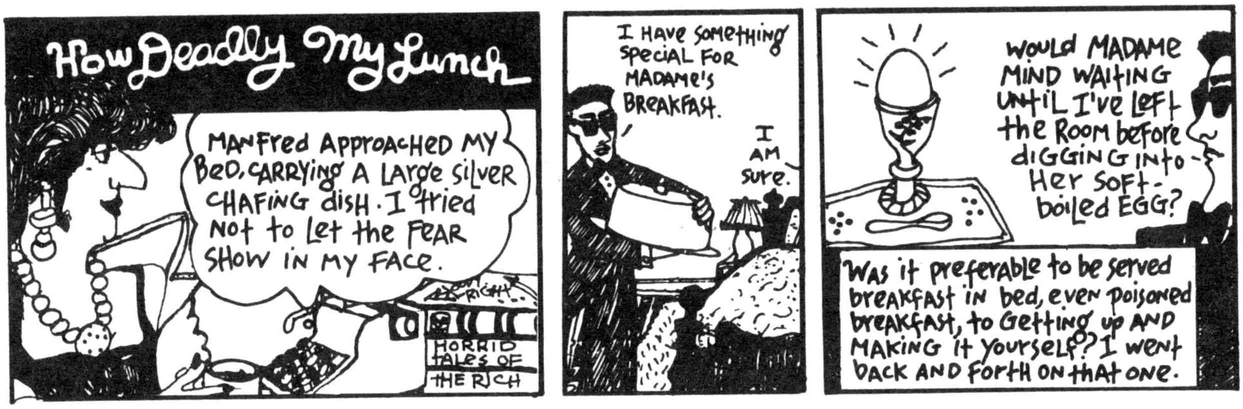
How Deadly My Lunch
MANFRED APPROACHED MY BED, CARRYING A LARGE SILVER CHAFING DISH. I TRIED NOT TO LET THE FEAR SHOW IN MY FACE.
HORRID TALES OF THE RICH
I HAVE SOMETHING SPECIAL FOR MADAME'S BREAKFAST.
I AM SURE.
WOULD MADAME MIND WAITING UNTIL I'VE LEFT THE ROOM BEFORE DIGGING INTO HER SOFT-BOILED EGG?
Was it preferable to be served breakfast in bed, even poisoned breakfast, to getting up and making it yourself? I went back and forth on that one.

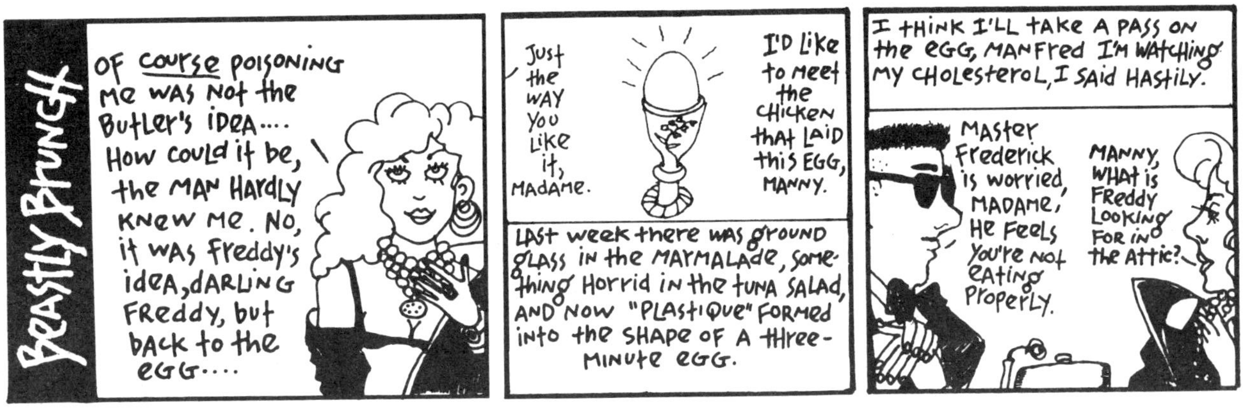
Beastly Brunch
OF COURSE POISONING ME WAS NOT THE BUTLER'S IDEA.... HOW COULD IT BE, THE MAN HARDLY KNEW ME. NO, IT WAS FREDDY'S IDEA, DARLING FREDDY, BUT BACK TO THE EGG....
JUST THE WAY YOU LIKE IT, MADAME.
I'D LIKE TO MEET THE CHICKEN THAT LAID THIS EGG, MANNY.
LAST WEEK THERE WAS GROUND GLASS IN THE MARMALADE, SOMETHING HORRID IN THE TUNA SALAD, AND NOW "PLASTIQUE" FORMED INTO THE SHAPE OF A THREE-MINUTE EGG.
I THINK I'LL TAKE A PASS ON THE EGG, MANFRED I'M WATCHING MY CHOLESTEROL, I SAID HASTILY.
MASTER FREDERICK IS WORRIED, MADAME, HE FEELS YOU'RE NOT EATING PROPERLY.
MANNY, WHAT IS FREDDY LOOKING FOR IN THE ATTIC?

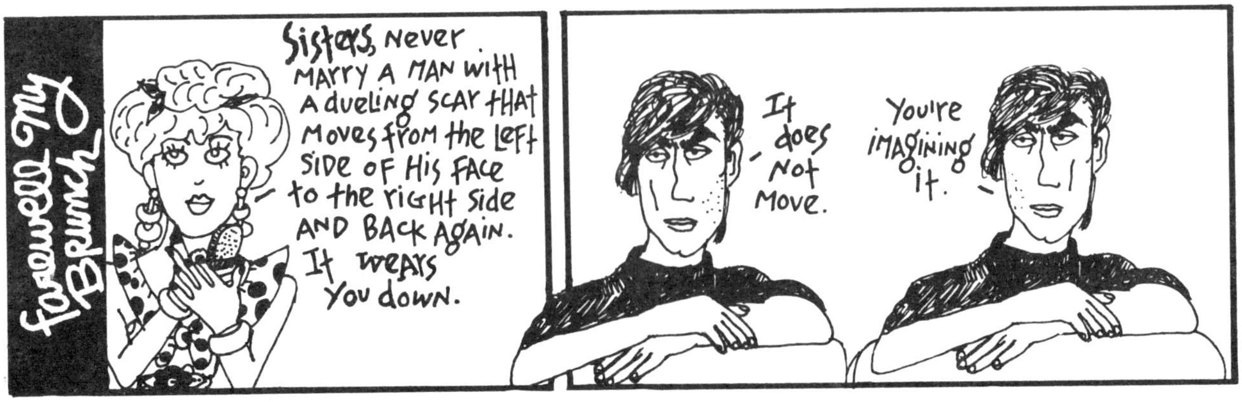
Farewell My Brunch
SISTERS, NEVER MARRY A MAN WITH A DUELING SCAR THAT MOVES FROM THE LEFT SIDE OF HIS FACE TO THE RIGHT SIDE AND BACK AGAIN. IT WEARS YOU DOWN.
IT DOES NOT MOVE.
YOU'RE IMAGINING IT.

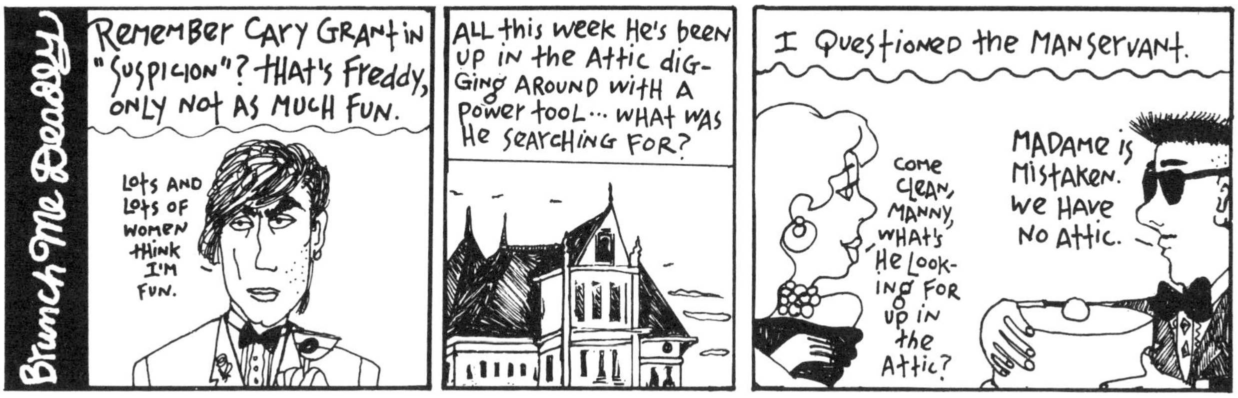
Brunch Me Deadly
Remember Cary Grant in "Suspicion"? That's Freddy, only not as much fun.
Lots and lots of women think I'm fun.
All this week he's been up in the attic digging around with a power tool... what was he searching for?
I questioned the manservant.
Come clean, Manny, what's he looking for up in the attic?
Madame is mistaken. We have no attic.

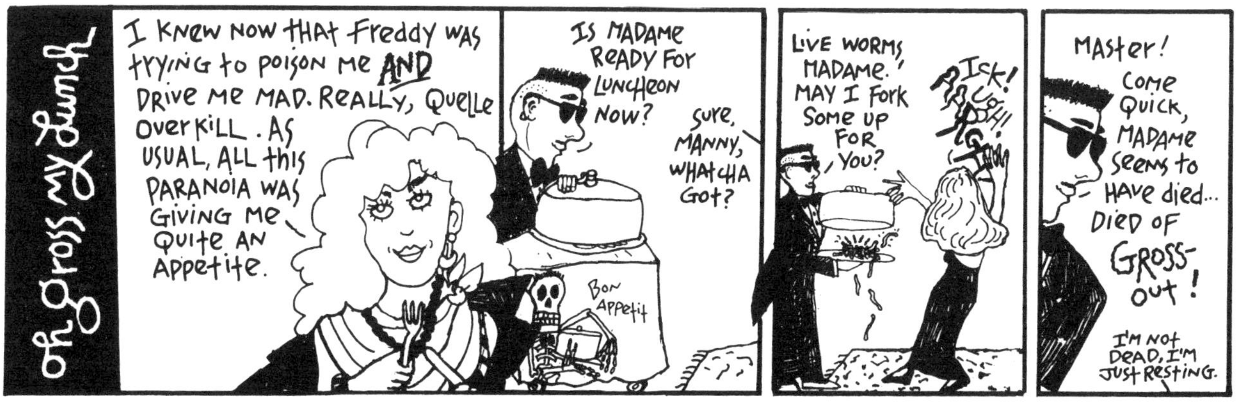
Oh Gross my Lunch
I knew now that Freddy was trying to poison me AND drive me mad. Really, quelle overkill. As usual, all this paranoia was giving me quite an appetite.
Is Madame ready for luncheon now?
Sure, Manny, whatcha got?
Bon Appetit
Live worms, Madame. May I fork some up for you?
Ick!
Master! Come quick, Madame seems to have died... died of gross-out!
I'm not dead, I'm just resting.

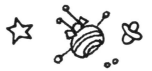

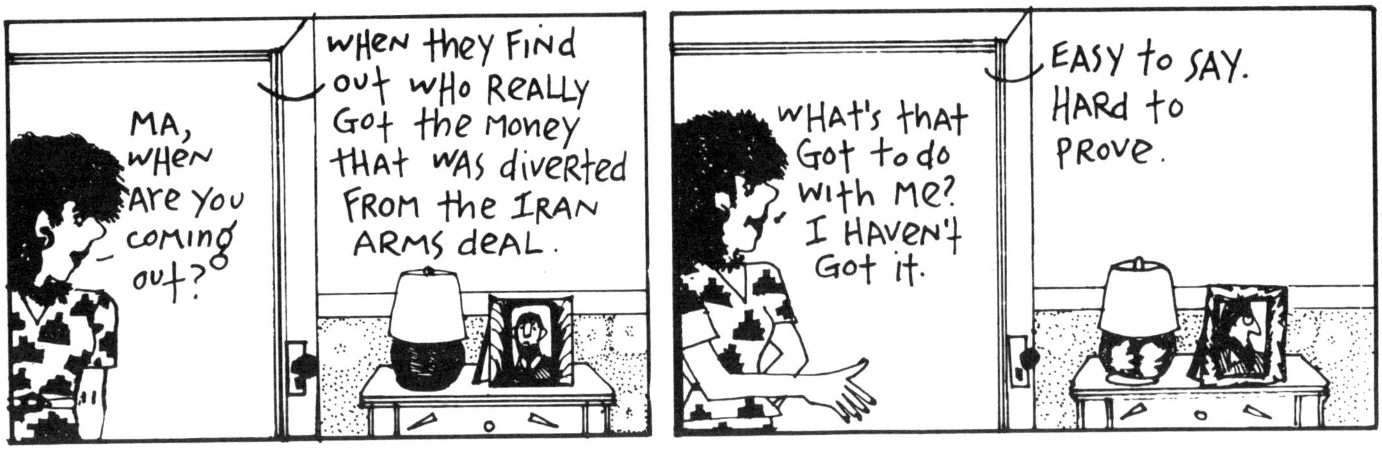

MA, WHEN ARE YOU COMING OUT?
WHEN THEY FIND OUT WHO REALLY GOT THE MONEY THAT WAS DIVERTED FROM THE IRAN ARMS DEAL.
WHAT'S THAT GOT TO DO WITH ME? I HAVEN'T GOT IT.
EASY TO SAY. HARD TO PROVE.

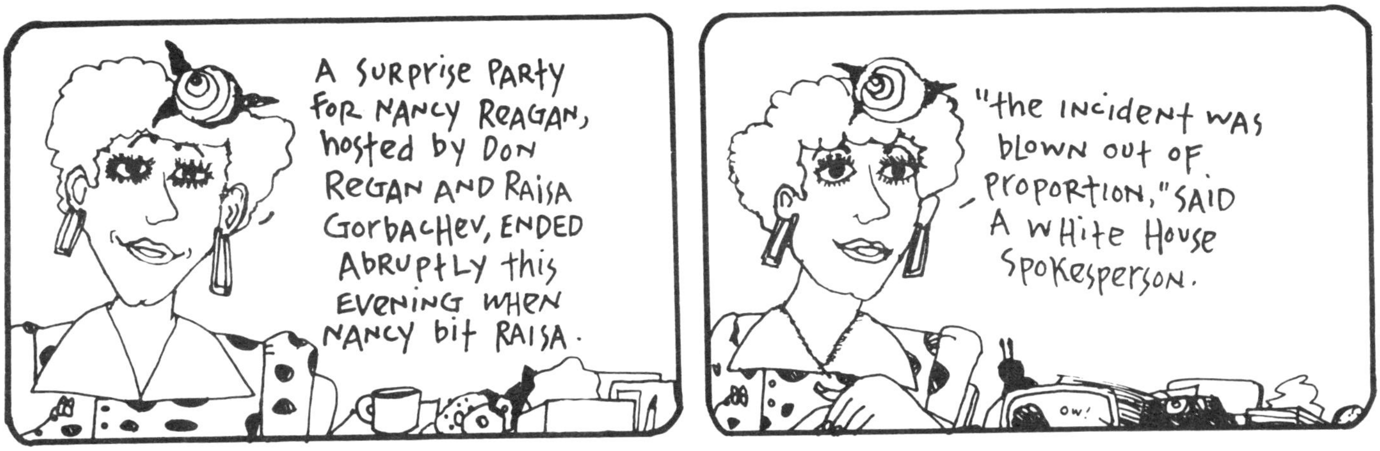

A SURPRISE PARTY FOR NANCY REAGAN, HOSTED BY DON REGAN AND RAISA GORBACHEV, ENDED ABRUPTLY THIS EVENING WHEN NANCY BIT RAISA.
"THE INCIDENT WAS BLOWN OUT OF PROPORTION," SAID A WHITE HOUSE SPOKESPERSON.
OW!

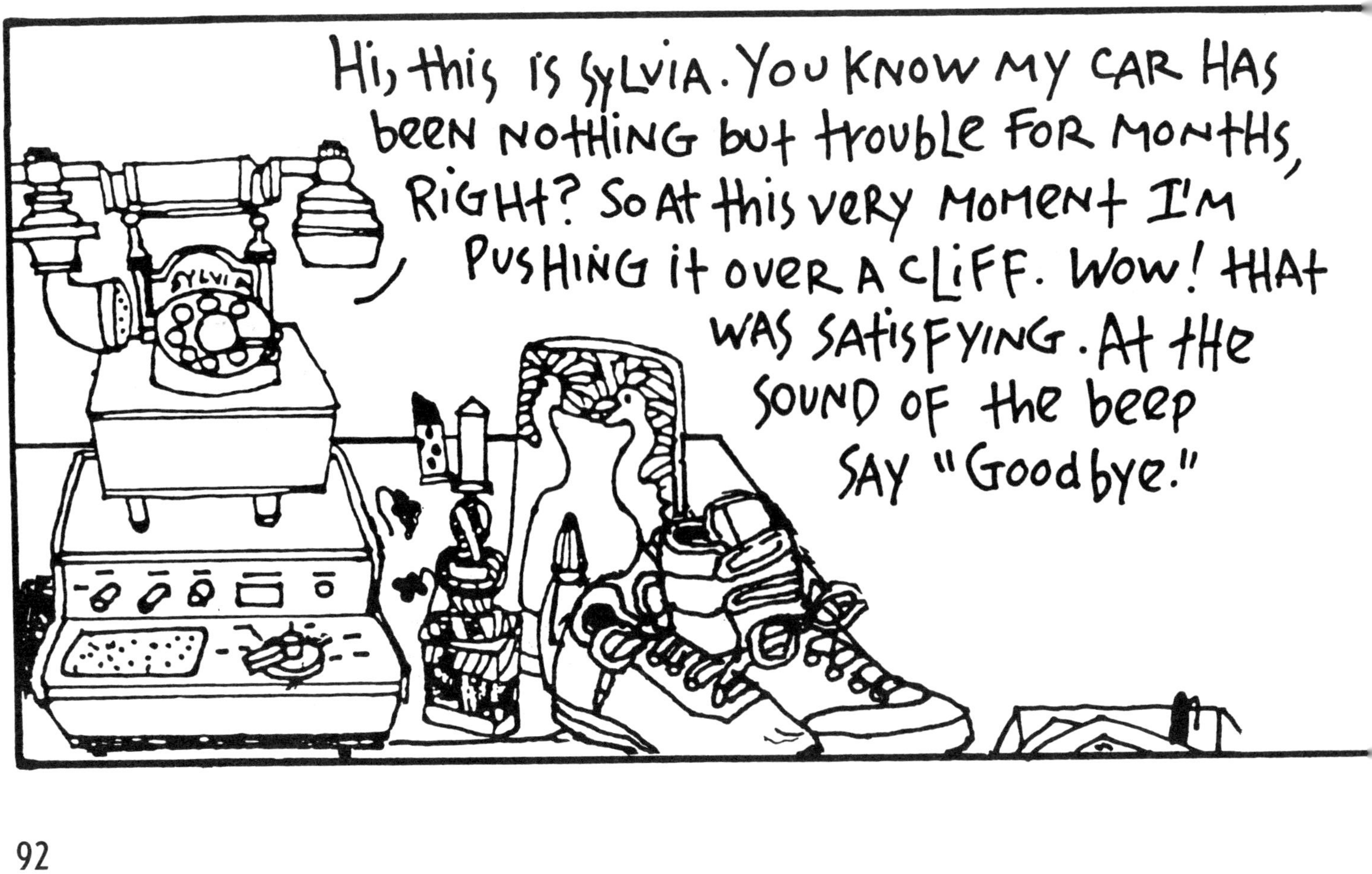

HI, THIS IS SYLVIA. YOU KNOW MY CAR HAS BEEN NOTHING BUT TROUBLE FOR MONTHS, RIGHT? SO AT THIS VERY MOMENT I'M PUSHING IT OVER A CLIFF. WOW! THAT WAS SATISFYING. AT THE SOUND OF THE BEEP SAY "GOODBYE."
SYLVIA

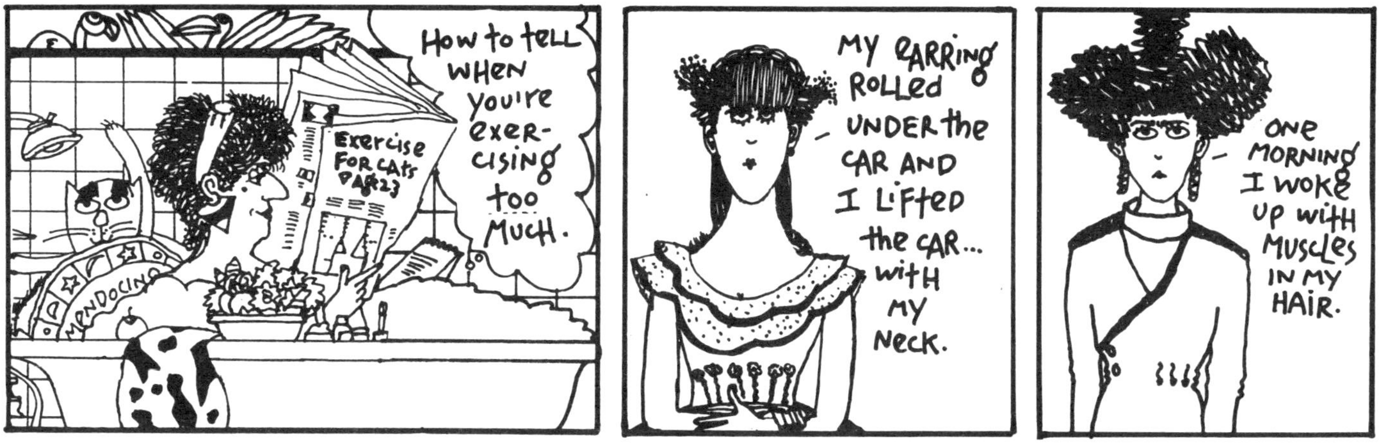
How to tell when you're exer-cising too MUCH.
Exercise For Cats
MENDOCINO
MY EARRING ROLLED UNDER the CAR AND I LIFTED the CAR... with MY Neck.
ONE MORNING I WOKE UP with MUSCLES IN MY HAIR.

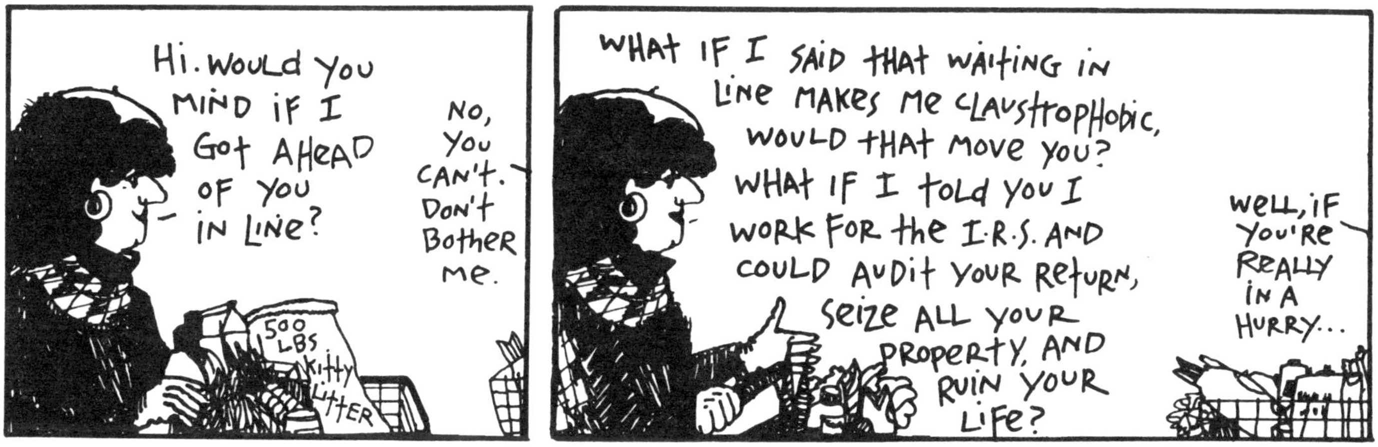
Hi. WOULD YOU MIND IF I GOT AHEAD OF YOU IN LINE?
No, You CAN'T. Don't Bother me.
500 LBS Kitty LITTER
WHAT IF I SAID THAT WAITING IN LINE MAKES ME CLAUSTROPHOBIC, WOULD THAT MOVE YOU?
WHAT IF I told YOU I WORK FOR the I.R.S. AND COULD AUDIT YOUR RETURN, SEIZE ALL YOUR PROPERTY, AND RUIN YOUR LIFE?
WELL, IF YOU'RE REALLY IN A HURRY...

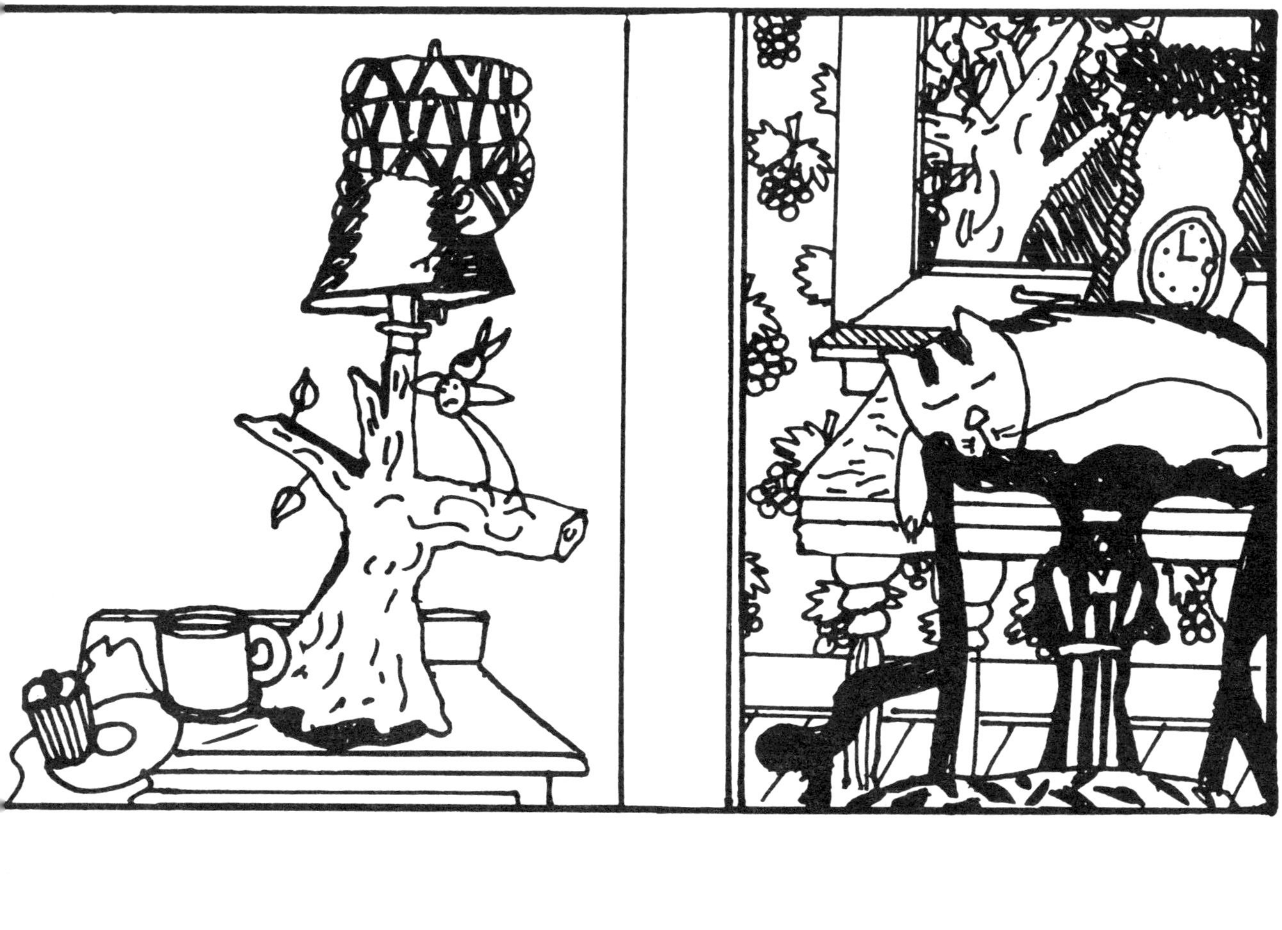

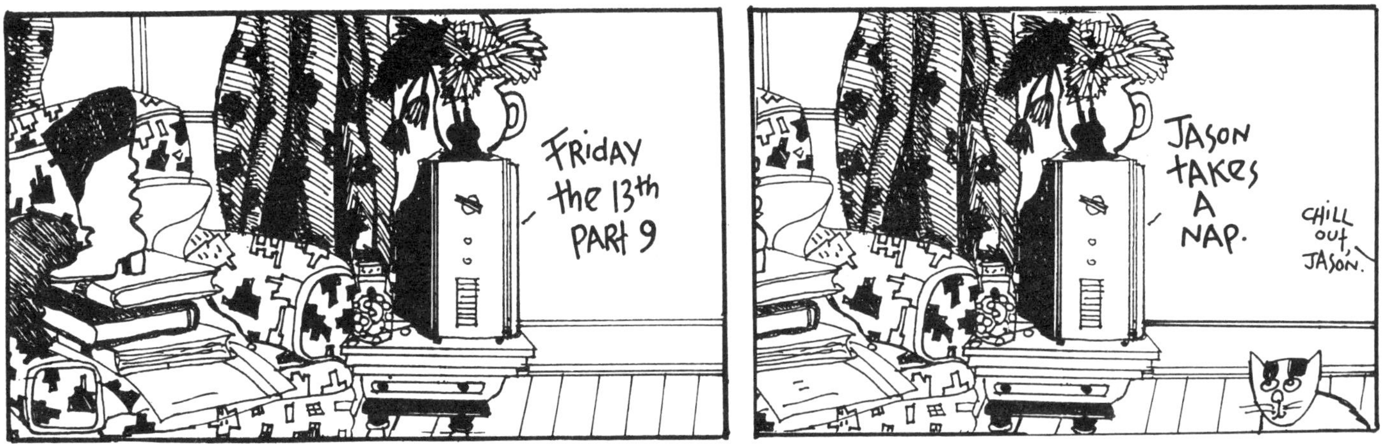
Friday the 13th Part 9
Jason takes a nap.
Chill out, Jason.

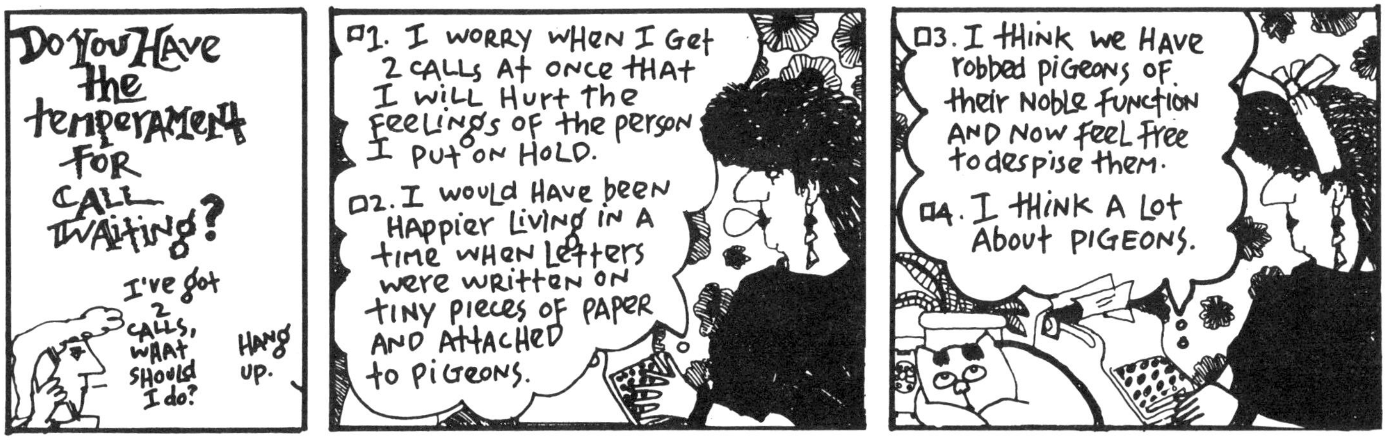
Do You Have the temperament for Call Waiting?
I've got 2 calls, what should I do?
Hang up.
☐1. I worry when I get 2 calls at once that I will hurt the feelings of the person I put on hold.
☐2. I would have been happier living in a time when letters were written on tiny pieces of paper and attached to pigeons.
☐3. I think we have robbed pigeons of their noble function and now feel free to despise them.
☐4. I think a lot about pigeons.

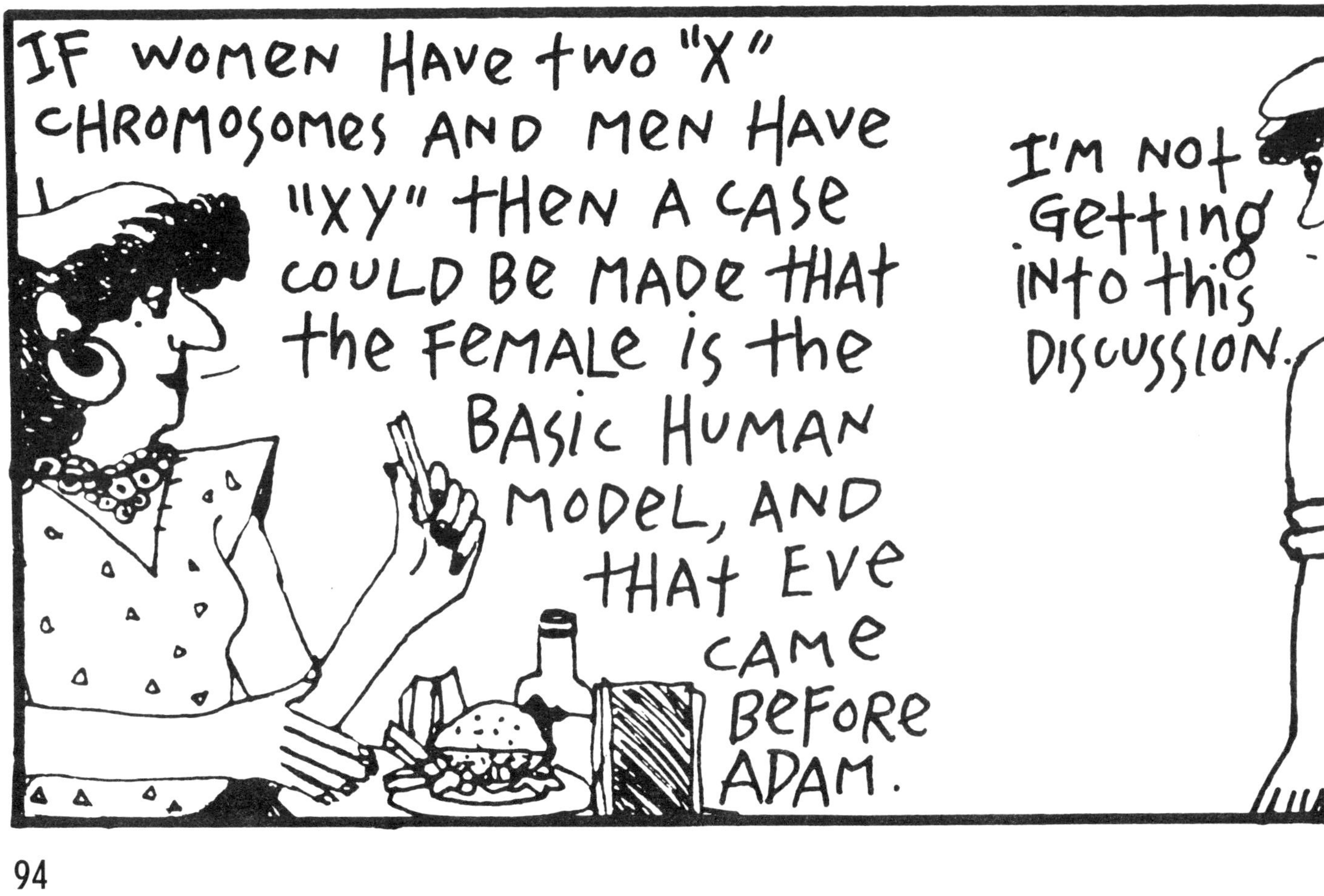
If women have two "X" chromosomes and men have "XY" then a case could be made that the female is the basic human model, and that Eve came before Adam.
I'm not getting into this discussion.

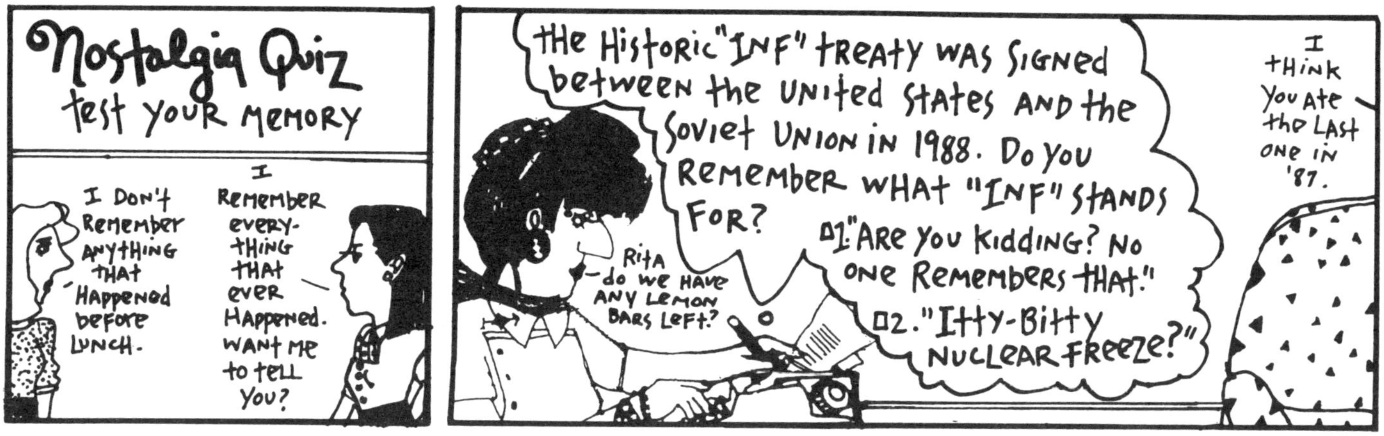
Nostalgia Quiz
test your memory
I Don't Remember anything that Happened before lunch.
I Remember everything that ever Happened. want me to tell you?
The Historic "INF" treaty was signed between the United States and the Soviet Union in 1988. Do you Remember what "INF" stands for?
□1. "Are you kidding? No one Remembers that."
□2. "Itty-Bitty Nuclear Freeze?"
Rita do we have any lemon bars left?
I think you ate the last one in '87.

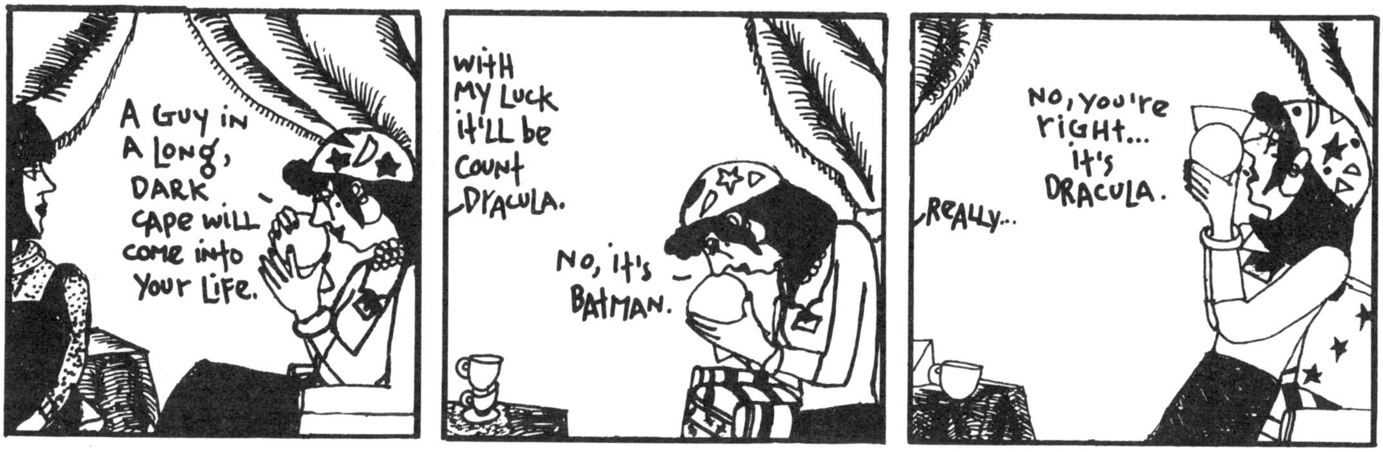
A Guy in a Long, Dark cape will come into your Life.
With my Luck it'll be Count Dracula.
No, it's Batman.
Really...
No, you're right... it's Dracula.

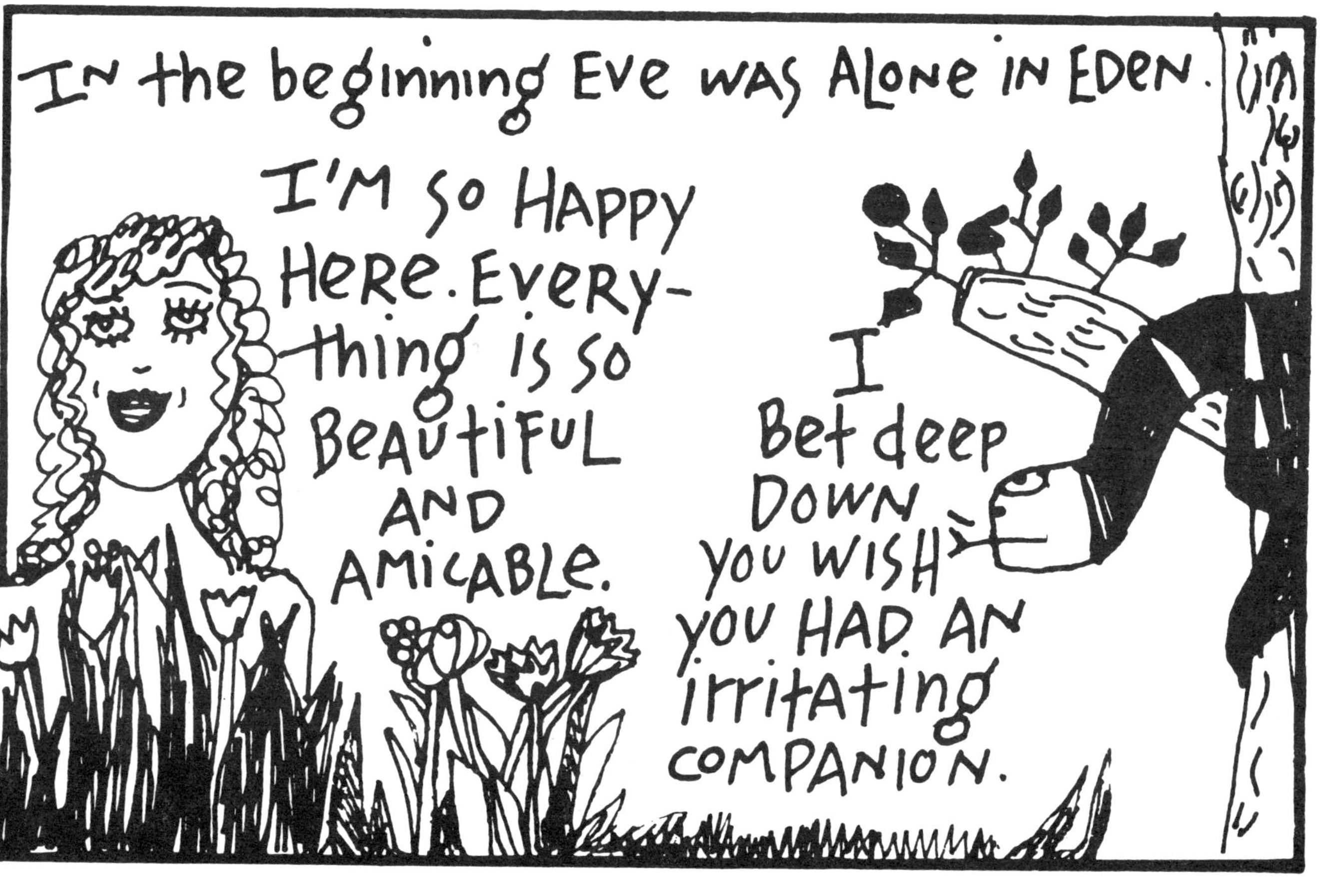
In the beginning Eve was Alone in Eden.
I'm so Happy Here. Everything is so Beautiful and Amicable.
I Bet deep Down you wish you had an irritating companion.

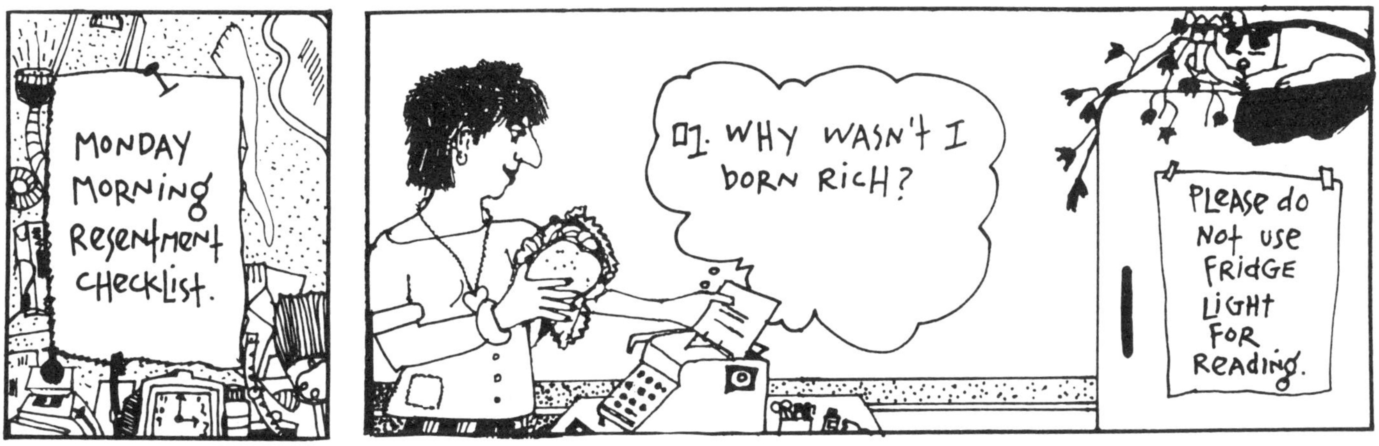
MONDAY MORNING Resentment checklist.
☐1. WHY WASN'T I born RICH?
Please do Not use FRIDGE LIGHT FOR Reading.

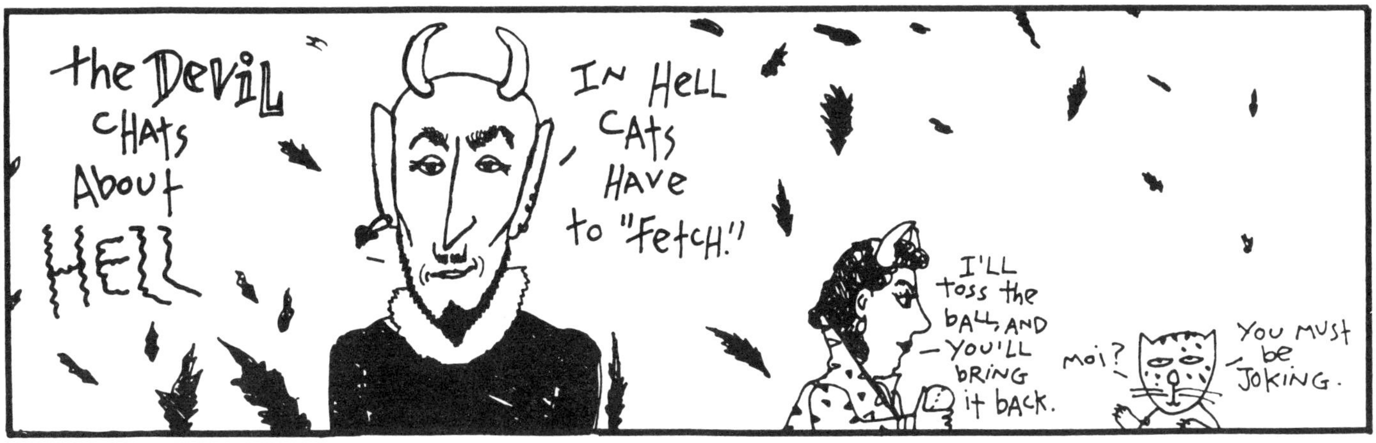
the DEVIL chats About HELL
IN HELL CATS HAVE to "FETCH."
I'LL toss the ball, AND YOU'LL bRING it back.
Moi?
YOU MUST be JOKING.

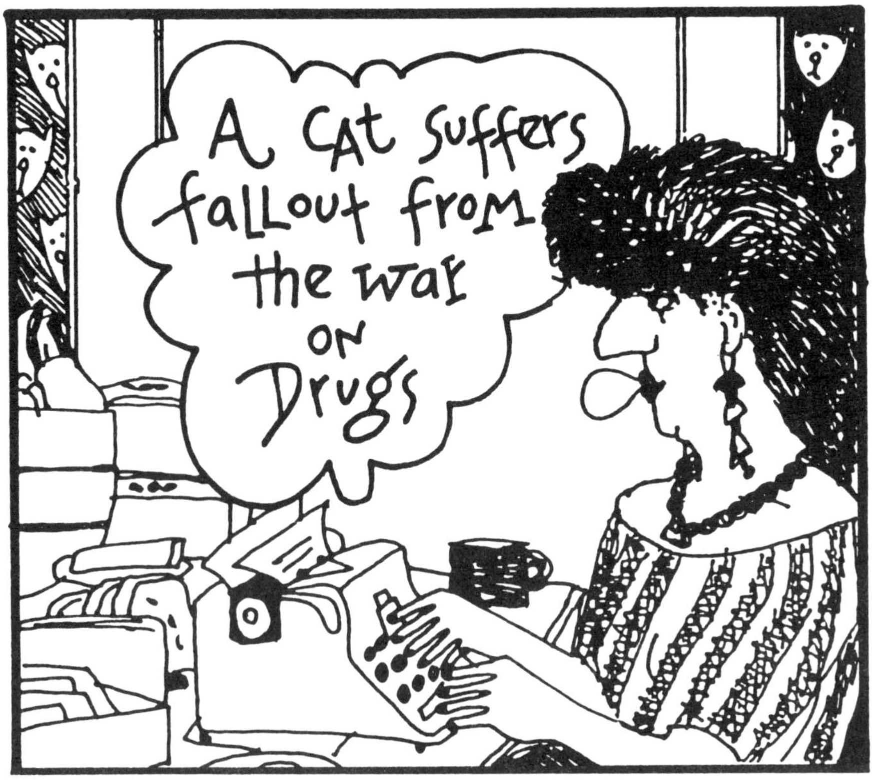
A cat suffers fallout from the war on Drugs

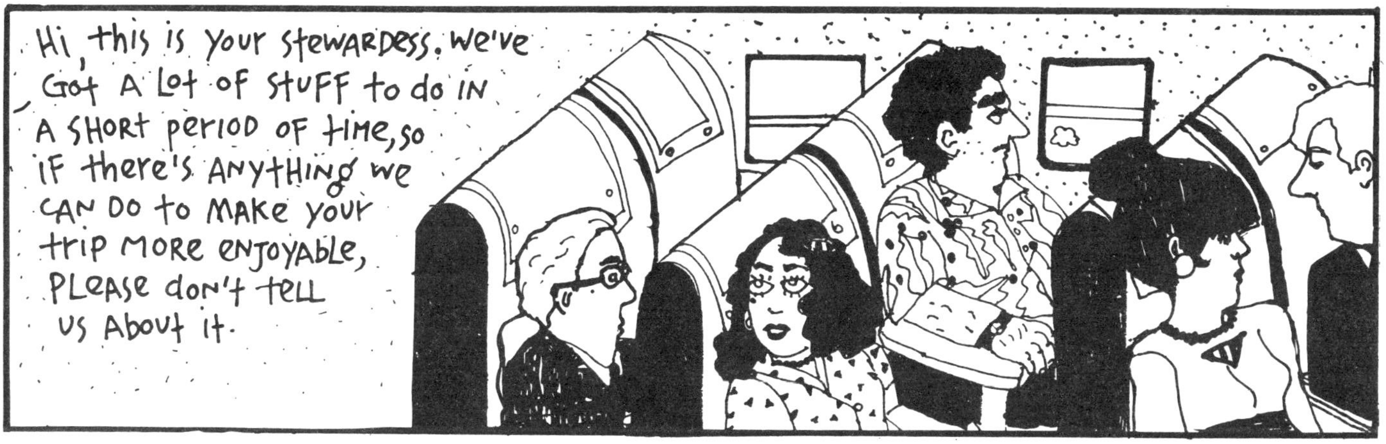
Hi, this is your stewardess. We've Got A Lot of STUFF to do in A SHORT period of time, so if there's ANYTHING we CAN DO to MAKE your trip MORE enjoyable, PLease don't tell us About it.

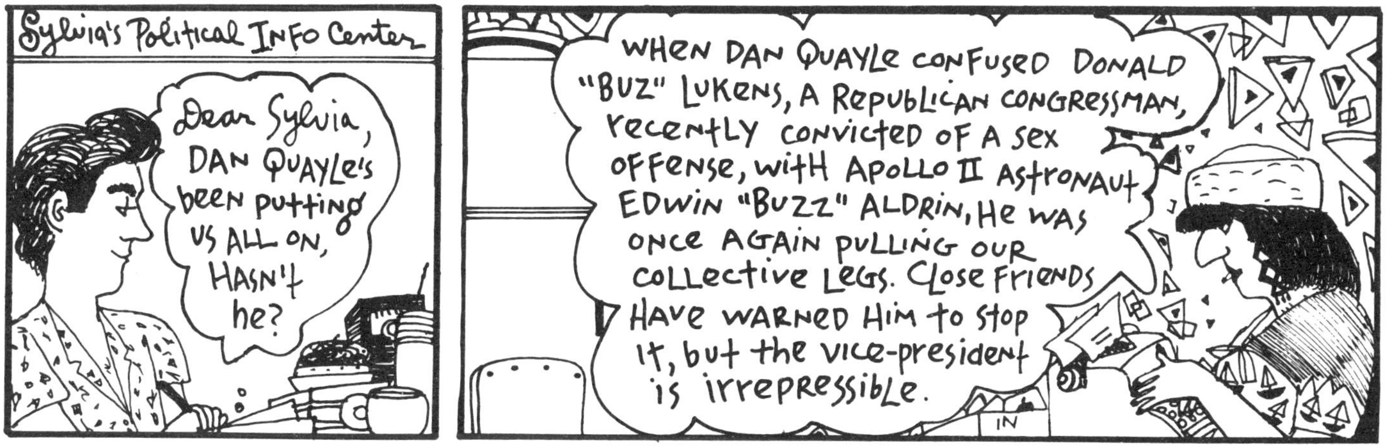
Sylvia's Political Info Center
Dear Sylvia, DAN QUAYLE's been putting us ALL ON, HASN't he?
WHEN DAN QUAYLE CONFUSED DONALD "BUZ" LUKENS, A REPUBLICAN CONGRESSMAN, recently convicted OF A SEX offense, with APOLLO II Astronaut EDWIN "BUZZ" ALDRIN, He was once AGAIN PULLING OUR collective Legs. Close Friends Have warned Him to stop it, but the vice-president is irrepressible.
IN

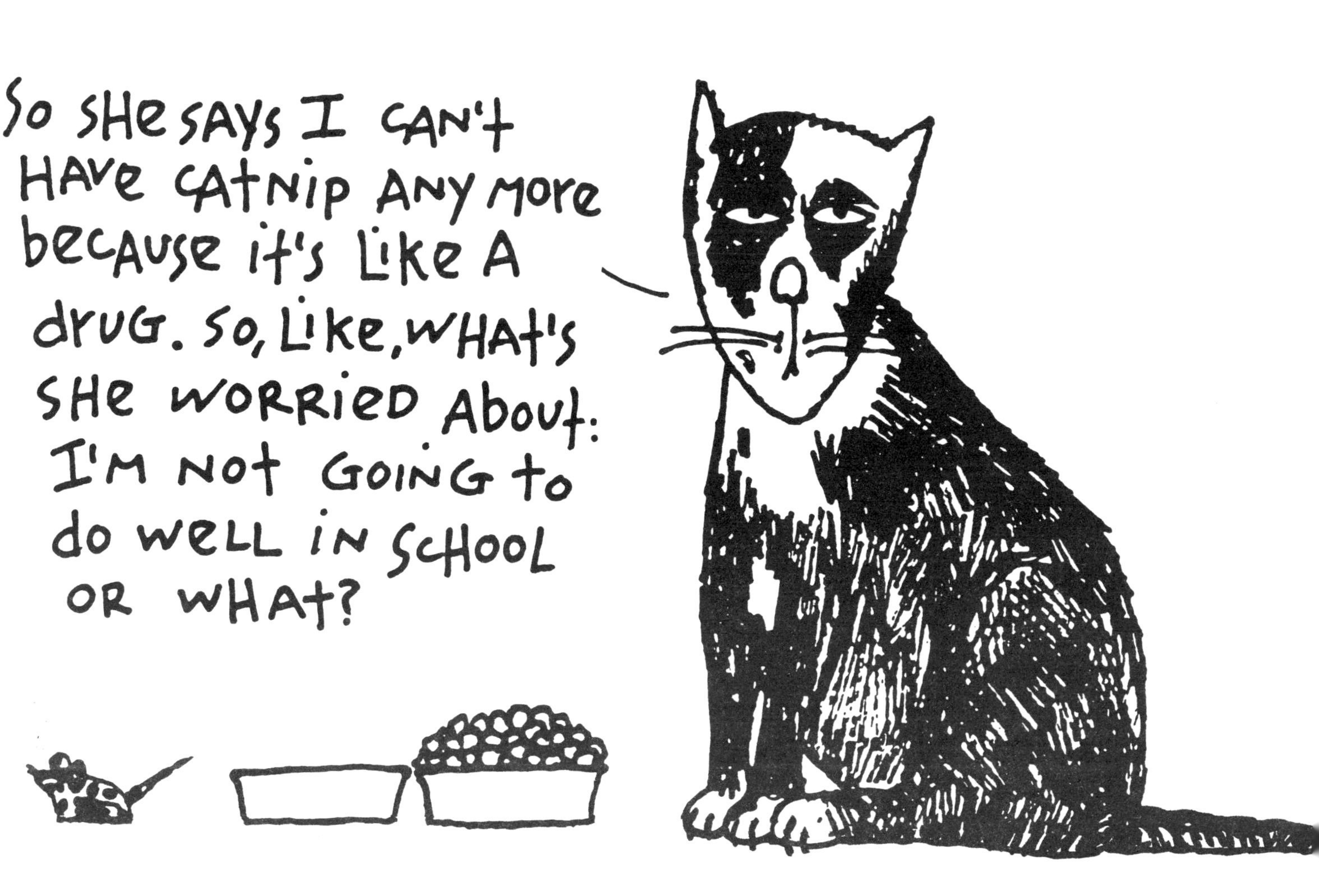
So SHE SAYS I CAN't HAVE CATNIP ANY MORE because it's Like A drug. So, Like, WHAT's SHE WORRIED About: I'M NOT GOING to do WELL IN SCHOOL OR WHAT?

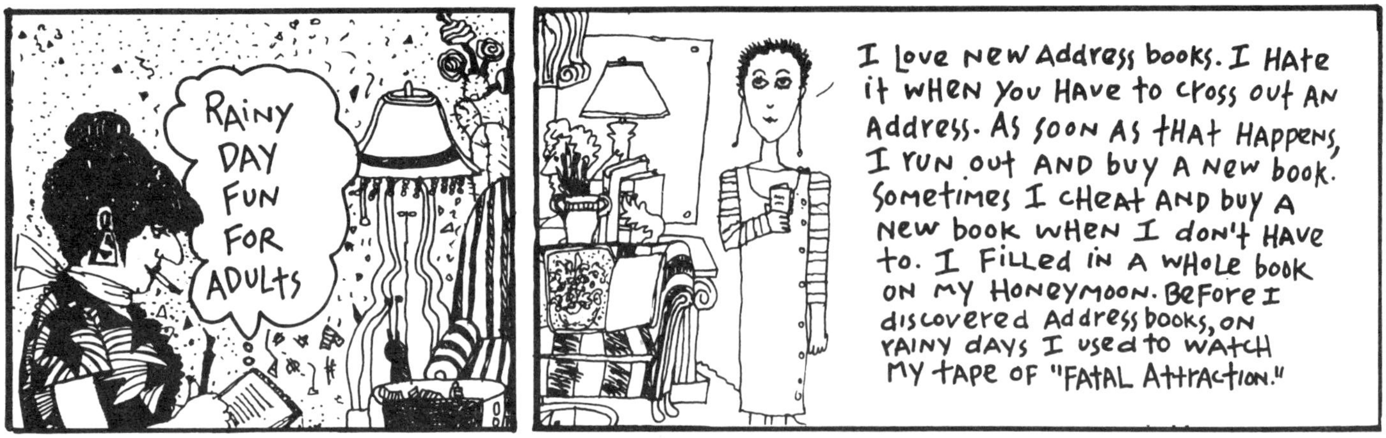
RAINY DAY FUN FOR ADULTS
I love new Address books. I hate it when you have to cross out an Address. As soon as that happens, I run out and buy a new book. Sometimes I cheat and buy a new book when I don't have to. I filled in a whole book on my Honeymoon. Before I discovered Address books, on rainy days I used to watch my tape of "Fatal Attraction."

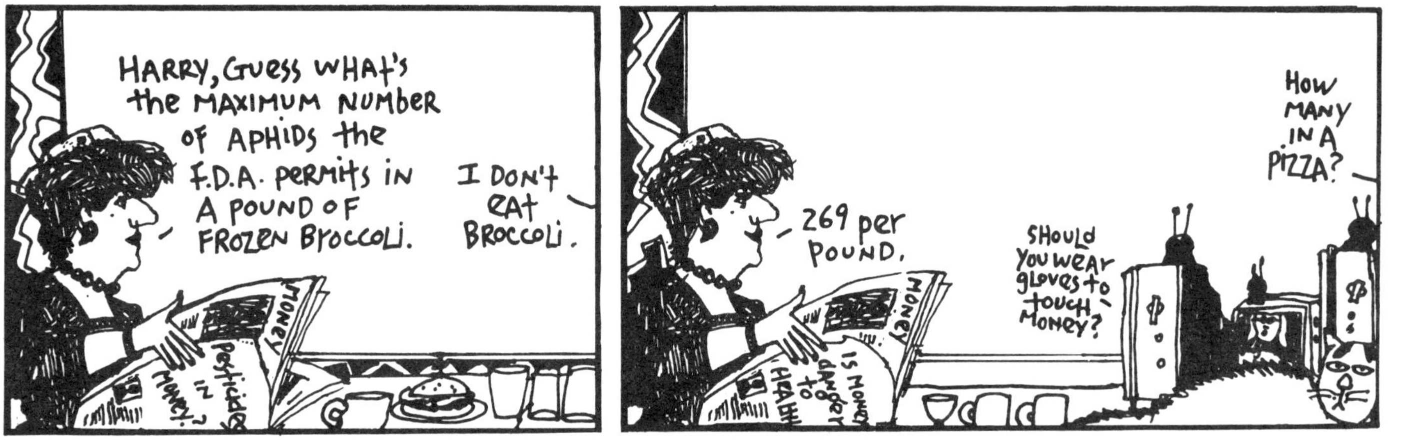
HARRY, GUESS WHAT'S the MAXIMUM NUMBER of APHIDS the F.D.A. permits in A POUND OF FROZEN Broccoli.
I DON'T eat Broccoli.
MONEY
Pesticides in Money?
269 per POUND.
MONEY
Should you wear gloves to touch Money?
How MANY IN A PIZZA?

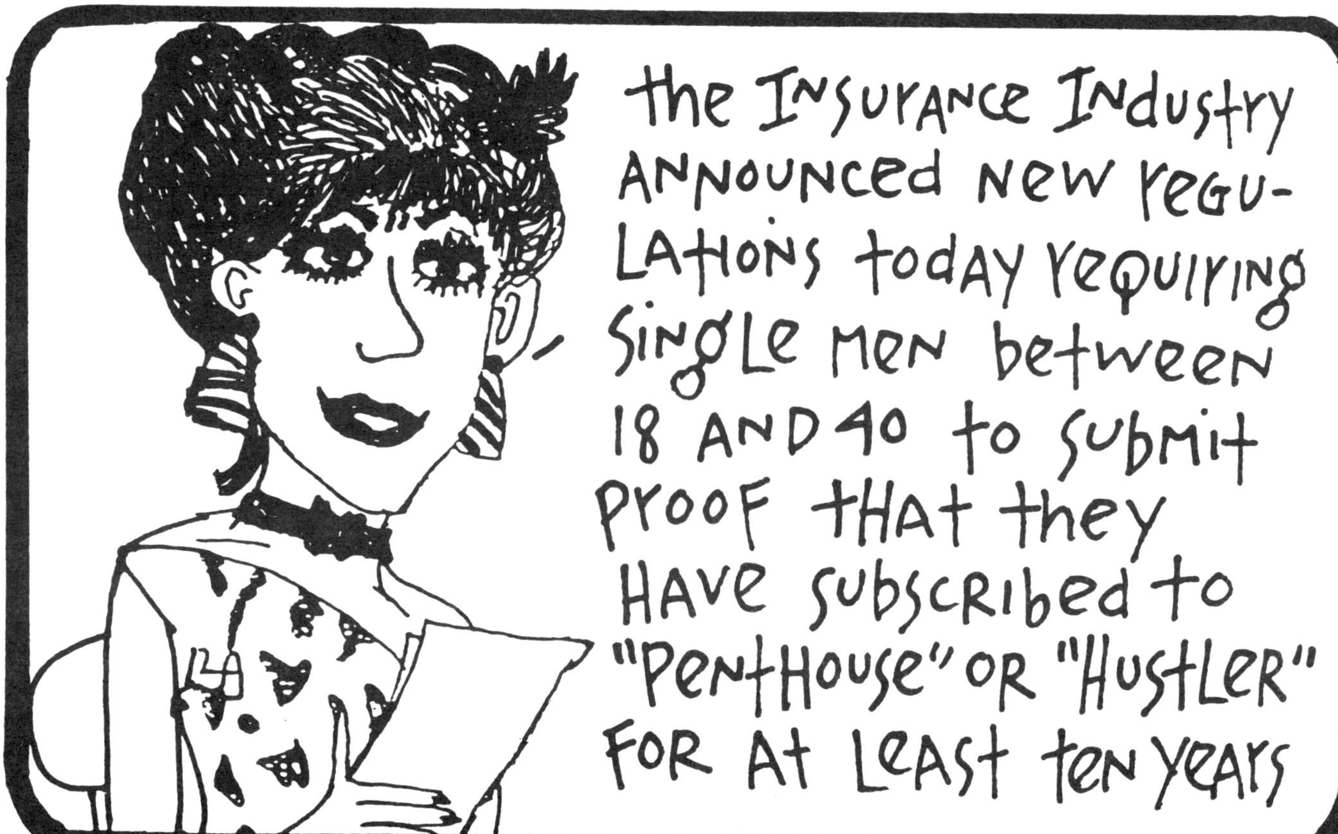
the Insurance Industry announced new regulations today requiring single men between 18 and 40 to submit proof that they have subscribed to "Penthouse" or "Hustler" for at least ten years

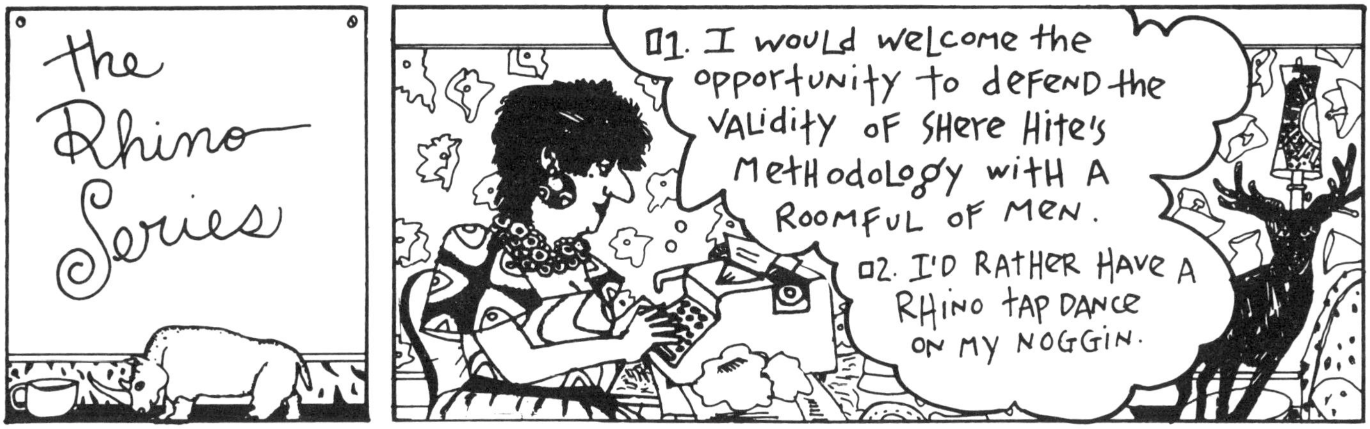
the Rhino Series
□1. I would welcome the opportunity to defend the validity of Shere Hite's methodology with a roomful of men.
□2. I'd rather have a rhino tap dance on my noggin.

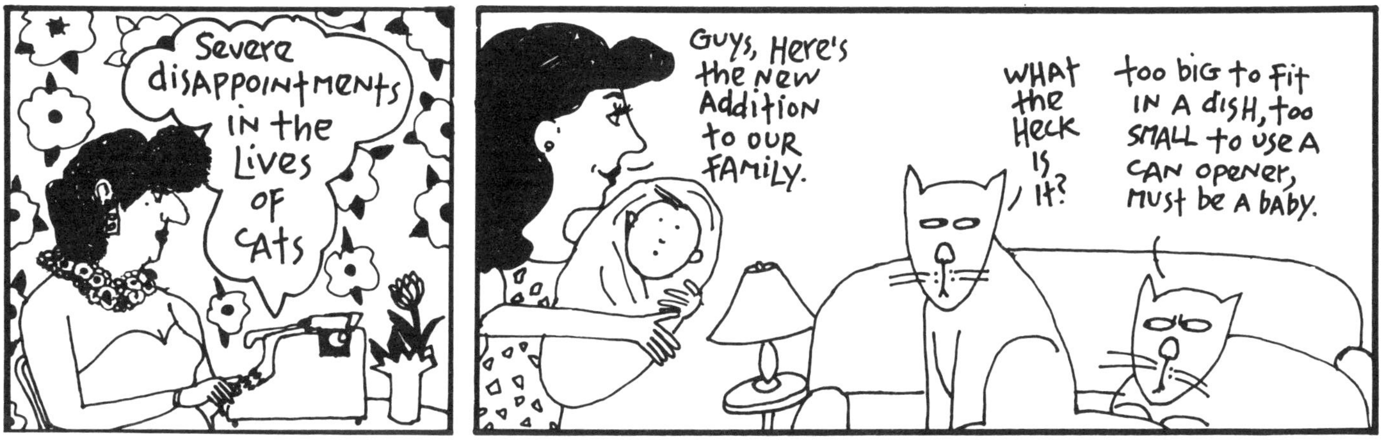
Severe disappointments in the lives of cats
Guys, here's the new addition to our family.
What the heck is it?
too big to fit in a dish, too small to use a can opener, must be a baby.

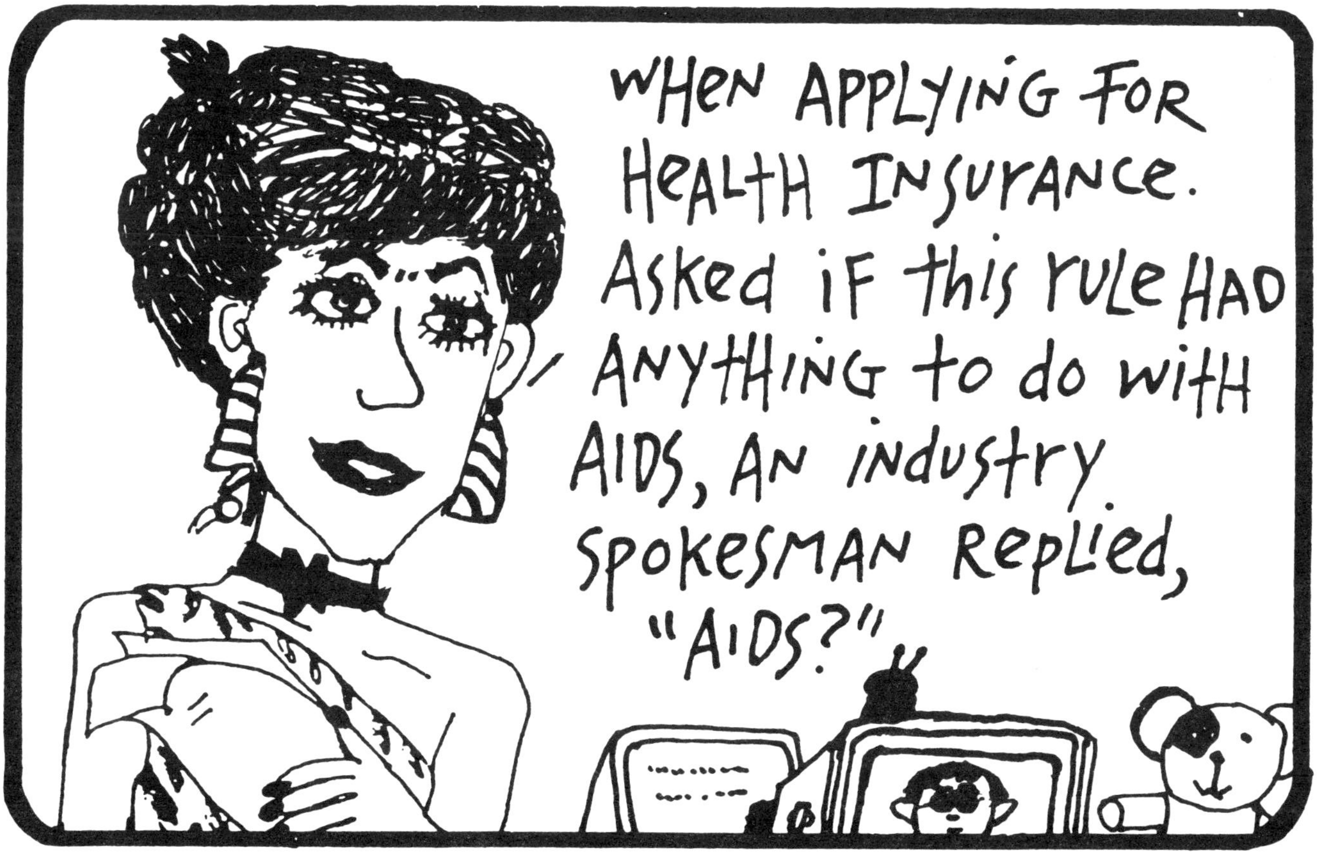
When applying for health insurance. Asked if this rule had anything to do with AIDS, an industry spokesman replied, "AIDS?"

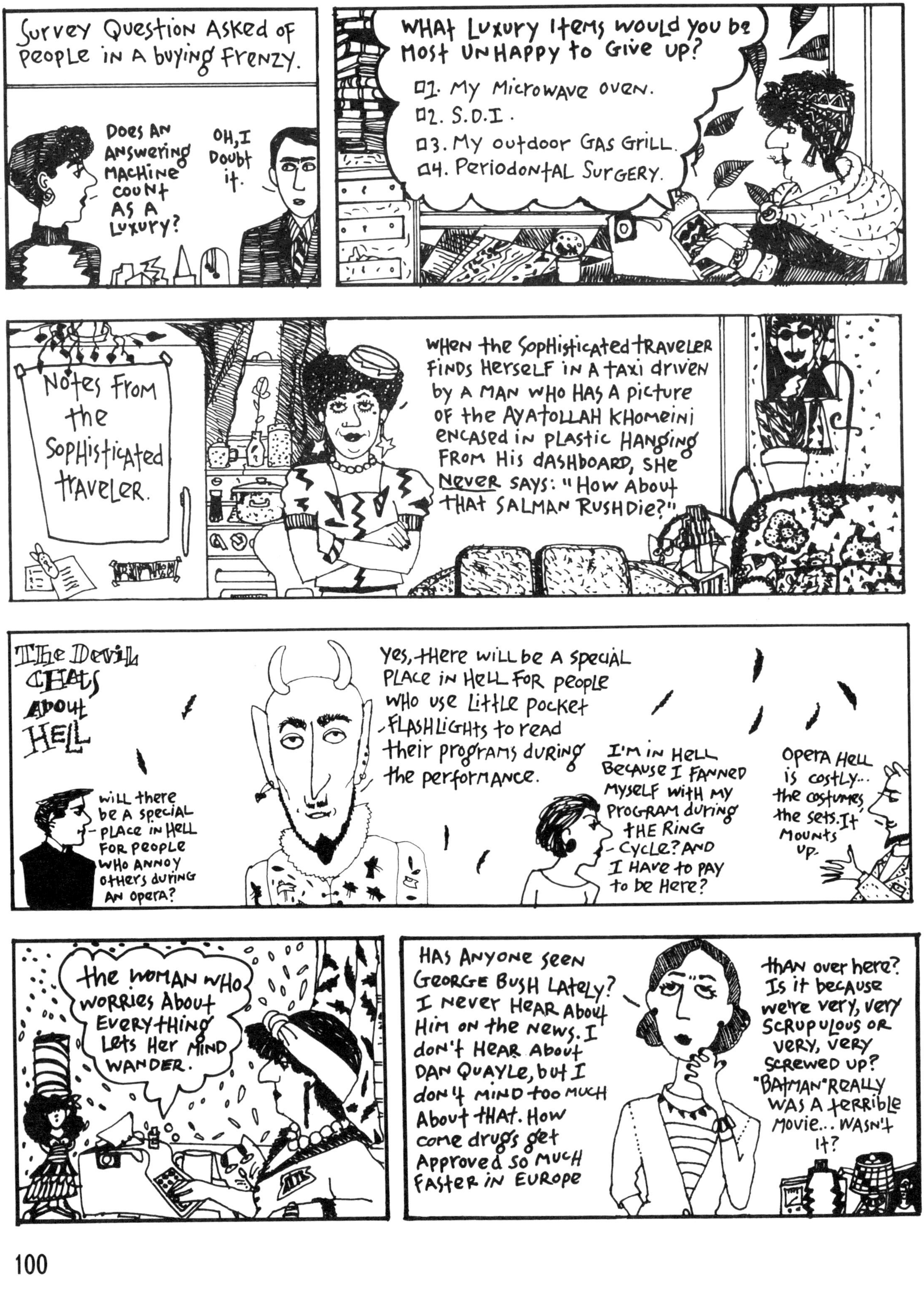
Survey Question Asked of people in a buying Frenzy.
Does an Answering Machine count as a Luxury?
Oh, I Doubt it.
What Luxury Items would you be Most unhappy to Give up?
□1. My Microwave oven.
□2. S.D.I.
□3. My outdoor Gas Grill.
□4. Periodontal Surgery.
Notes from the Sophisticated traveler.
When the Sophisticated traveler finds herself in a taxi driven by a man who has a picture of the Ayatollah Khomeini encased in plastic hanging from his dashboard, she Never says: "How About that Salman Rushdie?"
The Devil Chats About Hell
Will there be a special place in Hell for people who annoy others during an opera?
Yes, there will be a special place in Hell for people who use little pocket flashlights to read their programs during the performance.
I'm in Hell because I fanned myself with my program during the Ring Cycle? And I have to pay to be here?
Opera Hell is costly... the costumes, the sets. It mounts up.
The woman who worries about everything lets her mind wander.
Has anyone seen George Bush lately? I never hear about him on the news. I don't hear about Dan Quayle, but I don't mind too much about that. How come drugs get approved so much faster in Europe than over here? Is it because we're very, very scrupulous or very, very screwed up? "Batman" really was a terrible movie... wasn't it?

AIRPLANES & TAXIS

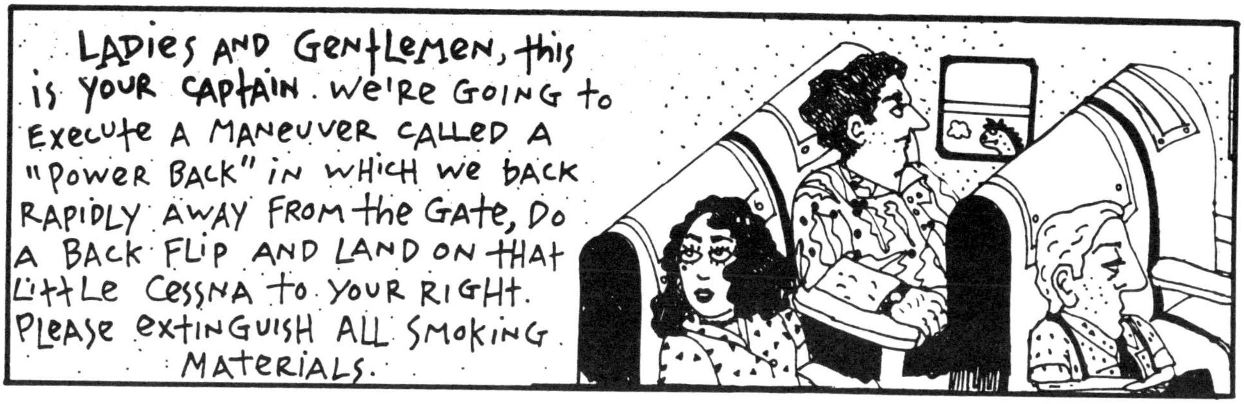
LADIES AND GENTLEMEN, this is YOUR CAPTAIN. WE'RE GOING to EXECUTE A MANEUVER CALLED A "POWER BACK" IN WHICH WE BACK RAPIDLY AWAY FROM the GATE, DO A BACK FLIP AND LAND ON THAT LITTLE CESSNA to YOUR RIGHT. PLEASE EXTINGUISH ALL SMOKING MATERIALS.

If I haven't been on a plane for a long time I forget how much I hate it. The only pleasant flight I ever had was when I sat next to a man who had been a pilot and he kept up a reassuring commentary throughout the trip. He reduced the terrifying sounds and dips of the plane to the ordinary. I had the illusion that I understood flight and it wouldn't hurt me. I can't remember a word he said when I'm actually on a plane. Whenever I come back from a trip, I purge myself by writing a cartoon about air travel.

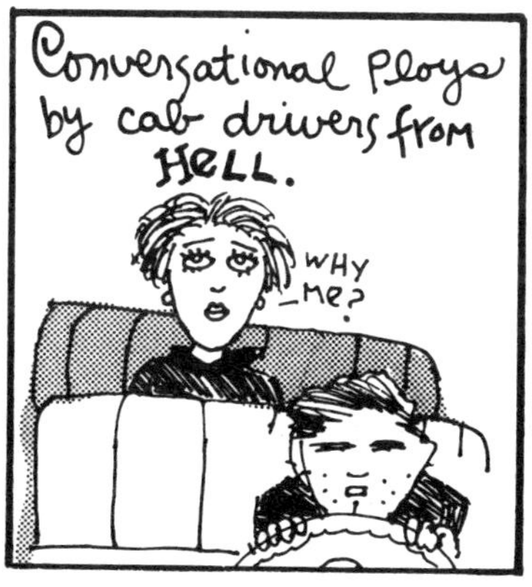
Conversational Ploys by cab drivers from HELL.
WHY ME?

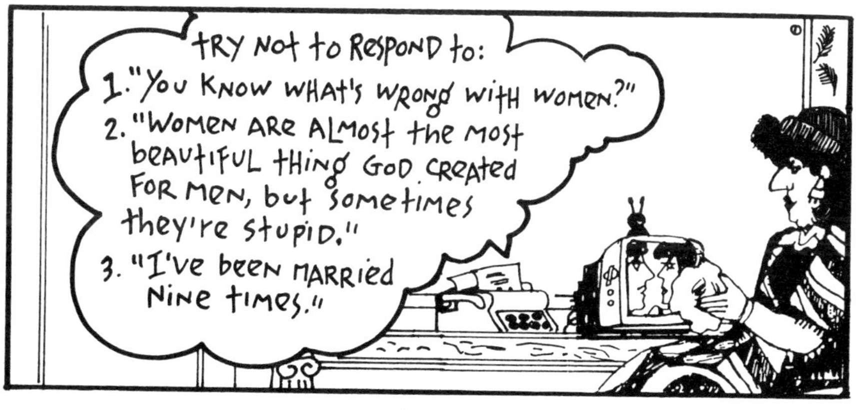
TRY NOT to RESPOND to:
1. "YOU KNOW WHAT'S WRONG WITH WOMEN?"
2. "WOMEN ARE ALMOST the MOST BEAUTIFUL THING GOD CREATED FOR MEN, but SOMETIMES they're STUPID."
3. "I've been MARRIED NINE TIMES."

Speaking of metal death traps, I have also had some rather unpleasant experiences in taxis chatting with the drivers. The exchange that really scared me was with a driver who weighed about three hundred pounds and who told me, in a voice filled with hate, that there was something funny about women, I asked him to stop the cab and I got out. I was never able to make a cartoon about that ride, but I have about some less intimidating ones. This first cartoon is verbatim. I was taking notes during the conversation.

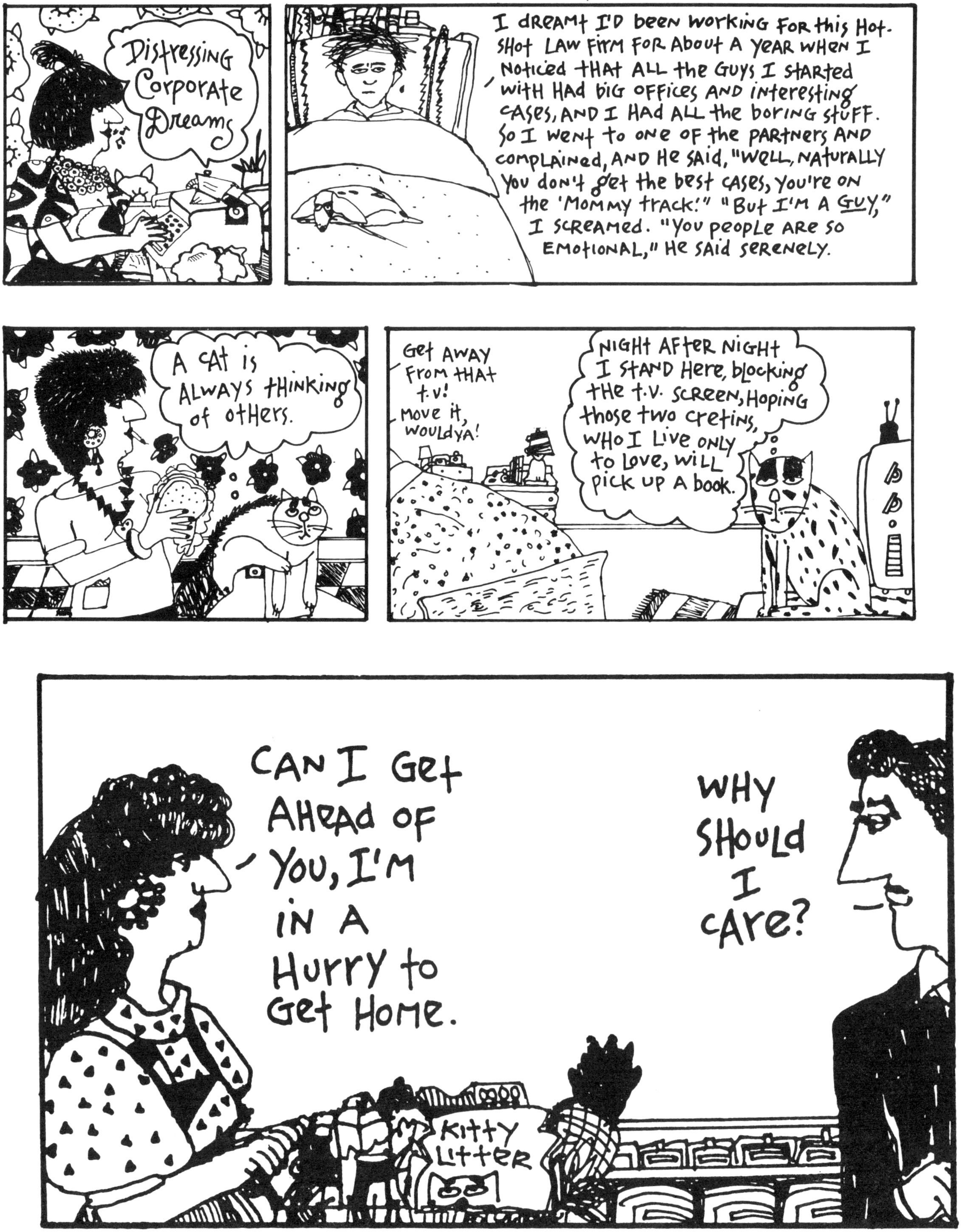
Distressing Corporate Dreams
I dreamt I'd been working for this Hot-shot law firm for about a year when I noticed that all the guys I started with had big offices and interesting cases, and I had all the boring stuff. So I went to one of the partners and complained, and he said, "Well, naturally you don't get the best cases, you're on the 'Mommy track.'" "But I'm a GUY," I screamed. "You people are so emotional," he said serenely.
A cat is always thinking of others.
Get away from that t.v! Move it, wouldya!
Night after night I stand here, blocking the t.v. screen, hoping those two cretins, who I live only to love, will pick up a book.
Can I get ahead of you, I'm in a hurry to get home.
Why should I care?
Kitty Litter

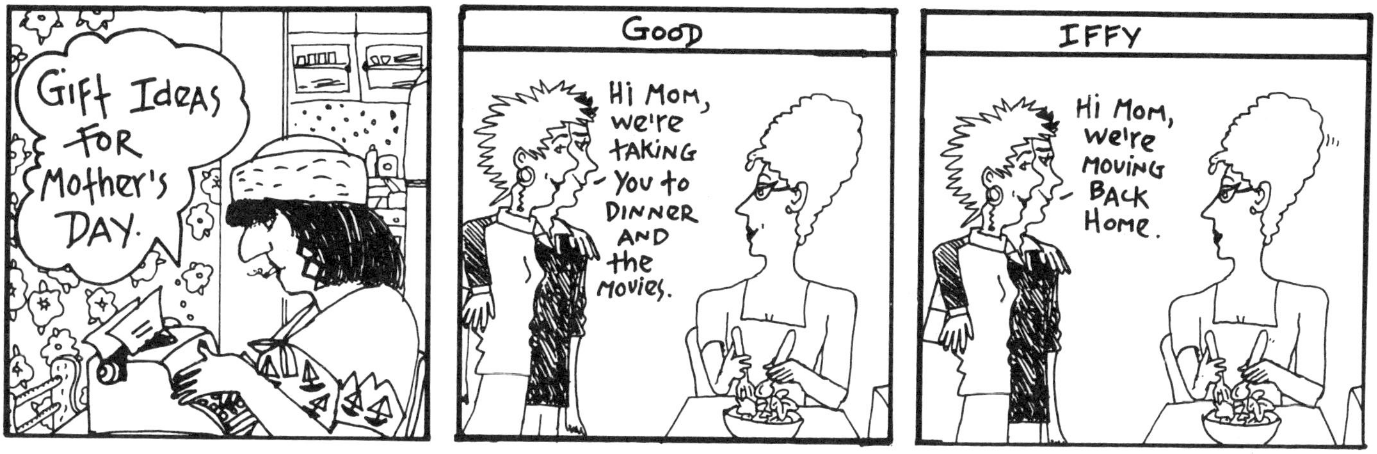
Gift Ideas For Mother's Day.
Good
Hi Mom, we're taking you to Dinner and the Movies.
Iffy
Hi Mom, we're Moving Back Home.

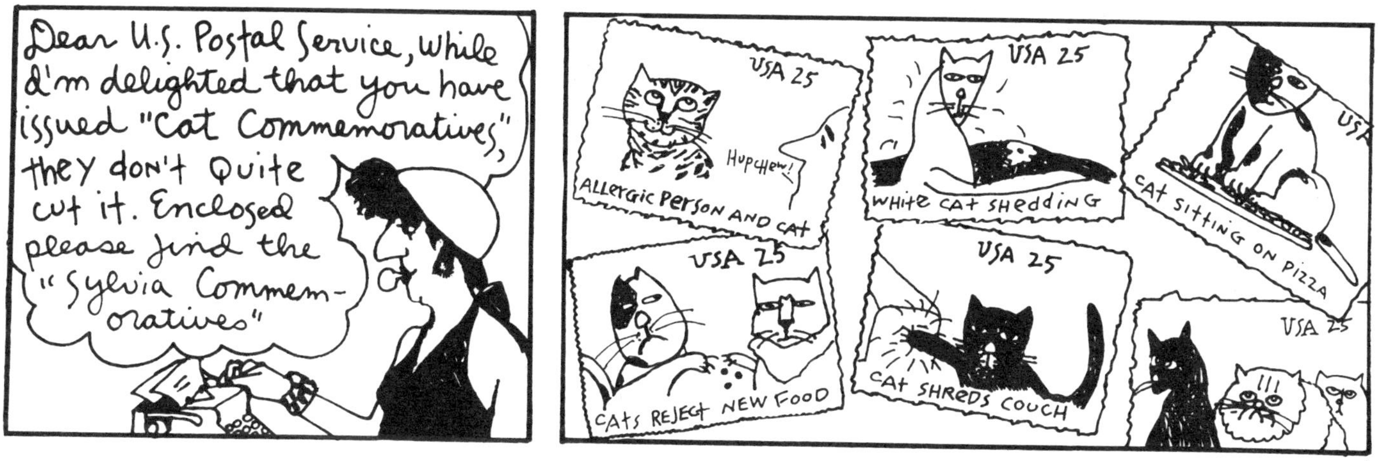
Dear U.S. Postal Service, while I'm delighted that you have issued "Cat Commemoratives," they don't quite cut it. Enclosed please find the "Sylvia Commemoratives"
USA 25
Hupchew!
Allergic Person and Cat
USA 25
White Cat Shedding
Cat Sitting on Pizza
USA 25
Cats Reject New Food
USA 25
Cat Shreds Couch
USA 25

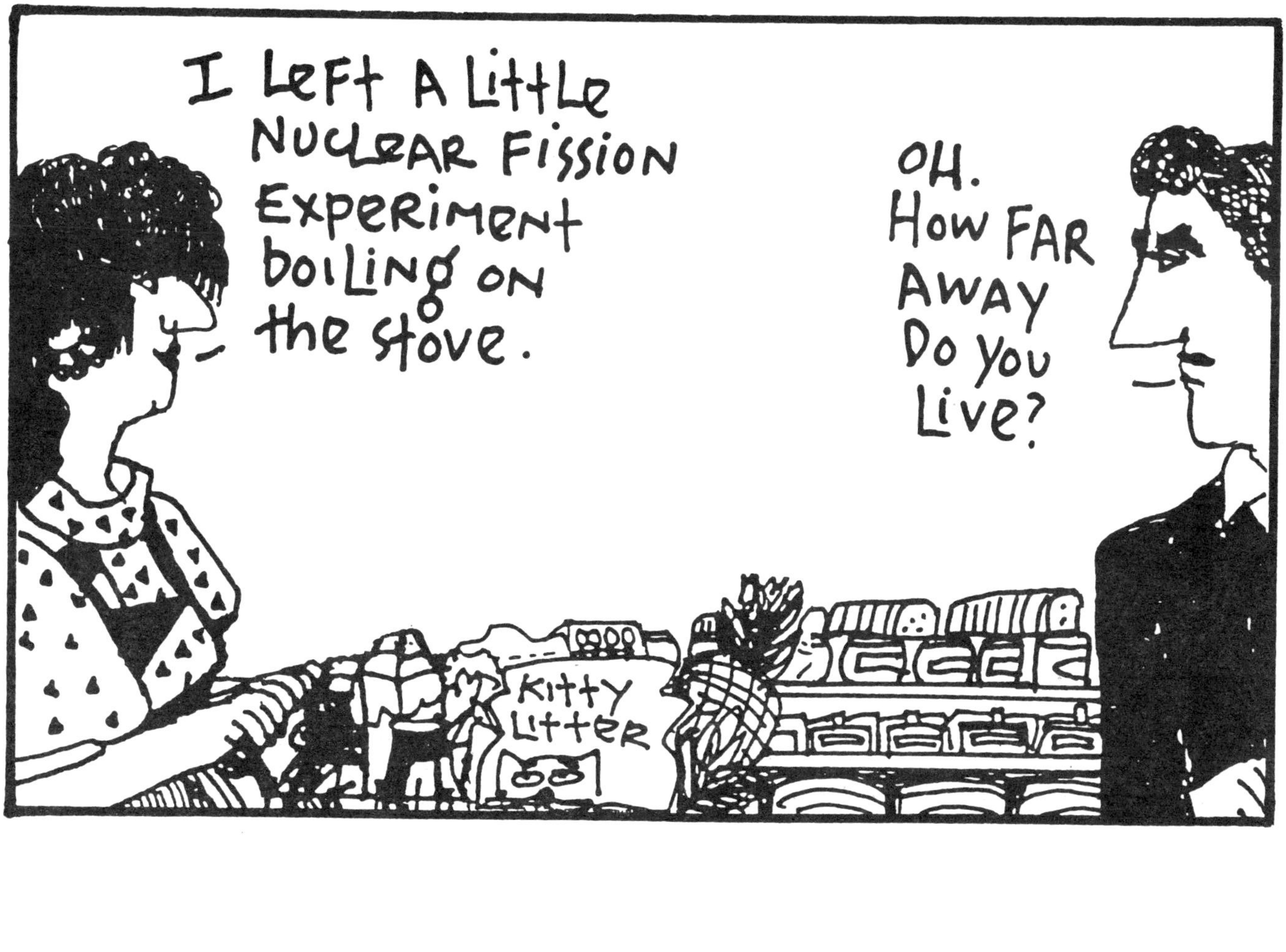
I left a little Nuclear Fission Experiment boiling on the stove.
Oh. How far away do you live?
Kitty Litter

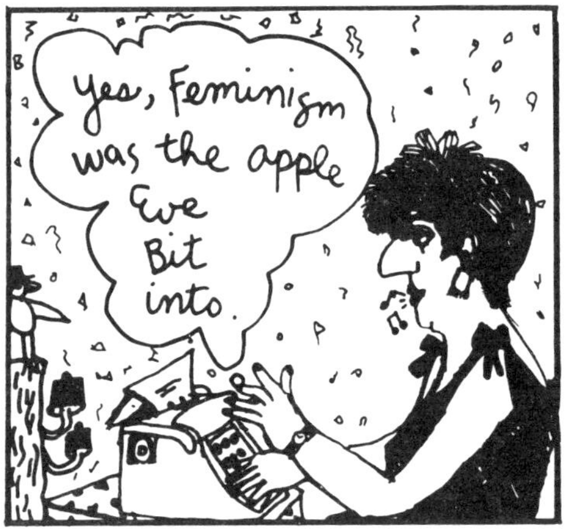
Yes, Feminism was the apple Eve Bit into.

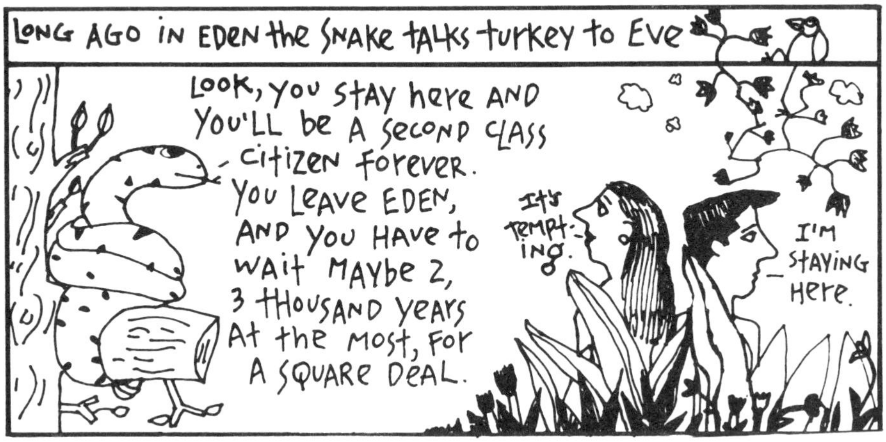
LONG AGO IN EDEN the SNAKE TALKS turkey to Eve
LOOK, you stay here AND YOU'LL be A SECOND CLASS citizen forever. You LEAVE EDEN, AND YOU HAVE to WAIT MAYBE 2, 3 THOUSAND YEARS At the MOST, FOR A SQUARE DEAL.
It's Tempting.
I'M STAYING Here.

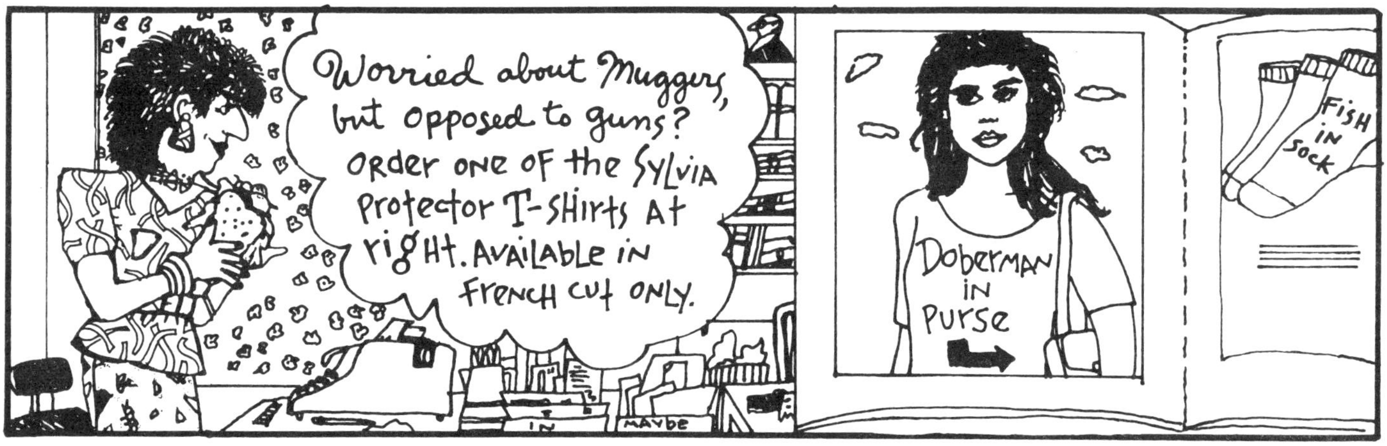
Worried about Muggers, but opposed to guns? Order one of the Sylvia Protector T-shirts at right. Available in French cut only.
IN
MAYBE
Doberman in Purse
Fish in Sock

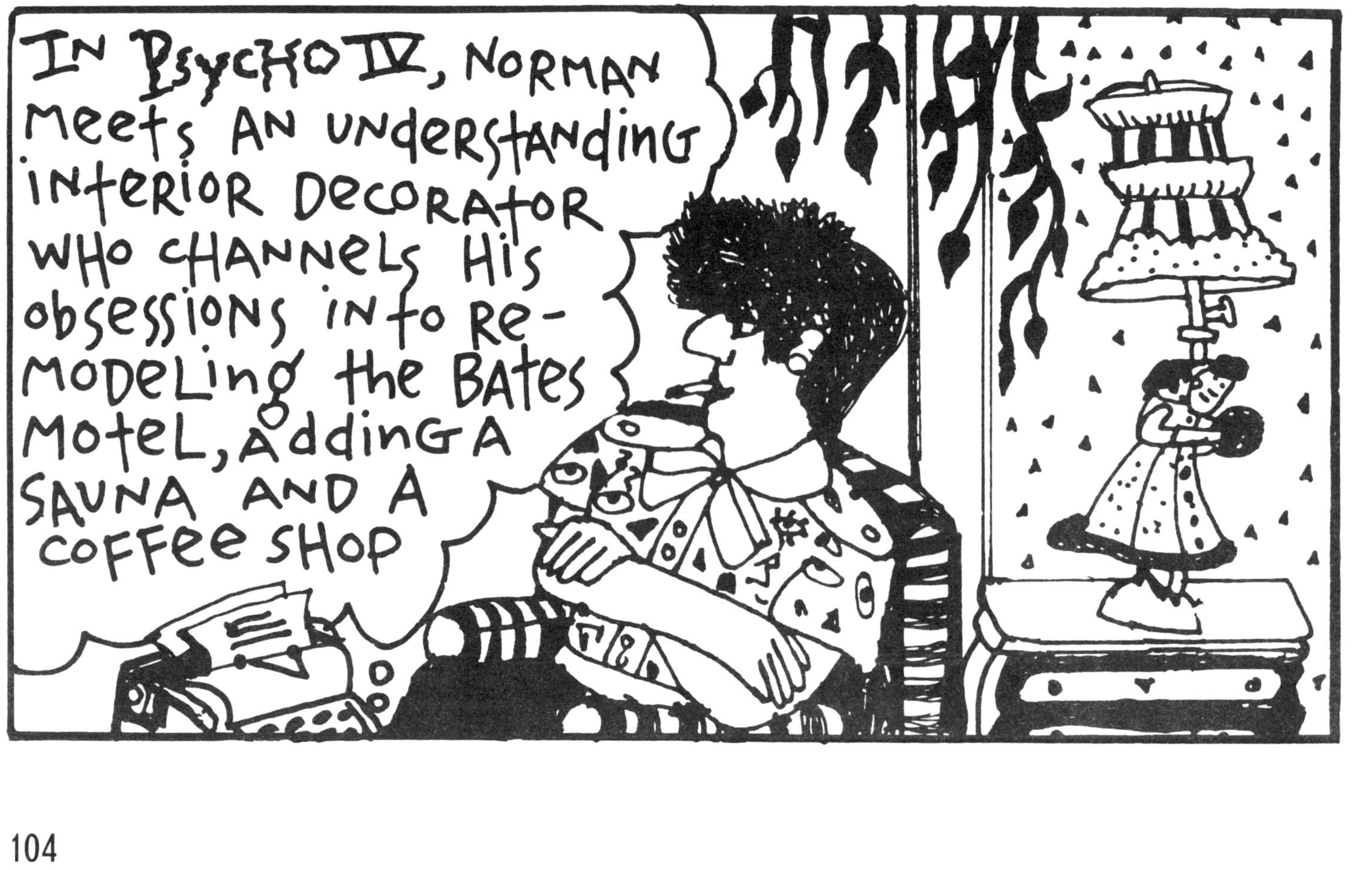
IN PSYCHO IV, NORMAN Meets AN understanding interior DECORATOR WHO CHANNELS HIS obsessions into RE-MODELING the BATES MOTEL, AddING A SAUNA AND A COFFEE SHOP

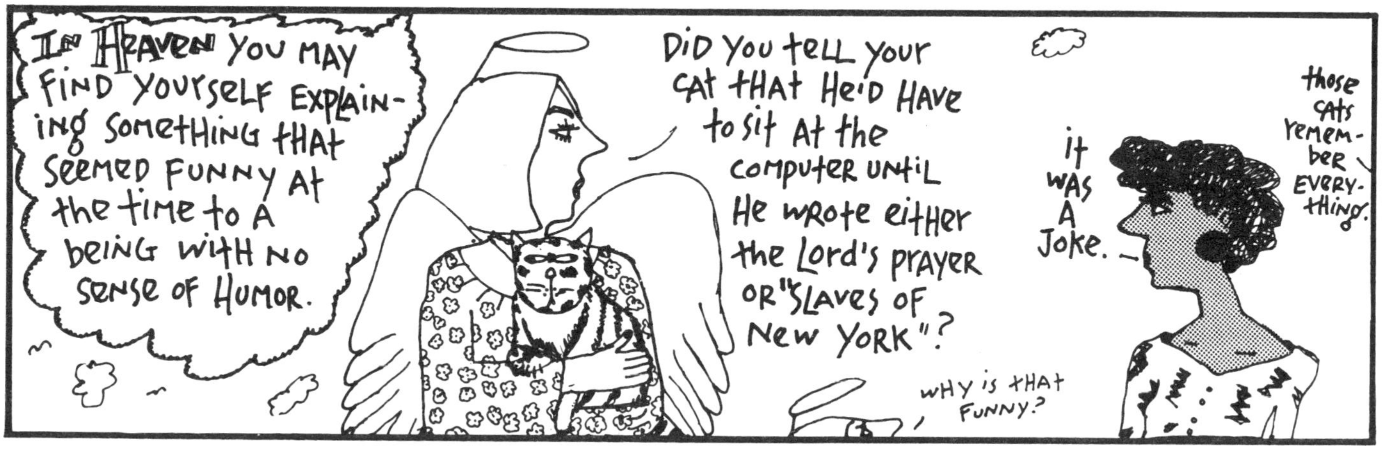
In Heaven you may find yourself explaining something that seemed funny at the time to a being with no sense of humor.
Did you tell your cat that He'd have to sit at the computer until He wrote either the Lord's prayer or "Slaves of New York"?
it was a Joke.
those cats remember everything.
why is that funny?

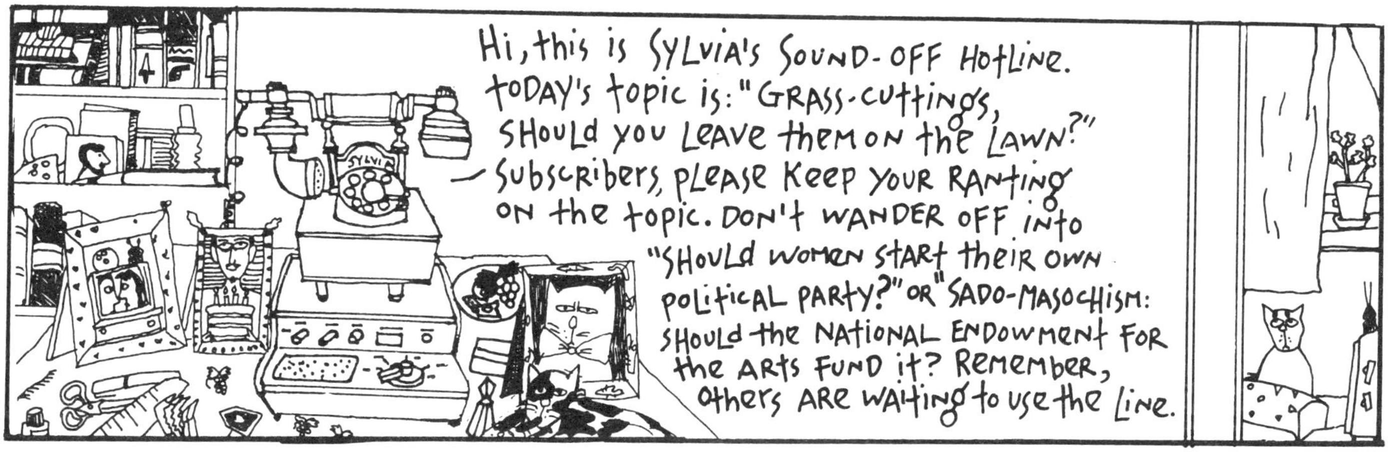
Hi, this is Sylvia's Sound-off Hotline. today's topic is: "Grass-cuttings, should you leave them on the lawn?" Subscribers, please keep your ranting on the topic. Don't wander off into "Should women start their own political party?" or "Sado-masochism: should the National Endowment for the Arts fund it? Remember, others are waiting to use the line.
SYLVIA

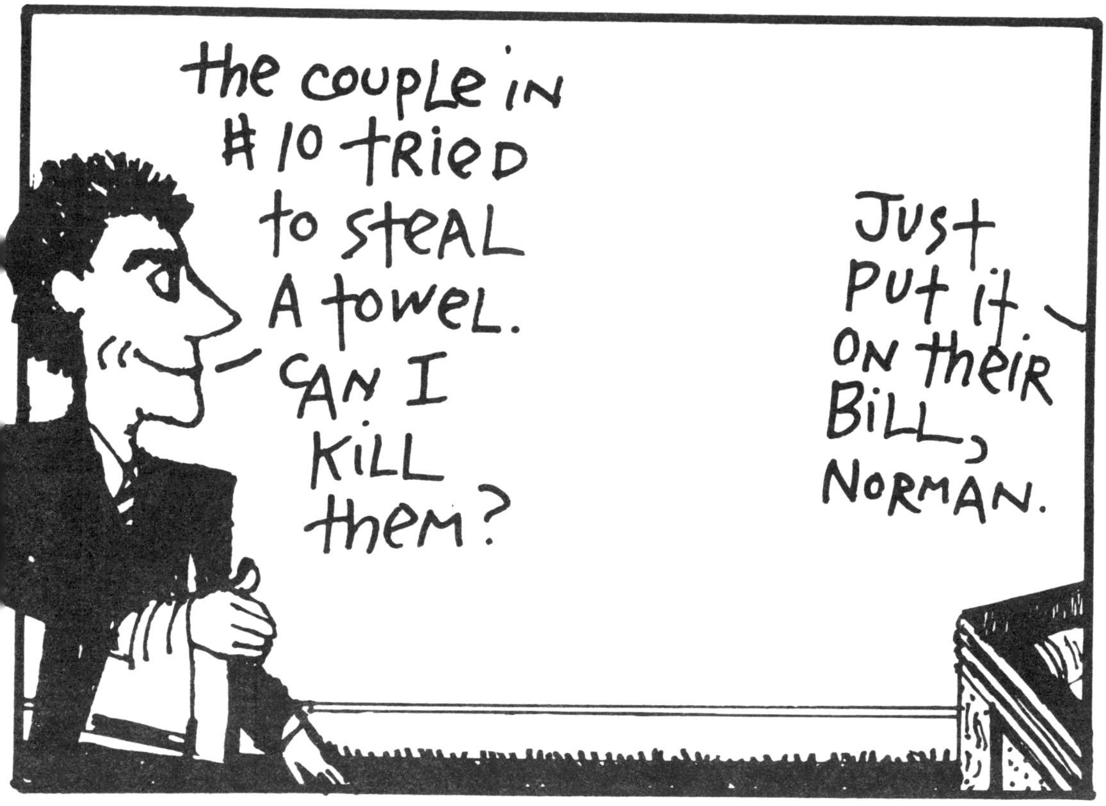
the couple in #10 tried to steal a towel. Can I kill them?
Just put it on their Bill, Norman.

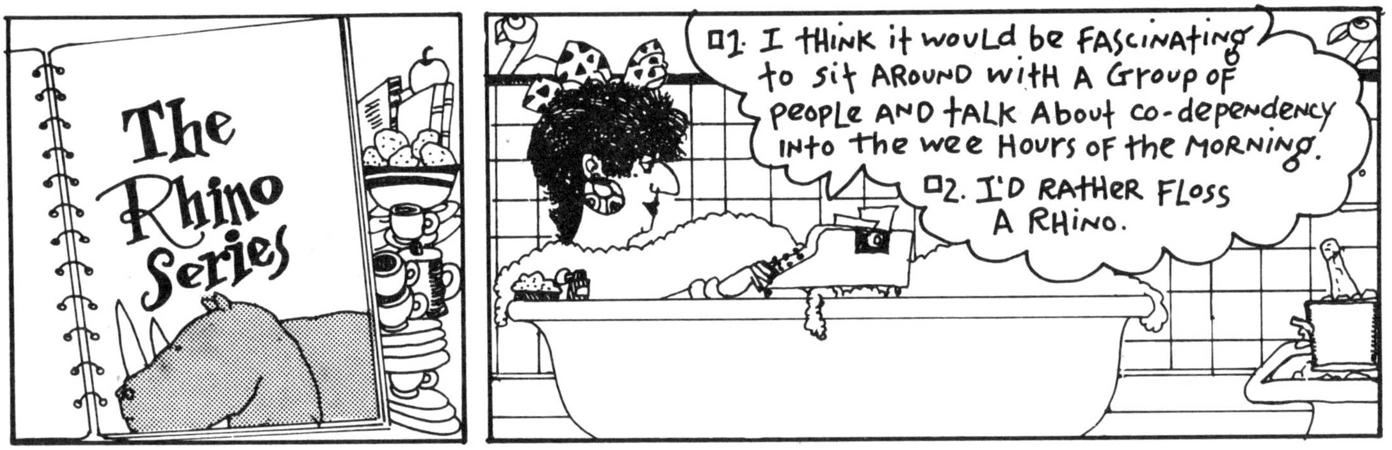
The Rhino Series
□1. I think it would be fascinating to sit around with a group of people and talk about co-dependency into the wee hours of the morning.
□2. I'd rather floss a rhino.

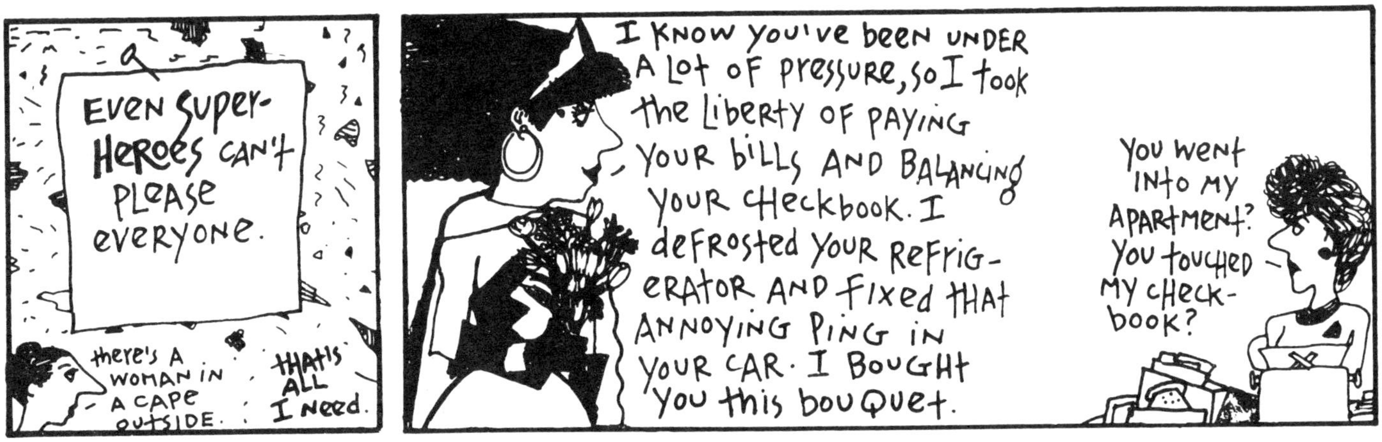
Even super-heroes can't please everyone.
there's a woman in a cape outside.
That's all I need.
I know you've been under a lot of pressure, so I took the liberty of paying your bills and balancing your checkbook. I defrosted your refrigerator and fixed that annoying ping in your car. I bought you this bouquet.
You went into my apartment? You touched my check-book?

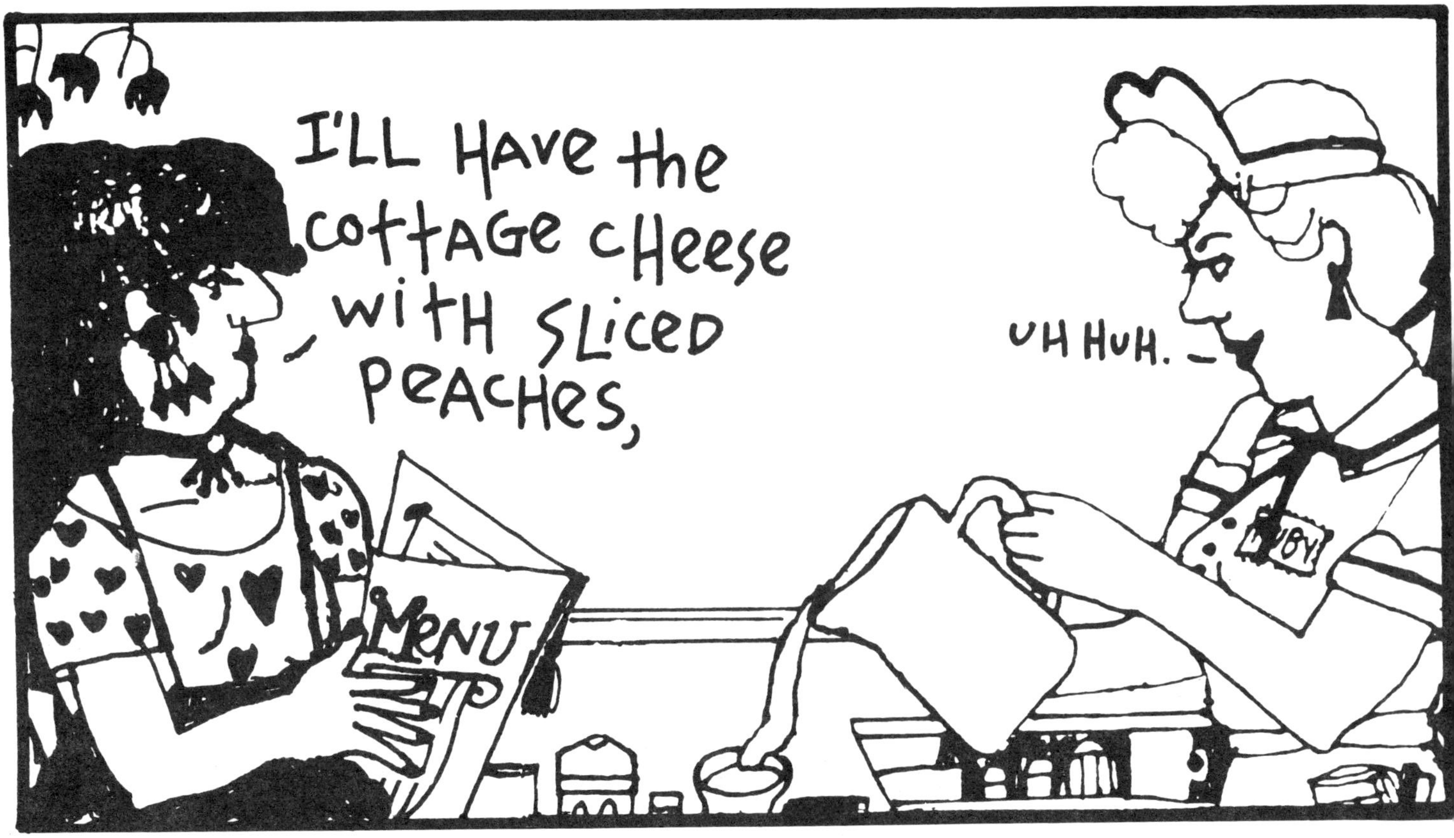
I'll have the cottage cheese with sliced peaches,
uh huh.
Menu

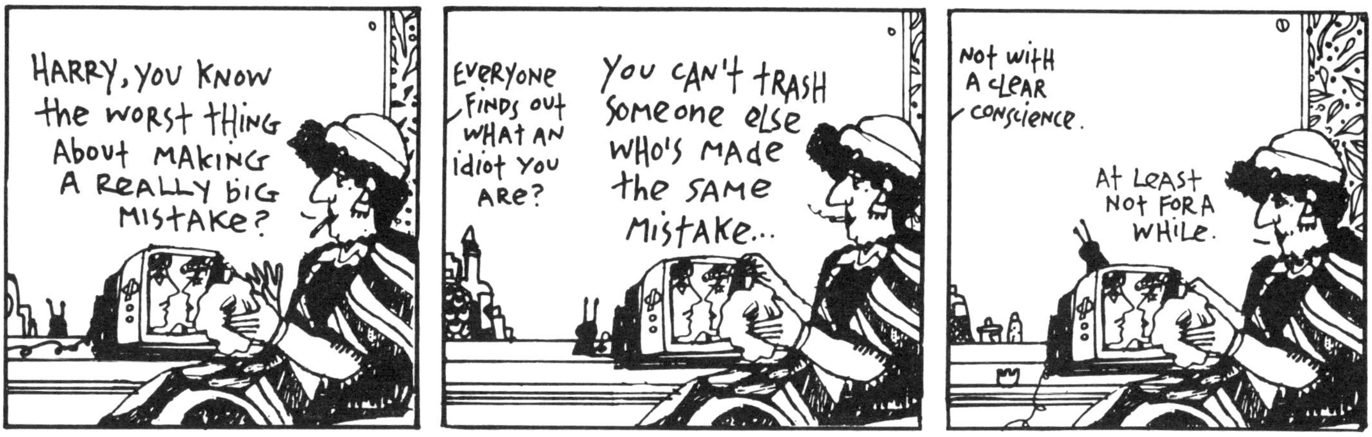
HARRY, YOU KNOW the WORST THING About MAKING A REALLY BIG MISTAKE?
EVERYONE FINDS OUT WHAT AN idiot YOU ARE?
YOU CAN'T TRASH SOMEONE ELSE WHO'S MADE the SAME MISTAKE...
NOT WITH A CLEAR CONSCIENCE.
At LEAST NOT FOR A WHILE.

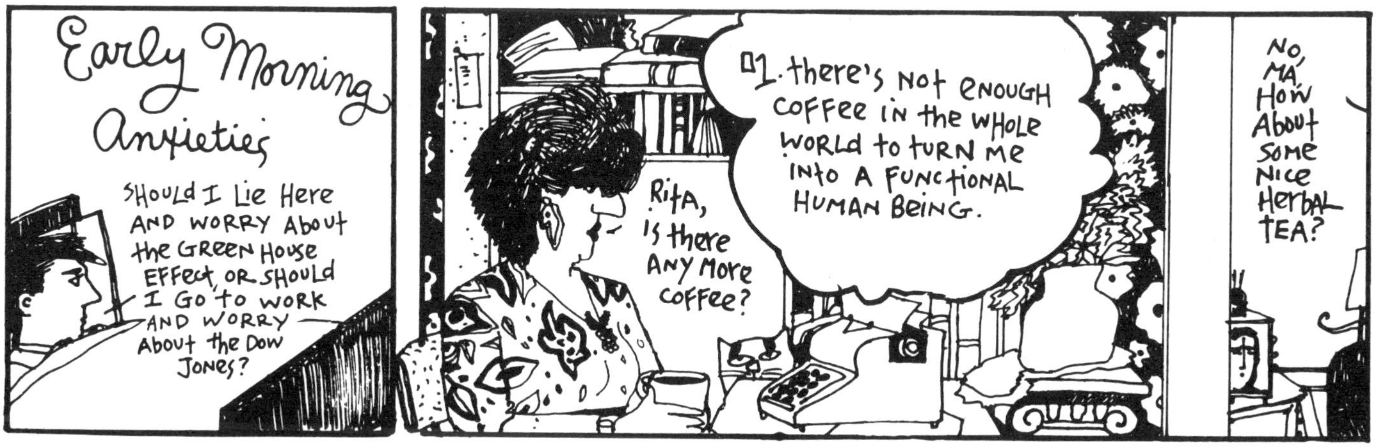
Early Morning Anxieties
SHOULD I LIE HERE AND WORRY About the GREEN HOUSE EFFECT, OR SHOULD I GO TO WORK AND WORRY About the DOW JONES?
RITA, IS there ANY MORE COFFEE?
1. there's NOT ENOUGH COFFEE IN the WHOLE WORLD to TURN ME INTO A FUNCTIONAL HUMAN BEING.
NO, MA. HOW About SOME NICE HERBAL TEA?

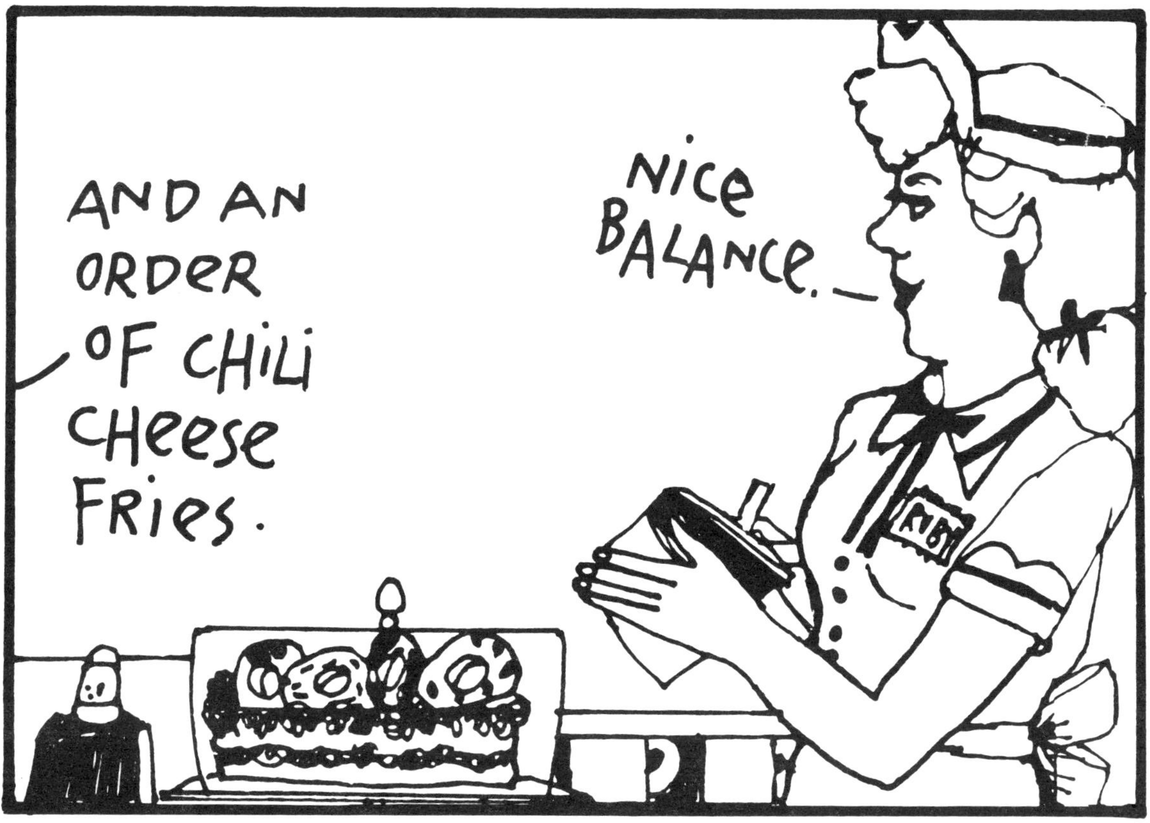
AND AN ORDER OF CHILI CHEESE FRIES.
NICE BALANCE.

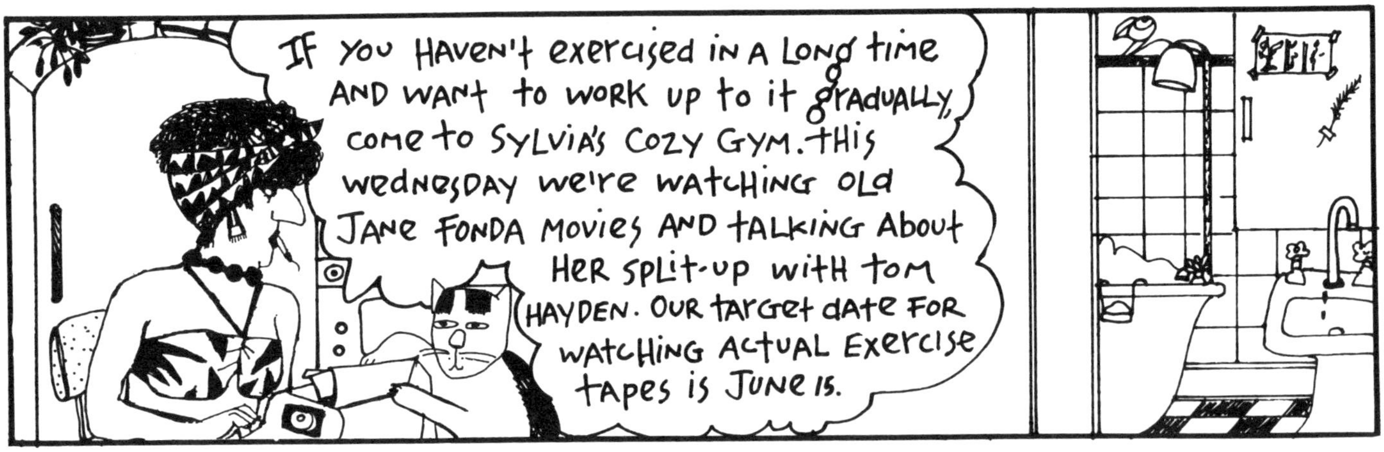
IF YOU HAVEN'T EXERCISED IN A LONG TIME AND WANT TO WORK UP TO IT GRADUALLY, COME TO SYLVIA'S COZY GYM. THIS WEDNESDAY WE'RE WATCHING OLD JANE FONDA MOVIES AND TALKING ABOUT HER SPLIT-UP WITH TOM HAYDEN. OUR TARGET DATE FOR WATCHING ACTUAL EXERCISE TAPES IS JUNE 15.

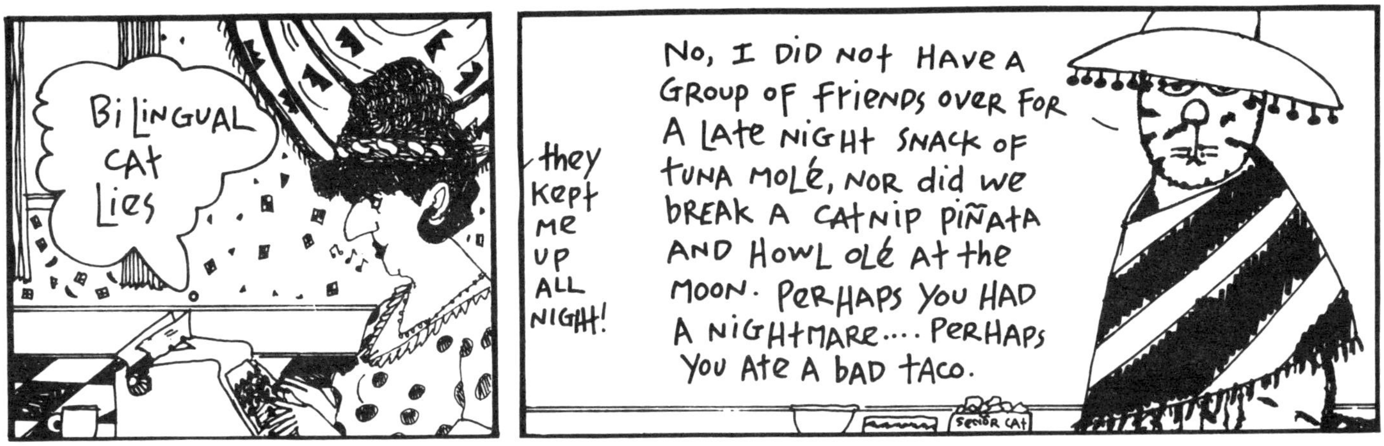
BiLINGUAL CAT LIES
they kept me up all night!
No, I DID NOT HAVE A GROUP OF FRIENDS OVER FOR A LATE NIGHT SNACK OF TUNA MOLÉ, NOR DID WE BREAK A CATNIP PIÑATA AND HOWL OLÉ AT THE MOON. PERHAPS YOU HAD A NIGHTMARE.... PERHAPS YOU ATE A BAD TACO.
SEÑOR CAT

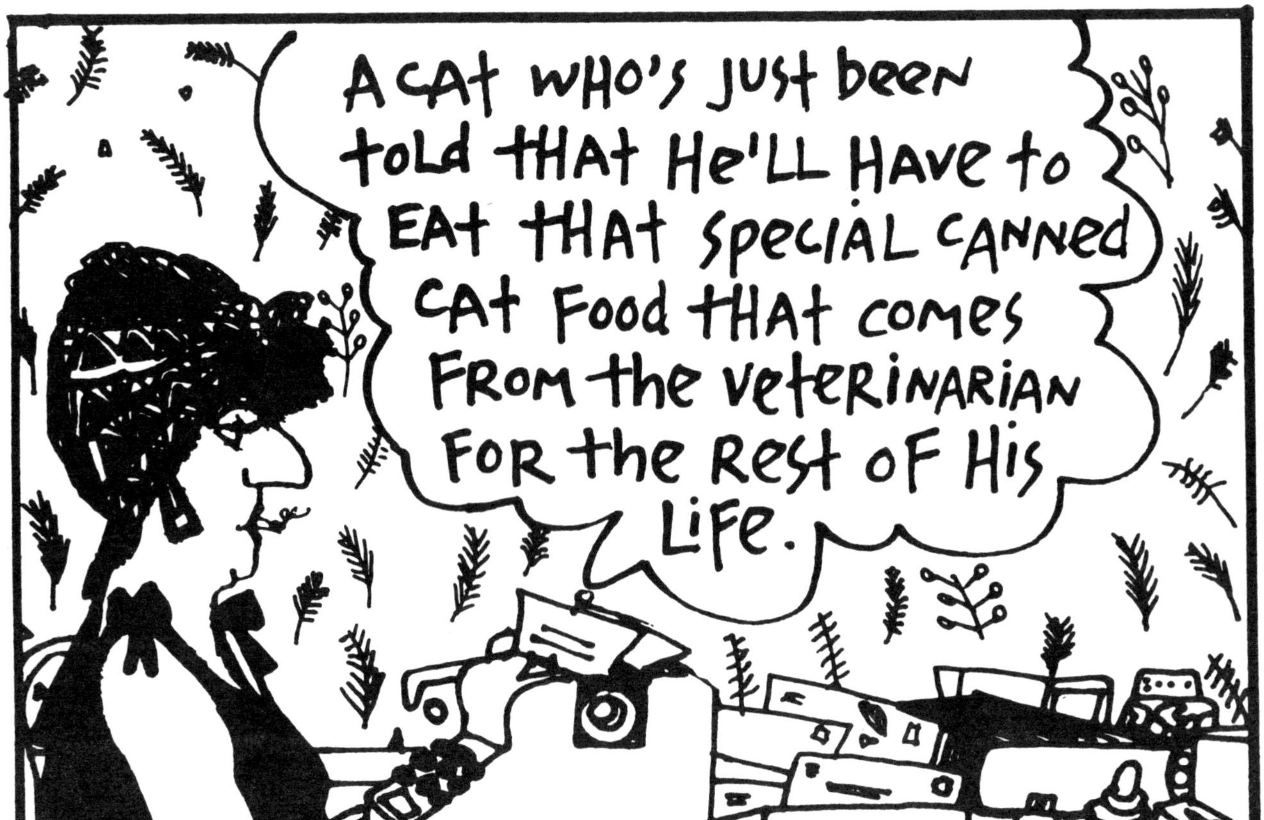
A CAT WHO'S JUST BEEN TOLD THAT HE'LL HAVE TO EAT THAT SPECIAL CANNED CAT FOOD THAT COMES FROM THE VETERINARIAN FOR THE REST OF HIS LIFE.

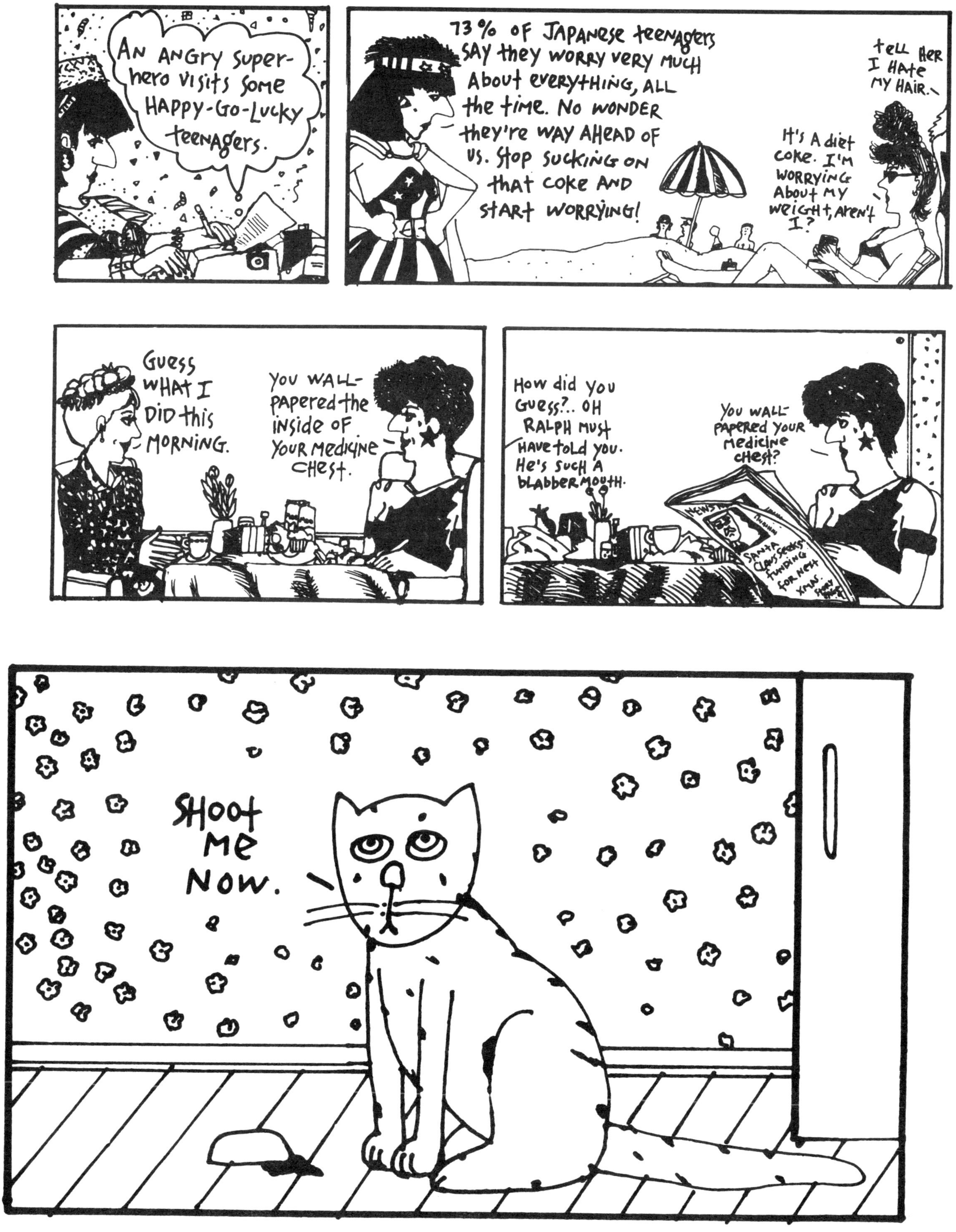
An angry super-hero visits some happy-go-lucky teenagers.
73% of Japanese teenagers say they worry very much about everything, all the time. No wonder they're way ahead of us. Stop sucking on that coke and start worrying!
Tell her I hate my hair.
It's a diet coke. I'm worrying about my weight, aren't I?
Guess what I did this morning.
You wall-papered the inside of your medicine chest.
How did you guess?.. Oh Ralph must have told you. He's such a blabbermouth.
You wall-papered your medicine chest?
SANTA CLAUS SEEKS FUNDING FOR NEXT XMAS
Shoot me now.

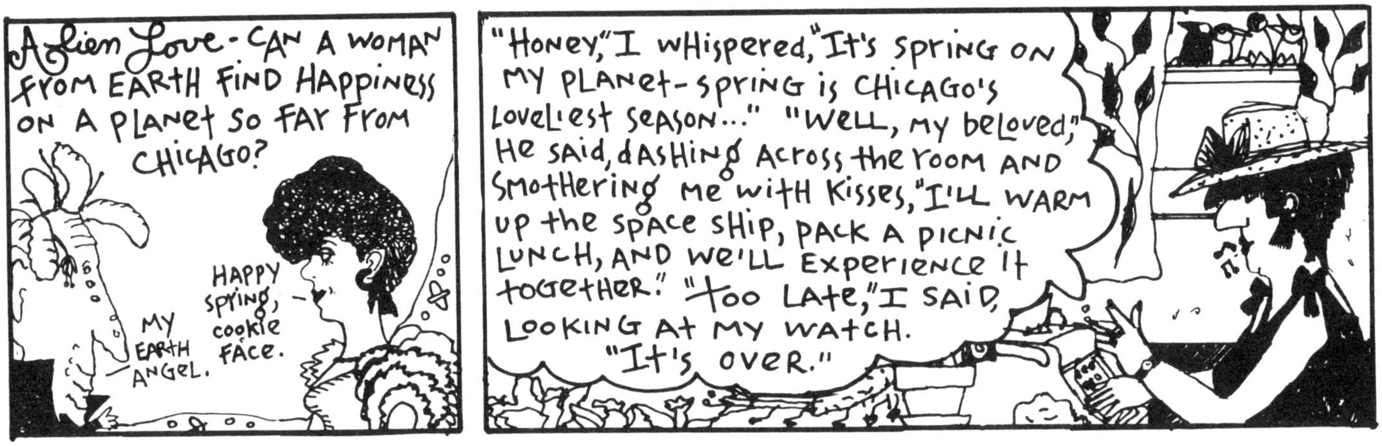
Alien Love - CAN A WOMAN FROM EARTH FIND HAPPINESS ON A PLANET SO FAR FROM CHICAGO?
HAPPY SPRING, COOKIE FACE.
MY EARTH ANGEL.
"Honey," I whispered, "It's spring on my planet - spring is Chicago's loveliest season..." "Well, my beloved," he said, dashing across the room and smothering me with kisses, "I'll warm up the space ship, pack a picnic lunch, and we'll experience it together." "Too late," I said, looking at my watch. "It's over."

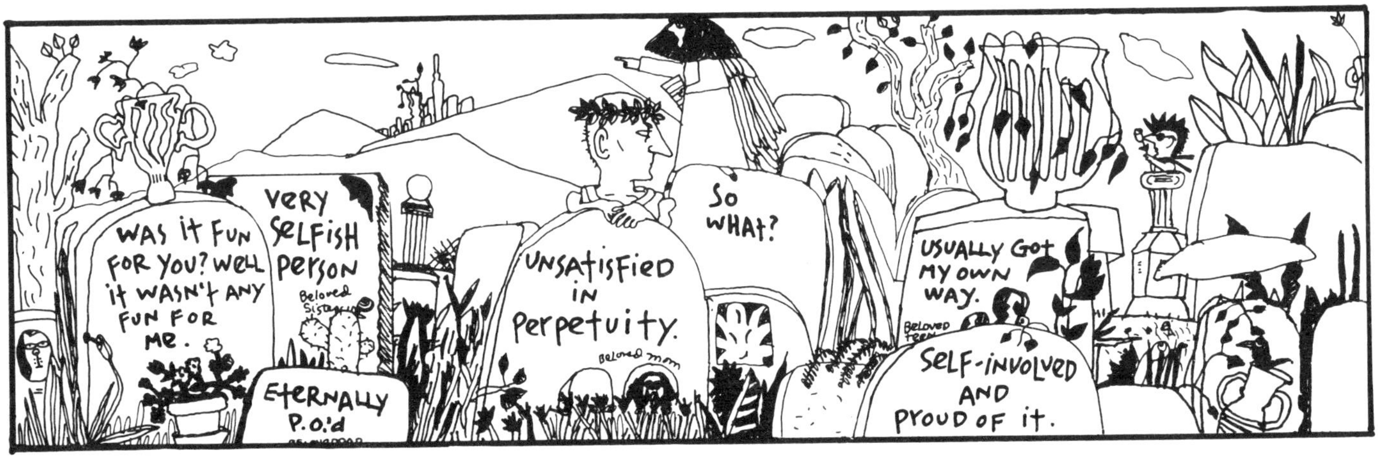
Was it fun for you? Well it wasn't any fun for me.
Very selfish person
Eternally P.O.'d
Unsatisfied in perpetuity.
Beloved Mom
So what?
Usually got my own way.
Self-involved and proud of it.

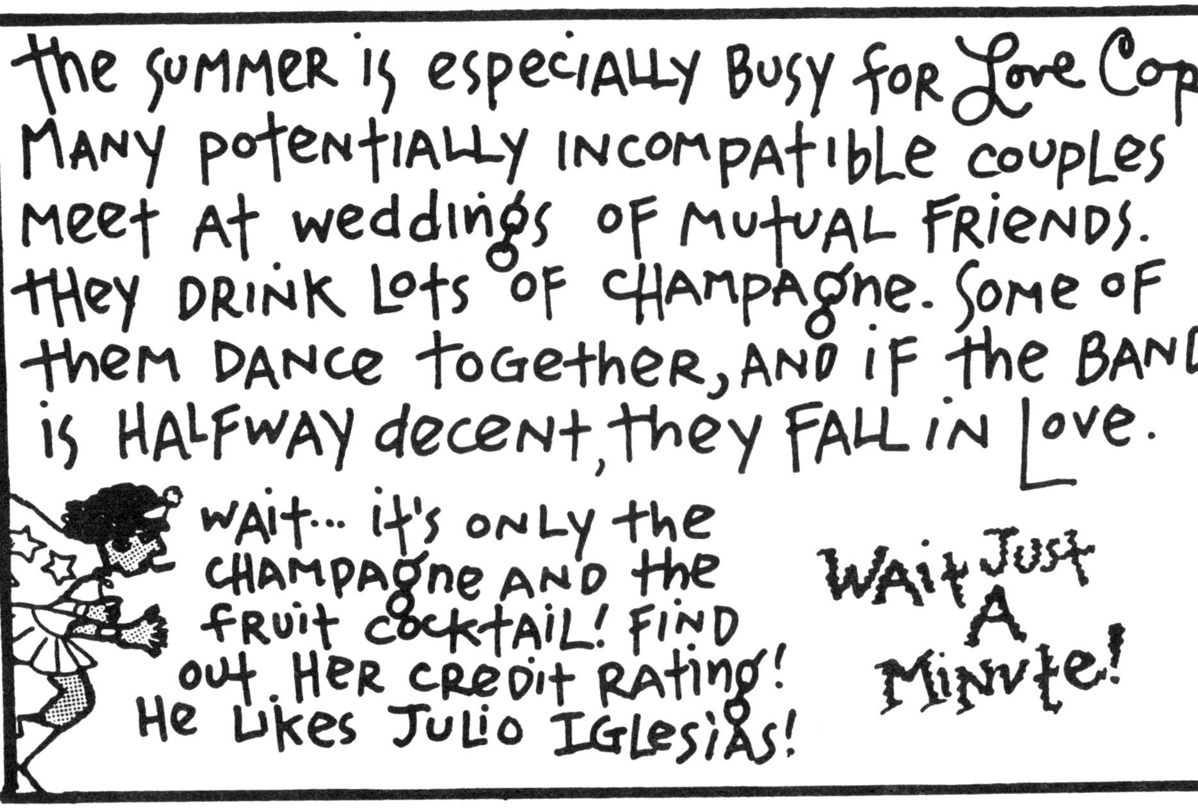
The summer is especially busy for Love Cop. Many potentially incompatible couples meet at weddings of mutual friends. They drink lots of champagne. Some of them dance together, and if the band is halfway decent, they fall in love.
Wait... it's only the champagne and the fruit cocktail! Find out her credit rating! He likes Julio Iglesias!
Wait Just A Minute!

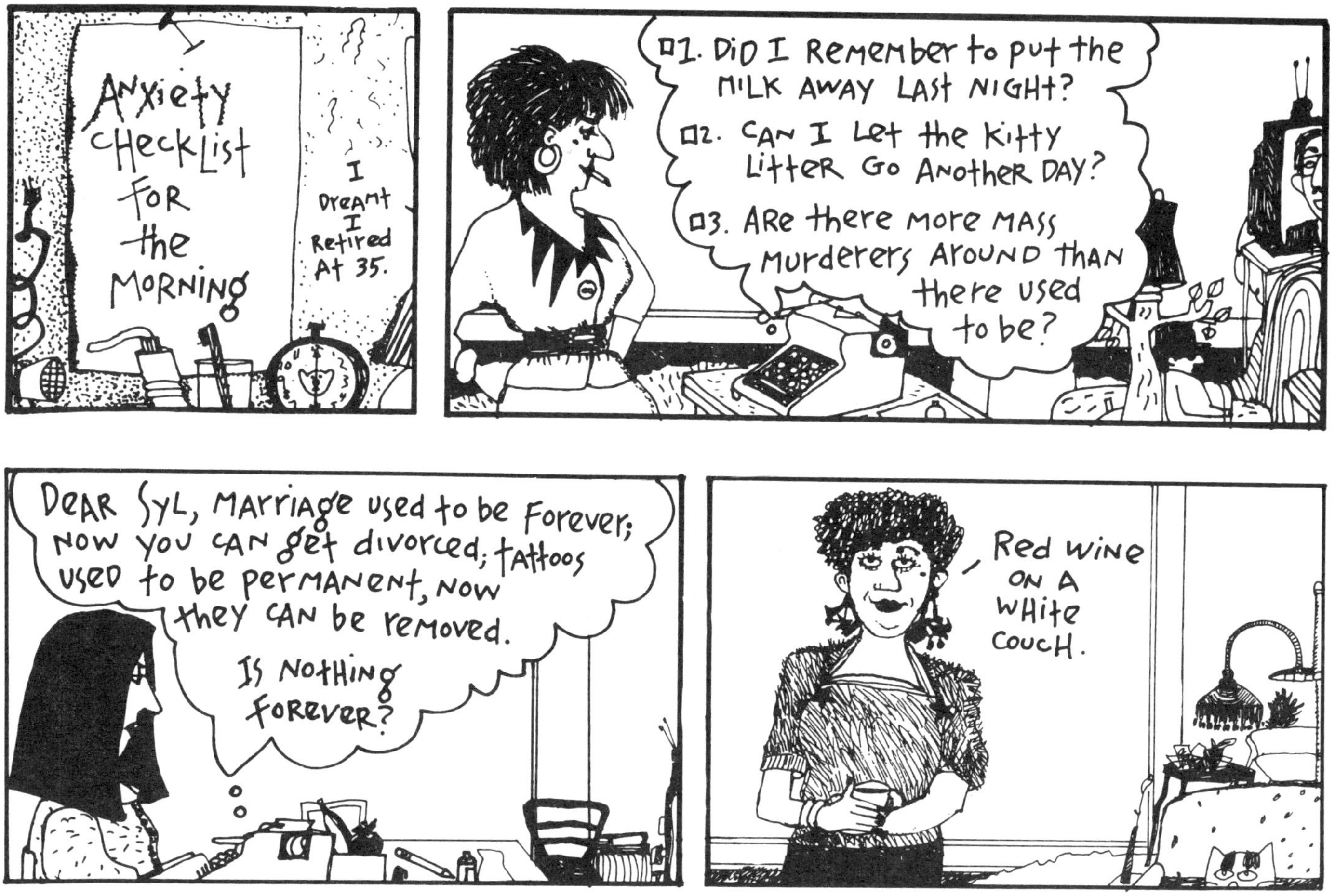
ANXIETY CHECKLIST FOR the MORNING
I DREAMT I RETIRED AT 35.
☐1. DID I REMEMBER to put the MILK AWAY LAST NIGHT?
☐2. CAN I LET the Kitty Litter GO ANOTHER DAY?
☐3. ARE there more MASS MURDERERS AROUND THAN there used to be?
Dear Syl, Marriage used to be Forever; now you can get divorced; tattoos used to be permanent, now they can be removed.
Is Nothing Forever?
Red wine on a white couch.

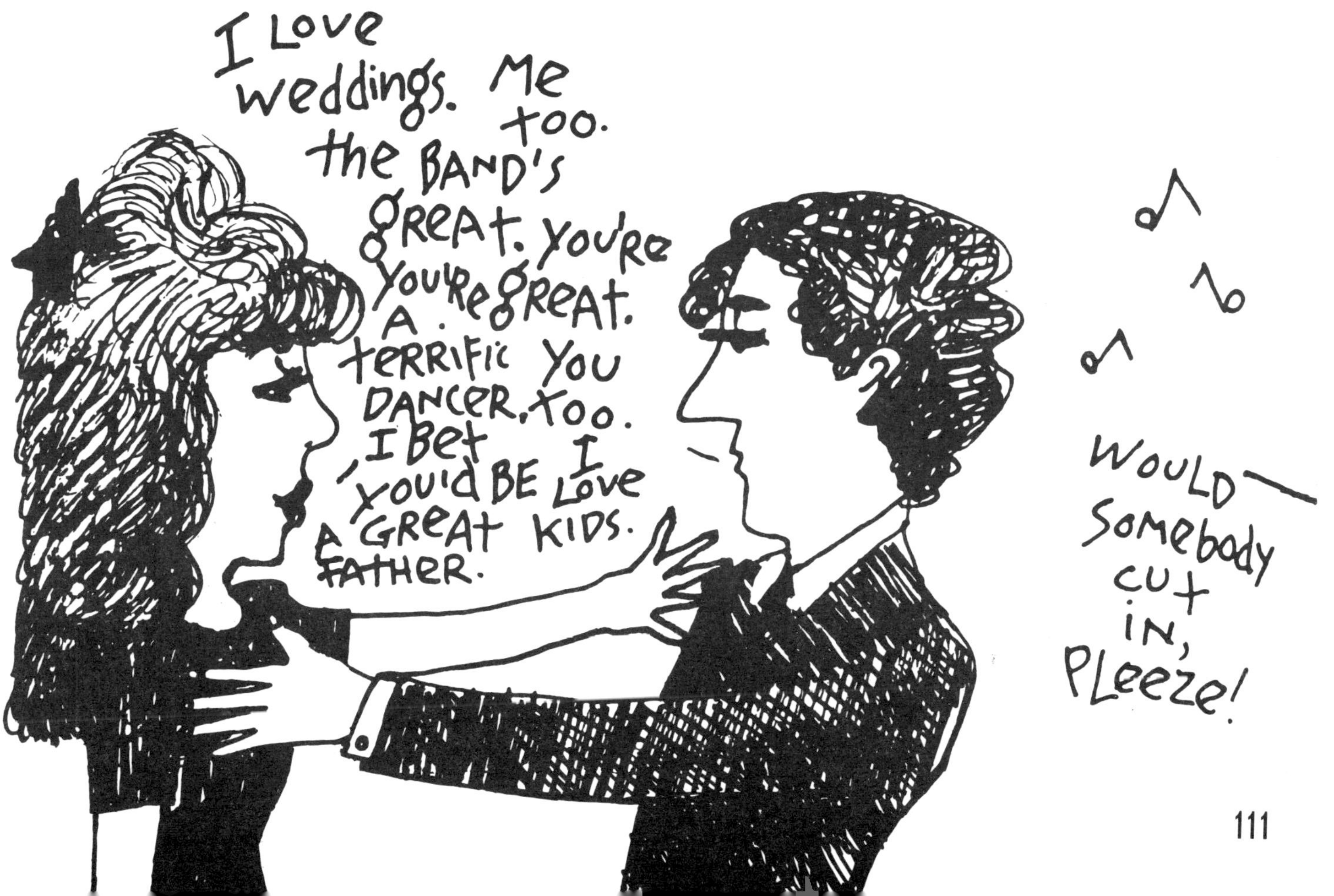
I Love weddings.
Me too.
the BAND's great.
You're great.
You're great.
A terrific DANCER.
You too.
I Bet you'd BE A GREAT FATHER.
I Love KIDS.
WOULD— Somebody cut in, PLEEZE!

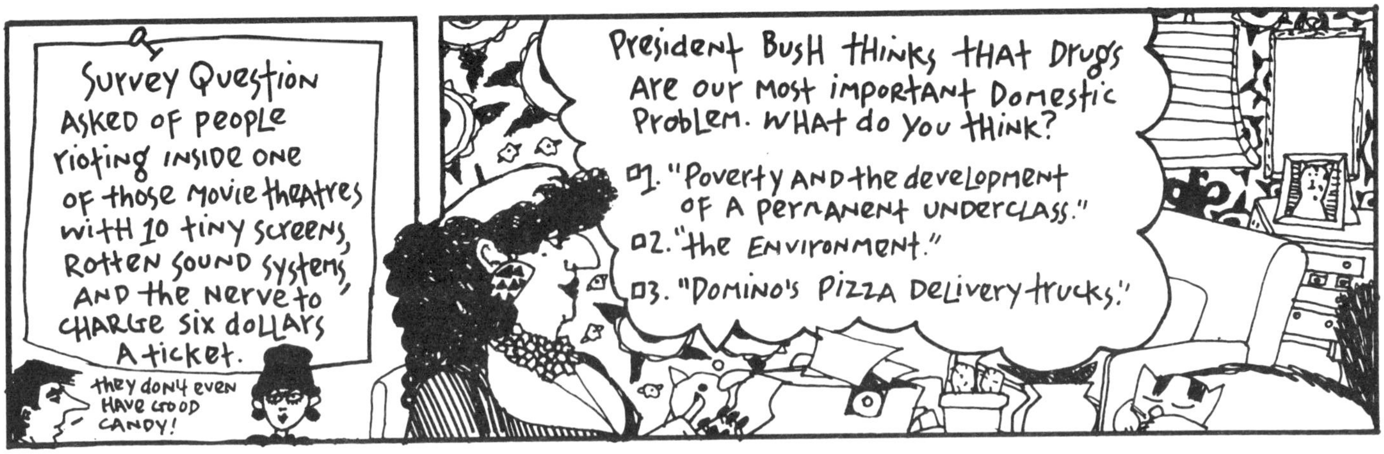
Survey Question Asked of people rioting inside one of those Movie theatres with 10 tiny screens, Rotten sound systems, And the Nerve to charge six dollars A ticket.
they don't even Have Good candy!
President Bush thinks that Drugs Are our Most important Domestic Problem. What do you think?
1. "Poverty and the development of A permanent underclass."
2. "the Environment."
3. "Domino's Pizza Delivery trucks."

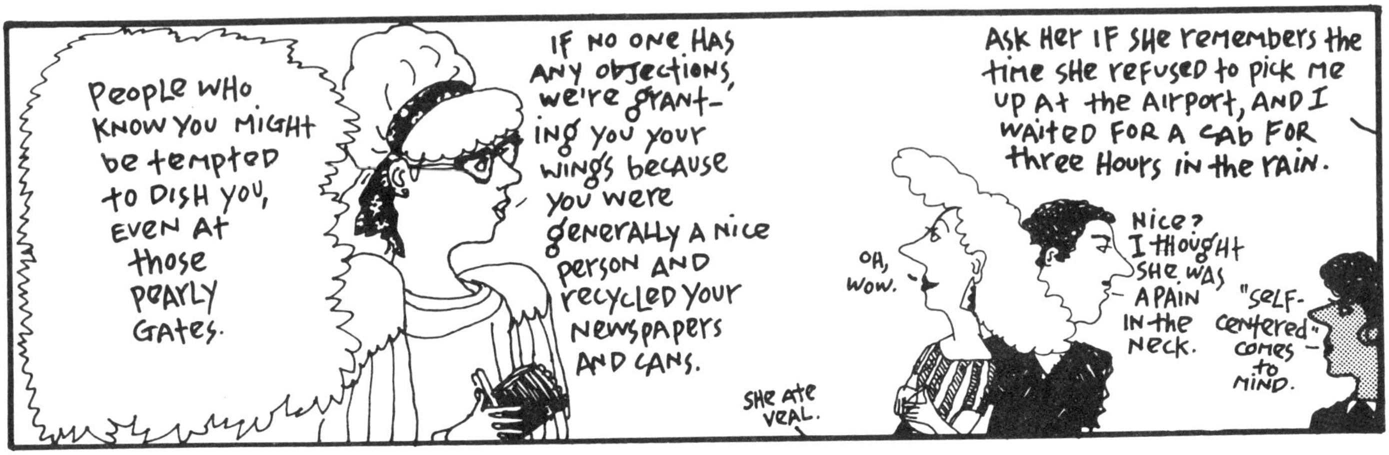
People who know you might be tempted to Dish you, even at those pearly gates.
If no one has any objections, we're granting you your wings because you were generally a nice person and recycled your newspapers and cans.
Ask her if she remembers the time she refused to pick me up at the Airport, and I waited for a cab for three hours in the rain.
Oh, wow.
Nice? I thought she was a pain in the neck.
"Self-centered" comes to mind.
She ate veal.

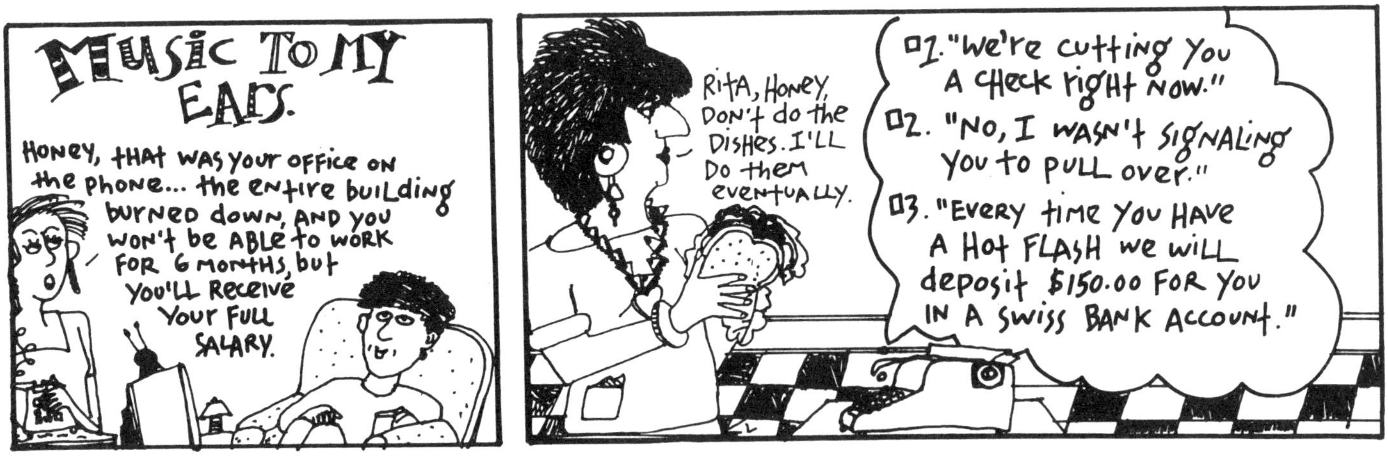
Music To My Ears.
Honey, that was your office on the phone... the entire building burned down, and you won't be able to work for 6 months, but you'll receive your full salary.
Rita, Honey, Don't do the Dishes. I'll Do them eventually.
1. "We're cutting you a check right now."
2. "No, I wasn't signaling you to pull over."
3. "Every time you have a hot flash we will deposit $150.00 for you in a Swiss Bank Account."

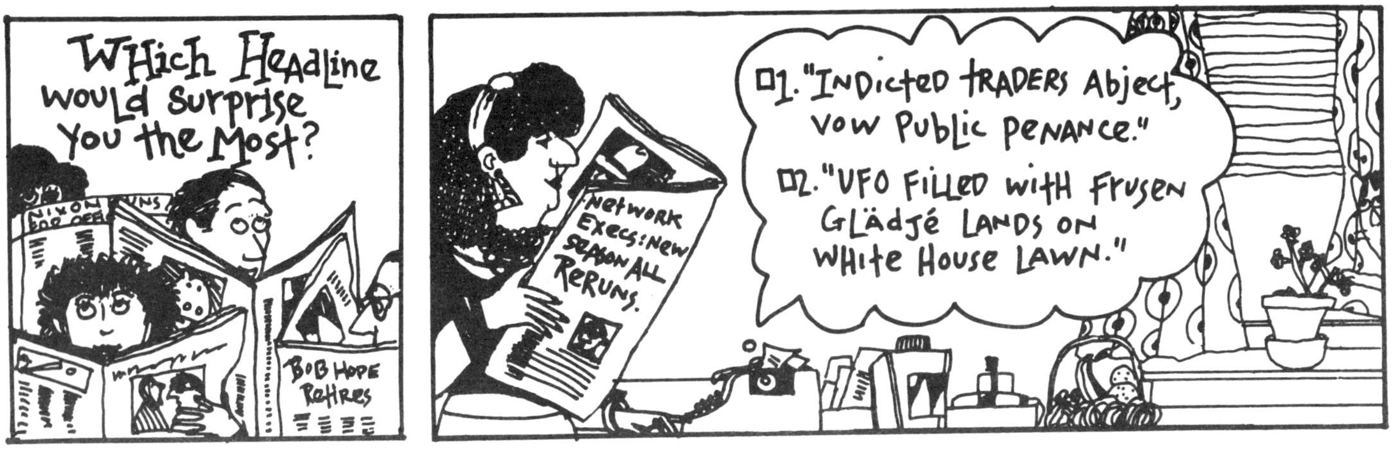
Which Headline would surprise you the Most?
Bob Hope Retires
Network Execs: New Season All Reruns.
1. "Indicted traders Abject, vow Public penance."
2. "UFO Filled with Frusen Glädjé Lands on White House Lawn."

TAXES

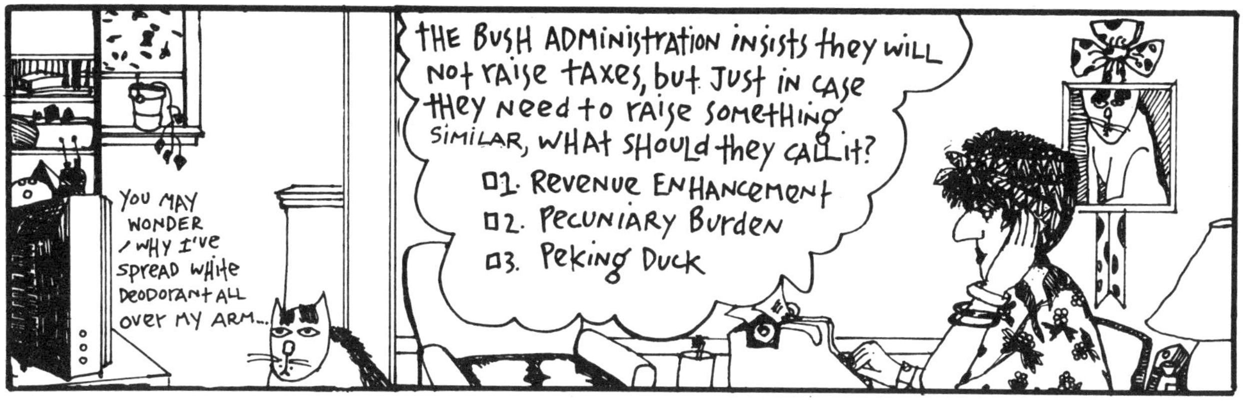
YOU MAY WONDER WHY I'VE SPREAD WHITE DEODORANT ALL OVER MY ARM...
THE BUSH ADMINISTRATION INSISTS THEY WILL NOT RAISE TAXES, BUT JUST IN CASE THEY NEED TO RAISE SOMETHING SIMILAR, WHAT SHOULD THEY CALL IT?
1. REVENUE ENHANCEMENT
2. PECUNIARY BURDEN
3. PEKING DUCK

Is it worse for a politician to admit that he will have to raise taxes or that he enjoys a line of coke now and then? No matter what Reagan and Bush say, taxes *were* raised during their administrations. They were just called something else. After I did this cartoon I didn't look at it again until much later, and when I did, I realized that my third choice was an unconscious parody of the old saying: "If it looks like a duck and walks like a duck, it's probably a duck."

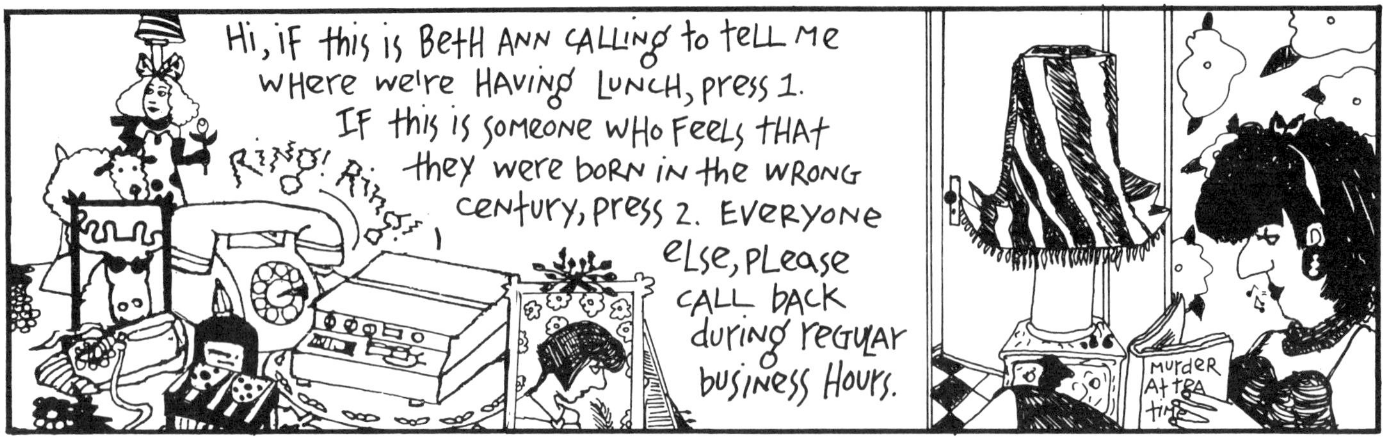
Hi, if this is Beth Ann calling to tell me where we're having lunch, press 1. If this is someone who feels that they were born in the wrong century, press 2. Everyone else, please call back during regular business hours.

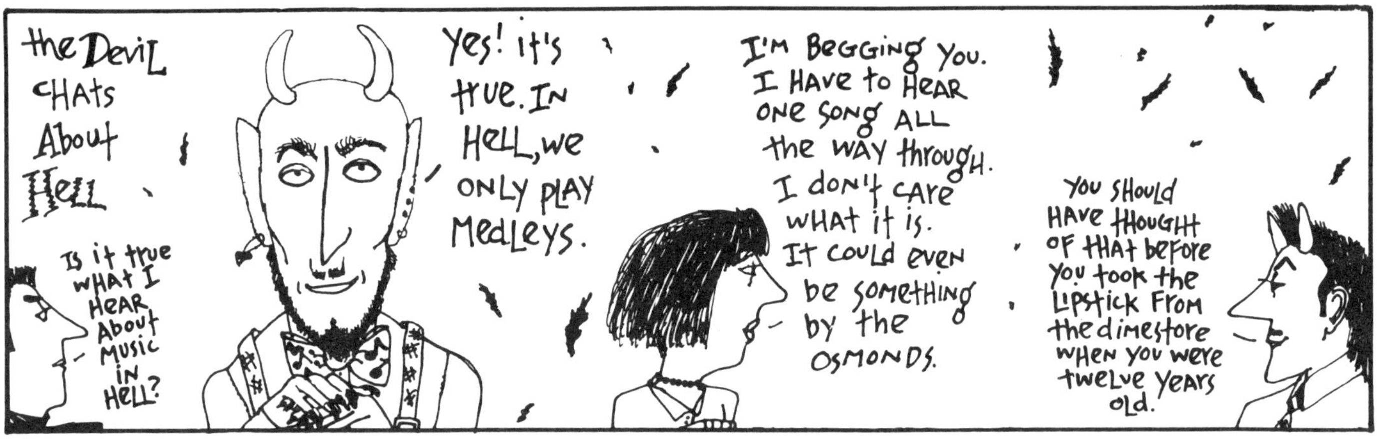
the Devil chats about Hell
Is it true what I hear about music in Hell?
Yes! it's true. In Hell, we only play medleys.
I'm begging you. I have to hear one song all the way through. I don't care what it is. It could even be something by the Osmonds.
You should have thought of that before you took the lipstick from the dimestore when you were twelve years old.

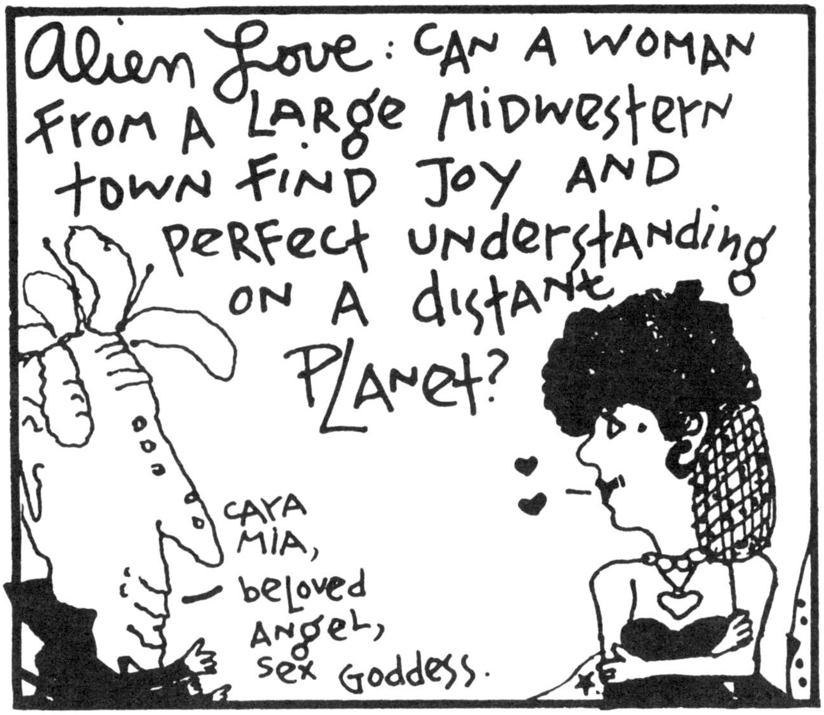
Alien Love: Can a woman from a large midwestern town find joy and perfect understanding on a distant planet?
Cara mia, beloved angel, sex goddess.

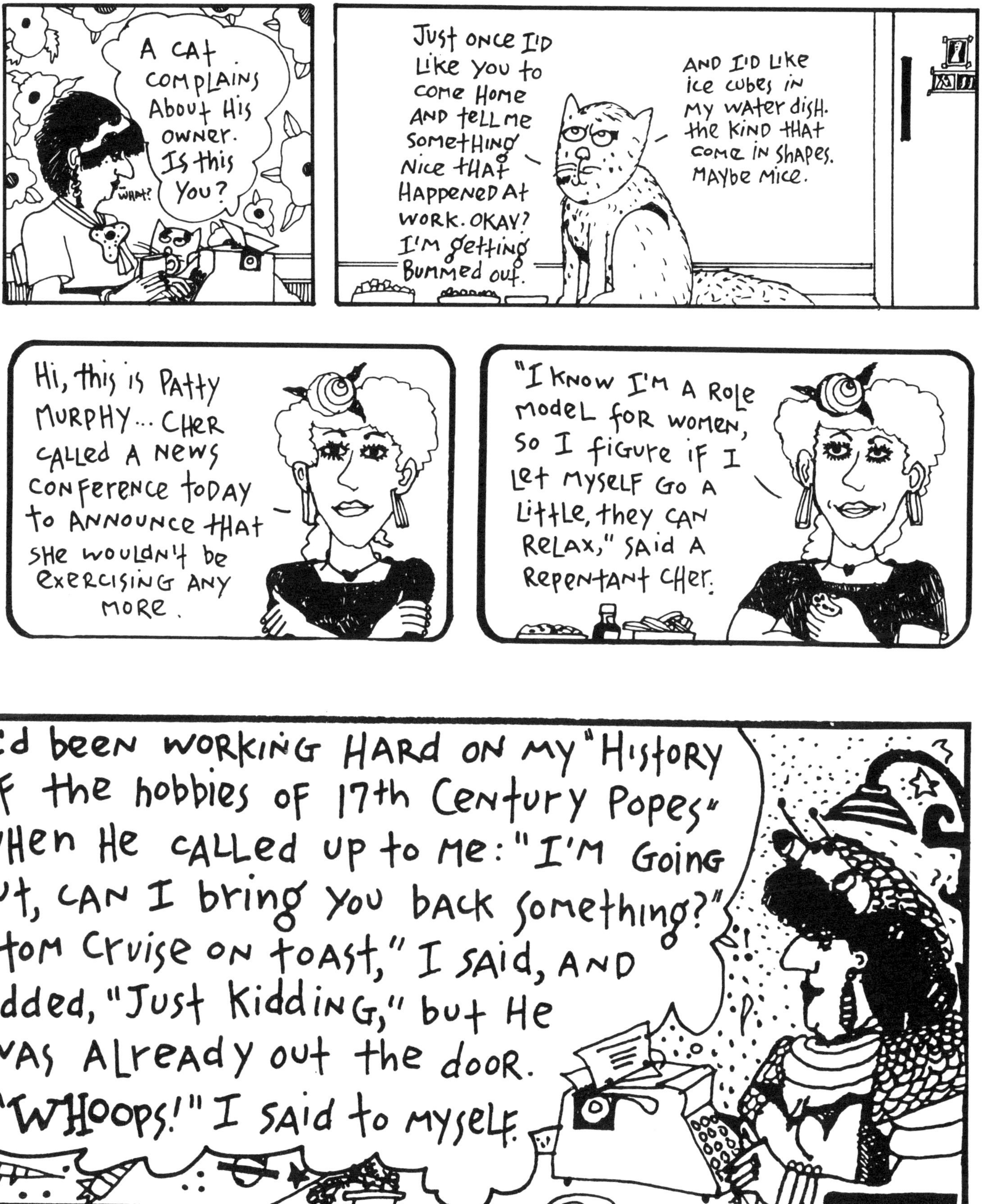
A CAT COMPLAINS ABOUT HIS OWNER. IS THIS YOU?
WHAT?
JUST ONCE I'D LIKE YOU TO COME HOME AND TELL ME SOMETHING NICE THAT HAPPENED AT WORK. OKAY? I'M GETTING BUMMED OUT.
AND I'D LIKE ICE CUBES IN MY WATER DISH. THE KIND THAT COME IN SHAPES. MAYBE MICE.
HI, THIS IS PATTY MURPHY... CHER CALLED A NEWS CONFERENCE TODAY TO ANNOUNCE THAT SHE WOULDN'T BE EXERCISING ANY MORE.
"I KNOW I'M A ROLE MODEL FOR WOMEN, SO I FIGURE IF I LET MYSELF GO A LITTLE, THEY CAN RELAX," SAID A REPENTANT CHER.
I'D BEEN WORKING HARD ON MY "HISTORY OF THE HOBBIES OF 17TH CENTURY POPES" WHEN HE CALLED UP TO ME: "I'M GOING OUT, CAN I BRING YOU BACK SOMETHING?" "TOM CRUISE ON TOAST," I SAID, AND ADDED, "JUST KIDDING," BUT HE WAS ALREADY OUT THE DOOR. "WHOOPS!" I SAID TO MYSELF.

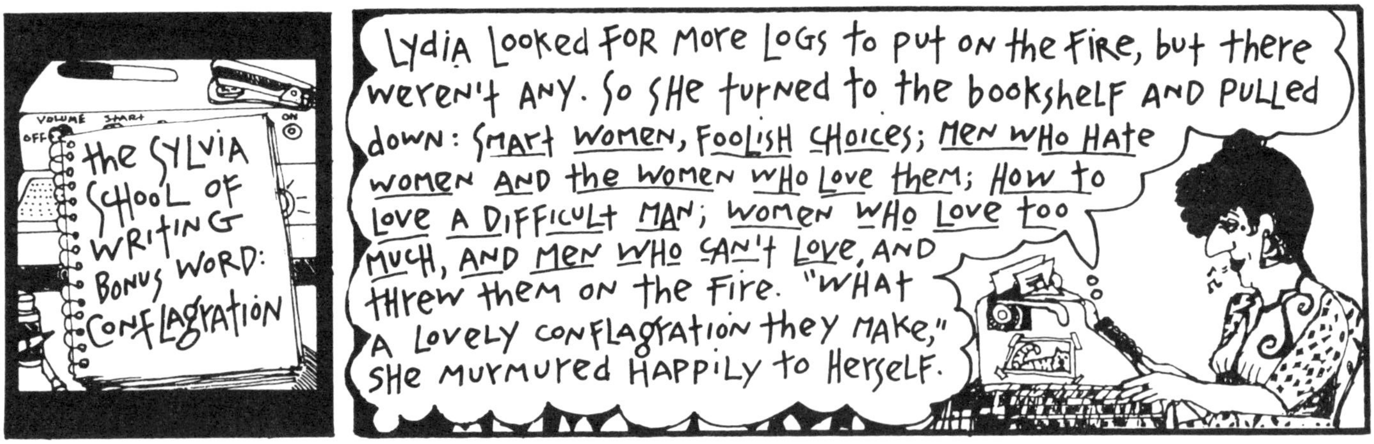
the Sylvia School of Writing Bonus Word: Conflagration
Lydia looked for more logs to put on the fire, but there weren't any. So she turned to the bookshelf and pulled down: Smart Women, Foolish Choices; Men Who Hate Women and the Women Who Love Them; How to Love a Difficult Man; Women Who Love Too Much, and Men Who Can't Love, and threw them on the fire. "What a lovely conflagration they make," she murmured happily to herself.

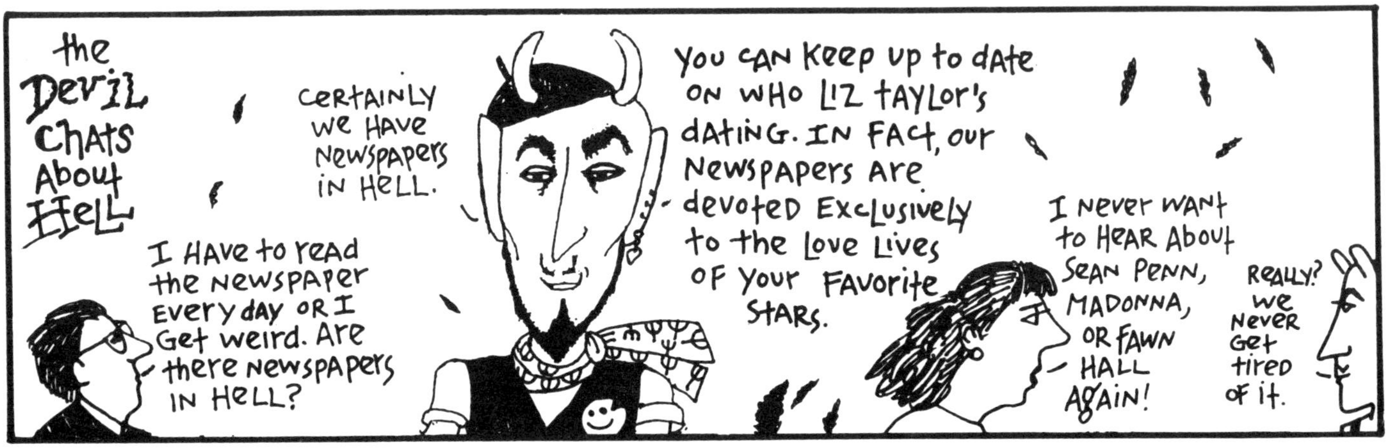
the Devil Chats About Hell
I have to read the newspaper every day or I get weird. Are there newspapers in hell?
Certainly we have newspapers in hell.
You can keep up to date on who Liz Taylor's dating. In fact, our newspapers are devoted exclusively to the love lives of your favorite stars.
I never want to hear about Sean Penn, Madonna, or Fawn Hall again!
Really? We never get tired of it.

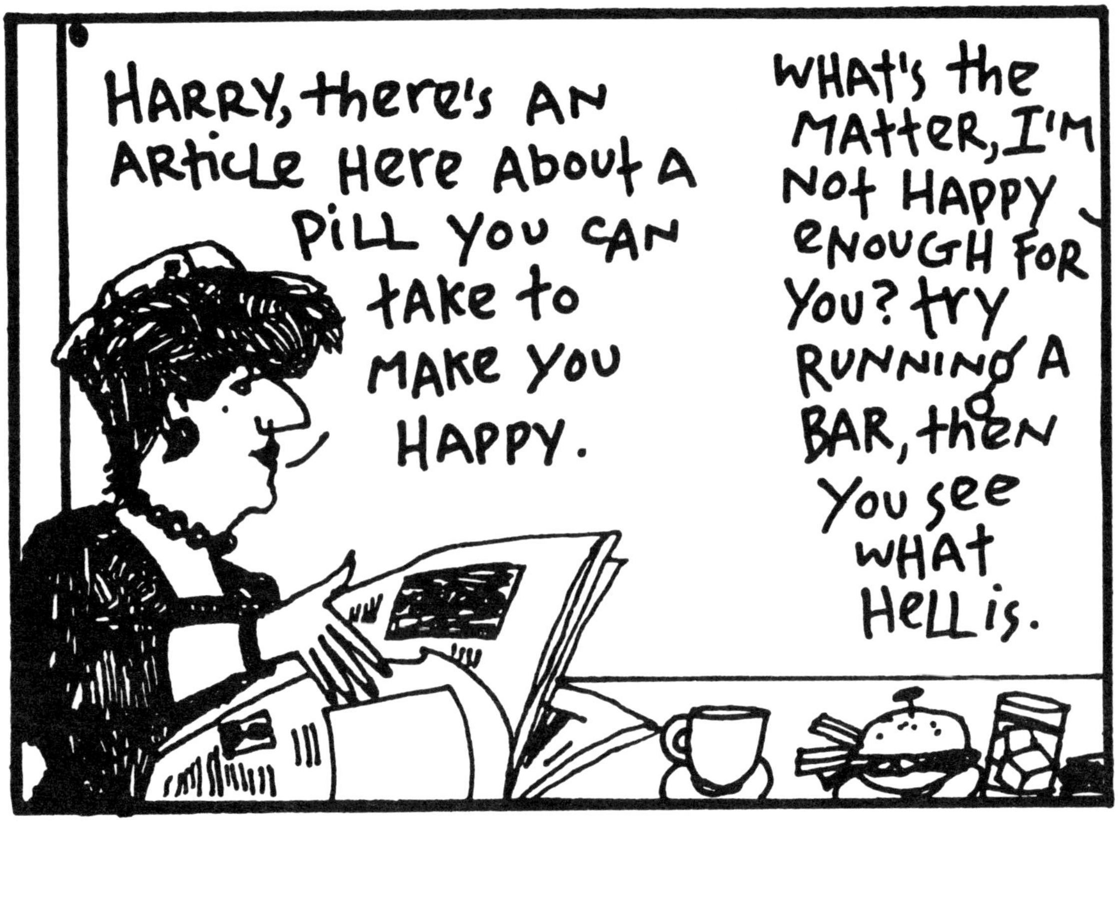
Harry, there's an article here about a pill you can take to make you happy.
What's the matter, I'm not happy enough for you? Try running a bar, then you see what hell is.

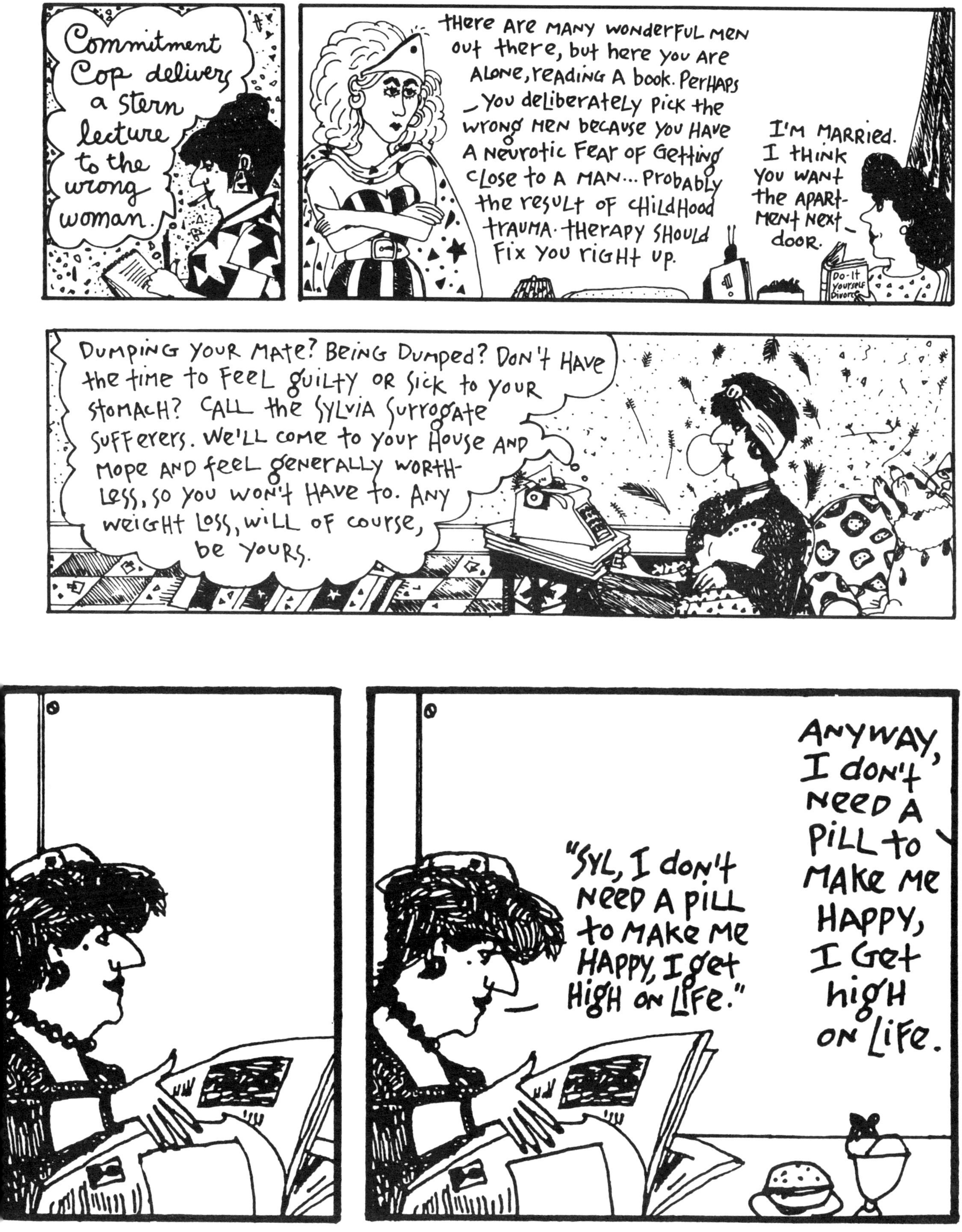

Commitment Cop delivers a stern lecture to the wrong woman.
There are many wonderful men out there, but here you are alone, reading a book. Perhaps you deliberately pick the wrong men because you have a neurotic fear of getting close to a man... probably the result of childhood trauma. Therapy should fix you right up.
I'm married. I think you want the apartment next door.
Do-It Yourself Divorce
Dumping your mate? Being dumped? Don't have the time to feel guilty or sick to your stomach? Call the Sylvia Surrogate Sufferers. We'll come to your house and mope and feel generally worthless, so you won't have to. Any weight loss, will of course, be yours.
"Syl, I don't need a pill to make me happy, I get high on life."
Anyway, I don't need a pill to make me happy, I get high on life.

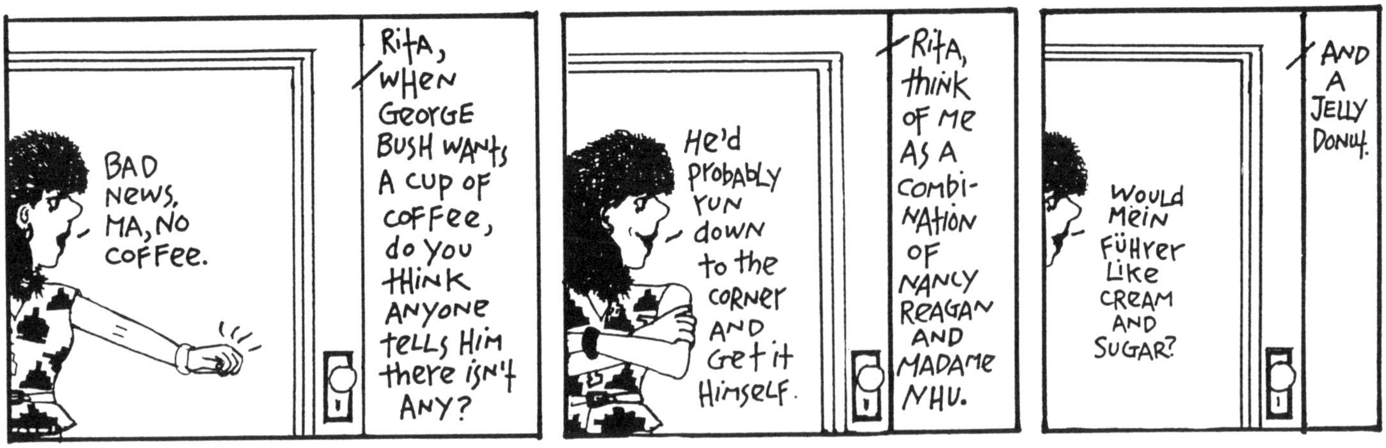
BAD NEWS, MA, NO COFFEE.
RiTA, WHEN GEORGE BUSH WANTS A CUP OF COFFEE, DO YOU THINK ANYONE TELLS HIM THERE ISN'T ANY?
He'd probably run down to the corner AND Get it Himself.
RiTA, think of me AS A combi-NATION OF NANCY REAGAN AND MADAME NHU.
Would mein Führer Like CREAM AND SUGAR?
AND A JELLY DONUT.

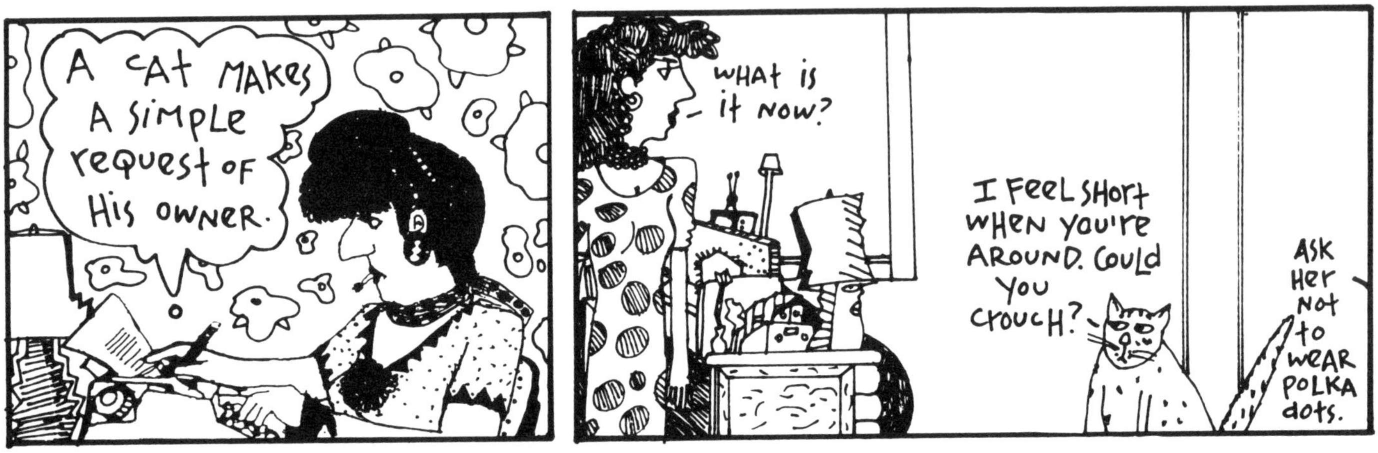
A CAT MAKES A SIMPLE request of His OWNER.
WHAT is it NOW?
I FEEL SHORT WHEN YOU'RE AROUND. COULD YOU CROUCH?
ASK Her NOT to WEAR POLKA dots.

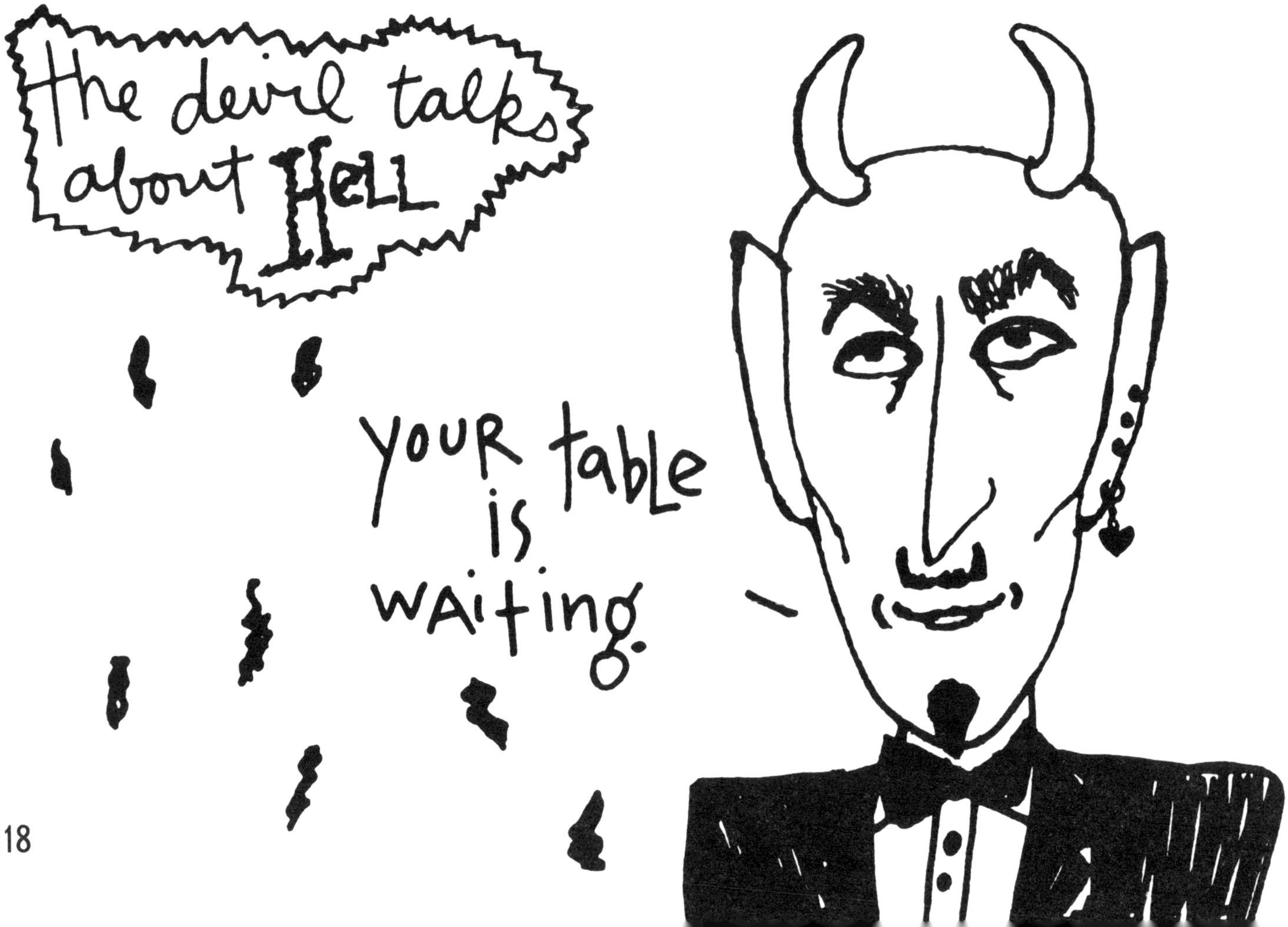
the devil talks about HELL
your table is waiting.

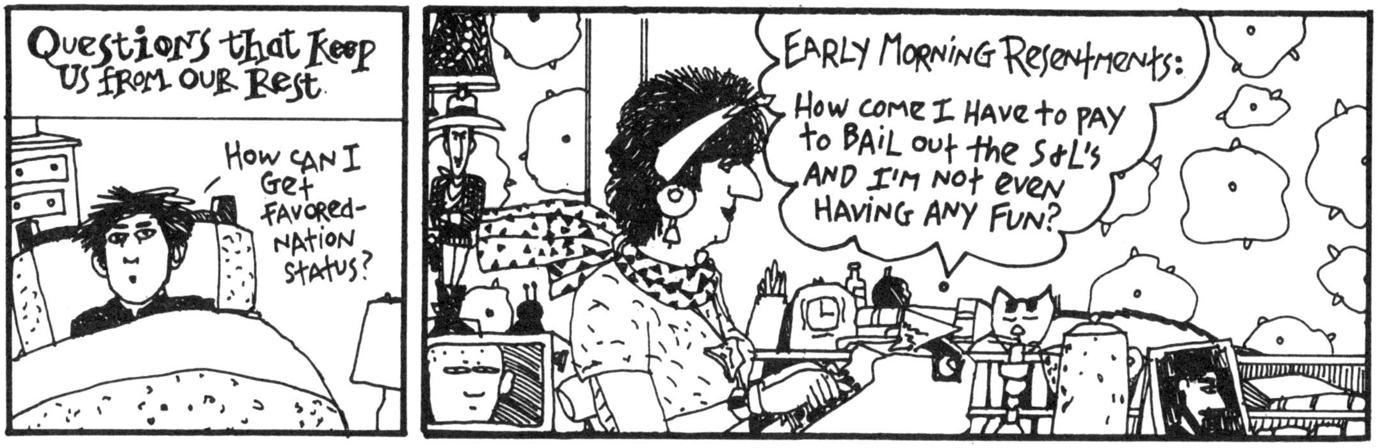
Questions that Keep Us from our Rest.
How can I Get Favored-Nation Status?
Early Morning Resentments:
How come I have to pay to bail out the S&L's and I'm not even having any fun?

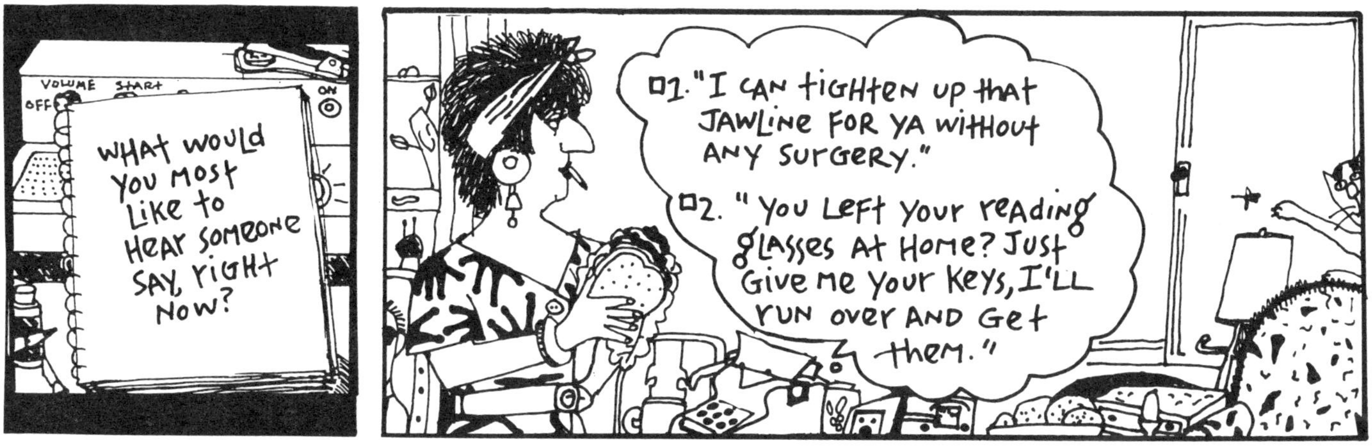
Volume
Start
Off
On
What would you most like to hear someone say, right now?
☐1. "I can tighten up that jawline for ya without any surgery."
☐2. "You left your reading glasses at home? Just give me your keys, I'll run over and get them."

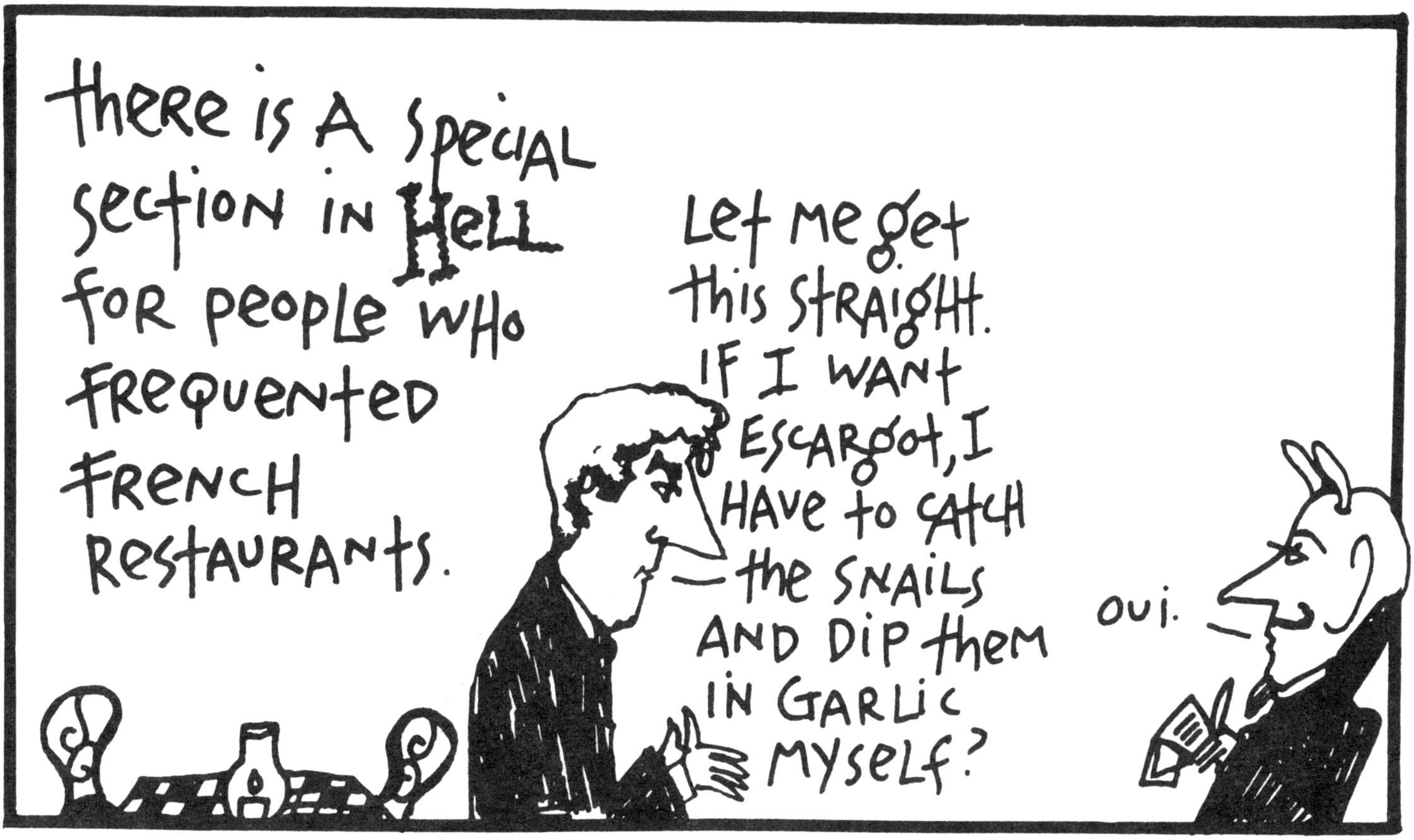
There is a special section in Hell for people who frequented French restaurants.
Let me get this straight. If I want escargot, I have to catch the snails and dip them in garlic myself?
Oui.

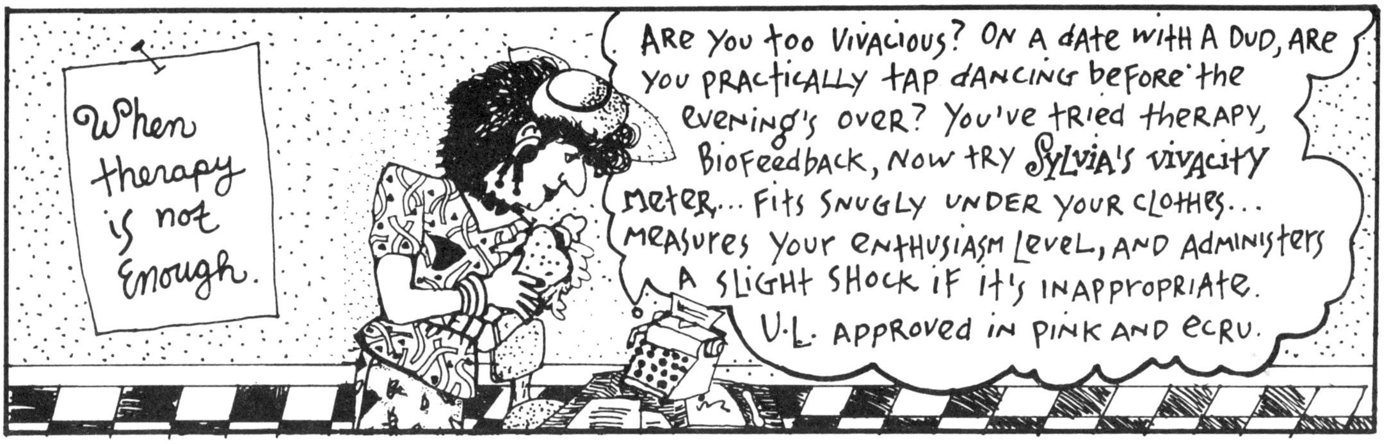
When therapy is not Enough.
Are you too Vivacious? On a date with a dud, are you practically tap dancing before the evening's over? You've tried therapy, Biofeedback, now try Sylvia's vivacity meter... Fits snugly under your clothes... measures your enthusiasm level, and administers a slight shock if it's inappropriate. U.L. approved in pink and ecru.

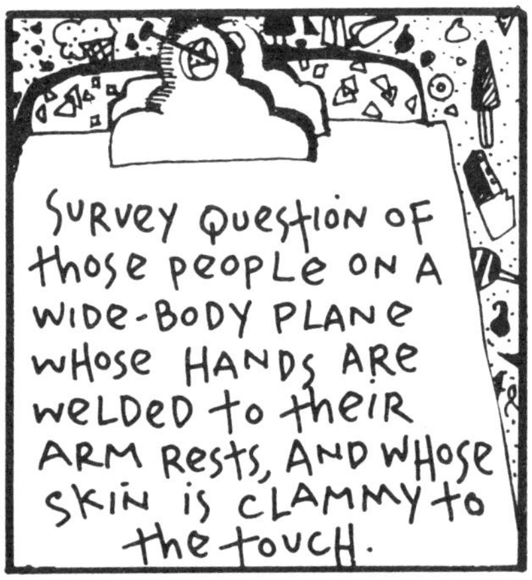
Survey question of those people on a wide-body plane whose hands are welded to their arm rests, and whose skin is clammy to the touch.

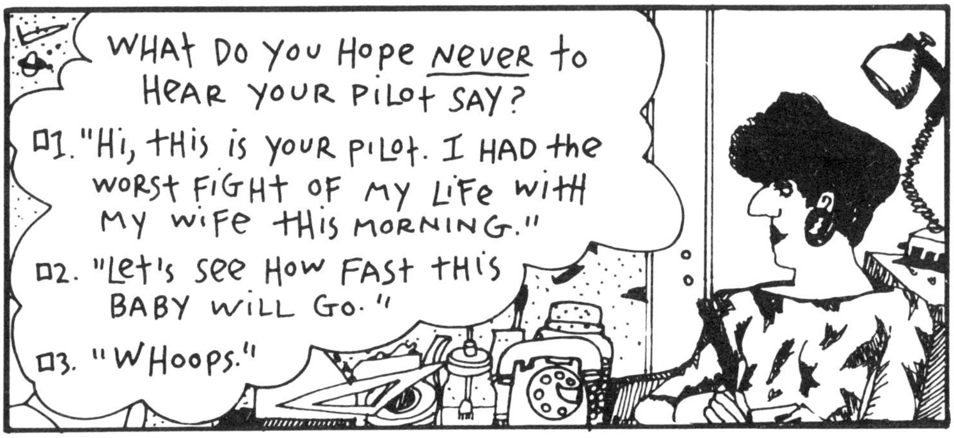
What do you hope never to hear your pilot say?
☐1. "Hi, this is your pilot. I had the worst fight of my life with my wife this morning."
☐2. "Let's see how fast this baby will go."
☐3. "Whoops."

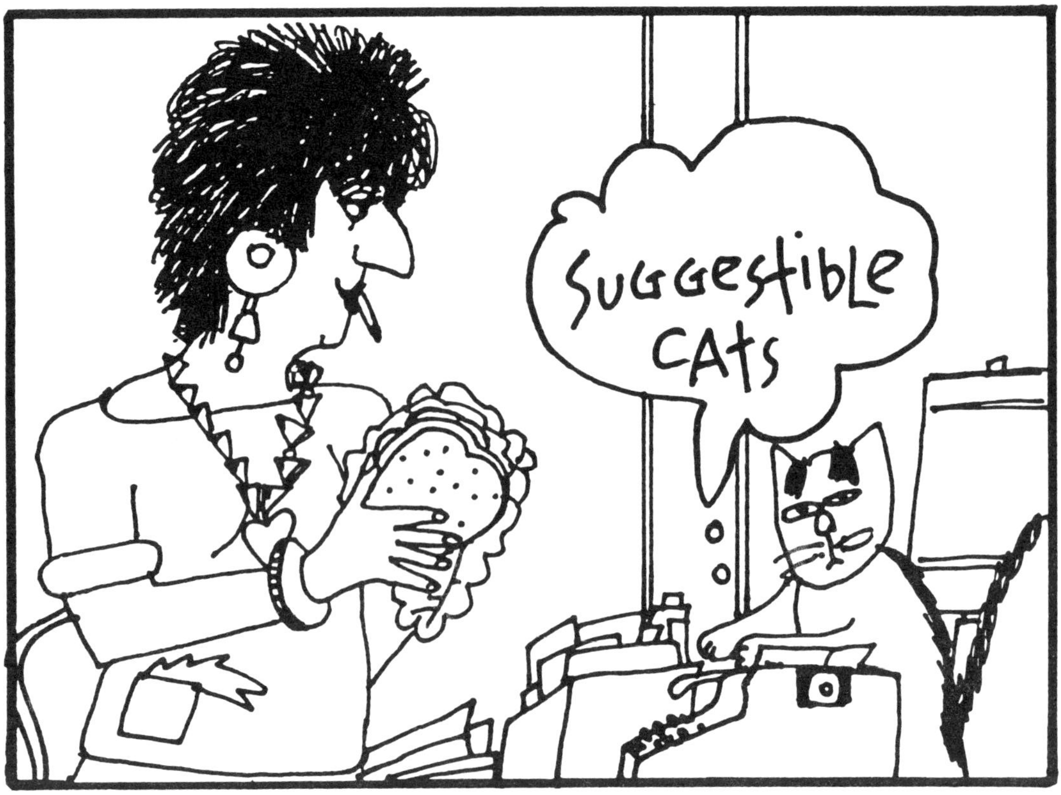
Suggestible cats

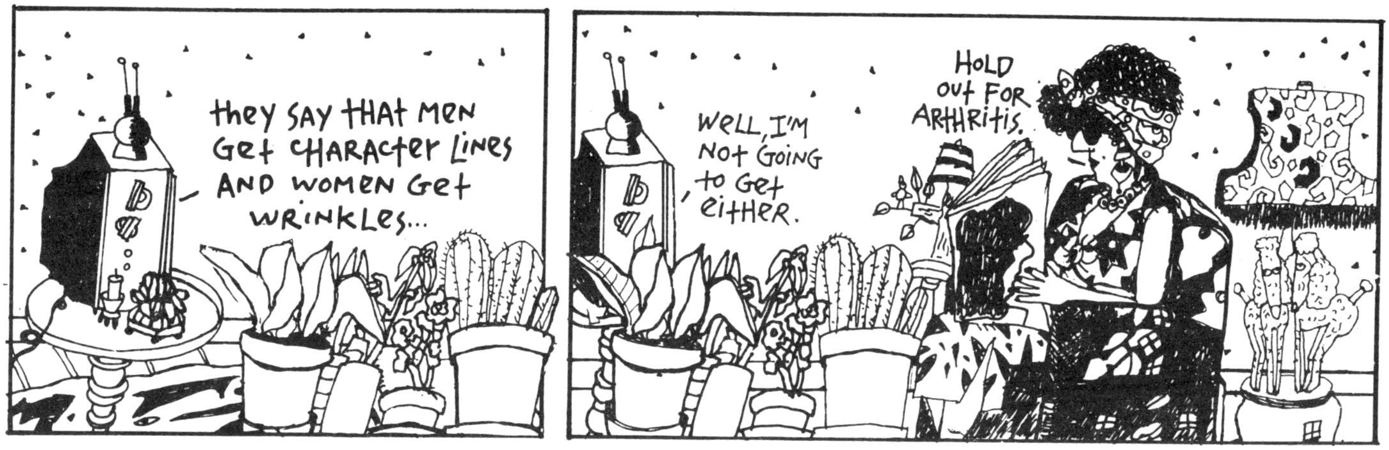
they say that men get character lines and women get wrinkles...
Well, I'm not going to get either.
Hold out for arthritis.

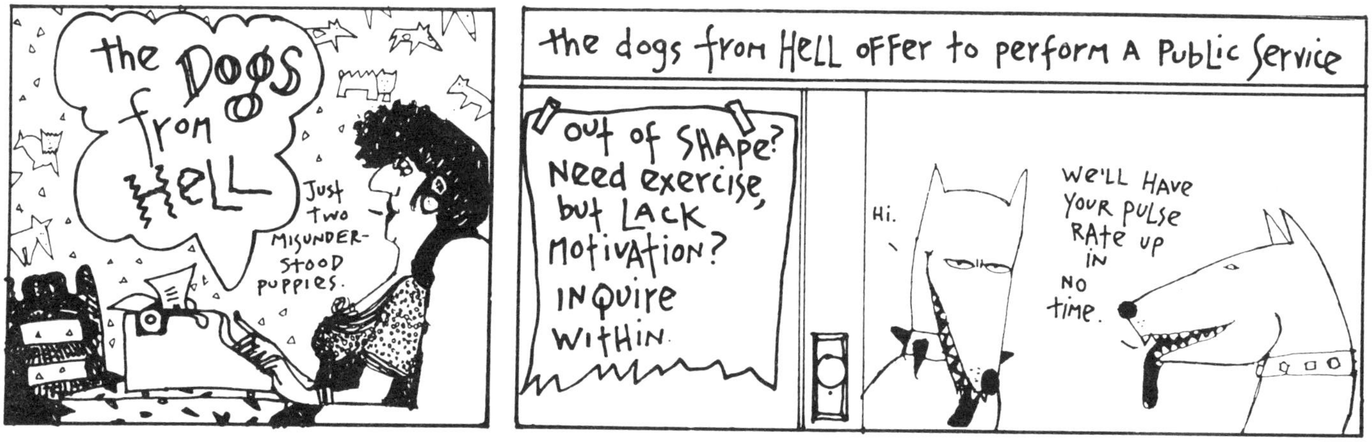
the Dogs from Hell
Just two misunderstood puppies.
the dogs from HELL offer to perform a Public Service
out of shape? Need exercise, but lack motivation? Inquire within.
Hi.
We'll have your pulse rate up in no time.

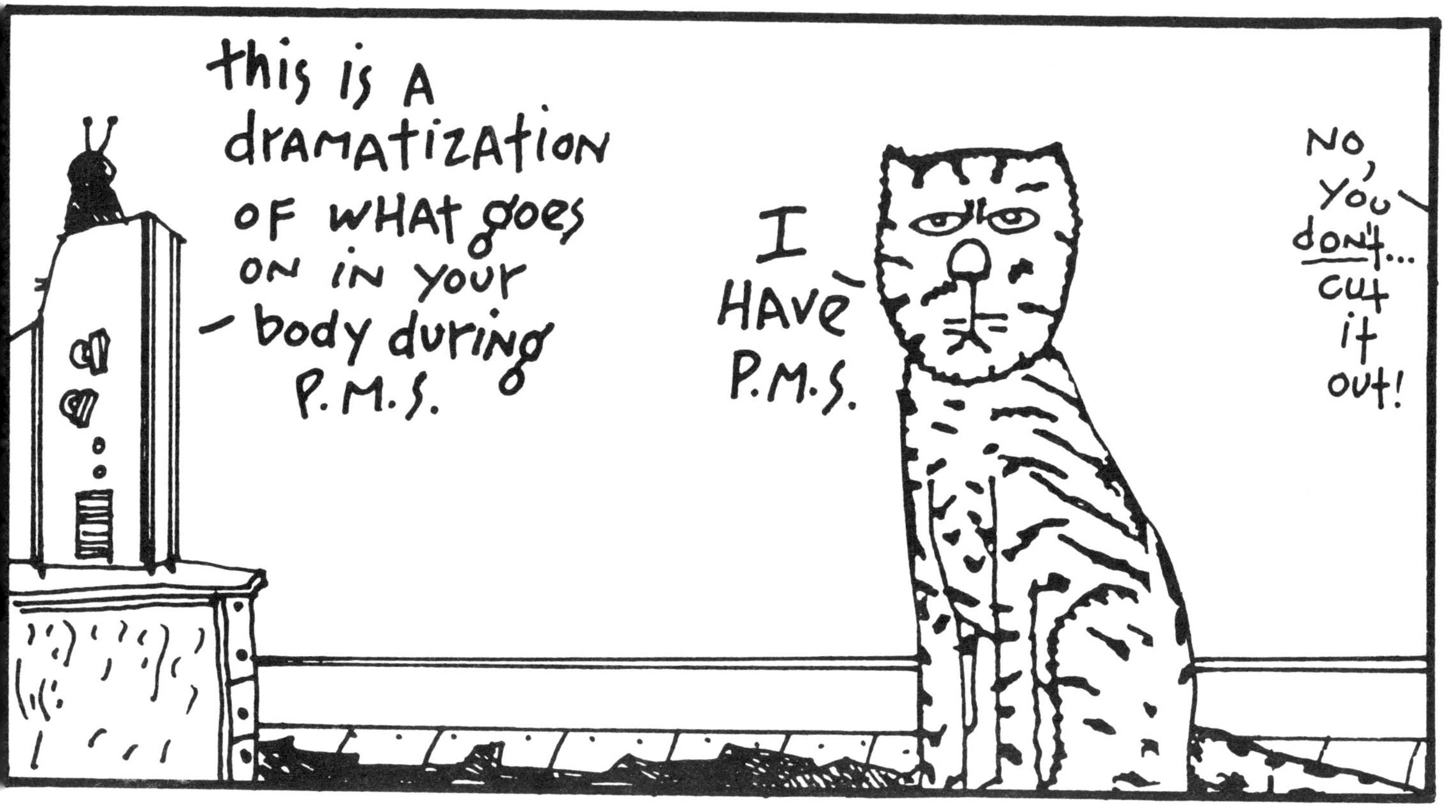
this is a dramatization of what goes on in your body during P.M.S.
I have P.M.S.
No, you don't... cut it out!

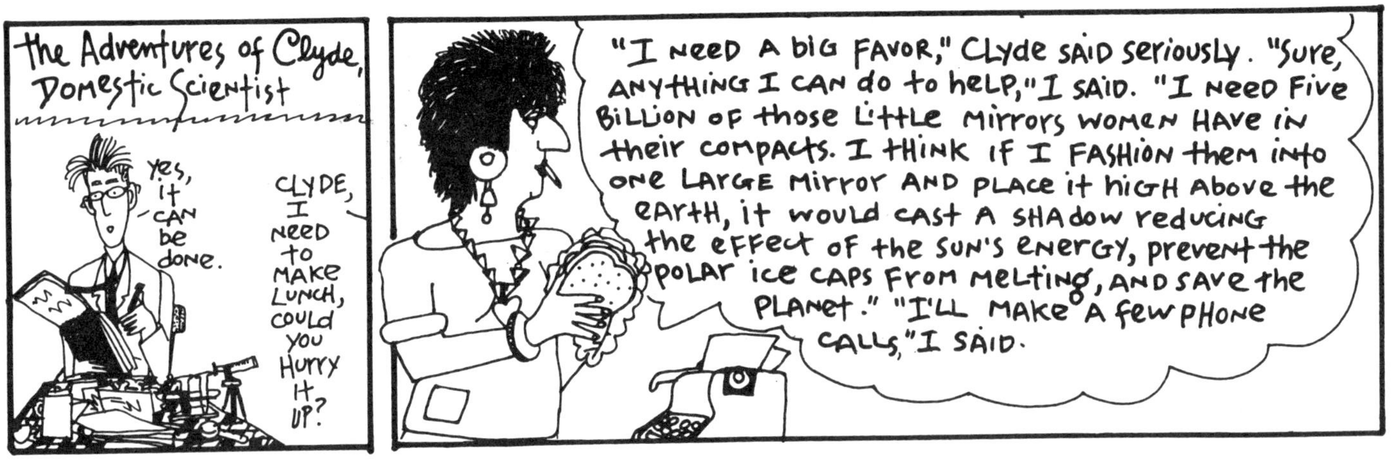
the Adventures of Clyde, Domestic Scientist
Yes, it can be done.
CLYDE, I need to make lunch, could you hurry it up?
"I need a big favor," Clyde said seriously. "Sure, anything I can do to help," I said. "I need five billion of those little mirrors women have in their compacts. I think if I fashion them into one large mirror and place it high above the earth, it would cast a shadow reducing the effect of the sun's energy, prevent the polar ice caps from melting, and save the planet." "I'll make a few phone calls," I said.

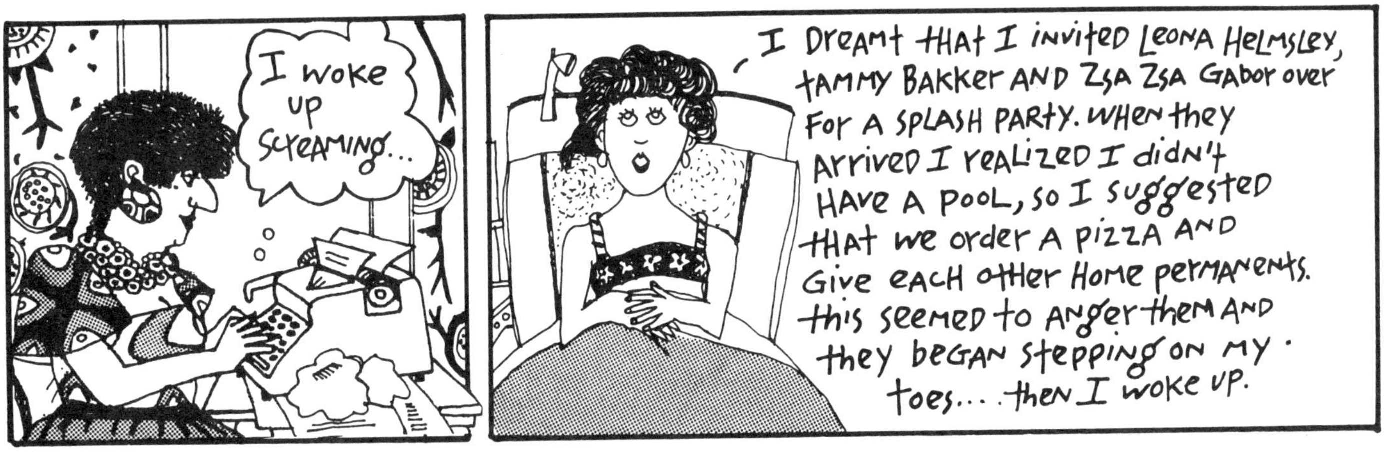
I woke up screaming...
I dreamt that I invited Leona Helmsley, tammy Bakker and Zsa Zsa Gabor over for a splash party. When they arrived I realized I didn't have a pool, so I suggested that we order a pizza and give each other home permanents. this seemed to anger them and they began stepping on my toes... then I woke up.

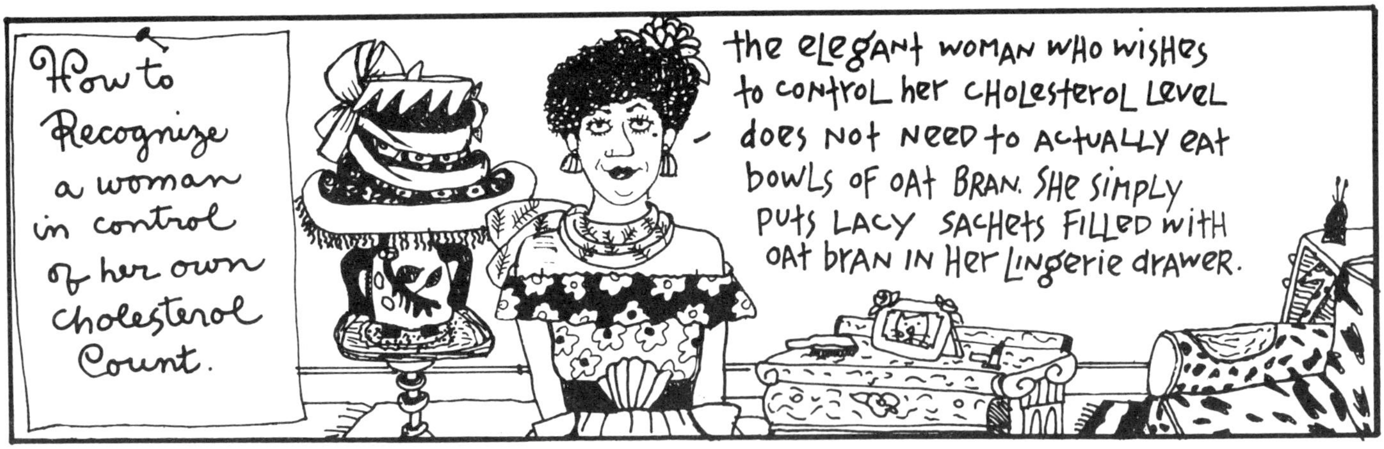
How to Recognize a woman in control of her own cholesterol Count.
the elegant woman who wishes to control her cholesterol level does not need to actually eat bowls of oat bran. She simply puts lacy sachets filled with oat bran in her lingerie drawer.

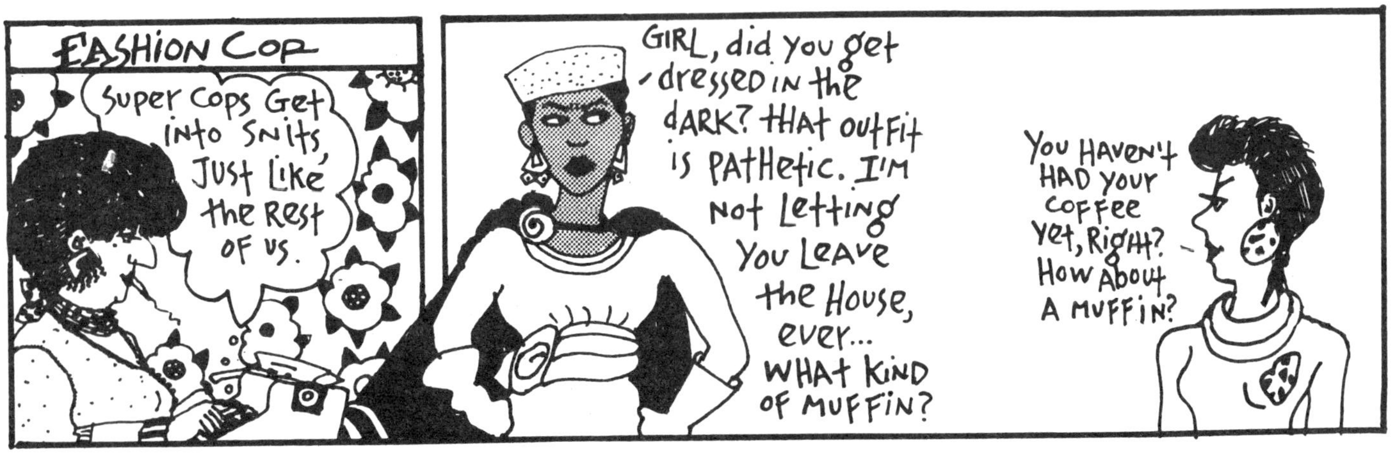
FASHION COP
Super Cops Get into Snits, Just like the Rest of us.
GIRL, did you get dressed in the dark? That outfit is pathetic. I'm not letting you leave the house, ever... WHAT KIND OF MUFFIN?
You haven't had your coffee yet, right? How about a muffin?

SYLVIA'S REAL GOOD ADVICE

There are two versions of why I wrote a musical comedy about Sylvia called *Sylvia's Real Good Advice. My* version is that over the years a number of people have asked me if they could adapt the Sylvia cartoons for the stage as a one-woman show or a cabaret act and I always said no. I realized that I was reluctant to let other people adapt the cartoons because I felt I was the only one who could do it.

So one day I walked up to Arnold Aprill, he's the artistic director of The City Lit Theater Company in Chicago and said, I want to write a Sylvia musical, and he said, I've been waiting a long time to hear that. So he and I and Tom Mula and Steve Rashid began collaborating. We were helped to finish the play by a request from University of Wisconsin to mount a workshop production of it in the summer of 1987. Deadlines are a great motivator.

Sylvia's version is that she made me do it. This is a monologue I wrote for her to help woo investors at a backers' audition.

☆ 🛸 ☆°

Hi, I'm Sylvia. You probably know me from the comic pages. I'm taller than you expected, right? More fully rounded; the kind of woman who would find two-dimensional life a little confining, a little flat? Believe it! I was looking for a more suitable venue, so I said to Nicole, write me a play. Make it a musical, I want to tap dance. I want to get out of that damned chair. She doesn't listen. I plead. Nothing. You know how stubborn she is. I hide her car keys, I nag her while she's asleep, I place personal ads in the newspaper that embarrass her. She gives in.

She writes a little while, then she says she has to go lie down. I bring in two guys I met in Kinko's to help her. I send her Steve Rashid to compose the music, the man understands me, I know him from a past life. Okay, the play. What's the plot? Nicole thinks the play should be a musical overview of

Twentieth Century feminism. I threaten suicide. We compromise. The play is about me.

You get to accompany me through a typical day where I chat with the Devil, entertain a visitor from another planet, and try to talk my daughter out of moving to her own apartment — in other words a richly faceted multilayered, twenty-four hour period in my life, a day that would kill a normal human being. Watch me as I solve the complicated personal problems of people who are far more neurotic than you.

You'll also get to meet my closest friends, like Harry. Harry owns the bar downstairs of my apartment. I have lunch there every day. Whether he likes it or not. We've been together through several marriages, fortunately, never to each other. You'll meet my straightest friend, my dearest pal, Beth-Ann. She's very neat. I've known her since kindergarten. When we all ate crayons together, she cut hers into small, bite-size pieces...And of course my lovely daughter Rita, named for Rita Hayworth. We have a difference of opinion. I was grooming her to be the foremeost Flamenco dancer of the century. She's decided to be a C.P.A. There are cats involved, of course. Cats, can't live with them, can't use them for collateral on a loan. You cat lovers will be happy to know that we've finally cracked the code of cat communication. Their entire language consists of two phrases delivered with varying degrees of intensity: "Hurry that dinner will ya," and "Everything here is mine."

✿ ☄ ☽ ✦

Here's a scene and a song from *Sylvia's Real Good Advice:*

 (Beth-Ann and Myrna at a greasy spoon, waiting for Sylvia)

BETH-ANN: Should we wait for her, or order now?

MYRNA: I'm tired of waiting for people. Let me see the menu.

 (Syl joins Beth-Ann & Myrna while they're looking at menus.)

SYL: I'm almost on time. There was an incredible accident on the express-

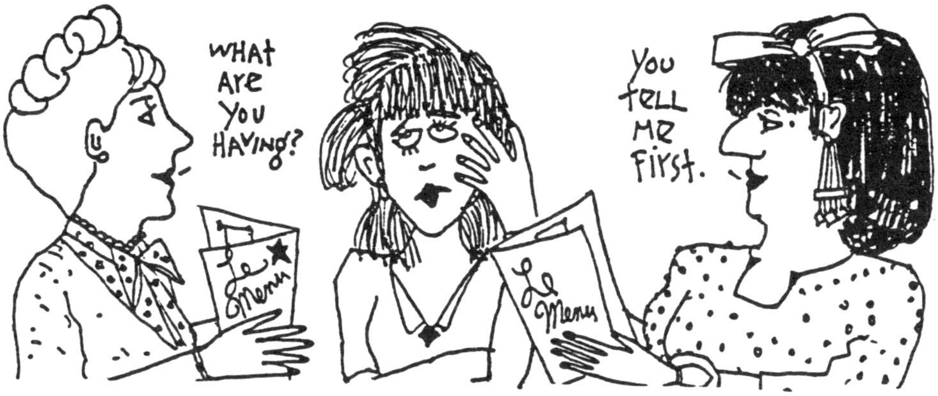
WHAT ARE YOU HAVING?
YOU TELL ME FIRST.

way… A truckload of condoms collided with a horse trailer. Condoms and horses all over the highway. Tied up traffic all the way to Utah.

MYRNA: I think I'll have the julienne salad.

SYL: The BLT is probably safe.

BETH-ANN: Oh! They have linguini with clam sauce!

SYL: You always order it.

MYRNA: You never like it.

BETH-ANN: I'm looking for the perfect linguini with clam sauce, and it's hard to find.

MYRNA: It's a quest. Nothing wrong with a quest. It's like looking for the right man. There's something noble about it, and stupid at the same time. (Myrna lays her head down on the table and begins sobbing.)

SYL: Are you going to order?

MYRNA: He's driving me crazy. I hate him. I'm miserable. Why me? I'm the most miserable person in the whole world!

SYL & BETH-ANN: Oh, poor baby. Did you pick an icky man again?

(They sing, making fun of her—Myrna gradually cheers up and joins them)

Some women live on a lonely island,
Somewhere out in the middle of a stormy sea

I live with a fella who would
rather die than,
ever do anything nice for me.

I need a guy who doesn't need me
Who always tells me NO!
Never put your arms around me
Oh my Sullen Romeo
I want a man who doesn't need me
a low-down so and so
Never put your arms around me,
Sullen Romeo

You may like a man who likes to send you roses
I guess my taste is somewhat more Baroque
You may like a man who treats you like a goddess
I like a man who treats me like a joke.

You like a man with social graces
witty, charming Fred Astaire.
I don't want no table manners,
slop that gravy in my hair
I like a guy who doesn't want me
Who always tells me NO!
Never put your arms around me
Oh my Sullen Romeo
I like a man who doesn't need me
a low-down so and so
Never put your arms around me,
Sullen Romeo

I want a guy who don't think of me,
kind of guy who grunts and pouts,
brags about how much he loves me,
'n forgets my name when the lights go out.

I want a man who spends my money,
always smokes a big cigar,

always calls my best friend honey,
moons my mother, wrecks my car.

I like a guy who doesn't want me
Who always tells me NO!
Never put your arms around me
Oh my Sullen Romeo
I want a man who doesn't need me
a low-down so and so
Never put your arms around me,
Sullen Romeo

You can have your blue-eyed crooners
Eagle Scouts who need a friend,
I prefer the Bogarts and the Brandos,
who look the same from either end.

And when I'm tired of being understanding
tired of forcing love to last
I'll gather up your toothbrush, oh my darling
'n toss you out upon your perfect ass.

I like a guy who doesn't want me
Who always tells me NO!
Never put your arms around me
Oh my Sullen Romeo
I want a man who doesn't need me
a low-down so and so
Never put your arms around me,
Sullen Romeo

Treat me dirty, treat me mean,
I don't want no Mr. Clean
Summer, spring, winter, fall
act like a Neanderthal
Make me scream, make me shout,
make me want to throw you out
I am at my very best
when I'm with someone I detest.